Liberal America
and the Third World

Robert A. Packenham

Liberal
America

and the Third World

Political Development Ideas in

Foreign Aid and Social Science

PRINCETON UNIVERSITY PRESS   PRINCETON, NEW JERSEY

LC: 72-1987
ISBN: 0-691-07549-2

This book has been set in Linotype Janson.
Printed in the United States of America
by Princeton University Press
Princeton, New Jersey

FOR MY PARENTS
AND FOR ANN, KEN, AND PAT

Contents

Tables

Acknowledgments

MANY INDIVIDUALS and organizations helped me during the course of my work on this book. I regret that I can acknowledge only some of them here. To those persons whose works are cited in the text I owe the most. The depth and scope of that debt will be apparent to the reader. My largest personal debts are to five colleagues in the Department of Political Science at Stanford University. Alexander George read the entire manuscript with exceptional care and thoughtfulness. He is the ideal colleague; although I can never hope to emulate his example, I am deeply grateful for it. David Abernethy read almost the entire manuscript in draft and provided lucid and detailed criticisms which improved the work substantially. Richard Fagen and Frank Bonilla have given me much good advice, on the manuscript and sundry other matters; for this, and for their good fellowship, they have my thanks. Last, but hardly least, Gabriel A. Almond has for more than a decade—as teacher, adviser, colleague, and friend—been a constant source of insight, good counsel, and encouragement. He has my admiration, gratitude, and affection. Without his support, and that of these other friends, this book might never have appeared.

I am also deeply grateful to several other colleagues and friends who during the last decade or so have shared my concern with Third-World political development and American foreign policy in relation to it, and who have, through conversations, their own published work, correspondence, and other forms of dialogue stimulated my thinking and changed my mind: Charles W. Anderson, Samuel P. Huntington, Helio Jaguaribe, Robert H. Johnson, Princeton Lyman, Joan M. Nelson, and Dankwart A. Rustow.

David Apter contributed an especially useful set of comments and suggestions about ways to improve the manuscript. Until he left California for pleasanter climes and better ecology, Sidney Verba was a ready source of encouragement, amusement, wisdom, and insight. Aaron Wildavsky gave me the benefit of his sage counsel regarding the penultimate draft of the manuscript. I also benefited from comments on particular points or chapters by Joel Bergsman, Bart Bernstein, Henry Bienen, Carl Degler, Louis Hartz, Albert O. Hirschman, John W. Lewis, Charles E. Lindblom, Frederick F. Simmons, and Frank McNeil. In the earliest stages of this work, Bradford Westerfield, Field Haviland, and Howard Wriggins provided suggestions and encouragement. Students at Stanford, both undergraduates and graduates, have listened to some of these ideas evolve; their reactions helped me to strengthen the book. I thank all these generous people.

Several organizations were also generous. From 1965, when I first came to the Department of Political Science at Stanford, until 1971 my work was partially supported by the University's Committee on International Studies and by its Committee on Latin American Studies, through funds for the Department and the Institute of Political Studies. I thank the chairmen of these committees, Professors Carl Spaeth and John J. Johnson, and their staffs. I am especially grateful to the Graduate Division of the University, and to its Dean, Lincoln Moses, for a Junior Faculty Research Leave grant for the autumn quarter of 1969. I also thank my two departmental chairmen during those years, Gabriel A. Almond and Heinz Eulau, for their support and entrepreneurship. During its early phases, this study was sustained by grants from the following organizations: the Chubb Fund of Timothy Dwight College, Yale University; the Foreign Area Fellowship Program, which is administered by the Social Science Research Council and the American Council of Learned Societies under a grant from the Ford Foundation; and the Ford Foundation. I owe a special debt to the Brookings Institution in Washington, D.C., where I was privileged to be a Research Fellow in 1962-1963 and a guest scholar in the summer of 1966.

xii

Sanford G. Thatcher and Lalor Cadley, my editors at Princeton University Press, have been extremely perceptive and thoughtful and have helped improve the book and ease my path in many ways. To Arlee Ellis, the administrative assistant of Stanford's Department of Political Science and Institute of Political Studies, and to her crew of typists, especially Elizabeth Rafferty, Helen Engle, Virginia Anderson, Barbara Sullivan, and Sharon Kimble, I can only express gratitude and admiration for competence and cool (theirs) amidst fire and stress (mine).

None of these individuals or organizations necessarily supports the views expressed in this book. They have helped me enormously, but none of them would have written this book as I have, and all shortcomings in it are my responsibility and mine alone.

I thank the editors of *World Politics* for permission to use a few passages from my articles in that journal in 1964 and 1966.

A version of Chapter 8 was published as a paper by the Southern California Arms Control and Foreign Policy Seminar under the title *The United States and Third World Development* (March 1973).

R.A.P.

Preface

....

THIS IS A BOOK about notions of political development held among two groups of people in the United States during the post-World War II years. By "notions of political development," I mean ideas regarding the nature, conditions, and consequences of highly valued types of political systems. The two groups are government officials concerned with economic and technical assistance programs abroad, and social scientists—mainly political scientists and sociologists—in the field of comparative politics. The notions of the policymakers are called *doctrines* of political development; those of the social scientists are designated *theories*.

This book will attempt to show that the doctrines and the theories were similar in important ways, and that both were profoundly affected by some largely inarticulated premises of American political ideology. Following Professor Louis Hartz, I call these assumptions the "liberal tradition" in America. Hartz and other "American exceptionalists" have offered insights about what happens when the liberal tradition confronts an obdurate foreign reality. This book sharpens and systematizes some of these exceptionalist hypotheses, tests them against both doctrines and theories, and finds them to be strongly supported by that evidence. The book thus advances beyond earlier exceptionalist writings in at least two ways. It broadens their hypotheses by suggesting that the liberal tradition affects the ideas of not only political actors and general political intellectuals, but also social scientists who have often been portrayed as more or less immune to such ideological influences. And by examining doctrines and theories systematically over a twenty-year period, it goes well beyond the exceptionalists' fragmented speculations and illustrations regarding the effects of the liberal tradition on American thinking about foreign political systems.

In addition, Chapters 1 and 2 provide the first analytic history of foreign aid doctrines concerning political development between 1947 and 1968. Since aid was a principal instrument of U.S. foreign policy toward underdeveloped countries, aid doctrines are good indicators of political development doctrines more generally embodied in U.S. foreign policy toward these countries. Finally, comparison of the largely implicit notions of the policymakers (the doctrines) with the explicit notions of the social scientists (the theories) makes possible an assessment of the utility and the limitations of social science for public policy. The central focus throughout is always on the notions of the officials and social scientists concerning political development: the nature of these ideas, their roots in American values and ideology, and their virtues and defects.

"Discovering" the Liberal Tradition: A Personal History. A very brief recounting of the history of this work is appropriate here for two reasons. First, a personal history is the best way I know to describe the process by which one "discovers" the liberal tradition. In a real sense, therefore, a sketch of this process describes an aspect of the methodology of the study. Second, these remarks provide an opportunity to set in proper context those aspects of the book that are critical, sometimes sharply critical, of the doctrines and theories.

My interest in the topics treated in this book began in the early 1960s. First as a graduate student in political science at Yale University, then as a summer intern in the Office of Program and Planning of the International Cooperation Administration (ICA), the forerunner of the Agency for International Development (AID), I thought I noticed some very substantial discrepancies between the stated goals of the U.S. economic aid program and the means and concepts employed to achieve those goals. In doing research for my doctoral dissertation, I discovered that those hunches were by and large correct. Although I was critical

xvi

of many of the Cold War aspects of U.S. policies, however, the developmental goals of the aid program seemed appropriate. The task seemed to be one of finding additional means to achieve those ends. In my dissertation and in articles based on it, therefore, I reported my major findings, and indicated my belief, which was widely accepted at the time, that social science might be able to make a significant contribution to the realization of the developmental objectives.[1]

The present work is almost completely different from those earlier writings. Only a few passages (mainly in Chapter 5) are incorporated from my dissertation and articles. The scope of the present study is much broader, both historically and thematically, and the stress on the liberal tradition as a unifying explanatory thread is completely new. Moreover, evaluations of the doctrines and theories in both normative and policy terms have altered sharply.

To be sure, the earlier descriptive and analytical conclusions about the gap between economic means and political development goals seem as valid today as ever. But, whereas I earlier argued that the means needed to be strengthened, I now believe that the overambitiousness of the goals constituted a more serious flaw. And whereas I used to be moderately optimistic about the contributions that social science theories could make to policy and policymakers, I am now struck by the similarities between doctrines and theories and the relative poverty of the theories as guides to improvements in policy.

In short, as I came slowly (and often painfully) to revise my earlier positions, I found that I myself had been the victim, in large measure, of the very fallacies the exceptionalists warned against and which now, in this book, I

[1] See Robert A. Packenham, "Foreign Aid and Political Development," Ph.D. dissertation, Department of Political Science, Yale University, 1964; "Approaches to the Study of Political Development," *World Politics*, 17, No. 1 (October 1964), 108-120; and "Political-Development Doctrines in the American Foreign Aid Program," *World Politics*, 18, No. 2 (January 1966), 194-230.

seek to identify and document among American policy-makers and scholars. Especially with respect to the theories, therefore, the criticisms of the writings of others constitute as well a critique of my own earlier work. I was not an influential "producer" of these theories; I was however a "consumer" who accepted many of them and who had exaggerated expectations about their policy utility. These facts may make more persuasive the claim that the intention of my criticisms is constructive and scholarly rather than recriminatory or polemical. For a long time political development literature reflected an uncritical acceptance of prevailing assumptions. I try not to repeat that error.

The Problem of Rhetoric and Reality. A variety of forces —some inevitable, some legitimate, some not—induce public officials to exaggerate, oversimplify, or appear more hopeful (or despairing) than they really are. Anyone who does research on doctrines has to come to grips with the problem of distinguishing attitudes and values that genuinely interacted with and shaped perceptions and actions from sheer rhetoric that had little meaning from a policy point of view.

A number of steps were taken to reduce the likelihood of confusing rhetoric and reality. For one thing, I have dealt not only with abstract doctrines but also with specific policies and activities. Doctrines have been examined at various levels of the policymaking machinery, not just at the top where rhetoric is more likely to be exaggerated. My study focuses not just on one agency or office of the U.S. government but on several. It draws upon a variety of source materials, including unclassified internal agency documents, congressional reports and hearings, memoirs, other scholarly studies, journalistic reports, interviews, participant observations, and personal contacts and correspondence with government officials and ex-officials over the last ten years. I have spent nearly two years in Washington doing research on foreign aid and as an AID employee. I also observed AID and State Department activities during a year in Brazil while doing research as a private scholar on other topics.

In making these decisions and in using these sources, I have tried constantly to take into account the environment of contention and "case-making" in which I knew the officials operated. I consciously employed multiple research strategies and sources in order to make better judgments concerning the thinking of the officials. Much of the material was disqualified, including a good deal that could have been used to support the book's theses, because it did not pass this judgmental but important test. Finally, I tried to abide by three simple but very useful and demanding guidelines for research and writing: keep digging; say what you mean; be fair.[2]

All this having been said, it remains true that to a considerable extent, the rhetoric *is* the reality. Much rhetoric was in fact firmly and widely believed by the officials. This was true of the economic and explicit democratic doctrines as well as the Cold War approach. Of course, not all the purposes of aid were developmental. Indeed, at no time was all economic and technical assistance used principally for developmental ends; during more than half the period under scrutiny—most of the fifties and the latter half of the sixties —more narrowly defined security ends were dominant. But these facts do not refute the contention that the rhetoric reflected genuine convictions to a very large degree; after all, Cold War aid had its own rhetoric, and it was quite genuine. Also, the Cold War goals of the aid programs overlapped considerably with the developmental ends and there is no doubt of the sincerity of the rhetoric regarding stable, anti-Communist political systems.

Moreover, even when officials do not mean all they say, their comments frequently have the effect of committing them to the stated goals and paradigms anyway. There are many reasons for this. Sheer repetition may induce belief. Articulating one course of action precludes, or at least reduces, articulation and thoughtful consideration of alterna-

---

[2] These good rules were derived from Eric F. Goldman, *The Tragedy of Lyndon Johnson* (New York: Knopf, 1969), p. vii.

tive courses. As Richard Neustadt has observed, "The tendency of bureaucratic language to create in private the same images presented to the public should never be underrated."[3] Further, public statements force the policymaker to work with the goals and expectations established by those statements because congressmen and various aid constituencies do not forget the rhetoric even if the official may want to. Thus, having "sold" doctrines, officials may be "stuck" with the consequences. And when attacked by critics of their public statements, policymakers may have to suspend their critical faculties and defend these statements unequivocally.[4]

Nor should it be forgotten that the doctrines and the liberal assumptions of the officials resonated harmoniously with dominant values in the wider political culture. An analysis by Donald J. Devine of mass public opinion surveys in the United States between 1936 and 1970 concludes that the Hartz thesis about the liberal tradition is confirmed for the political culture at large during this period.[5] Thus it is plausible to argue that officials articulated things as they did in part because they knew their words harmonized with the larger cultural tradition; once said, moreover, their comments reinforced the tradition and made it harder to change.

What This Book Is Not. It is worthwhile to state clearly what this book is *not.*

The principal focus, to repeat, is on the nature and the roots of ideas about political development among policymakers and scholars in the United States. In treating this

[3] Richard E. Neustadt, *Presidential Power: The Politics of Leadership* (New York: Wiley, 1960), p. 139.

[4] For additional testimony and evidence on these tendencies, see Anthony Lake, "Lying Around Washington," *Foreign Policy*, No. 2 (Spring 1971), 99; Jerome Slater, *Intervention and Negotiation: The United States and the Dominican Republic* (New York: Harper and Row, 1970), pp. 215-16.

[5] Donald J. Devine, *The Political Culture of the United States: The Influence of Member Values on Regime Maintenance* (Boston: Little, Brown, 1972).

topic, it has been necessary to touch on a number of others, but it is the doctrines and the theories themselves which are central. Thus, the book is not mainly about political development per se in the Third World, or in the United States, nor about the domestic politics of foreign aid, nor the impact of U.S. aid on Third-World countries—even though each of these subjects receives some attention. It is not so much a study of foreign aid as an instrument of U.S. foreign policy, where the stress is on aid as an element of international relations, as it is a study of American values and ideology. Between 1947 and 1968 the U.S. government became deeply involved in the affairs of much of the rest of the world, including underdeveloped countries. In this book I try to show the kinds of ideas that emerged among policymakers and scholars when, through this involvement, liberal America confronted a largely illiberal world. These ideas had, of course, been present all along; they "emerged" at this time, however, in the sense that they became more sharply defined and comprehensible as a consequence of foreign contacts.

This period was not, of course, the first in which liberal America encountered an illiberal world, but it was by far the most wide-ranging and intensive encounter. Whatever their other characteristics, defects, and virtues, these postwar international entanglements have helped to reveal some of the inarticulated premises about political development that are embedded in the liberal tradition.

Nor is it suggested here that the liberal tradition explains *all* American thinking on the subject of Third World development. Even less can one contend that the liberal tradition explains all U.S. policies and activities toward Asia, Africa, and Latin America. Obviously, other political, social, economic, military, and cultural factors are also relevant and necessary as explanations of American attitudes and policies. Security needs and perceptions (often grossly distorted and exaggerated) were particularly potent causal variables in producing an anti-Communism that at times seemed almost obsessive. The intention here, then, is not to deny that the roots of American policies and activities toward the Third

World are many and complex. Rather, it is to establish the existence of a powerful and hitherto ill-understood relationship between a cultural tradition, on the one hand, and ideas and policies about political development in other cultures, on the other.

Least of all is this book intended as a vehicle for the presentation of my own theory of political development. I define political development, for present purposes, as the will and capacity to cope with and to generate continuing transformation toward whichever specific values seem appropriate in particular contexts. This definition, which is as open-ended as I think it has to be but not nearly so vapid as it may seem to those who are unfamiliar with the alternatives, is elaborated somewhat in Chapter 8. Readers who wish to know more about my own views might look ahead to the relevant portions of that chapter and to Chapters 4 and 6, where the doctrines and theories are explicitly evaluated. Of course, anyone who reads any part of this book is bound to learn a good deal—whether he wants to or not—about the author's empirical and normative views on political development. Indeed, since these views inevitably inform the entire work and inevitably constitute a large part of the standard against which the doctrines and theories are evaluated, implicitly and explicitly, in this book,[6] it is desirable that the reader be aware of this and understand my position as far as possible. Nevertheless, my main intention is to describe, analyze, account for, and evaluate doctrines and theories, rather than systematically to elaborate a theory of how political development takes place or what course it ought to follow.[7]

[6] More precisely, this political development standard is based on the theoretical social science literature, as of now, as interpreted by me. This yardstick is not as strong, certain, and unambiguous as one would like, to be sure; but it is hard to think of a better way to proceed. The literature is never adequate to serve as the standard; yet it is indefensible not to learn from it what one can.

[7] For additional details about definitions, scope, and method in the treatment of the doctrines and the theories, see the Appendix.

Liberal America
and the Third World

Introduction

FOR MORE THAN two decades after World War II, the United States government carried on large foreign aid programs directed first to Europe and soon thereafter to the underdeveloped countries of the Third World.[1] During this same period American social scientists began to study and theorize about these Third World countries on an unprecedented scale. Both the policymakers and the scholars had conceptions about the kinds of political systems they considered to be desirable and feasible. Although the views of the policymakers were usually not stated so explicitly as those of the social scientists, they existed and could easily be identified. Both groups also had ideas about the conditions which supported these kinds of political systems and about the socioeconomic and other consequences of such systems for the wider community.

The main questions addressed in this book are these: What precisely were the conceptions of the officials and the social scientists about the nature, conditions, and consequences of desirable and feasible types of political systems? Where did their ideas come from? How appropriate were these conceptions for the reality they were meant to describe, explain, and set standards for? Why, in the face of abundant evidence that should have called many of these ideas into question, did they persist? How can Americans better understand and relate to political development in the Third World? And in the United States?

Both officials and theorists defined political development

[1] "Third World" comes from the French "Tiers Monde." It refers to all the underdeveloped countries of Asia, Africa, and Latin America, not just to those which are neutral in the Cold War. "Underdeveloped" is a term of convenience, not a judgment about the quality of all aspects of life in Third World countries. It is a synonym for "Third World," and one which is commonly used even among people from those countries.

3

in terms of democracy, stability, anti-Communism, peace, world community, and pro-Americanism. To a considerable degree, they also agreed on the conditions and the consequences of political development so defined. Their ideas were sometimes appropriate but very often they were naïve, ethnocentric, and rigid. As a consequence, under certain conditions American actions that seemed progressive could turn out to be conservative or even reactionary.

To account for the origins and persistence of such ideas, no single explanation is adequate. The stress in the present book is on certain premises embedded in American culture and political thinking which are collectively designated here as the American liberal tradition. By coming to understand the force of these liberal assumptions in shaping our views about Third World political change and development, and by seeing how these premises distort American perceptions and actions, we may be able to improve the quality of our relationships with these countries. We may also learn something about political development in the United States.

Doctrines and Theories

Doctrines. Three main approaches to political development were embodied in U.S. economic and technical assistance programs between 1947 and 1968. The first of these may be called the economic doctrine. According to this approach economic and technical assistance contributed to economic development; and economic development in turn was seen as contributing to political development. Economic development was defined in terms of growth of per capita product and other conventional measures; political development was defined in terms of stability, democracy, anti-Communism, "world community," peace, pro-Americanism. This economic approach to political development was strong throughout this entire period, especially in the Agency for International Development (AID) and its predecessors.

A second doctrine was the Cold War or security approach.

The assumption here was that aid should be used not so much to achieve economic development and with it a host of congenial political results, but more as an instrument of security more narrowly defined. Aid was thus seen as a Cold War tool that could be used to promote political stability, win alliances for the United States, and impede the emergence of radical or Communist regimes. A variety of conditions and consequences of political development so defined were also specified. This approach was most influential in the periods from 1951 to 1960 and from 1964 to 1968.

The third and least influential doctrine, but the only other one that became explicit and salient among at least some policymakers, was the explicit democratic one. According to this view, the economic and Cold War doctrines should be adjusted so as to maximize the likelihood that aid might contribute to the growth and strengthening of liberal democratic political systems in the Third World. The explicit democratic approach was manifested most clearly in the Latin American policy of the Kennedy Administration in 1962 and 1963, and again after 1966, when Congress added Title IX ("Utilization of Democratic Institutions in Development") to the Foreign Assistance Act.

In describing these approaches, I have combined two types of American perspectives on political development that are analytically separable: the views of American officials about desirable and feasible political trends in the Third World; and their views about the probable effects of American aid on these trends. At various points in the text it will again be necessary to discuss these two types of views at the same time. This necessity derives from the fact that the ideas about political development covered in this book are those embodied in an instrument of U.S. foreign policy—economic aid and technical assistance. It is almost impossible to discuss these ideas without at the same time implying something about the effects of this instrument, and about people's views of these effects.

However, it is important to remember that views about the trends in political systems (i.e. views about political development) are analytically quite sharply distinguishable from views about the effects of aid on those trends. Similarly, actual trends and effects are also analytically distinguishable from ideas about them. My main concern in this book is with just one of these topics: the views of aid officials (and social science scholars) about political development. In other words, I am interested in what the officials and social scientists wanted the trends to be, what conditions they thought promoted these trends, and what they supposed to be the consequences of such desirable trends. I am less interested in the trends themselves, the effects of aid on the trends, or the views of the officials regarding such effects, even though for a variety of reasons it becomes useful to say something at various points about each.

Theories. The theories of the scholars were in many respects remarkably similar to the doctrines of the practitioners. Thus, the social scientists and the officials defined Third World political development mainly in terms of stable, nonradical, constitutional, and, if possible, peaceful and pro-American polities. In their analyses of the conditions that gave birth to and sustained these types of political systems, the theorists like the officials were to a large degree economic determinists: they too saw political development as flowing from economic development. The scholars and the policy-makers supplemented economic determinism with sociological and psychological determinism. Both groups also largely assumed the converse, namely, the beneficence for socio-economic transformations of stable, constitutional political systems. For both groups, reform tended to be good, but revolution and attempts at revolution were almost always bad. Neither group saw much virtue under any circumstances in intense conflict, especially for radical ends. The theorists were more ideological than they were generally perceived to be or conceded themselves to be during the period, and

6

their ideology, like that of the officials, was strongly affected by the style and substance of the Cold War. The list of parallels could fairly easily be extended.

There were, of course, differences as well, not only between officials and academicians but also within each of these groups; but the differences were not nearly so great as the similarities. Accordingly, this book does not deny differences, but it does focus on the *prevailing* similarities and continuities, not only within and between these two principal groups, but also over time, across party lines, and among various administrations and political leaders. In this sense most American politicians and academicians are liberals (or "Liberals"): Richard Nixon as well as Hubert Humphrey, John Foster Dulles as well as Dean Acheson or Dean Rusk or Harry Truman, Lyndon Johnson as well as John Kennedy.[2] Such, at any rate, is the perspective from which this book is written. This does not deny, of course, the existence of differences in policies, personalities, and attitudes among these men, or among administrations, or over time. From other perspectives these differences might be very interesting and important. Nor, of course, does it deny that these differences can produce policies and actions with very significant contrasts in their consequences. It does say that for a variety of reasons both explicit and implicit in this book the similarities prevail and are pertinent to the kinds of insights the book seeks to convey.

How appropriate were these doctrines and theories? Appropriateness involves many things: feasibility, desirability, empirical reliability and validity, flexibility and firmness, parsimony and completeness, among others. Obviously, appropriateness is a complex question. It is scarcely possible to deal with all aspects of the matter here. The most detailed

[2] An arresting interpretation of Richard Nixon from this perspective is Garry Wills, *Nixon Agonistes: The Crisis of the Self-Made Man* (Boston: Houghton Mifflin, 1970). Wills feels that Nixon may be the "last liberal," contending (perhaps too strongly) that he has reduced the liberal creed to "absurdity."

treatment of this question can be found in Chapters 4 and 6 (where the doctrines and theories, respectively, are evaluated) and in Chapter 8 (where a working definition of political development is elaborated and prescriptions are suggested). However, even though most of the evaluative content of this book is concentrated in those chapters, it is possible to begin here to assess the doctrines and theories by focusing on just one aspect of their appropriateness, namely, their feasibility.

The Feasibility of the Goals

Feasible goals are goals that are capable of being carried out; they are practicable, "realistic," nonutopian. How feasible were the goals embodied in the political development doctrines of the American aid program (and, by extension, in the social-scientific theories) from 1947 to 1968? One way to answer this question is to replace it with another, more operational one: to what extent were the goals of the programs actually realized during this period? Answers to this question by themselves will not, of course, enable us to assess the feasibility of the goals, much less their appropriateness. But they are surely relevant to any such assessment. So let us see how great the gap was between the objectives and the reality that emerged.

In the case of the European Recovery Program, the main approach was economic, and it seemed to work very effectively. The United States provided aid; the economies revived; Communist parties did not come to power; stability and democracy were the political results, by and large, in Western European political systems. NATO was set up and flourished—at least for a time.

In the Third World, however, neither the economic doctrine nor either of the other two doctrines has worked nearly so well. Economic development proceeded more slowly than most people had expected. Moreover, aggregate annual rates of economic growth declined in underdeveloped countries from 1950 to 1966. And in most countries population growth rates either increased or remained sufficiently high so that, while there were variations among countries, overall annual increases in per capita product were lower than annual increases in gross domestic product (see Table 1). These are absolute rates of growth; relative to the rich countries, underdeveloped nations fell even further behind as the income gap between rich and poor countries widened.[3] In terms of the political development goals, the record was no better and perhaps worse. Few of the political development goals set from the late 1940s on were achieved by the late 1960s. Some of them appeared even more distant at the end of this period than they had at its beginning. Take political stability, "world community," and peace. During the two decades after World War II, according to Samuel Huntington, successful coups d'etat occurred at least once (and often several times) in 17 of 20 Latin American countries, in 6 North African countries, and in 7 Asian societies. In general, political instability and violence increased: "Violence and other destabilizing events were five times more frequent between 1955 and 1962 than they were between 1948 and 1954. Sixty-four of 84 countries were less stable in

[3] Gunnar Myrdal, *Rich Lands and Poor* (New York: Harper and Row, 1957), p. 6; George D. Woods, "The Development Decade in the Balance," *Foreign Affairs*, 44, No. 2 (January 1966), 207, both cited in Samuel P. Huntington, *Political Order in Changing Societies* (New Haven: Yale University Press, 1968), p. 2. Woods, then the president of the World Bank, suggested that at current rates of growth the gap in per capita national income between the United States and 40 underdeveloped countries would increase 50% by the year 2000.

For excellent general discussions of these tendencies, see Theodore Caplow, "Are the Rich Countries Getting Richer and the Poor Countries Poorer?" *Foreign Policy*, No. 3 (Summer 1971), 90-107; and Barbara Ward, J. D. Runnalls, and Lenore D'Anjou, eds., *The Widening Gap: Development in the 1970's* (New York: Columbia University Press, 1971); this is a report on the "Columbia Conference on International Economic Development" held in February 1970 to consider the recommendations of the Pearson Report (*Partners in Development*).

TABLE 1

AVERAGE ANNUAL RATE OF ECONOMIC GROWTH IN UNDERDEVELOPED
COUNTRIES, 1950-1966
(*in percentages*)

	Gross Domestic Product	Per Capita GNP
1950-1955	4.9	2.8
1955-1960	4.5	2.1
1960-1966	4.4	1.8

SOURCES: Statistical Office of the United Nations, *Yearbook of National Accounts Statistics 1967* (New York: United Nations, 1968), p. 808; Luther H. Evans and others, *The Decade of Development: Problems and Issues* (Dobbs Ferry, N.Y.: Oceana Publications, 1966), p. 17. See also John Pincus, *Trade, Aid and Development: The Rich and Poor Nations* (New York: McGraw-Hill, 1967), p. 72. Pincus' figures are broken down differently but are in line with these. Cf. *Partners in Development*, Report of the Commission on International Development, Lester B. Pearson, Chairman (New York: Praeger, 1969), pp. 28, 358. The Pearson Report shows a 5 percent average annual rate of growth in gross domestic product from 1960 to 1967. The discrepancy between this figure and the one given above is partly due to the inclusion in the Pearson Report of Southern Europe (Cyprus, Greece, Portugal, Spain, Turkey, and Yugoslavia) as part of the Third World. The figure given for that region is 7.1 percent. Also, the Pearson Report has an unusually high rate of growth (7.2 percent) for the Middle East. Pincus' figure for this region is 5.5 percent for 1957/58 to 1963/64.

the latter period than in the earlier one." In 1958, there were "some 28 prolonged guerrilla insurgencies, four military uprisings, and two unconventional wars. Seven years later, in 1965, 42 prolonged insurgencies were underway; ten military revolts occurred; and five conventional conflicts were being fought." Between 1958 and 1961, there were 155 military conflicts of all types; between 1962 and 1965, the number increased to 219.[4]

[4] Huntington, *Political Order*, pp. 3-4.

Or consider the record with respect to another goal and anticipated consequence of the aid program—democracy. Almost all of the 37 colonies that attained independence between 1945 and 1960 were equipped with a written constitution providing for democratic government. But at the beginning of 1967, according to calculations from Rustow's data, only 4 of these (11%) "had regimes based on three or more consecutive, popular, and competitive elections." These were Ceylon, India, Israel, and the Philippines. If we add 3 countries that Rustow omitted—Malaysia, Turkey, and Venezuela—the proportion rises to only 19%. By contrast, of the 47 countries which became independent between 1776 and 1943, 17 (36%) were democratic by Rustow's criteria in 1967. Of the 22 countries which became sovereign before 1775, 10 (45%) were democratic (see Tables 2 and 4).

Of course many underdeveloped countries (about half in 1960, less than half after 1960) became independent before 1945. At the end of 1960 there were 75 underdeveloped countries and 31 developed countries. Twenty-one (68%) of the developed countries were democratic at the beginning of 1967; by contrast, only 10-13 (13%-17%), of the underdeveloped countries were democratic at that time. Nor does it appear that the proportion of democracies among underdeveloped countries increased significantly between 1945 and 1967. About 15% of underdeveloped countries had democratic political systems in 1945. The proportion rose to approximately 25% between 1950 and 1955; but it dropped in 1960 to about 16% or 19%, depending on who was counting; and it fell still further to about 13%-17% at the beginning of 1967 (see Tables 3 and 4).

It is possible, of course, to quarrel with these classifications, but such quarrels would change the results only marginally. And the case for changes that would increase the number of democracies is probably weaker than the case for changes that would decrease it. Moreover, adding those underdeveloped countries which gained independence after

11

TABLE 2

SOVEREIGN COUNTRIES IN 1960: DATE OF INDEPENDENCE
AND NUMBER DEMOCRATIC IN 1967

Independence Gained	Number of Countries	Number Democratic in 1967	Percent Democratic in 1967
Before 1775	22	10	45
Europe	12	9	75
E. and S. Asia	5	1	20
Mid-East and N. Africa	5	0	0
1776-1943	47	17	36
Europe	14	7	50
N. America and Oceania	4	4	100
E. and S. Asia	1	0	0
Mid-East and Africa	8	1	13
Middle and S. America	20	5	25
1945-1960	37	4	11
E. and S. Asia	12	3	25
Mid-East and N. Africa	9	1	11
Tropical and S. Africa	16	0	0
TOTAL	106	31	29

SOURCE: Calculated from data in Dankwart A. Rustow, *A World of Nations: Problems of Political Modernization* (Washington, D.C.: The Brookings Institution, 1967), Appendix Tables 5 and 6. Democratic countries are "all countries which at the beginning of 1967 had regimes based on three or more consecutive, popular, and competitive elections." *Ibid.*, p. 290. This table excludes all countries which became independent between 1961 and 1966 because they were not independent long enough to satisfy Rustow's criteria.

TABLE 3

DEVELOPED AND UNDERDEVELOPED COUNTRIES IN 1960 AND
DEMOCRATIC POLITICAL SYSTEMS IN 1967

	Number of Countries in 1960	Number Democratic in 1967	Percent Democratic in 1967
Developed Countries	31	21	68
Europe	26	16	62
E. Asia	1	1	100
N. America and Oceania	4	4	100
Underdeveloped Countries	75	10	13
E. and S. Asia	17	3	18
Mid-East and Africa	38	2	5
Middle and S. America	20	5	25
TOTAL	106	31	29

SOURCE: Same as Table 2. Developed countries are defined as all of Europe (including the USSR, Spain, Portugal, and the 7 Communist countries of Eastern Europe), Japan, the United States, Canada, and Oceania (Australia and New Zealand). Underdeveloped countries are all of Africa, Asia (except Japan), the Middle East, and Middle and South America. If it is unfair to saddle the underdeveloped world with South Africa and Rhodesia (which are counted as nondemocracies), this seems offset by the inclusion of Portugal and all of the East European countries as part of the developed world. Also, Greece is classified as developed and democratic because the military dictatorship began there in April 1967; Israel and Uruguay are counted underdeveloped democracies. If anything, this table exaggerates the degree of stable, liberal democracy (Rustow's definition) in the Third World.

It should be emphasized that this table is intended to describe the frequency of democracy in the two groups of countries; it is not intended to suggest explanations for these differences.

13

TABLE 4

DEMOCRATIC POLITICAL SYSTEMS IN THE THIRD WORLD, 1945-1967

	1945	1950-1955	1960 (Coleman)	1967 (Rustow)
Argentina			X	
Brazil		X	X	
Ceylon	NI	X	X	X
Chile	X	X	X	X
Colombia			(X)*	X
Costa Rica	X	X	X	X
India	NI	X	X	X
Israel	NI	X	X	X
Lebanon	Xª	X	X	X
Malaya/ Malaysia	NI	X	X	(X)**
Mexico	X	X		X
Philippines	NI	X	X	X
Turkey	X	X	X	(X)**
Uruguay	X	X	X	X
Venezuela			(X)*	(X)**
Number Democratic	6	12	12 (14)	10 (13)
Total 3rd World	39	48	73ᵇ	75ᶜ
Percent Democratic	15	25	16 (19)	13 (17)

NI = Country not yet independent.

* Colombia and Venezuela are not on Coleman's list but are added here because both seem to have been democratic by his criteria in 1960. The numerical and percentage figures given below in parentheses are based on these additions.

** Malaysia, Turkey, and Venezuela are not on Rustow's list but are added here. Rustow omitted Malaysia because it was so new a nation, and Turkey because of the brief interruption of democratic government in 1960-61. Venezuela seems to have satisfied Rustow's criteria since 1958. The numerical and percentage figures given below in parentheses are based on these additions.

ª Classified as democratic even though independent only since 1943.

14

^b Coleman's list, p. 534.
^c Rustow's list, Appendix Table 6.

SOURCES: For 1945 and 1950-1955: Monograph sources and Dankwart
A. Rustow, *A World of Nations: Problems of Political Modernization*
(Washington, D.C.: The Brookings Institution, 1967), Appendix
Table 6.
For 1960 (Coleman): James S. Coleman, "Conclusion," in James S.
Coleman and Gabriel A. Almond, eds., *The Politics of the Developing
Areas* (Princeton: Princeton University Press, 1960), pp. 534, 562-567.
Coleman notes that his classifications are "gross" and "both tentative
and disputable." The present list includes only the 7 Asian and African
countries Coleman classifies as "political democracies" and the 5 Latin
American countries he classifies as "competitive" political systems. It ex-
cludes the 7 regimes he calls "tutelary democracies" and the 18 he
classifies as "terminal colonial democracies."
For 1967 (Rustow): Rustow, *op.cit.*, Appendix Tables 5 and 6.
Rustow classifies as democratic "all countries which at the beginning
of 1967 had regimes based on three or more consecutive, popular, and
competitive elections."

1960 to the total would not increase the proportion of democracies greatly. For example, 21 Third World countries
became sovereign between 1961 and 1966.[5] The earlier history of decolonization suggests that it is risky to classify
such countries as democratic on the basis of only a few
years experience; but let us assume that 8 of them (say, the
4 Caribbean countries, Singapore, and 3 of the African countries) were democratic in 1967. This would increase the
number of democracies in the Third World to 21 out of 95
nations, or only 22%. And the more recently independent
countries have smaller populations than all the other countries. The median population of the 1961-1966 group was 2
million in 1964. In the same year the median population of
the pre-1775 group was 22.6 million; of the 1776-1943 group,
5.2 million; of the 1945-1960 group, 4.7 million.[6] In general,

[5] These were: Singapore, Maldive Islands, Algeria, Kuwait, Tan-
zania, Kenya, Uganda, Rhodesia, Malawi, Zambia, Rwanda, Burundi,
Sierra Leone, Lesotho, Botswana, Gambia, Barbados, Guayana, Ja-
maica, and Trinidad and Tobago.
[6] Calculated from Dankwart A. Rustow, *A World of Nations: Prob-*

15

only a minority ranging from about 10% to, at the very most, 25% of Third World countries has been democratic at any one time since World War II. This experience suggests that prospects are not bright for a rapid or substantial increase in the incidence of democratic politics in these countries.[7]

The one political development goal of the aid program that was substantially realized in the Third World was the anti-Communist one. Excluding East European countries, only mainland China, North Korea, North Vietnam, Cuba, and (arguably) Chile may be said to have "gone Communist" between 1947 and 1968. The final goal cited—pro-Americanism—is harder to define and measure. However, a good case could be made that esteem and friendship for the United States were never at a lower ebb during those two decades than at the end of 1968.

All this is not to say either that foreign aid was primarily responsible for these outcomes, or that the goals were unrealizable in all instances. The first question, on the influence of aid, is very complex. The best global generalization is that this influence varied considerably over time, and according to several variables, but that in most cases the impact was not very great. Even if, in terms of the foregoing political development goals, aid's influence was more positive than negative—so that it slowed down the "bad" trends—this influence was not usually sufficient to make a sizable difference in the extent to which the goals were actually realized.

---

lems of Political Modernization (Washington, D.C.: The Brookings Institution, 1967), Appendix Tables 6 and 7.

[7] This conclusion seems evident from an inspection of Tables 2 through 4 above. For very similar projections, see Robert A. Dahl, *Polyarchy: Participation and Opposition* (New Haven: Yale University Press, 1971), pp. 200, 246-48, and Reinhold Niebuhr and Paul E. Sigmund, *The Democratic Experience: Past and Prospects* (New York: Praeger, 1969), esp. pp. 183-84. Dahl's list of "contemporary polyarchies" (p. 248) is, as he notes, "almost identical" with Rustow's list of contemporary democracies; Rustow's list was, in turn, used by me in Tables 2 through 4 above.

16

In fact, though the available studies are not very satisfactory, there appears to be no clear correlation between aid and economic development, to say nothing of aid and political development. Some of those countries which received substantial aid have realized no significant economic development, while some of the most impressive cases of economic growth and development occurred without the benefit of foreign assistance.[8]

As to the second question, it is not suggested that stability, democracy, and the other goals could never have been achieved in any countries of the Third World during this period. As a matter of fact, some of them were achieved in some countries at some times. The point is that in most countries most of the time the probability that they could have been realized was low.[9] Many of these objectives were optimistic even if taken singly; taken together, they constituted a form of naiveté bordering on utopianism.

[8] *Partners in Development*, Report of the Commission on International Development, Lester B. Pearson, Chairman (New York: Praeger, 1969), p. 49; John Pincus, *Trade, Aid and Development: The Rich and Poor Nations* (New York: McGraw-Hill, 1967), p. 73. Of course, correlations are at best suggestive as to causal relationships. The magnitude and direction of aid's influence on economic and political development are topics so complex and difficult that it is necessary to examine country studies as well as general surveys and to consider qualitative as well as quantitative factors. A brief discussion of aid's influence and citations to a variety of empirical studies using different kinds of techniques are given in Chapter 4. As I try to show there, the impact of aid on the recipients is, so to speak, the great unanswered question in the field, at least in terms of serious research. A fairly comprehensive representation of the variety of answers given to this question appears in Ward, Runnalls, and D'Anjou, eds., *The Widening Gap*, esp. pp. 1-14, 238-42, and 275-345.

For the argument that U.S. economic aid has fostered political instability in the Third World, see Huntington, *Political Order*, pp. 4, 461.

[9] See n. 7 above. Chapter 8 contains a discussion of and response to the possible objection that this conclusion is overdeterministic, overpessimistic, and pseudorealistic.

Thus, according to this evidence the feasibility of most of the goals does not seem to have been very great. We Americans thought that by applying these doctrines political trends would improve; instead they tended to get worse or improve more slowly than expected. We thought we knew more about the conditions of political stability, democracy, and other goals than we really did. We thought we knew which types of political systems were desirable in these countries; now we are not so sure, and wonder whether we were not formerly ethnocentric. On all these matters, earlier views now seem to have been too optimistic, too parochial, too rigid.

Why was this so? To the extent that such errors and misjudgments existed, what were their origins? Why did they persist? A great variety of explanations is possible, and certainly more than one explanation is necessary. Without in any way denying the multiple causes of these phenomena, I shall argue that the origins and persistence of the doctrines —and, to a slightly lesser extent, of the theories—may be explained in substantial measure by reference to some largely implicit but powerful assumptions embodied in what Louis Hartz has called the "Liberal Tradition" in America.[10]

THE LIBERAL TRADITION IN AMERICA

Louis Hartz's book, *The Liberal Tradition in America*, begins with a statement from the great nineteenth-century French student of American democracy, Alexis de Tocqueville: "The great advantage of the Americans is, that they have arrived at a state of democracy without having to endure a democratic revolution; and that they are born equal, instead of becoming so." Tocqueville's view is the foundation for the hypotheses contained in Hartz's book, which is aptly described as "an extended illustration of the conse-

[10] Louis Hartz, *The Liberal Tradition in America: An Interpretation of American Political Thought Since the Revolution* (New York: Harcourt, Brace, and World, 1955).

quences of this democracy without revolution for American political thought," and as "basically . . . a study of the unconscious mind of America, conditioned by a peculiar historical and social experience."[11]

What was the nature of this "peculiar historical and social experience"? According to Hartz, and other members of the school of historical interpretation known as "American exceptionalism,"[12] American society was founded by migrants who had fled the class and religious conflicts of Europe and had come to a continent of great size and unusual economic potential. Feudalism and intense class conflict, if not wholly absent, were important only at the margins of this new society. The ideas—if not always the practice—of equality and individual liberty were established early and took deep roots. The American Revolution, when it came, was relatively speedy, easy, and above all conservative. It was a revolution that sought to maintain "the rights of Englishmen" rather than to reject the political values of English society. The political institutions of the new American nation reflected the traditional American distrust of author-

[11] Marvin Meyers, "Louis Hartz, *The Liberal Tradition in America*: An Appraisal," *Comparative Studies in Society and History*, Vol. 5 (1962-1963), pp. 262, 264.

[12] Especially Carl N. Degler, "The American Past: An Unsuspected Obstacle in Foreign Affairs," *The American Scholar*, 32, No. 2 (Spring 1963), 192-209, David M. Potter, *People of Plenty: Economic Abundance and the American Character* (Chicago: University of Chicago Press, 1954); and Daniel J. Boorstin, *The Genius of American Politics* (Chicago: University of Chicago Press, 1953).

Other useful sources of Hartz's ideas have been his testimony in *The Nature of Revolution*, Committee on Foreign Relations, U.S. Senate, Hearings, 90th Cong., 2nd Sess., February 19, 21, 26, and March 7, 1968 (Washington: Government Printing Office, 1968), pp. 109-152; and his essay, "A Comparative Study of Fragment Cultures," in Hugh Davis Graham and Ted Robert Gurr, eds., *Violence in America: Historical and Comparative Perspectives* (New York: Bantam, 1969), pp. 107-127. A symposium on *The Liberal Tradition in America*, with essays by Marvin Meyers, Leonard Krieger, Harry V. Jaffe, and Hartz, appears in *Comparative Studies in Society and History*, Vol. 5 (1962-1963), pp. 261-84, 365-77.

ity and the belief that political power should be checked and balanced and decentralized rather than accumulated and concentrated. And for almost a century and a half after independence America was fortuitously blessed, by geography and the technology of the time, with isolation from most of the political and military conflicts of Europe.

What kinds of beliefs about economic and political development did this singular and relatively happy history engender among Americans? These four propositions, among others:

1. Change and Development Are Easy
2. All Good Things Go Together
3. Radicalism and Revolution Are Bad
4. Distributing Power Is More Important Than Accumulating Power

Hartz might not state the propositions in precisely this form. Other writers have influenced this formulation.[13] And it is hard to be certain just where their views leave off and my own begin. In any event, the main point to be emphasized is that the data reported here provide considerable empirical support for certain hypotheses that flow from the school of historical interpretation known as "American exceptionalism," just as the hypotheses help to order and make sense of the data. The insights that Hartz and others have derived from their historical studies of American political thought and institutions seem to be confirmed by the record of U.S. aid doctrines from 1947 to 1968, and by the theories.

Moreover, the "American exceptionalist" perspective, particularly as enunciated by Hartz, implies two corollaries that are also confirmed by the historical record since World

[13] In addition to those authors cited in the previous note, I must mention Samuel P. Huntington, especially his *Political Order*. Though Huntington is a political scientist rather than a historian, his work is richly informed by historical scholarship and draws frequently on Hartz's major study. I am indebted to him for many ideas and for helping me to see the revelance of Hartz's work to the present study.

War II. One is that political ideas that looked radical to Americans were in fact well within the liberal tradition. Since the American liberal tradition is, on a world scale, a rather conservative type of political thought, these "radical" ideas were also rather conservative, even though they did not appear so to Americans. In other words, variations in political development ideas in the doctrines and theories seem large when viewed from within the liberal tradition, but they appear much smaller when viewed from outside it.

Another corollary is that we Americans do not realize how powerful the grip of the liberal tradition is on our thinking. Hence we tend to think we have "escaped" it when in fact we have not. The liberal tradition, in other words, has many *layers* of meaning. To peel away one layer is by no means to remove its ethnocentric effects, for there is almost always another layer of meaning underneath.

As a final preliminary word, it should be emphasized that the degree to which these four premises have accurately described the American experience as far as political and economic development is concerned, and the extent to which liberal ideology has been good or bad for America per se (as distinguished from America's involvement with Third World countries) are not questions treated in this book. An adequate discussion of these important, but complex topics would take us far afield. At this point let it be said only that the postulates of the liberal tradition are not and never have been wholly accurate descriptions of the American experience. Although the liberal premises are substantially more accurate and appropriate when applied to the United States than they are when applied to the rest of the world, especially poor countries, in important and sometimes tragic ways they have also coincided poorly with the realities of our own society. Moreover, the liberal ideology has not been nearly so unambiguous a blessing for this country as we tend to think. Nevertheless, the principal tasks here are to describe the origins of these premises in the American experience (however selectively perceived), to argue that they have

21

considerable utility for understanding why the doctrines and theories took the shape they did, and to criticize their extension to and application in the Third World, rather than to assess their validity with respect to the nature and quality of American political life.

PART I   Doctrines

1   Political Development
Doctrines, 1947-1960

The Fifteen Weeks was one of those rare times in history when shackles fall away from the mind, the spirit, and the will, allowing them to soar free and high for a while and to discover new standards of what is responsible, of what is promising, and of what is possible. It was a time when men thought not in terms of what could be done but of what should be done, when only the timid idea was banished and all others welcomed, a time of courage, of bold decision, of generous response. It was a time when American democracy worked with unexampled efficiency and inspiration to produce national agreement. It was a great time to be alive.[1]

THE Fifteen Weeks went from February 21 to June 5, 1947. They began the day Great Britain informed the Department of State of its inability to maintain its commitments in Greece and Turkey, and ended when General George C. Marshall, the U.S. Secretary of State, delivered his famous commencement address at Harvard University. Out of those hundred days two programs emerged: the Truman Doctrine for aid to Greece and Turkey, and the Marshall Plan of aid for the economic recovery of Europe. Moreover, the planning that was done, the statements that were made, and the actions that were taken by the U.S. government in relation to these two programs formed the basis for much of the continuity in American foreign policy during the next two decades. Among the many subsequent policies and actions that "had their roots [in part] in the national conversion of the Fifteen Weeks"[2] were the Point Four Program, the

[1] Joseph Marion Jones, *The Fifteen Weeks: February 21–June 5, 1947* (New York: Harcourt, Brace and World, 1955), p. 259.
[2] *Ibid.,* p. 262.

25

Mutual Security Program, the Development Loan Fund, the composite Foreign Assistance Act of 1961, the Alliance for Progress, and the whole range of massive American aid programs and intervention in South Vietnam.

THE TRUMAN DOCTRINE

On March 12, 1947, President Harry S. Truman stood before a special joint session of Congress and requested $400 million for economic, technical, and military assistance to Greece and Turkey. Journalists, comparing its boldness and sweeping implications to the Monroe Doctrine, promptly dubbed the speech the "Truman Doctrine." They had a point. For the Truman Doctrine signaled a fundamental change in the grand foreign policy strategy of the United States. It was the first clear public statement of what came to be known as the "containment policy." (The containment label came from George Kennan's formulation which was published a few months after Truman's speech.)[3] The policy was directed especially at the Soviet Union, but it was stated in general terms: "I am fully aware," Truman said, "of the broad implications involved if the United States extends assistance to Greece and Turkey. . . . I believe that it must be the policy of the United States to support free peoples who are resisting attempted subjugation by armed minorities or by outside pressures." And he added: "I believe that we must assist free peoples to work out their own destinies in their own way. I believe that our help should be primarily through economic and financial aid which is essential to economic stability and orderly political processes."[4]

[3] H. Bradford Westerfield, *The Instruments of America's Foreign Policy* (New York: Thomas Crowell, 1963), p. 102. Kennan's article, published anonymously, was Mr. X, "The Sources of Soviet Conduct," *Foreign Affairs* (July 1947).

[4] *Public Papers of the Presidents of the United States, Harry S. Truman, 1947* (Washington, D.C.: Government Printing Office, 1960), pp. 178-79.

The immediate stimulus for President Truman's request had been the precarious economic and political situation in Greece and the decision by Great Britain in late February 1947 to withdraw its economic and military support from Greece and Turkey. The main concern was Greece. The war had almost literally decimated the Greek economy. Virtually all the railways, roads, port facilities, communications, and merchant marine were destroyed. Inflation was rampant. A thousand villages had been burned, and almost all livestock had disappeared. Eighty-five per cent of the children were tubercular.[5] Moreover, guerrilla bands, thought by the American government to be led by Communists directed from Moscow, roamed the northern mountains; in the cities and towns, "Communist newspapers and agitators carried on a scarcely less effective war of words against the Greek government."[6] All of this occurred against the background of increasing friction and deteriorating diplomatic relations between the United States and the Soviet Union between 1945 and 1947. The situation seemed urgent. As Truman saw it, "Greece must have help to import the goods necessary to restore internal order and security so essential for economic and political recovery.... Greece must have assistance if it is to become a self-supporting and self-respecting democracy. The United States must supply this assistance.... There is no other country to which democratic Greece can turn."[7] After considerable discussion, Congress appropriated about $300 million for Greece and about $100 million for Turkey.

The broad rationale for the Truman Doctrine was not pure humanitarianism but the national interest of the United States. This was not novel; foreign policies are almost always justified in terms of national interest. What matters is how

---

[5] According to President Truman, *ibid.*, p. 176.

[6] William Hardy McNeill, *Greece: American Aid in Action, 1947-1956* (New York: Twentieth Century Fund, 1957), p. 34.

[7] *Public Papers, Harry S. Truman, 1947*, pp. 176-77.

27

that interest is defined.[8] Truman's speech was ambiguous on this score. He defined the American interest in both relatively narrow security terms and in broader developmental terms. He included the support of not just Greece and Turkey but other "free peoples" as part of the U.S. interest. In short, he defined the American interest in both specific and universal terms on both geographic and Cold-War/development dimensions. The ambiguity was in some measure intentional in order to warn the Soviet Union.[9] But another consequence was to pave the way for other aid programs to other areas for broader development purposes according to uncertain criteria.

The most salient political development objective of the Truman Doctrine was that of maintaining and strengthening non-Communist, pro-American governments in Greece and Turkey. "The United States had to make a choice between supporting temporarily a bad democratic government and allowing an armed minority under Soviet direction to fasten a Communist dictatorship permanently on Greece," is the way Joseph Marion Jones, who wrote the original draft of Truman's speech, explains it: "It was not a choice between black and white, but between black and a rather dirty grey."[10] The anti-Communist objective seemed important enough to justify publicly minimizing the undemocratic character of the Greek regime. Jones, who wrote later that the Greek government was "corrupt, reactionary, inefficient, and indulged in extremist practices,"[11] nevertheless drafted a speech which had Truman note only briefly that the Greek government was "not perfect," and then point out that it represented 85% of the members of Parliament chosen in a fair election the previous year. (Others

[8] Robert A. Packenham, "Foreign Aid and the National Interest," *Midwest Journal of Political Science*, 10, No. 2 (May 1966), 214-21; John Kautsky, "The National Interest: The Entomologist and the Beetle," *ibid.*, 222-31.

[9] Jones, *The Fifteen Weeks*, p. 159.

[10] *Ibid.*, p. 186.   [11] *Ibid.*, p. 185.

have contested the fairness of the election; no one has disputed the liabilities of the Greek government.) There is also some question as to whether the rebels were "under Soviet direction" or even receiving aid from Russia. Certainly there was little time in late February and early March 1947 for a searching inquiry into the character of the rebel movement, its *raison d'être*, or its relations with Communist countries. To the American government the answers seemed obvious at the time.[12]

The combination of the broad language of the Truman Doctrine and the loose definition of a "free people" in the Greek case had important consequences. As George Kennan was later to remark:

> Throughout the ensuing two decades the conduct of our foreign policy would continue to be bedeviled by people in our own government as well as in other governments who could not free themselves from the belief that all another country had to do, in order to qualify for American aid, was to demonstrate the existence of a Communist threat. Since almost no country was without a Com-

[12] See especially Richard J. Barnet, *Intervention and Revolution: The United States in the Third World* (New York: World, 1968), pp. 107-121. Also Jones, *The Fifteen Weeks*, pp. 67-77, 129-47, 185-87; Dean Acheson, *Present at the Creation: My Years in the State Department* (New York: Norton, 1969), pp. 219-25; and George F. Kennan, *Memoirs: 1925-1950* (Boston: Little, Brown, 1967), p. 316. Barnet contends that the Soviet Union neither aided nor directed the Greek rebels and that Stalin opposed the Greek uprising and in fact tried in vain to prevent the Yugoslavian government from continuing its assistance to the rebels. There is little if anything in the accounts by Jones, Kennan, and Acheson to contradict Barnet's conclusion that: "During the feverish days of preparation for the Truman Doctrine speech, no one in the national-security bureaucracy appears to have ventured a political analysis of the Greek rebels, their relations with Russia, Yugoslavia, or the other Balkan neighbors. The fifth-column analogy from World War II dominated official thinking. The possibility that men had taken to the hills for reasons of their own and not as agents of a foreign power was never seriously considered" (p. 121).

29

munist minority, this assumption carried very far. And as time went on, the firmness of understanding for these distinctions on the part of our own public and governmental establishment appeared to grow weaker rather than stronger. In the 1960s so absolute would be the value attached, even by people within the government, to the mere existence of a Communist threat, that such a threat would be viewed as calling, in the case of Southeast Asia, for an American response on a tremendous scale, without serious regard even to [the] main criteria that most of us in 1947 would have thought it natural and essential to apply."[13]

And aid to Greece on the premise that it was a free people fighting off a coercive dictatorship opened the door to aid to other dubious democracies, also in the name of freedom.

A second salient political development objective was democracy. The desire to promote freedom in Greece and Turkey was not all rhetoric. If the United States had to stretch the definition of democracy in Greece in order to support it at the outset, this did not mean the Americans would not try to bring about a more genuine democracy later on. In Jones's words, "With United States aid and pressure the gray might become a respectable white."[14] The effort was made, not once but repeatedly. For example, at the end of the civil war American officials found the Greek version of democracy "very hard to take." They "embarked upon a determined and distinctly high-handed effort to get a government that would more nearly suit their wishes." They insisted that elections be held immediately, and in March 1950 they were. The American hope was that a group of democratic centrist parties would win, organize a stable government, and carry on reform, recovery, and development programs. Their hopes were not realized: no clear majority resulted, and the new prime minister was un-

[13] Kennan, *Memoirs*, p. 322.
[14] Jones, *The Fifteen Weeks*, p. 186.

acceptable to them. They pressured him into resigning, but the next man was no better. Other techniques were tried—economic pressures, pressures on legislators, changes in electoral laws—but they were equally unsuccessful. In September 1950 a new American ambassador, John Peurifoy, "declared that the United States government was completely neutral in matters of internal Greek politics. This pious falsehood was in effect a public confession of defeat."[15] Thus the explicit efforts to engineer democracy from the top in Greece were frustrated.

The final set of political development objectives were vague and diffuse hopes for freedom, world peace, stability, and community. As American involvement around the world increased and our aid programs expanded, these objectives continued to be prominent. Economic and technical assistance were seen as important for economic development in the Third World, and economic development in those countries was regarded as conducive to a host of other good things.

The main instruments by which the goals of the Truman Doctrine were to have been achieved were economic: funds, materials, technical assistance. In Turkey, funds were used to enable the Turks to spend their own money for military purposes: thus economic aid to Turkey was an early version of what came to be known later as defense support (i.e. economic aid for security purposes). In Greece, the assumption was that economic aid would strengthen the economy, and that the strengthened economy would produce greater political stability and reduce the appeals of Communism. However, events in Greece made this theory obsolete even before its implementation began. Full-scale civil war broke out in July 1947 between the government and the rebels. Consequently, "willy-nilly the American mission found itself compelled to wage war also."[16] From 1947 to 1949, military considerations and programs came first and almost everything else had to wait.

[15] McNeill, *Greece*, pp. 61-63, 187.   [16] *Ibid.*, p. 38.

What were the results? The main objective of the program—containing the Communists—was achieved. The national army, with American help, won the civil war in Greece. But the cost was great. The original sum of $300 million had swelled to appropriations totaling more than a $1½ billion through fiscal year 1950/51; still more followed later. And this was only part of the real cost. "The country as a whole was worse off in 1949 than it had been in 1944 and 1945, when the severe losses of the occupation years were still fresh. Clearly, the task of reconstruction and construction was going to be much larger than United States officials had estimated in 1947. Except for main roads and ports, which had been rebuilt and improved during the course of the fighting, almost everything planned in 1947 still remained to be done in 1949."[17] Almost two decades later, when the total amount of American military and economic aid is said to have reached almost $4 billion, socioeconomic inequities and political instability were still grave problems.[18] An out-and-out military dictatorship came to power in April 1967. American aid had ended, or at least deferred, civil war, and it had prevented a Communist takeover; but these were the only unambiguous successes of the Truman Doctrine and its successor programs in Greece.

THE MARSHALL PLAN

The Marshall Plan was part of the same grand strategy and had the same general rationale and political development objectives as the Truman Doctrine. Undersecretary of State Dean Acheson and President Truman were already thinking about a program for European recovery and other aid programs even as the Truman Doctrine was being formulated. When speechwriter Joseph Jones was drafting President Truman's address and found himself perplexed over whether to restrict references specifically to Greece and Turkey or

17 *Ibid.*, pp. 45, 229.
18 Barnet, *Intervention and Revolution*, p. 128.

to include more sweeping and general policy statements, he went to Acheson for advice. Acheson told him: "If F.D.R. were alive, I think I know what he'd do. He would make a statement of global policy but confine his request for money right now to Greece and Turkey."[19] Truman, asked almost two years later by newsmen for some "background on the origins of Point Four," replied: "The origin of point four has been in my mind, and in the minds of members of the government, for the past 2 or 3 years, ever since the Marshall Plan was inaugurated. It originated with the Greece and Turkey proposition. Been [*sic*] studying it ever since. I spend most of my time going over to that globe back there, trying to figure out ways to make peace in the world."[20]

There were some important differences, of course, between the Marshall Plan and the Truman Doctrine. In the first place, the scale of the problem and of the eventual solution was much greater. There were many European countries—the original invitation by Secretary Marshall extended even to the Communist East European countries—and much more aid would be required. Western Europe was even more important strategically than Greece and Turkey. We had closer and more long-standing ties there, and probably humanitarian and economic motives played a greater role in the Marshall Plan than they had in the Truman Doctrine. Last but certainly not least, notwithstanding its grave economic difficulties, in 1947 Europe had a far more advanced technical, social, and political base than did Greece or Turkey; and it offered much better prospects for efficient use of aid resources and for coordinated regional planning and implementation among the recipient nations.

The fundamental theory about political development contained in the Marshall Plan was explicitly and unambiguously that political health in Europe depended on economic

[19] Jones, *The Fifteen Weeks*, p. 159.
[20] *Public Papers, Harry S. Truman, 1949*, p. 118. See also *ibid., 1948*, p. 178.

medicine. In all the planning memoranda, speeches, and legislation connected with the Marshall Plan—from Acheson's relatively little-noticed but important speech in Cleveland, Mississippi in May 1947 through the Economic Cooperation Act passed in March 1948, which legislated the European Recovery Program into existence—there was remarkable agreement on this basic proposition.[21] The same fundamental theory underlay the implementation phase. The aid instruments were almost exclusively economic: raw materials, industrial equipment, and international liquidity.[22] These were allocated to the Organization for European Economic Cooperation (OEEC), a planning agency which in turn reallocated the aid, subject to final American approval, among the 16 member nations. Political progress meant a whole array of things: anti-Communism, pro-Americanism, stability, democracy, and popularly supported center and left-of-center political leadership.[23] All the goals were salient. If anti-Communism and pro-Americanism were the first goals, they were a sort of first-among-equals, at least until the Korean War changed the foreign policy posture of the United States.

What is more, virtually all the goals were achieved; and they were achieved *within* the projected four-year time span and at a cost about $4 billion *below* the $17 billion appropriated by Congress. The Marshall Plan remains the most successful program in the history of American foreign aid. Nowhere else have conditions been so appropriate for the economic approach to political development. These conditions included: technical and financial expertise, relatively highly institutionalized political parties, skillful and visionary politicians, well-educated populations, strong national identi-

[21] Jones, *The Fifteen Weeks*, *passim*, esp. pp. 24-36, 239-56, 265-66.
[22] Legislative Reference Service, Library of Congress, *U.S. Foreign Aid: Its Purposes, Scope, Administration, and Related Information*, House Document No. 116, 86th Cong., 1st Sess. (Washington, D.C.: Government Printing Office, 1959), pp. 41-43.
[23] Jones, *The Fifteen Weeks*, pp. 243-44.

fications, democratic traditions (in most instances except Germany). The missing ingredients were economic, and when they were supplied, the political development goals began to emerge. In Asian, African, and Latin American countries, however, the same sets of conditions usually did not—and do not—obtain.

TRANSFER OF MARSHALL PLAN CONCEPTS

Between 1948 and 1950 the concepts of the Marshall Plan were transferred, through the administrative machinery of the Economic Cooperation Administration (ECA), to East and Southeast Asia. Later many of them were extended to Africa and Latin America. Today, the vast differences between the European and the less-developed regions, and the consequent inappropriateness of the transfer, are obvious. Evidently, however, they were not so obvious at the time. Although some of the initial illusions were soon dispelled, others were not; and once the United States had committed itself to a set of assumptions for developing the Third World, it was difficult to alter those premises. So the United States found itself pursuing a variety of ends, many worthy, some not, of which a very large proportion could not be achieved. While the impetus for the transfer may have been strongest in the Congress, many executive branch officials— including the President—were strongly behind it. And in the United States, the dominant influence on foreign policy comes from the White House.

The transfer occurred not through a unified, comprehensive plan for aid to a large group of underdeveloped countries. Rather, it began with aid to one country—China —and then proceeded incrementally until the total number of countries was very large indeed. This incremental expansion was due in part to the simple convenience of using the administrative machinery of the ECA to carry out seemingly similar tasks in Asia. The China Aid Act of 1948 was Title IV of the Economic Cooperation Act of the same

35

year. The aid programs in Burma, Indochina, Thailand, and the Philippines began when ECA suggested to Congress that funds left over from the mainland China program be expanded in "the general area of China." American aid to South Korea before January 1, 1949, had been administered by the Department of the Army as a Government Relief to Occupied Areas program (GARIOA). After that date, it was administered by ECA.[24] It is not surprising that the ERP machinery often brought some ERP concepts along with it.

In the case of China, American objectives were more modest than those of the ERP. The main thrust of ECA's efforts in China was to do "all it could, with limited means, to arrest the rate of economic deterioration"[25] in the hope of strengthening the Nationalist cause in the civil war. Despite these efforts the Chinese Communists won a year later.

ECA aid to Korea, however, had much more ambitious aims. The purpose of military aid under the GARIOA program had been "to facilitate the military objective of preventing disease and unrest." The much broader objective of ECA aid was "to assist the Korean people in establishing a sound economy and educational system as essential bases of an independent and democratic state."[26] The theme of using aid to build and strengthen political independence and stable democracy was stated over and over again by ECA and the Department of State. For example, in one general statement submitted by these two agencies to the Congress the words "democracy" and "democratic" appeared seven times in four sentences.[27]

President Truman drew heavily on the Marshall Plan

[24] Harry Barnes Price, *The Marshall Plan and Its Meaning* (Ithaca: Cornell University Press, 1955), pp. 179-200.

[25] *Ibid.*, p. 184.

[26] Charles Wolf, Jr., *Foreign Aid: Theory and Practice in Southern Asia* (Princeton: Princeton University Press, 1960), p. 48; and Price, *The Marshall Plan*, p. 196.

[27] The quotation appears in Price, *The Marshall Plan*, p. 197.

36

model in his statements about Korean aid. In June 1949 he told the Congress that ". . . the aid granted should not be for mere relief but for recovery. The kind of program which is needed is the kind which the Congress has authorized for the countries of Western Europe and under which these countries have achieved such rapid progress toward recovery during the past year. Full advantage should be taken of the broad and successful experience in Western Europe by continuing responsibility for the administration of the Korean aid program in the Economic Cooperation Administration."[28] The achievement of democracy was a central objective for President Truman not only in Korea but in all the Far East. Aid, he said, was ". . . not only the soundest course economically but also the most effective way from the standpoint of helping to achieve the objectives of peaceful and democratic conditions in the Far East. . . . Korea has become a testing ground. . . . The survival and progress of the Republic toward a self-supporting, stable economy will have an immense and far-reaching influence on the people of Asia."[29]

It was thought that a recovery program designed to increase productive capacity could make South Korea economically self-reliant "within a relatively few years." By contributing a moderate amount of funds—$110 million plus $30 million in leftover GARIOA resources up to June 30, 1950—plus some comparatively inexpensive technical assistance, the optimistic view was that in "a relatively few years" the United States could help Korea achieve democracy, stability, governmental capacity to promote economic development, and other goals.[30] The Communist assault on South Korea in June 1950 altered entirely the Korean situation and the relationship of the United States to it. Thus it is impossible to be certain whether the rather limited American instruments could have achieved the rather unlimited goals. It seems doubtful, however.

[28] *Public Papers, Harry S. Truman, 1949*, pp. 278-79.
[29] *Ibid.*   [30] Price, *The Marshall Plan*, pp. 196-97.

From Europe, China, and Korea, ECA aid programs skipped to Southeast Asia—Burma, Indochina, Thailand, and the Philippines. In these countries the objective was "the survival of moderate democratic governments"; and this objective depended in turn on the capacity of the Southeast Asian regimes "to provide constructive leadership . . . resist communist subversion . . . and to participate in friendly and cooperative relations with the United States and other free nations. The ECA emphasized these points on many occasions."[31] Here again, there were a host of salient political development goals, including democracy.

A "major aim" of these programs was "to develop institutions and practices which would not require prolonged American support." The main instruments were conceived to be "extensive technical assistance and relatively small quantities of material aid."[32] This was in line with the new emphasis on technical assistance which had been enunciated in Point Four of President Truman's 1949 inaugural address. Since technical assistance was relatively inexpensive, aid to Southeast Asia would cost less than aid to Europe, and it would be used in such a way that American support would not have to be "prolonged." The limited-time idea was understandably appealing. This had been the concept in Europe, and it was working; why not use it also in Southeast Asia, and with cheaper technical assistance to boot? Americans had not yet grasped just how different conditions were in the Third World, and how much harder it was to bring about change there.

By now, of course, it is almost a cliché to assert that Marshall Plan concepts were transferred inappropriately to the Third World. So much is this the case, in fact, that on reflection one begins to doubt that misconceptions so profound could actually have existed, and even to wonder whether the passage of time and the cliché may not distort more than they reveal about what really happened in the

[31] *Ibid.*, pp. 205-6.   [32] *Ibid.*, p. 206.

late forties and early fifties. Yet, when one examines the attitudes and activities of high American officials, both in the administration and Congress during those years, what is most striking is just how close to the truth the cliché is, and how many layers of meaning it has. Even today many Americans do not seem to realize how profound are their illusions and how persistent are their proclivities to exaggerate the applicability of their own experience and that of Europe to other areas. The brief history just sketched has hopefully provided a glimpse into these proclivities and illusions.[33] Perhaps we can sharpen the picture a bit more by examining the evaluation of ECA programs in Asia offered by Harry Bayard Price, author of the most searching study to date of the Marshall Plan and ECA aid. For while Price's analysis, published in 1955, reveals that American officials had learned a good deal from 1948 to 1952, it also reveals how fundamental were some of the misconceptions that remained even several years later.

Price begins by noting some of the "illusions" Americans had at the beginning of the ECA effort in Asia. He describes them vividly. "American experience . . . was far less relevant than had been supposed. Advice from foreigners was not awaited with bated breath. Pat solutions toppled like tenpins." But "hard realities" in Asia "quickly dispelled" such illusions, and gradually American officials gained "greater insight into the problems that had to be faced." Let us see what had been learned.

The first "problem" that had to be faced was that of "Communism versus Democracy." In order to understand this critical problem the first question to be answered was why Communism had such a "powerful appeal" in Asia and

[33] See also Kennan, *Memoirs*, p. 353; and Wolf, *Foreign Aid*, pp. 34ff. Both Kennan and Wolf state that the administration distinguished conditions in Europe from those in the Third World more clearly than did Congress. But Wolf states that "Congressional pressure for aid to Southern Asia was also due to the fact that ECA's objectives and premises, as expressed in the ECA Act, seemed to be quite general in their implications" (p. 35).

the rest of the underdeveloped world. The explanation "seemed obvious at the outset": "hunger and want [were] so severe and widespread that people were ready to grasp at any new hope, any utopian promise. What was there to lose?" In the "battle" of "competing civilizations" in Asia, the Communists had an "initial advantage." They could turn nationalism in Asia to their advantage because they dealt in "deception" and sought "radical revolution through dictatorship," whereas the democracies dealt in "facts" and sought "solid advancement by peaceful consent." However, the democracies—the United States—did have one big advantage: "an approach geared to gradual but *genuine* fulfillment of the aspirations of the people, not to their ultimate enslavement."[34]

It would be wrong to use the benefit of hindsight only to criticize views which to many people seemed plausible enough at the time and which as guidelines to a narrowly defined national security policy had some merit under the existing conditions. But it would be foolish not to use the benefit of hindsight to try to assess the validity of this type of diagnosis of developmental problems and thus to gain perspective on the strengths and weaknesses of our policies. As diagnosis in this sense Price's analysis, which probably reflects fairly accurately the thinking of aid officials in the early fifties, leaves a great deal to be desired.

In the first place, Communism has not had a very strong appeal in Third World countries. Among them only China, North Korea, North Vietnam, and Cuba have acquired Communist regimes since World War II. Only North Korea has had consistently warm and friendly relations with the Soviet Union; in the cases of Cuba and Communist China relations have varied from very cordial to intensely hostile. Even conceding that the paucity of Communist regimes may be due in some (unknown and possibly small) measure to American aid, it seems highly dubious today that the

[34] Price, *The Marshall Plan*, pp. 369-71 (emphasis in original).

appeal of Communism to the underdeveloped countries or the threat of Communism to the United States was ever as great as Price claims.

Nor has liberal democracy been the only or even the main alternative to the "competing civilization" of Communism. At no time since the end of World War II has the proportion of democracies in the Third World been greater than 25%; most of the time it has been between 10 and 20%. The modal types of political system in the Third World are neither Communist nor democratic but rather undemocratic and unstable types of regimes—military, single-party, multiparty, monarchical, etc. "Hunger and want" do not necessarily lead to Communism, and the satisfaction of hunger and want does not necessarily lead to democracy. While it remains difficult to state the respective sets of conditions under which democratic and Communist regimes occur, it seems quite safe to say that neither is a direct function of the degree of economic development.

If any single force is fundamental to an understanding of the behavior of underdeveloped countries in this regard, it is nationalism. The main concerns in such countries are to acquire the capacity to act independently to achieve economic and social development and to maintain and evolve their own ways of life. These concerns do not necessarily lead the peoples and the elites of these countries to distinguish, as Price does, American "facts" from Communist "deception"; or to equate "solid advancement" with "peaceful consent" rather than "radical revolution"; or to think that only "gradual" change brings "genuine fulfillment" while radical change always brings "enslavement." To make such distinctions in an analysis of the fundamental problems of development in the Third World is to force the facts onto a procrustean Cold-War and liberal bed.

Price emphasized that the answer to the "deep peril" of Communism did not lie either in total withdrawal or in military strength alone. Where then did it lie? "Where but in recognizing the dimensions of the problem and the extent of the intelligence, determination, and patience that would be required to meet it?" This particular conclusion was sound enough, but for Price and for many officials in the early fifties, the prescription that flowed from the diagnosis was, it now seems clear, quasi-utopian and therefore pernicious. To express it he chose language from the report of a prestigious presidential commission, the International Development Advisory Board, headed by Nelson Rockefeller: "Our strategy must be a positive one, based on constructive progress and a genuine sense of humanity's needs for common effort toward the future. It must be both *global*, embracing every part of the world, and *total*, with political, psychological, economic, and military considerations integrated into one whole."[35]

It is in this type of prescription, based on this kind of diagnosis, that one finds some of the roots of the morass into which the United States had gotten itself in Vietnam and elsewhere by the middle and latter part of the 1960s. Toward the end of his evaluation, Price correctly points out that the shortcomings of American foreign aid doctrines lay even more "in ignoring moral and spiritual aspects of social development" than they did in purely economic and technical matters. This failure to provide moral leadership was, he speculated, "perhaps the greatest single weakness in the programs for assistance to underdeveloped areas during the period of ECA operations. The full explanation for this weakness, and the means whereby it might have been overcome, remained largely unsolved problems."[36] Part of the explanation, it is suggested, may be found in the constraints imposed upon Americans by the inarticulate assumptions of their liberal tradition, which the quotations from Price illustrate so well, and which we shall analyze in more detail in Chapter 3.

[35] International Development Advisory Board, *Partners in Progress* (Rockefeller Report; Washington, 1951), p. 4, quoted in Price, *The Marshall Plan*, p. 372.

[36] Price, *The Marshall Plan*, p. 391.

POINT FOUR

In his inaugural address in 1949 President Truman had announced that there were four main elements in American foreign policy: (1) support for the United Nations; (2) the European Recovery Program; (3) military defense assistance; and (4) "a bold new program for making the benefits of our scientific advances and industrial progress available for the improvement and growth of underdeveloped areas." The legislative program which issued from the fourth point was supposed to do two things: first, to establish "the objectives and the broad policy to guide the whole program of American aid to underdeveloped areas,"[37] and, second, to authorize a worldwide expansion of technical advisory missions in such fields as health, education, public administration, agriculture, mining, and industrial development. The missions came to be the distinctive element of the program, so that Point Four became synonymous with "technical assistance." But the significance of the Point Four is much greater than that of the missions themselves. The speeches and testimony in support of it are good indicators of the thinking of American officials in 1949-1950 regarding the purposes, probable consequences, and techniques for achieving the purposes of aid. More than a year of preparation went into the Point Four legislation. Numerous Congressmen, private groups, and 43 agencies of the federal government were consulted. According to Secretary Acheson, the Point Four legislation represented "the best combined judgment of all who were concerned in shaping it." And the law which emerged—rather grandly called the Act for International Development—established "economic development of un-

[37] Secretary of State Dean Acheson in *Act for International Development*, Committee on Foreign Relations, U.S. Senate, Hearings, 81st Cong., 2nd Sess., March 30 and April 3, 1950, p. 5. President Truman's four points and the most relevant portion of Secretary Acheson's testimony are reprinted in David A. Baldwin, ed., *Foreign Aid and American Foreign Policy: A Documentary Analysis* (New York: Praeger, 1966), pp. 60-66.

derdeveloped areas for the first time as a national policy" of the United States.[38]

As expressed in Truman's address, congressional testimony by administration officials, and the Act itself,[39] the justifications for Point Four were national security, humanitarianism, and the idea that it was "a sound economic investment" for the United States. The more specific goals which flowed from these rationales—although most of them were not very specific—were manifold. By helping "the free peoples of the world" to produce more food, more clothing, more materials for housing, and more mechanical power, the United States would contribute to "freedom and democracy," "prosperity," "dignity," "international understanding and goodwill," "world peace," and other vaguely defined good things.

For President Truman, such words were evidently not just rhetoric; he really believed what he said. Speaking later that year to a group of civil engineers, the President asked that all "technical men" inform themselves "on just exactly what I mean by point 4." He wanted them to know that if the United States could "make a contribution in the know-

[38] Acheson in *Act for International Development*, pp. 4-5. Although this policy had its roots in the Truman Doctrine and other programs, the Act for International Development was at the time the most explicit and unqualified commitment by the U.S. to the policy of developing underdeveloped countries. The Truman Doctrine itself was more ambiguous and the law that emerged from the Truman Doctrine speech was more specifically directed to Greece and Turkey than was the Act for International Development.

[39] For the Senate Hearings, see *ibid*. The Committee on Foreign Affairs of the House of Representatives had two sets of hearings: *International Technical Cooperation Act of 1949* ("*Point IV*" Program), 81st Cong., 1st Sess., September and October 1949; and *Act for International Development* ("*Point IV*" Program), 81st Cong., 2nd Sess., January 1950. For the Act itself, see "Act for International Development" (Title IV, Foreign Economic Operations Act of 1950), June 5, 1950, in *American Foreign Policy, 1950-1955*, Vol. II (Washington, D.C., Government Printing Office, 1956), pp. 3,047-3,054.

how, and [thus] raise the standard of living *just* 2 percent of the *rest of the world*, [then] our factories and our businesses never could catch up with the demand that would be on them. Just think of that! That's *all* we need to do. It is not beyond the bounds of possibility. . . . And if these resources produce things . . . to keep the world from being hungry, then no one would have any idea of carrying on a destructive war for the purpose of obtaining something that didn't belong to them. That's what the cause of wars has been . . . the idea of grasping something that the other fellow has."[40] The theory here was that technical assistance could quite possibly lead to an increase of 2% in the standard of living in the Third World; and that this increase would lead to a sharp increase in demand for American exports and to the end of war on earth.

It should be noted that the more grandiose political development goals were apparently less salient for other officials who testified on the Point Four legislation than they were for President Truman and Secretary of State Acheson. Officials such as Undersecretary of State James Webb, Assistant Secretary of State for Economic Affairs Willard Thorp, and Ambassador-at-Large Philip Jessup spoke mostly of the economic development and security objectives of technical assistance; they said less about democracy, international understanding and good will, and the end of wars. Moreover, when the law was finally passed it had only a very general statement at the beginning to the effect that "the economic and social progress of all peoples" could further "the secure growth of democratic ways of life, the expansion of mutually beneficial commerce, the development of international understanding and good will, and the maintenance of world peace."[41] Thereafter the Act dealt almost exclusively with economic development. For example, it defined technical assistance programs as "programs

[40] *Public Papers, Harry S. Truman, 1949*, pp. 546-47 (emphasis added).

[41] Section 402(a) of the Act.

for the international interchange of technical knowledge and skills designed to contribute to the balanced and integrated development of the economic resources and productive capacities of economically underdeveloped areas."[42] Here as elsewhere nothing was said about how economic development was linked to the ostensible political development goals.

There was thus a huge gap between the goals of the program—both the strictly economic goals and the more grandiose political development goals—and the potential of the instrument of technical assistance for achieving them. President Truman had argued that "For the first time in history humanity possesses the knowledge and the skill to relieve the human suffering" of people in underdeveloped countries, and that while the material resources of the United States were limited, its "imponderable" resources in technical knowledge were "constantly growing and . . . inexhaustible." But American resources were evidently not "inexhaustible." The Administration asked for a $45 million appropriation in the first year; it got $35 million. Until the 1960s, the appropriation for technical assistance never rose much above $150 million per year; usually it was less than that. A chronic problem in implementing Point Four even at these levels of expenditure was the great difficulty of recruiting qualified personnel, especially in fields like transportation, mining, and industry where competition from private enterprise was even keener than it was in health, education, and agriculture.[43] Much more important, however, is the fact that even if appropriations had been ten or twenty times greater than they were, and personnel had been more readily available, technical assistance still could not have relieved human suffering caused by economic underdevelopment in all the world.

[42] Section 418(a) of the Act.

[43] See Truman's Point Four speech; William Adams Brown, Jr. and Redvers Opie, *American Foreign Assistance* (Washington, D.C.: The Brookings Institution, 1953), pp. 394-96; and Westerfield, *America's Foreign Policy*, pp. 356-62.

In the hearings, however, the ambitiousness of the goals was hardly noticed or discussed. Little attention was paid to either the political or the economic development goals as such. Few if any legislators (or administrators) raised the seemingly obvious argument that the goals of the technical assistance program, while worthy, were almost absurdly unrealistic. In the hearings the goals were generally accepted as expressed; most of the attention and controversy centered instead on which techniques were better suited for achieving them. Would the Point Four program emphasize public or private measures, be multilateral or bilateral, utilize technical assistance exclusively or investment capital as well?[44] Many congressmen were concerned about the cost of technical assistance, but few if any of them doubted that the United States could achieve the lofty goals if enough money were spent; they just opposed spending it. Almost exclusively, the legislators raised instrumental questions; to the extent that their questions had theoretical or ideological dimensions they related not to the linkages between aid, economic development, and political development, but rather to such matters as concern about free enterprise versus socialism in our own government (as in the debate over public versus private investment) or about national sovereignty versus world government (as in the debate over multilateral versus bilateral aid). As Brown and Opie put it a few years later, the United States had failed "*even to attempt* to assess realistically how much could be done at relatively small cost to raise the standard of living in economically backward areas merely by spreading 'knowledge and skill.' "[45] And this judgment applies as much to the Congress as it does to the executive branch.

In summary, then, the theory of Point Four was that technical assistance contributes to economic development, and economic development contributes to a host of politi-

[44] Brown and Opie, *Foreign Assistance*, make this same point at p. 393.

[45] *Ibid.*, p. 394 (emphasis added).

cally good things—democracy, peace, non-Communist governments, good will, international understanding. No clear linkage between economic and political development was offered by the administration, and Congress demanded none. The possibility that some of these goals might be conflicting, and that priorities among them might have to be set, was little noticed or discussed. Even the linkage between technical assistance and economic development was not challenged as such. The important question was not whether technical assistance could contribute to economic development, but which techniques or instruments were better suited for achieving that end.

Some years later, some of the broader questions began to dawn. Philip Glick wrote, in a study published in 1957, that "the national decision to go forward with a technical assistance program was not based on a sharply formulated, or even very clear, notion either of the policy itself or of the reasons for going forward with it." In 1956 a committee of the House of Representatives concluded, not much too strongly, that "the blunt fact of the matter appears to be that most technical cooperation programs are conducted on a basis such that starting from an unknown point for an unknown goal they can tell neither how far they have progressed nor when they have got there."[46] But it is fair to note that in 1949 and 1950, when the law was debated and passed and the programs were begun, neither the administration *nor* the Congress raised such questions.

What was mainly wrong with Point Four was not the idea of using American knowledge and skill to help underdeveloped countries, but the failure to appraise realistically what could be accomplished thereby. More specifically, Point Four exaggerated greatly the ease and speed with

[46] Philip Glick, *The Administration of Technical Assistance: Growth in the Americas* (Chicago: University of Chicago Press, 1957), p. xi; Committee on Government Operations, U.S. House of Representatives, "U.S. Technical Assistance in Latin America," 14th Intermediate *Report*, House Report No. 1985, March 29, 1956, p. 13.

which change and development in the Third World could be achieved. It also tended to assume that economic development always has congenial consequences in terms of all its political development objectives. In part, these failings and misconceptions were manifestations, on an international scale after World War II, of the liberal tradition in America.

"MUTUAL SECURITY" AND THE EISENHOWER YEARS

In the decade after the attack on South Korea by North Korean troops on June 25, 1950, Cold War considerations weighed heavily in the rationales and objectives of American aid. In 1949, the ratio of economic to military aid was about four to one; by the end of 1950, that ratio had been reversed, and throughout the fifties the ratio of military to economic aid averaged about two to one. Even in the case of Marshall Plan aid from 1950 to 1952, the main officially stated aim changed from economic recovery to rearmament. The shift in emphasis from economic development to security was expressed not only in the reduction in the percentage of economic aid as compared to total aid, but in the uses to which economic aid was to be put.

After 1950, the efforts of the Economic Cooperation Administration, the Technical Cooperation Administration (the Point Four agency), and the Mutual Defense assistance program (the military aid component) were regarded as "mutually supporting aspects of a single effort in strengthening the free world in its resistance to Communism."[47] The Mutual Security Act of 1951 gathered under one legislative authorization all of these activities and agencies; only the Export-Import Bank, among American aid activities, was excluded. This Act, which remained the main basis for the American aid effort until 1961, had the following purpose:

. . . to maintain the security and promote the foreign policy of the United States by authorizing military, eco-

[47] Brown and Opie, *Foreign Assistance*, p. 505.

nomic, and technical assistance to friendly countries to strengthen the mutual security and individual and collective defenses of the free world, to develop their resources in the interest of their security and independence and the national interests of the United States, and to facilitate the effective participation of those countries in the United Nations system for collective security.

The emphasis throughout this statement of purpose is on security. Both the strengthening of defenses and the development of economic resources are objectives which follow and depend upon the phrase "friendly countries." The "friendly countries" criterion had bite. For example, in 1951 India requested two million tons of grain to ward off an impending famine. The request was held up for four months because of concern that India had demonstrated a "neutral" posture in the Cold War. This congressional resistance was described by Mr. Sam Rayburn, the Speaker of the House of Representatives and a political realist if ever there was one, as "one of the most amazing things I have ever witnessed."[48] This is how deep the preoccupation with security went in 1951.

Throughout the decade, the most salient political development objectives of American aid continued to be those that flowed from the Cold War concern. A study of presidential messages and congressional testimony by leading administration witnesses from 1951 to 1958 showed that five major arguments were advanced in support of aid "with rather consistent frequency and emphasis" during the period.[49] These five arguments claimed that aid would:

(a) Help build a strong free world alliance which is essential to United States security.
(b) Help United States allies build adequate defenses without imperiling their basic economy.

[48] *Congress and the Nation: 1945-1964* (Washington, D.C.: Congressional Quarterly Service, 1965), p. 169.
[49] Legislative Reference Service, *U.S. Foreign Aid*, p. 84.

(c) Provide a more economical defense for the United States in terms of money and manpower.

(d) Help deter Soviet aggression and to meet it more effectively if deterrence should fail.

(e) Help raise living standards in the less developed areas and thus make Communist claims less attractive.

The same study also discovered ten other arguments cited in support of foreign aid. In descending order of emphasis these objectives were:

(f) Help insure continued access to vital raw materials.

(g) Help maintain strength for a long-term struggle with the Soviet bloc.

(h) Raise living standards in the less-developed areas and thus help lay the foundation for a world of prosperity, political freedom, and international cooperation.

(i) Help build self-sustaining economies, including the defense establishment, in allied countries.

(j) Help provide the United States with military bases at strategic points around the world.

(k) Speed up European defenses to meet the immediate crisis. (Mostly 1951-1953.)

(l) Help develop a favorable attitude toward the United States, especially in Asia and the Middle East. (Mostly 1951-1953.)

(m) Help stimulate increased American private investments in underdeveloped areas.

(n) Help increase American exports and develop markets for future exports in the currently underdeveloped areas.

(o) Help provide employment for hundreds of thousands of Americans. (Mostly 1958.)

As in the case of Point Four aid, the linkages between mutual security aid and its goals were often unclear or open to question. Military aid and economic aid used for short-term political purposes probably did contribute to defensive alliances, at least in the short run. But the claim that aid can "help raise living standards in the less-developed areas and *thus* make Communist claims less attractive" may be challenged. It was challenged, in fact, in the very study by the Legislative Reference Service of the Library of Congress that identified the fifteen major arguments advanced in support of aid. The study observed that:

> The simple assumption that communism flows from poverty is so widely accepted in America that it is almost an article of faith. The evidence of history suggests, however, that while there is a relationship between poverty and the growth of communism this is a highly complex relationship and that it is not possible to assert as a generalization of universal validity that poverty leads to communism. . . . A stagnant society of illiterate people, mired in poverty, living on a near starvation diet, with little expectation of progress, and with only enough energy for work is not likely to produce a large group of communist revolutionaries.[50]

But the challenge to this "article of faith" was largely unanswered and unheeded. Officials continued to suppose that poverty has a positive and linear relationship to Communism: i.e. that as poverty decreases, Communism decreases. As late as 1965, for example, a closely related theory, that poverty has a positive and linear relationship to political instability, and that economic development produces stability, was to be advanced by Robert S. McNamara, then Secretary of Defense and later President of the World Bank. He argued that this relationship between violence and economic backwardness was "irrefutable." But the fact that the most economically developed countries tend to be stable does not mean that as poor countries develop economically they will necessarily become more stable. The relationship between

[50] *Ibid.*, pp. 84-85.

development and stability seems rather to be curvilinear: stability is greatest when countries are either relatively rich or very poor; instability is greatest when relatively poor countries are trying to become richer. Most Third World countries fall into the latter category, and most are unstable.[51]

Although the most salient goals during the fifties were closely linked to the Cold War, the aid program had many other fairly notable objectives. Some were manifestly political in substance: e.g. democracy and freedom. Other were vague, fairly humanitarian goals: prosperity for all, international cooperation, self-sustaining economies. Still others were directed at the American economy: access to raw materials and increased American exports, markets, and domestic employment. In other words, although greater emphasis now lay on the Cold War objectives, most of the other types of goals that the United States had set for its aid in the 1947-1951 period were still present in the whole decade of the fifties (as they would be again in the sixties).

During this period the total amount of American economic assistance to the Third World increased significantly. The total amount of American economic aid to all countries

[51] For the McNamara "poverty thesis," see Joan M. Nelson, *Aid, Influence, and Foreign Policy* (New York: Macmillan, 1968), pp. 13, 19-20; and Huntington, *Political Order*, pp. 40ff. Huntington offers a good critique of this thesis. The best comparative quantitative analyses of strife, violence, and political instability have been done by Ted Robert Gurr and by Ivo Fcicrabend, Rosalind Feierabend, and Betty Nesvold. Their studies appear in Graham and Gurr, eds., *Violence in America*, Chaps. 17 and 18. The conclusion of the second of these two studies, based on data from 84 nations over a 30-year period, is that "Political violence is least in traditional and modern societies, greatest in societies in the process of more or less rapid social change that we call 'modernization.' The evidence is that the more rapid are economic, social, and political change, the greater is political unrest—but with significant qualifications and exceptions" (p. 571). One significant qualification has to do with the levels of strife in the United States in recent years.

53

was larger in the Marshall Plan period (1948-1952) than in the fifties, and the proportion of economic aid over total aid decreased after 1950. However, the total amount of economic assistance to the Third World increased substantially in the latter period because a smaller share of total economic assistance was directed to Europe and a larger share to underdeveloped countries. From 1949 to 1952, total U.S. economic assistance to all countries averaged $3.4 billion annually, but 86% of it went to Europe and only 14% to the Third World. In 1953-1957, the total annual average was down to $1.8 billion, but only 25% was directed to Europe and the rest went to underdeveloped countries. In 1958-1961, the total annually was $1.85 billion, with only 6% going to Europe; by 1962-1966, the average annual total rose to $2.3 billion and all of it went to the Third World.[52]

However, despite these increases in aid to the Third World in the 1960s, many of the goals remained far beyond the means utilized by the United States. This was due partly to the fact that the number of countries receiving aid expanded even faster than the total amount of economic aid. Only a handful of Third World countries were receiving substantial amounts of economic assistance in the late 1940s; by 1959, some 60 foreign countries and territories were recipients. In the same year there were technical assistance missions in more than 50 countries.[53] In 1958 the Department of State claimed that technical assistance programs served "... both the basic interests of the cooperating countries, and in varying degrees, the primary foreign policy interests of the United States: Our moral interest in helping less fortunate people to improve their lot; our economic interest in having prosperous and progressive nations as sources of raw materials and markets for our goods; our political interest in having stable, friendly, and democratically inclined neighbors in the world community; and our

[52] Nelson, *Aid, Influence*, p. 5.
[53] Legislative Reference Service, *U.S. Foreign Aid*, pp. 88, 72-73.

strategic interest in having the nations of the free world strong and determined to resist aggression."[54]

Even with the qualifying phrase, "in varying degrees," this array of goals was a tall order for a program with an expenditure of a paltry $129 million a year for over 50 countries! And although economic assistance in the same year was about 15 times that amount, the goals of peace, democracy, stability, prosperity, international cooperation, and friendliness to the United States were still quite ambitious. They were also based on theoretical assumptions about the relationship between aid and aid's goals that were often extremely dubious. Thus the linkages between aid, economic development, and political development were even less clear and strong in the portion of the aid program that utilized the economic approach than they were in the portion that utilized the Cold War approach.

Moreover, the goals often conflicted with one another. For example, the Cold War objectives of anti-Communism and stability sometimes conflicted with the goal of democracy. Partly this inconsistency is endemic in general foreign policy statements: different countries have different priorities and needs, and some conflict among goals is inevitable and not necessarily wrong. Partly it occurred because aid officials, in order to get what they wanted from Congress, often had to accept the legislators' goals as well. However, the inconsistency was also due in some measure to the unfounded conviction among aid officials that all good things do indeed go together without conflict. Professor Stanley Hoffmann has likened this tendency to a "smokescreen" which saves the policymaker from having to work out a policy. One smokescreen, he suggests, "substitutes objectives for policy—defines ends but not the combination of ends, means, and alternatives that a long-range policy entails. This substitution . . . gives many discussions of long-range issues

[54] U.S. Department of State, "The Mutual Security Program, Fiscal Year 1959, A Summary Presentation," February 1958, pp. 44-45, quoted in *ibid.*, p. 73.

an air of wishful unreality in which uncertainty and risks are blandly smothered under clichés." A statement by President Eisenhower illustrates the point: "For some decades our purposes abroad have been the establishment of universal peace with justice, free choice for all peoples, rising levels of human well-being, and the development and maintenance of frank, friendly, and mutually helpful contacts for all nations willing to work for parallel objectives." As Hoffmann observes such statements offer a "liberal vision of harmony and accommodation," but they do not recognize the conflicts that exist among ostensibly salient objectives.[55]

From beneath the clichés emerged two main political development doctrines in the Eisenhower years: the dominant Cold War approach, and the secondary economic approach. Dissatisfaction in some quarters, especially in the Senate, with the dominance of the Cold War approach led to a number of government-commissioned studies and research reports on the aid program in 1956 and 1957. Perhaps the best known and probably the most influential of these was a report prepared by a group of social scientists, led by Max F. Millikan and W. W. Rostow, at the Center for International Studies of the Massachusetts Institute of Technology. The main argument in their report was that aid for economic development should be separated entirely from other forms of aid and allocated to "free world" countries according to the strictly economic criterion of whether the country had the capacity to "absorb" the capital, i.e. to use it effectively for development. The MIT group argued further that such a program would produce stable, effective, and democratic political systems. Most of the other studies were generally in agreement with the Millikan–Rostow thesis, and the upshot of the whole process of studies and political bargaining

[55] Stanley Hoffmann, *Gulliver's Troubles, Or the Setting of American Foreign Policy* (New York: McGraw-Hill, 1968), p. 163; he quotes from Dwight D. Eisenhower, *Waging Peace: 1956-1960* (New York: Doubleday, 1965), p. 621.

and maneuvering was the creation in August 1957 of the Development Loan Fund (DLF).[56]

The purpose of the DLF was to make loan capital available for economically sound projects in "friendly" underdeveloped countries at lower rates and over longer repayment periods than were possible from other sources. Although Millikan and Rostow had explicitly predicted that stable, democratic, and effective governments would result from the economic development which this aid would presumably promote, the charter of the Fund itself specified only economic development goals, except for a vague reference to the "strengthening" effect development would have on the "friendly" countries. Another aim of the Fund was to encourage private enterprise and the investment of private foreign capital in the Third World.[57]

Some advocates of the economic approach still were not satisfied, however. On August 25, 1958, eight Democratic members of the Senate Committee on Foreign Relations sent a public letter to President Eisenhower in which they expressed their belief that there was "a serious distortion in the present relative importance which is attached to military and related aid on the one hand and technical assistance and self-liquidating economic development assistance on the other." They urged him to study the Mutual Security Program, and in November the President appointed William H. Draper, Jr., an investment banker with prior military and government experience, to head a ten-man committee. The mission of the committee was "to appraise the military

[56] A thorough description of the 1957 reappraisal is given in H. Field Haviland, Jr., "Foreign Aid and the Policy Process: 1957," *American Political Science Review*, 52, No. 3 (September 1958), 689-724. Max F. Millikan and W. W. Rostow, *A Proposal: Key to An Effective Foreign Policy* (New York: Harper, 1957), is a revised version of the MIT study.

[57] Legislative Reference Service, *U.S. Foreign Aid*, pp. 74-75. For the charter of the Fund, see Section 201, Mutual Security Act of 1954 as Amended.

assistance program and the relative emphasis the United States should place on economic aid."

The Draper Committee submitted its report in August 1959. Its conclusions were different from those hoped for by the Senate group. The committee denied the allegation that the military assistance program was too great in relation to the economic assistance program. It recommended that economic aid be increased and that military aid be increased even more. With respect to the former, it reasserted the doctrine that economic aid "assists less developed nations to achieve economic progress within the free world, thereby decreasing opportunities for communist political and economic domination."[58]

[58] President's Committee to Study the United States Military Assistance Program, *Committee Report* (Washington, D.C.: August 17, 1959), pp. 185-87, ix, 135.

2

Political Development Doctrines, 1961-1968

THE KENNEDY YEARS

John F. Kennedy was one of the eight Senate Democrats who in 1959 had urged President Eisenhower to reassess the importance of military and security aid relative to economic assistance for long-term development. When he became President, Kennedy had the opportunity to rearrange these priorities himself. To a considerable extent, he did. In his first message to the Congress on foreign aid, he declared that existing programs and concepts were "largely unsatisfactory and unsuited" to the needs of the sixties; and that the United States, along with other industrialized countries, should seek to "move more than half the people of the less-developed nations into self-sustained economic growth, while the rest move substantially closer to the day when they, too, will no longer have to depend upon outside assistance." He by no means denied the existence of the Cold War and its close relationship to the Third World: "Without exception," he asserted, the new nations "are under Communist pressure." But he sought to shift the emphasis of the aid program. The "fundamental task of our foreign aid program in the 1960's," he said, "is not negatively to fight Communism: Its fundamental task is to help make a historical demonstration that in the twentieth century, as in the nineteenth—in the southern half of the globe as in the north—economic growth and political democracy can develop hand in hand."[1]

The words were dramatic, ambitious, and somewhat exaggerated. Kennedy hung onto many concepts developed out of the earlier aid experience, including some of the

---

[1] *Public Papers of the Presidents of the United States, John F. Kennedy, 1961* (Washington, D.C.: Government Printing Office, 1962), pp. 203, 205.

59

optimistic assumptions of the Truman era and others overly tinged by the Cold War. Moreover, many of the new concepts—such as the notion of a "take-off" stage into self-sustained economic growth—were highly dubious, although they seemed less so at the time. But the shift in emphasis was genuine. Statistics tell some of the story. Total economic aid commitments increased from an annual average of $2.5 billion between 1956 and 1960 to an average of over $4 billion per year between 1961 and 1963. A larger proportion of economic assistance was used for developmental as contrasted with security purposes. In the fifties military assistance and "that part of economic aid which financed defense support or other security objectives" had been roughly double the level of developmental aid; during the first half of the sixties, that ratio was reversed.[2]

To carry his ideas into effect, Kennedy initiated significant changes in legislation, organization, and concepts. The legislative change was the Foreign Assistance Act of 1961. It replaced the Mutual Security Act as the fundamental law for American economic and military aid. Its "Statement of Policy" both reflected the shift to an emphasis on developmental assistance and maintained the tradition—begun in the late forties—of listing a great many ambitious goals, some of which inevitably conflicted. The list was revised and supplemented each year. In 1963, for example, the Statement of Policy "contained at least twenty-four shelf items, of varying scope and importance, arranged in no apparent order of priority. . . . This 'Statement of Policy,' instead of being a clarion call to the conscience, wisdom, and will of the citizenry, [was] more like the wheeze from a player

[2] Nelson, *Aid, Influence*, pp. 4, 45, 121; Kenneth M. Kauffman and Helena Stalson, "U.S. Assistance to Less Developed Countries, 1956-65," *Foreign Affairs*, 45, No. 4 (July 1967), 719. Cf. Barnet, *Intervention and Revolution*, p. 20. Barnet's data give lower ratios of economic to military and security aid; but the shift in emphasis is in the same direction.

piano too often repaired."[3] Beyond these general goals, there were in the same year a dozen other specific objectives; 7 negative objectives, such as a prohibition on aid to countries trading with Cuba; and a 41 item checklist of statutory criteria for loans under the Alliance for Progress![4]

The main organizational change was the creation of the Agency for International Development (AID). It absorbed the functions of the International Cooperation Administration and the Development Loan Fund and was organized principally on a geographic (e.g. Near East and South Asia, Africa) rather than a functional (e.g. agriculture, community development) basis. Henceforth most grant, loan, and technical assistance programs were administered by AID. The administrator of the agency, who was responsible only to the Secretary of State and the President, had the rank of Undersecretary of State, and the four regional assistant administrators had the rank of Assistant Secretaries of State.

THE CHARLES RIVER APPROACH

Kennedy's new concepts for long-term developmental aid were, according to Arthur Schlesinger, Jr., "most fully explored along the banks of the Charles River" with a group of social scientists, mainly economists, from MIT and Har-

[3] Frank M. Coffin, *Witness for Aid* (Boston: Houghton Mifflin, 1964), pp. 96-97.

[4] In 1967 the Senate Committee on Foreign Relations repealed the entire Statement of Policy, which had grown to a length of sixteen bulky paragraphs with literally dozens of objectives. The Committee claimed, among other things, that statements of policy "too often become the tools of special bureaucratic interests," and that it was an "insult" to the Congress for the executive branch "to send up draft legislation which purports, in a statement of policy, to set forth what the Congress believes." In part at least this was hypocritical, since Congress itself had contributed greatly to the ever-expanding list of goals. Probably the main reason for the Senate action was diffuse distrust and anger over the war in Vietnam. See the Report of the Committee on Foreign Relations, U.S. Senate, "Foreign Assistance Act of 1967," Report No. 499, 90th Cong., 1st Sess., 1967, p. 16.

vard. These "action intellectuals" felt that economic development "required the modernization of entire social structures and ways of thought and life—and for this capital was not enough." Rather than the project orientation of the International Cooperation Administration, according to which the main unit of analysis and action was the individual project—a dam, a highway, or a factory—they favored the concept of comprehensive country programming. Country programming was to be a total, integrated aid effort, comprised of technical, capital, and commodity assistance, all tailored to the particular circumstances of the individual country. (In practice, country programs to a large extent became packages wrapped around the things that would have been done under the project approach.) Efforts were also made to develop more specific, quantitative criteria for assistance, and some progress was made in this direction in terms of strictly economic criteria. Self-help, a stress on loans rather than grants, and new incentives for private investment were among the other concepts that were emphasized by the Kennedy team.[5]

The message of the "Charles River group"—which directly influenced Kennedy and with which he agreed— was that aid should be designed to enable the underdeveloped countries to "take off" into self-sustaining economic growth. They believed that "take off" was feasible in most countries; when it was reached, the need for aid would end. To achieve "take off" and to "reduce the explosiveness of the modernization process" required not only economic inputs but also social change—land reform, tax reform, more voluntary organizations, greater political participation. The re-

[5] For a description (and to some extent, a celebration) of the "Charles River" approach, see Arthur M. Schlesinger, Jr., *A Thousand Days: John F. Kennedy in the White House* (Boston: Houghton Mifflin, 1965), pp. 586-89 and ff. For a generally favorable but balanced discussion of country programming, see Nelson, *Aid, Influence,* Chap. 3. The term "action intellectuals" is taken from the laudatory series of articles by Theodore H. White, "The Action Intellectuals," *Life,* 62, Nos. 23-25 (June 9, 16, 23, 1967).

sult of all of this, they believed, would be a host of good things politically: more democracy, less Communism, greater national independence, and greater political stability—ultimately, a "world community" of stable, independent, democratic and peaceful states. As Schlesinger observed later in a revealing passage,

> All this, it must be confessed, had occasionally a certain blandness. It sometimes made the process sound a little too easy and continuous. . . . The Charles River approach represented a *very American effort* to persuade the developing countries to base their revolutions on *Locke* rather than Marx. . . . It may have fallen short of the ferocities of the situation. But, *given the nature of our institutions and values, it was probably the best we could do.*[6]

This "very American effort" to export Locke to the Third World did not consist of rhetoric alone. It is true that there was (not surprisingly!) a huge gap between the goals and U.S. capacity to implement them. Nevertheless, the goals themselves were salient and widespread among the middle and higher levels of the American aid establishment during the Kennedy years. Congress accepted Kennedy's plea for a "historic demonstration that economic growth and political democracy can go hand in hand," incorporating that exact language into the Foreign Assistance Act of 1961. Secretary of State Rusk stated repeatedly during the Kennedy and the Johnson years that the overriding goal of American foreign policy was the creation of a world community of independent, stable, self-governing nations. Economic and social development, he said many times, "can best occur under free institutions with a mobilized effort of peoples by consent, and not through direction from an authoritarian society." The *Program Guidance Manual* of AID for 1963 stated

[6] Schlesinger, *A Thousand Days*, pp. 588-89 (emphasis added). See also Theodore C. Sorensen, *Kennedy* (New York: Bantam, 1966), pp. 596-97.

that the goal of aid was to assist in the development "of a community of free nations cooperating on matters of mutual concern, basing their political systems on consent and progressing in economic welfare and social justice. Such a world offers the best prospect of security and peace for the United States."[7]

Moreover, although the relationships between substantial American aid, economic growth, and political democracy in the recipient countries are certainly unclear and probably weak, aid officials sometimes tried to make them appear clear and strong. A notable instance of this occurred in 1963, in testimony by the AID administrator, David E. Bell. He presented the results of an analysis by his staff of the economic and political performance of 41 countries that "had received substantial amounts of economic aid since 1945," and divided the countries into four groups according to their growth rates and performance in reducing dependence on external aid. He inferred from these data that the relationship between economic growth and political "progress" was "decidedly favorable." His conclusions and his reasoning are as follows:

> In virtually all of the 24 countries in the first two groups of economically successful aid programs, democratic institutions have been strengthened or less democratic regimes liberalized. At the other extreme, unsatisfactory economic conditions have clearly contributed to political instability in [security deletion] some of the countries in group D. Although the possibility of economic progress leading to political backsliding cannot be ruled out, there is no clear case of this among the countries to which we have extended substantial amounts of

[7] Dean Rusk, "The Bases of United States Foreign Policy," *The New Look in Foreign Aid*, Proceedings of the Academy of Political Science, Vol. 27 (January 1962), p. 110; Agency for International Development, *Program Guidance Manual* (August 1, 1963), p. 1, quoted in Edward S. Mason, *Foreign Aid and Foreign Policy* (New York and Evanston: Harper, 1964), p. 49.

economic assistance. The relationship is overwhelmingly in the other direction and it strengthens our belief in the underlying premise of the aid programs; namely, that while there is no guarantee that improved political institutions will follow in any automatic way, it seems clear that without economic progress the chances for strengthening democratic processes in the less developed countries would be greatly diminished.[8]

This analysis is extremely interesting and significant for several reasons. The last two phrases of the final sentence are probably valid, but it is doubtful indeed that the "underlying premise" of other officials (both above and below Mr. Bell) was as cautious and precise as he expressed it in those phrases. Even more open to question, however, is the assertion that the relationship between economic growth and political development is "overwhelmingly" positive. Bell's evidence for this statement was that in "virtually all" of the 24 countries in the first two groups, "democratic institutions have been strengthened or less democratic regimes liberalized" by economic growth abetted by American aid.

Now, of the 14 countries in the first group, 11 were European countries that received Marshall Plan aid; one was Spain; the others were Lebanon and Japan. So the only underdeveloped country in that group was Lebanon, which was democratic. Group B, countries with "substantial growth and adequate or increasing self-sufficiency," included Israel and 9 less-developed countries, of which no more than 5 (Colombia, India, Mexico, the Philippines, and Venezuela) may be considered democratic.[9] (Greece, Iran, Taiwan, and

[8] Bell's testimony is in *Foreign Assistance Act of 1963*, Committee on Foreign Affairs, U.S. House of Representatives, Hearings, 88th Cong., 1st Sess., Part II, April 23, 24, 25, and 26, 1963, pp. 185-91 and ff. The quotation appears at p. 188.

[9] This count uses the rather easy criterion (from the Introduction, Table 2) of "three or more consecutive, popular, and competitive elections." By using more demanding criteria the number would decrease even further.

Thailand were not and are not democracies.) But 3 of the 5 were Latin American countries, where substantial American aid began only in the early sixties: democracy there obviously could not be attributed to aid-induced economic development. Group C, 9 Third World countries with substantial growth but continuing external dependence, contained no stable democracies at all; but Bell minimized this because "adequate or increasing self-sufficiency" suddenly became an ad hoc additional condition of democracy, even though there was "substantial growth" in the countries. Group D—9 Third World countries without substantial growth—had two firm democracies, both Latin American (Chile and Costa Rica). Bell also notes without explanation that he excluded at least 6 Third World nondemocracies (Korea, Vietnam, Laos, Cambodia, Libya, and Morocco) from the analysis, presumably because they had been receiving larger quantities of supporting assistance[10] than of developmental aid. But the mix of aid in these countries was not different from that in countries like Taiwan, Jordan, Thailand, Greece, and the Philippines, which he included.

Thus, the same data may be interpreted in very different and at least equally plausible ways. It would seem entirely proper to throw out the 11 Marshall Plan countries, Spain, and Japan: the present concern was the Third World, where conditions were so obviously different as to make inferences from the European and Japanese cases dubious in the extreme. That would leave 28 countries, of which 8 were democratic. One should also throw out the Latin American countries: since they had been receiving substantial economic aid for only a year or two at the time, democracy there could not possibly have been due to aid-induced economic development. That would reduce the universe to 15 countries, of which only 3 (or 4, if Israel were included) were democratic. The 3 were Lebanon in Group A and the Philippines and India in Group B. Bell's appropri-

[10] "Supporting assistance" was the new name for "defense support," or, economic aid principally for immediate security purposes.

ately cautious final phrases may still stand, but the relationship between aid-induced economic development is no longer "decidedly favorable" or "overwhelming." It is very
shaky indeed, and if one brings in the other 6 or more
countries with heavy proportions of supporting assistance,
the relationship becomes even more tenuous (3 or 4 democracies out of 21 countries).

Two other points related to Bell's analysis are noteworthy
as evidence of the lack of clarity and rigor among officials in
the Kennedy administration about the relationship between
economic and political development. The first is the vague
and shifting character of the definition of political "progress" and its opposite, "backsliding." In the short space of
four sentences, Bell defines political progress first as
"strengthening democratic institutions or liberalizing less
democratic regimes," then as political stability, then back
to democracy again. Obviously, however, democracy and
stability are discrete phenomena, and they may exist independently of one another. The second point is the degree to
which this piece of analysis was evidently accepted without
critical examination by Congress and officialdom. Although
the full analysis was presented in Bell's prepared written
statement, and he summarized it orally before the congressional committee, no congressman challenged or even
mentioned it. However, two high officials in the Kennedy
administration—Frank M. Coffin, the Deputy Administrator
of AID, and Arthur Schlesinger, Jr., a special assistant to
the President on foreign affairs—completely accepted Bell's
analysis and drew upon it uncritically in books they published in 1964 and 1965, respectively.[11]

Despite the weaknesses of Bell's analysis, it was a far more
explicit and sophisticated examination of the theory underlying the aid program than usually occurred in the early
sixties. Interviews and other research carried out in 1962-
1963 showed that the majority of officials in AID believed

[11] Coffin, *Witness for Aid*, p. 153; and Schlesinger, *A Thousand
Days*, pp. 599-600.

that if they could promote economic development, political development would follow automatically.[12] They devoted little attention to the second link in the chain, but few doubted its strength. A minority of no more than a third of the AID officials gave some indication of having thought about political development sufficiently so that it might have influenced some of their decisions. In such cases political development was usually defined as democracy and officials tended to stress the ways in which aid might strengthen cooperatives, credit and trade unions, "responsible" journalism, bargaining skills among politicians, and other forces in a pluralistic political system. But these doctrines had a relatively small effect on AID programming. Later AID could and did list a vast array of such pluralism-promoting activities as evidence of concern for political development. In fact, however, these activities had been undertaken almost entirely as part of the effort to promote economic development, not for political development purposes.

Besides AID (and the White House), the other main locus of decisionmaking about economic aid was the Department of State. Political analysis in the State Department was restricted for the most part to "plots and personalities" rather than in-depth studies of systemic political change. Officials there tended to perceive aid as an instrument for achieving short-run political purposes rather than long-term economic and political development. Thus the State Department tended to use aid to win friends, punish enemies (by withdrawing aid), maintain alliances, influence elections, and otherwise protect and advance American security in the short run. Most often, these short-run purposes were defined in Cold War terms. AID also used aid for such purposes, but the practice was much more widespread in the Department of State. Since aid for short-run security purposes also had long-run political consequences, the Cold War concerns of

[12] The tendencies summarized in this paragraph are documented in Packenham, "Political-Development Doctrines," 209-229. See also Nelson, *Aid, Influence*, pp. 134-42.

the Department of State constituted a significant political development doctrine—after the economic approach, the most powerful one of the Kennedy years.[13]

DIPLOMACY-FOR-DEMOCRACY IN LATIN AMERICA

The third significant approach during the Kennedy years may be called the explicit democratic approach. Whereas the economic approach assumed that democracy and other favorable political results would flow from economic development, and the Cold War approach implied support for almost any kind of government that was neither radical nor Communist, the explicit democratic approach designated specific steps to encourage and support liberal constitutional regimes. The explicit democratic approach was utilized most often and most clearly in President Kennedy's policies toward Latin America. This diplomatic effort is significant for a number of reasons. It resembled but went beyond the repeated efforts during the Truman administration to try to promote democracy in Greece; in this sense it was probably the most sustained explicit attempt since the late forties to foster democracy in the Third World. It was a typically "liberal American" effort, which defined political development as constitutional democracy and excluded radical as well as Communist politics from that definition. It was a learning experience, of considerable importance for President Kennedy, about the limits of America's capacity to promote democracy in the Third World. Finally, it was a more self-conscious and explicit doctrine of political development than the two dominant approaches; as such it therefore reveals much about typical American responses to the

[13] For a good discussion of the short-run political uses of aid, see Nelson, *Aid, Influence*, Chap. 5. The "plots and personalities" characterization is taken from Richard Neustadt's memorandum to Roger Hilsman, the Director of Intelligence and Research in the Department of State, quoted in Packenham, "Political-Development Doctrines," 219. Neustadt, writing as a consultant, was describing the kind of political analysis demanded by Washington of its Thailand mission; but his characterization had broader applicability.

69

problem of how to promote political development in the Third World.

With much fanfare, President Kennedy had initiated the Alliance for Progress in March 1961 as an inter-American effort for social and economic progress through democratic politics in the hemisphere. Democracy was a very salient goal for him from the beginning. Speaking to the Latin American ambassadors in the White House on March 13, 1961 (the "birthdate" of the Alliance), Kennedy quoted the prophecy of the nineteenth-century Mexican liberal, Benito Juárez: "Democracy is the destiny of humanity." The task of the Americas, Kennedy said, was "to demonstrate . . . that man's unsatisfied aspiration for economic progress and social justice can best be achieved by free men working within a framework of democratic institutions." Arthur Schlesinger and Theodore Sorensen make it abundantly clear that Kennedy considered constitutional democracy to be a critical goal, "fundamental to the success of the Alliance."[14]

Kennedy believed that economic and social progress by themselves would go a long way toward increasing the likelihood of democracy. For example, while the "Declaration to the Peoples of the Americas" and the Preamble to the Charter of the Alliance specified such goals as "personal liberty," "representative democracy," and the improvement and strengthening of "democratic institutions," the body of the Charter itself specified only economic and social goals, and it was on these goals that the Latin American bureau of AID and the Department of State placed their emphasis. Kennedy felt that if he could promote economic and social reform, he would thereby strengthen the forces of the "democratic left"[15] and thus avoid tyranny of either the

[14] Schlesinger, *A Thousand Days*, pp. 759-93, quotation at p. 769; Sorensen, *Kennedy*, pp. 599-604. The quotation from Juárez is taken from *President Kennedy Speaks on the Alliance for Progress* (Washington: AID, n.d.), p. 4.

[15] Schlesinger, *A Thousand Days*, pp. 766, 194ff. The assumption

Right (landed oligarchs and the military) or the Left (radicals and Communists) in the region.

But six military coups d'etat in 1962 and 1963 induced Kennedy to employ complementary, diplomatic techniques.[16] After a rather perfunctory objection to the Argentinian coup, he made his most intense diplomatic effort in Peru. There the military had taken power when it appeared that Víctor Raúl Haya de la Torre, the leader of the Aprista Party, had received a plurality (not a majority) in the presidential election. According to a formula worked out in advance with the American ambassador, James Loeb, Jr. (a dedicated liberal intellectual and founder of the Americans for Democratic Action), Kennedy suspended diplomatic relations, cut off economic aid, and ordered technical assistance personnel not to go to their jobs. He let it be known that he was considering the suspension of Peru's sugar quota. The State Department issued an unusually strong statement: "We deplore this military coup d'etat which has overthrown the constitutional government of Peru."[17] Kennedy told a news conference: "We are anxious to see a return to constitutional forms in Peru. . . . We feel that this hemisphere can only be secure and free with democratic governments."[18]

Many Americans expected, along with Kennedy and his advisers, that other Latin American countries would come

---

here was that reform is a substitute for revolution and possible tyranny rather than a catalyst. This assumption is often valid but sometimes open to question. For an excellent discussion of this problem, see Huntington, *Political Order*, pp. 362ff.

[16] The coups were in Argentina (March 1962), Peru (July 1962), Guatemala (March 1963), Ecuador (July 1963), the Dominican Republic (September 1963), and Honduras (October 1963). For summary discussions of the coups and the United States' responses, see Edwin Lieuwen, *Generals vs. Presidents* (New York: Praeger, 1963, 1965), pp. 10-69, 114-20; Schlesinger, *A Thousand Days*, pp. 769-73, 783-88, 1001. I have also relied heavily on newspaper reports, especially the *New York Times*, and the *Hispanic American Report*, for the descriptions that follow.

[17] *New York Times*, July 19, 1962.

[18] Quoted in Schlesinger, *A Thousand Days*, p. 787.

71

to the support of the United States when it used its influence to support democracy rather than dictatorship in the region. For example, on the day after the coup the *New York Times* said in an editorial: "The State Department could do no less than it did yesterday in suspending diplomatic relations with Lima and in cutting off further Alliance for Progress aid. Every government in Latin America that respects constitutionality and democracy will surely also make its condemnation [of the coup] clear."[19]

However, not all the "condemnations" were those that had been predicted. The three largest Latin American nations—Brazil, Mexico, and Argentina—all protested the American "intervention" in Latin American affairs. The Chilean foreign minister warned the United States against being "more royalist than the king." Four countries, led by Venezuela, whose President Rómulo Betancourt was an old friend of Haya de la Torre, initiated a meeting of the Ministers of the Organization of American States to consider the Peruvian situation; but lack of support prevented them from even raising the question of the junta, and the meeting became instead an occasion for a resolution against the hemispheric designs of Cuba. In Peru, the public greeted the junta apathetically. The Aprista-controlled Peruvian Labor Confederation called a general strike which failed utterly. Both of the other two candidates in the election (Fernando Belaúnde Terry and Manuel Odría) accepted the military government and criticized the American stand. Most other politicians, government officials, and interest groups also went along with the new regime; not even the students were united in opposition.[20]

The effect of Kennedy's actions on Peruvian politics is difficult to measure. The junta promised to hold elections within a year, and it kept the promise.[21] Whether this was

[19] *New York Times,* July 19, 1962.

[20] *Hispanic American Report,* 15, Nos. 7 and 8 (July and August 1962), 638-39, 737-38; Schlesinger, *A Thousand Days,* p. 787.

[21] Belaúnde Terry was elected in June 1963, and deposed in another military coup in October 1968.

because of American pressure is uncertain.[22] In any event, the United States accepted the promise at face value, restored diplomatic relations (with a new ambassador—Loeb by this time was thoroughly *persona non grata*), and resumed economic and military aid.

Kennedy seemed to learn from the Peruvian experience and the ones that followed. He took less severe stands toward the coups in Ecuador and Guatemala, partly because the alternatives there were perceived as equally undesirable. In the Dominican Republic and Honduras, he again took a firmer position, but again with only partial success. In Guatemala, for example, as in Peru, the military promised to hold elections later; the promise was honored; and in March 1965 a liberal democratic leader, Julio Méndez Montenegro, was elected president. But liberal democracy was by no means established either in Guatemala, Peru, the Dominican Republic, or any of the other countries, and the Kennedy administration had learned something of the limits of its capacity to promote democracy in Latin America.

These lessons were to be codified in an important and relatively little-noticed statement by Edwin M. Martin, the Assistant Secretary of State for Inter-American Affairs, on October 5, 1963. This "Official U.S. Policy for Latin America" was sent to every diplomatic post in Latin America with the notation, "This statement by Mr. Martin constitutes U.S. policy vis-à-vis military governments in Latin America." It was also made public in toto the next day.[23]

Martin's statement began by emphasizing that "By tradi-

[22] A Foreign Service officer with experience both in Lima and on the Peru Desk in Washington argues that "the Junta laid down the conditions of its rule in the first public statement it made upon taking over the government. Its further reiteration of these terms cannot be considered a major victory for the policy of sharp disapproval from Washington." Curtis C. Cutter, "The United States Role in the Peruvian Elections of 1962," seminar paper, Stanford University, 1968, pp. 9-10. Cf. Schlesinger, *A Thousand Days*, pp. 787-88.

[23] The statement appears in the *New York Herald Tribune*, October 6, 1963, p. 30, and in the *Department of State Bulletin*, 49 (November 4, 1963), 698-700.

73

tion and conviction as well as a matter of policy, the United States opposes the overthrow of constitutional and popular democratic governments anywhere. This is especially true in Latin America," because of historic ties and because of the Alliance for Progress. He then struck his main theme about the limits of American power and the inherent moral ambiguities of political choices in an imperfect world.

> We all have respect for motherhood and abhor sin. We may observe, however, that while motherhood has prospered, so has sin. In an increasingly nationalistic world of sovereign states, a U.S. frown doesn't deter others from committing what we consider to be political sins. . . .
>
> I fear there are some who will accuse me of having written an apologia for coups. I have not. They are to be fought with all the means we have available. Rather . . . I am insisting . . . that democracy is a living thing which must have time and soil and sunlight in which to grow. We must do all we can to create these favorable conditions, and we can and have done much. But we cannot simply create the plant and give it to them; it must spring from seeds planted in indigenous soil.

What Martin sought to achieve was a middle position between what he called "impatient idealists" and "defeatist cynics." On the whole, he succeeded. The statement did not alter the U.S. position on radical movements; however, with respect to the issue of democratic versus military rule, it was realistic without abandoning the democratic goals entirely. It thus reflected the learning experience through which the Kennedy administration had just come. Newsmen asked the President himself on October 9 if the statement represented a "reversal of his policy on dictatorships in Latin America." He replied that it did not; that he supported the statement; that it was consistent with the Alliance and general U.S. policy; and that sending the Marines into Honduras (the site of the most recent coup) was "not the way for democracy to flourish . . . we did the best we could."[24]

Any existing concern that Martin's statement constituted an apologia for coups seemed largely to disappear soon thereafter. Certainly reactions to it could not compare to those which followed a much more extreme statement by Martin's successor, Thomas Mann, in March 1964. In fact, the so-called Mann Doctrine and other policies of President Johnson toward Latin America—especially the warm embrace of the military government in Brazil after April 2, 1964, and the massive intervention in the Dominican Republic a year later—have obscured the fact that the Kennedy administration was already taking a less ambitious position regarding coups in the hemisphere even before Johnson took office.[25]

A WORLD OF DIVERSITY?

If Kennedy's learning experiences in the Alliance for Progress and in the foregoing instances of diplomacy-for-democracy represented the "affirmative side" of his Latin American policy, his dealings with Dr. Cheddi Jagan in British Guiana represented another, darker side that differed little from the most inflexible Cold War doctrines.[26] Seemingly an "insignificant" case, Kennedy's relations with the Jagan government of tiny British Guiana (population 600,-000) in fact illustrate how hardened and dogmatic the Lockean ideology can be. They also lay bare an extraordi-

[24] *New York Times*, October 10, 1963.

[25] For more evidence in support of this point, see Slater, *Intervention and Negotiation*, pp. 16-17.

[26] Except where indicated otherwise, the source for this account and the quotations in it is Schlesinger, *A Thousand Days*, pp. 773-79. Latin American matters were one of Schlesinger's main responsibilities in the White House, and he played an uncommonly important role in the Jagan affair. Since neither Theodore Sorensen nor Roger Hilsman, Kennedy's other "inside" biographers, mention this episode, it seems appropriate to rely heavily on Schlesinger.

nary divergence between the Kennedy administration's pretensions of support for "a world of diversity" and its actual performance. Theodore Sorensen reports that Kennedy

> . . . did not insist that every nation be marked as either Communist or anti-Communist, or even be interested in the Cold War. . . . Nor did he try to fix an aid recipient's domestic policy. Although he did seek basic reforms . . . he knew that our own system could not be universally imposed or accepted in a world where most of the people [quoting Kennedy] "are not white . . . are not Christians . . . [and] know nothing about free enterprise or due process of law or the Australian ballot." All must adopt their own system, and their freedom to do so was the heart of his policy. Without specifically contradicting Wilson's phrase of "a world made safe for democracy," he began in 1963 to refer in his speeches to "a world made safe for diversity." That single phrase summed up much of his new thinking in foreign policy.[27]

Let us see how this was applied to British Guiana.

Kennedy had to take some sort of a position about Jagan, the prime minister of then still-colonial British Guiana, when he visited Washington in late October 1961 to meet Kennedy and to seek economic assistance. Jagan was an East Indian dentist (Guiana had a slight Indian majority population and a Negro minority), trained at Howard University in Washington. He was "some sort of Marxist" and had an American wife whom he had met while a student and who had once been a member of the Young Communist League. He had been elected to the legislature three times, most recently in 1961. Jagan and his party stood for independence

[27] Sorensen, *Kennedy*, pp. 605-6. See also Schlesinger, *A Thousand Days*, Chap. 22, "The World of Diversity," on Kennedy's policies toward the Third World. Understandably, neither Jagan nor British Guiana is mentioned in this chapter.

from Great Britain, racial harmony, a vague socialism, and constitutional democracy.

The Americans evidently had little information and no strong opinion about Jagan prior to his visit. The British, however, on whose information Schlesinger and Kennedy apparently relied until their meeting with Jagan, were "not unsympathetic" toward him. "Though they had earlier imprisoned him more than once, they now claimed that it was possible to work with him and that he was more responsible than his rival, the Negro leader Forbes Burnham." Until Burnham came to Washington himself in May 1962, the United States had accepted the British description of him as "an opportunist, racist, and demagogue intent only on personal power." On the other hand, "the AFL-CIO people in British Guiana thought well" of Burnham; Hugh Gaitskell liked him; and he impressed Schlesinger, who was deeply involved in the affair, as "an intelligent, self-possessed, reasonable man, insisting quite firmly on his 'socialism' and 'neutralism' but stoutly anti-communist." He also talked as if he would try to temper racial animosities in his country and give his own party, which was predominantly African while Jagan's was more mixed, a "bi-racial flavor."

The reasons Schlesinger gives for the American turning-away from Jagan are these. British Guiana was "the main target of convenience" for "Communism" in Latin America in 1961. This statement is simply alleged: Schlesinger offers no evidence whatever to support it. "Senator Dodd of Connecticut had pronounced him [Jagan] a communist agent, but then he had said the same thing about Sékou Touré." On the television program "Meet the Press" the Sunday before his meeting with the President, Jagan had "resolutely declined to say anything critical of the Soviet Union and left an impression of either wooliness or fellow traveling." In the private meeting in the White House, Jagan seemed to Schlesinger "endowed . . . to those of us present, with an unconquerable romanticism or naiveté."

The most damning evidence of all came after Jagan affirmed his admiration of the political ideas of the British socialists Laski and Bevan. Schlesinger reports:

> We all responded agreeably to this, citing Bevan's faith in personal freedom and recalling his belief that the struggle of the future would be between democratic socialism and communism. Jagan, after avowing his commitment to parliamentary government, went on to say that he also admired the *Monthly Review* and the rather pro-communist writings of Paul Sweezy, Leo Huberman, and Paul Baran. [Undersecretary of State] George Ball and I pressed him on this point, declaring there was a large difference between Bevan and the Sweezy group. Jagan finally said, "Well, Bevanism, Sweezyism, Hubermanism, Baranism—I really don't get those ideological subtleties." Kennedy observed later that this was the one time when his exposition rang false.[28]

After this, Kennedy would not see Jagan again. The President instructed Schlesinger to try to placate him and the British by working out a mutually agreeable statement, but to avoid any aid commitment. Kennedy also observed that he had "a feeling that in a couple of years he will find ways to suspend his constitutional provisions and will cut his opposition off at the knees. . . . With all the political jockeying and all the racial tensions, it's going to be almost impossible for Jagan to concentrate the energies of his country on development through a parliamentary system."

[28] Huberman and Baran, now deceased, and Sweezy are all American economists with Marxist but non-Communist orientations. Sweezy and Huberman published a book in 1961 decidedly favorable to the Castro regime; in 1969 they co-authored another, much more critical volume. Baran was then professor of economics at Stanford University. Their writings and the *Monthly Review* are standard fare among non-Communist Latin American progressives and radicals, much as the works of John Kenneth Galbraith and Arthur M. Schlesinger, Jr., were among North American liberals.

78

The final reason Schlesinger cites is the most revealing of all. After Jagan's visit, he reports:

> . . . events had convinced us that Jagan, though perhaps not a disciplined Communist, had that kind of deep pro-communist emotion which only sustained experience with communism could cure; and the United States could not afford the Sékou Touré therapy when it involved a quasi-communist regime on the mainland of Latin America. Burnham's visit left the feeling, as I reported to the President, that "an independent British Guiana under Burnham (*if* Burnham will commit himself to a multi-racial policy) would cause us many fewer problems than an independent British Guiana under Jagan." (Emphasis in original.)

What, on the other hand, did Jagan have going *for* him? Schlesinger's own account reveals a great deal. "Jagan was plainly the most popular leader in British Guiana." His party had won 57% of the parliamentary seats on the basis of 42.7% of the vote in 1961. The British found him substantially superior to his nearest rival, Burnham. Jagan's party was more biracial than Burnham's. Jagan "spoke as a nationalist committed to parliamentary methods"; he readily consented to a public statement at the end of his American visit, pledging himself to "uphold the political freedoms and defend the parliamentary democracy which is his country's political heritage."

Moreover, Schlesinger does not mention that

> . . . although a Marxist [not a Communist] in outlook, [Jagan] had made no move to become part of the Soviet orbit. Indeed, he had in seven years succeeded in doing virtually no socialist planning and had continually applied to the United States for aid. Despite the visits of trade missions from the U.S.S.R., Cuba, and Hungary, a contract with Cuba for rice at an advantageous price and

79

Castro's offer of thirty-five million dollars in loans (which the British refused to let Jagan accept), the Kennedy administration itself had no hard evidence that Jagan was about to make a "Cuba" of his country.[29]

Nor does Schlesinger say anything about the activities of either the American Institute of Free Labor Development (AIFLD)—the Latin American arm of the AFL-CIO, whose $6 million yearly budget was financed almost entirely by U.S. funds—or the Central Intelligence Agency. AIFLD and Gerald O'Keefe, the CIA agent, helped to plan and finance a variety of stratagems—strikes, riots, lockouts, blockades, racist campaigns—aimed at bringing down the Jagan government. Yet only when American oil companies cooperated with the strikers in refusing to unload petroleum did Jagan appeal to Cuba, which sent him some oil.[30]

In their talk, Kennedy had told Jagan:

I want to make one thing perfectly clear. We are not engaged in a crusade to force private enterprise on parts of the world where it is not relevant. If we are engaged in a crusade for anything, it is national independence. That is the primary purpose of our aid. The secondary purpose is to encourage political freedom. But we can't always get that; and we have often helped countries which have little personal freedom, like Yugoslavia, if they maintain their national independence. This is the basic thing. So long as you do that, we don't care whether you are socialist, capitalist, pragmatist, or whatever. We regard ourselves as pragmatists.

But in the end, national independence was not "the basic thing," and Kennedy cut him down. Although there is

[29] Barnet, *Intervention and Revolution*, p. 239.

[30] *Ibid.*, pp. 240-42. See also Leo A. Despres, *Cultural Pluralism and Nationalist Politics in British Guiana* (Chicago: Rand McNally, 1967), pp. 182-83, 199; and the essay by Frank McDonald in Tad Szulc, ed., *The United States and the Caribbean* (Englewood Cliffs, N.J.: Prentice-Hall, 1971), p. 145.

nothing whatever in Schlesinger's account which conflicts with Kennedy's criteria or supports Schlesinger's view that Jagan was either a Communist "target" or a pro-Communist himself, Jagan had to go. The reasons were the ones indicated: he had a pro-Communist "emotion," he refused to criticize the U.S.S.R., he liked radical (but non-Communist) authors. The way to get rid of him was open and obvious: get the British to establish a system of proportional representation, which worked against Jagan and to Burnham's advantage. It was an unusually effective piece of "political development" engineering. After "prolonged discussion," the British government finally made the electoral change, and it worked. Despite the AIFLD- and CIA-supported attacks on him, Jagan increased his popular vote and his party received almost 6% more popular support than any other single party; but Burnham became premier in a coalition government with two other parties.[31] "With much unhappiness and turbulence," concludes Schlesinger, "British Guiana seemed to have passed safely out of the communist orbit."

British Guiana was not, of course, the only country in which the Cold War doctrine of political development was employed by the Kennedy administration. It was used all around the world; and since the Cold War existed, this was probably justified in some instances. There were, however, other instances besides British Guiana in which Kennedy used it badly and too strongly. Among the more obvious of these were Cuba, especially in the Bay of Pigs episode, and Vietnam. Without challenging the explanations which Kennedy's biographers have offered for the debacle at the Bay of Pigs (mainly the reluctance of the new Kennedy staff advisers to challenge the CIA and Pentagon "experts"), it is interesting to note Kennedy's own ambivalent views before April 1961 about the Castro regime. On the one hand he had

[31] For additional evidence that the change to a system of proportional representation hurt Jagan and his party, see Despres, *Cultural Pluralism*, pp. 262-67, 282-84.

described Fidel in his book, *The Strategy of Peace*, as "part of the legacy of Bolivar," as part of "the frustration of that earlier revolution which won its war against Spain but left largely untouched the indigenous feudal order." On the other hand, he played politics with Cuba in his campaign in 1960. For a while he appeared "to adopt the thesis that the State Department should have listened to its pro-Batista ambassadors and recognized the revolution as a communist conspiracy from the outset." He had a "deep feeling against Castro (unusual for him) . . ." which contributed, in Sorensen's view, to his big mistake in April 1961.[32]

In Vietnam, too, Kennedy was ambivalent; eventually, however, he fell prey to fallacious assumptions stemming in part from the liberal tradition, which in turn led him to unworkable Cold War "solutions." In 1954, Senator Kennedy had declared that a "unilateral action by our own country . . . without the support of the great masses of the peoples [of Vietnam] . . . would be virtually impossible in the type of military situation which prevails in Indochina . . . [that is,] an enemy which is everywhere and at the same time nowhere, 'an enemy of the people' which has the sympathy and covert support of the people."[33] But in December 1961, President Kennedy made the very same kind of mistake he had counseled against from the Senate floor seven years earlier when he increased the number of military advisers to South Vietnam and placed the main American emphasis on the military effort. Like Eisenhower before him and Johnson after him, Kennedy, working within the broad set of assumptions that flowed from the Fifteen Weeks of 1947, which in turn reflected liberal America's response to worldwide political involvement, followed the incremental policy of "one more step—each new step always promising

[32] Schlesinger, *A Thousand Days*, pp. 224-25; Sorensen, *Kennedy*, p. 343.

[33] Sorensen, *Kennedy*, p. 737.

the success which the previous last step had also promised but failed to deliver."[34]

Even the so-called "political" alternative to a military solution in Vietnam was highly optimistic and reflected a curious mix of forced-labor and liberal-constitutionalist tactics. The main concept was "strategic hamlets," which called for the "relocation of peasants into fortified villages, surrounded by barbed wire fences and ditches filled with bamboo spikes. . . . Each hamlet would elect its political representative by secret ballot."[35] The first element of this formula seems to have been implemented more consistently than the second. The strategic hamlets program was to be supplemented by social and economic modernization programs and by guerrilla tactics.[36] But these were either not tried or not effective. Although Kennedy "had always believed there was a point at which our intervention might turn Vietnamese nationalism against us and transform an Asian civil conflict into a white man's war,"[37] he evidently never believed that point had been reached during his presidency. Perhaps he would have, but he did not have the chance after November 22, 1963; and his successor never saw it that way at all.

Not only in Vietnam but in many parts of the Third World, one of the most important expressions of the Cold War approach in the Kennedy administration was the expansion and intensification of counter-insurgency programs. Presidential advisers like Roger Hilsman, Robert Kennedy,

[34] Arthur M. Schlesinger, Jr., *The Bitter Heritage: Vietnam and American Democracy, 1941-1966* (New York: Fawcett Crest, 1967), pp. 39, 47; Schlesinger, *A Thousand Days*, p. 548. Cf. Daniel Ellsberg, "The Quagmire Myth and the Stalemate Machine," *Public Policy*, 19, No. 2 (Spring 1971), 217-74; Leslie H. Gelb, "Vietnam: The System Worked," *Foreign Policy*, No. 3 (Summer 1971), 140-67.

[35] Schlesinger, *A Thousand Days*, p. 549.

[36] These are described in Roger Hilsman, *To Move a Nation: The Politics of Foreign Policy in the Administration of John F. Kennedy* (Garden City, N.Y.: Doubleday, 1967), pp. 431-35.

[37] Schlesinger, *A Thousand Days*, p. 998.

and Walt W. Rostow (and even the President himself) prided themselves on their ingenuity and expertise in initiating and extending these programs. American counter-insurgency doctrines admitted no circumstances under which radical politics were justified. In this very important respect they were highly consistent with the American liberal tradition. These programs, which seemed necessary and progressive to the Kennedy administration, now seem in many instances to have been superfluous and regressive.

Thus, the administration of John F. Kennedy utilized all three of the main approaches to political development: the economic approach, the Cold War approach, and the explicit democratic approach. President Kennedy seemed buoyantly confident during his first months in office about the potential of American economic assistance, and of U.S. foreign policy in general, to bring about major change in the Third World. As time wore on, however, his optimism waned. Using a word "rare in his vocabulary" (according to Theodore Sorensen), Kennedy said publicly that he felt "depressed," not only about Vietnam, but about Latin America and the Alliance for Progress. So far as foreign aid was concerned, the President was coming to the conclusion sometime in 1962 that the "basic weakness lay in the program itself and its execution" rather than just administrative organization. As early as November 1961 he first made a statement he was to repeat with increasing frequency:

> We must face the fact that the United States is neither omnipotent nor omniscient—that we are only 6 per cent of the world's population—that we cannot impose our will upon the other 94 per cent of mankind—that we cannot right every wrong or reverse each adversary—and that therefore there cannot be an American solution to every problem.[38]

[38] Sorensen, *Kennedy*, pp. 601-2; Schlesinger, *A Thousand Days*, pp. 596, 615.

84

President Kennedy thus displayed a capacity to learn, to let events affect his assumptions, to be, as he so often alleged himself to be, a pragmatist—an "idealist without illusions." He learned, but he learned incompletely and inconclusively. For example, both his efforts to promote democracy in Latin America and his most serious mistakes in Vietnam came *after* he first pronounced the "6 per cent" maxim in Seattle in November 1961. Learning takes time. It would have taken a long period of time to learn enough through pragmatic, step-by-step, incremental testing to challenge seriously the basic assumptions of the Fifteen Weeks. And John Kennedy's time was limited. At the time of his death, he was groping, but he had not made a fundamental reassessment about the political development doctrines in American foreign aid. And after November 22, 1963, the awesome responsibility fell to Lyndon Johnson: child of the New Deal, relatively untutored in foreign affairs, without even the benefit of Kennedy's three years of pragmatic learning. He would project the liberal tradition, with all the massive energy and conviction he possessed, even further onto the world stage.

THE JOHNSON YEARS

President Lyndon Johnson retained the same basic legislative, organizational, and conceptual bases for the aid program that he inherited from President Kennedy. All of the foreign assistance laws during his administration were amended versions of the Foreign Assistance Act of 1961. The Agency for International Development continued to be the main foreign aid administrative unit. The two administrators of AID during the Johnson years were David E. Bell, whom Kennedy had appointed in late 1962 and who continued in the post until mid-1966, and William S. Gaud, whom Kennedy had appointed assistant administrator for Near East and South Asian affairs and who moved up to the top job when Bell resigned. (Gaud had already taken the post of deputy administrator when Frank Coffin resigned in 1964.) Dean Rusk remained Secretary of State until January 20, 1969.

During the Johnson years AID retained and at least theoretically gave even greater emphasis to concepts that President Kennedy had stressed: self-help, country programming, incentives for private investment, country concentration, loans rather than grants. Johnson reviewed the program in early 1964 and then again, more intensively, in 1966, with the "help" of a Cabinet committee and other advisory groups originally established by his predecessor. This review was the basis for his aid proposals in 1966, which he presented as a revamped program. While they gave new emphasis to the areas of food, health, and agriculture, the 1966 proposals were for the most part extensions of trends already under way. Congress recognized them as such; no mention was made, for example, in either of the reports of the relevant committees in the Senate and the House of Representatives in 1966 of any revamped or "revolutionary" new aid program.[39] By contrast, the changes made by an increasingly angry Congress in 1967 made the latter program, in the Senate's eyes, "the most significant revision of the aid program in many years." But even the congressional adjustments in 1967 were not conceptual changes so much as attempts to restrict the Johnson administration and to require closer legislative review.[40]

[39] See Committee on Foreign Affairs, U.S. House of Representatives, "Foreign Assistance Act of 1966," House Report No. 1651, 89th Cong., 2nd Sess., June 23, 1966; Committee on Foreign Relations, U.S. Senate, "Foreign Economic Assistance," Senate Report No. 1359, 89th Cong., 2nd Sess., July 7, 1966. Cf. Philip Geyelin, *Lyndon B. Johnson and the World* (New York: Praeger, 1966), who calls President Johnson's 1966 proposals "revolutionary" (p. 260). Geyelin also contends that the "help" of the cabinet committee and advisory groups was minimal or nonexistent, except in the restricted sense of giving more legitimacy to what the President wanted to do anyway (p. 264).

[40] Committee on Foreign Relations, U.S. Senate, "Foreign Assistance Act of 1967," Senate Report No. 499, 90th Cong., 1st Sess., August 9, 1967, p. 15. See also Geyelin, *Lyndon Johnson*, pp. 80, 163ff.

Until 1966, the level of expenditures for economic aid remained more or less constant. Gross expenditures for all economic assistance oscillated around $3.5 billion annually; gross AID expenditures hovered around $2 billion. Up to 1966 or 1967, according to a well-informed estimate, about 65% of American economic aid was used to promote "long-term economic and social progress," 20-25% to "combat immediate and continuing security problems," and 10-15% for "limited objective" purposes. After 1966, however, increased expenditures in Vietnam raised the proportion of economic aid used for immediate security purposes to about 40%, which left less than half for long-term development.[41] Congressional dissatisfaction with Johnson's foreign policies, especially in Vietnam, severely reduced the total amount of aid in the last two years. His final economic aid request (for fiscal year 1969) was for $2.5 billion; it was cut by almost a billion dollars, in percentage terms the biggest reduction by the Congress of a presidential request for foreign aid in the history of the program.

In terms of official statements—presidential messages, executive testimony in Congress, and the like—the aid goals and the means by which to achieve them also remained largely the same. What was distinctive about the Johnson years, as contrasted with the Kennedy period, was not so much the pattern of abstract goals espoused by the President, the Secretary of State, and high aid officials, or the working concepts of the aid bureaucracy. Rather, the most distinctive features of the Johnson years are to be found in the personality, assumptions, and general approach to international affairs of the new President; the shift in practice back to a greater emphasis on security objectives for foreign aid (while not completely abandoning the economic approach); and the emergence, especially in Congress and quite independently of presidential interest or initiative, of an explicit and fairly intense concern with political devel-

[41] Kauffman and Stalson, "U.S. Assistance," 719, 723-24; Nelson, *Aid, Influence*, pp. 45, 121.

opment, in the form of the Title IX amendment to the Foreign Assistance Act of 1966.

JOHNSON'S DIPLOMACY

When he came to the presidency, Lyndon Johnson was more interested in national than international affairs. He could not ignore foreign policy, of course, but he much preferred to concentrate his energies on the domestic problems for which his background, talents, and natural inclinations were better suited. Aside from trips to Mexico and his wartime military service, Johnson had never been outside the United States prior to 1961. The trouble with foreigners, he said, "is that they're not like the folks you were reared with." Throughout his presidential tenure he wished that foreign policy problems would go away so that he could achieve his goals at home.[42]

This relative disinterest, together with Johnson's much discussed "pragmatism," seems to make it difficult to identify any "operational code" or Johnson doctrine for dealing with other nations. However, as Philip Geyelin (the one author who has treated Johnson's general approach to foreign policy at book length) has observed, Johnson's actions and statements reveal "a recognizable pattern of response and performance, a method of operation, a code of conduct for the international arena derived from domestic political experience and applied, with remarkably little adjustment, to relations with the world."[43] Among the principles in "Lyndon Johnson's Common Law," as codified by Geyelin, none is more amply supported in his handling of the aid program than this: "Doing something for nothing is a violation of every law of practical politics." Or, as he put it elsewhere, "Lyndon Johnson was for doing favors to those who showed themselves to be appreciative . . . in what they did for them-

---

[42] Geyelin, *Lyndon Johnson*, pp. 15-17; Eric F. Goldman, *Tragedy of Johnson*, pp. 275, 378ff.

[43] Geyelin, *Lyndon Johnson*, p. 153.

selves . . . and what they did, or did not do, that might run counter to the larger interests of the benefactor."[44]

For Johnson, this rule of barter was basic. And he "served notice" to aid recipients that actions counter to American interests as *he* perceived them, and to his domestic political interests, "would not be countenanced." Within three days after Kennedy's death, for example, he warned the Pakistani foreign minister that continued sympathy for Communist Chinese causes and antipathy toward those of the West could produce a discontinuance of American aid in Pakistan. In 1966, he made Pakistan and India "object lessons" for any nation receiving or expecting U.S. aid. He let it be known publicly that the United States would maintain its aid— but only at the price of more support from them for the American effort in South Vietnam. Johnson could be "generous"; but the recipients had to come through too. "Johnson was not against foreign aid; he was merely against handing it out without a clear cut return, either in terms of demonstrable economic improvement, or in political favors, or both."[45] Johnson's aid diplomacy was thus an extension of the game of national politics. It involved both persuasion and pressure. Its Biblical justification and banner were not only Isaiah 1:18—"Come now, and let us reason together, saith the Lord"—but also Isaiah 1:19-20—"If ye be willing and obedient, ye shall eat the good of the land: But if ye refuse and rebel, ye shall be devoured with the sword: for the mouth of the Lord hath spoken."[46]

[44] *Ibid.*, pp. 156, 39.   [45] *Ibid.*, pp. 39, 3, 267ff, 30.
[46] Goldman, *Tragedy of Johnson*, p. 63; Geyelin, *Lyndon Johnson*, p. 141. Goldman also writes:

President Johnson brought to the White House [the] traditional American assumption that Americans and the peoples of the rest of the world had in common a bedrock interest in ruling themselves and in advancing economically and socially. As a result, sensible foreign policy was to be based on the working out of the shared attitude in concrete ways. As far as foreign leaders were concerned, LBJ carried over from his experience in domestic affairs a convic-

Another Johnson rule was that one should make oneself very clear, avoiding misunderstandings and miscalculations at all costs. Both Geyelin and Eric Goldman, who served on Johnson's White House staff for almost three years, made the startling contention that Johnson had little "respect" for American foreign relations since the Truman administration, and that he thought little had been accomplished since then. This judgment explicitly included the Kennedy years. Johnson felt, they report, that the United States was too easily misunderstood abroad; that foreigners tended to think of the United States as "fat and fifty, like the country club set"; and that the most important task for the President was to prevent this sort of "miscalculation." What had to be done "was like a Senate maneuver; you had to show that you were ready to play your cards." The President had to insure "respect for the flag," and, above all, stop "aggression." Therefore, before anything else, he meant to do just that. If the operational implications of these imperatives were ambiguous to others, they were perfectly clear to Lyndon Johnson, and he had little patience with those who did not define them as he did.[47]

Out of these perspectives emerged two principal political development doctrines: the economic approach and the Cold War approach. The latter was the more salient, but let us first consider the former briefly.

---

tion that techniques must exist to reach them and to arrive at accommodations with them. If they were men of good will, this could be done by concentrating on their genuine concern for the advancement of their nations toward democracy and a higher standard of living. If the leaders were types unmoved by such considerations, the need was for some of the many forms of arm twisting available in the international sphere, not excluding the form of dropping bombs. Then the leaders would give way to the popular desires which Lyndon Johnson was sure existed, or their replacement would be forced (p. 385).

[47] Goldman, *Tragedy of Johnson*, p. 379; Geyelin, *Lyndon Johnson*, p. 44.

THE ECONOMIC APPROACH

President Johnson wanted aid to help solve the age-old problems of "ignorance, poverty, hunger, and disease." Relatively uninterested in Africa and the Middle East, he was eager to advance these ends in Latin America and, especially, in Asia. In a curious way, Asia had been a special mission in the American tradition of overseas involvement, and so it was also for Lyndon Johnson. His ten-day trip to Southeast Asia in the spring of 1961 was "the most satisfying episode in his whole three years as Vice President."[48] When Johnson looked at Asia, "he saw central Texas—its needs and what had been done about them." "That Asia," he said "—things can be done there." He became especially interested in and knowledgeable about the Mekong River project for flood prevention, electric power, irrigation, fisheries, and better navigation in the lower delta. Here was a chance to duplicate on a grand scale what he had done for central Texas in the thirties, and to make a bigger and better TVA. With this project, with the Asian Development Bank established in 1966, and with his overall program of economic and social development for the region, Lyndon Johnson "had proposed what amounted to a crash Marshall Plan for Southeast Asia."[49]

There was unbounded optimism in all of this. Johnson at times seemed to believe, as his wife put it, "that anything can be solved, and quickly." He stressed the concept of self-help, and just as emphatically violated it by his own actions. Returning from his Southeast Asian tour, Vice President Johnson counseled Kennedy that "these nations cannot be saved by United States help alone." But he violated this self-help precept and other of his 1961 recommendations when he was President. By late 1966, when he was well down the

[48] Goldman, *Tragedy of Johnson*, p. 388; Geyelin, *Lyndon Johnson*, p. 35.
[49] Goldman, *Tragedy of Johnson*, pp. 387, 409, 443.

91

road to his defeat, he wanted his grandchildren to think of him, in his own words, "as the man who *saved* Asia and Vietnam."[50] It is possible to argue that the context had changed in such a way as to render his earlier guidelines no longer relevant—certainly he thought it had. Nevertheless, the United States took on the major burden for the effort in Vietnam. The change from Johnson's prescriptions about self-help in early 1961 to his performance as President in 1965-1968 is curiously reminiscent of John Kennedy's casting aside his own 1954 maxims by sending military advisers to Vietnam in late 1961.

Johnson was pleased when the economic approach worked well and led, as the liberal assumptions said it would, to democracy, stability, non-Communism, and peace. In some respects the description of him as "a 'global populist' with a genuine yearning to bring to the backward areas everywhere what had been brought to the backward areas of Texas three decades earlier"[51] was an accurate one. Yet he never spent a large share of his political capital for development-oriented aid. In this, to be sure, he differed little from his predecessors, but it was particularly characteristic of Lyndon Johnson to qualify sharply his commitment to aid for development. He was loath to give something for nothing. And since economic development was slow, what the underdeveloped countries had to offer him was mainly support for his anti-Communist objectives. Johnson would hope for economic development; but if (as often occurred) he did not get it, or it led to instability or radicalism or anti-Americanism, he felt "almost betrayed."[52] The one-dimensional caricatures of Johnson's personality are obviously not acceptable, but it is impossible not to see his personal insecurity as an important determinant of his foreign policy attitudes, especially as the Vietnamese situation became more

[50] *Ibid.*, pp. 357, 391-92, 511 (emphasis added); Geyelin, *Lyndon Johnson*, p. 40.

[51] Geyelin, *Lyndon Johnson*, p. 276.

[52] *Ibid.*, p. 136.

threatening.[53] Thus his assumptions and his personality both tended to lead him to favor the Cold War approach to political development over any other.

COLD WAR DOCTRINES

The most important manifestations of the Cold War doctrine came in Johnson's policies toward Latin America and Vietnam. As Vice President, he had privately felt that John Kennedy's Latin American policy was "a thorough-going mess." As President, Johnson aimed to do something about it. His criticisms were numerous. He felt that Kennedy's approach toward the region was too "ideological," especially insofar as it stressed government spending (both by the United States and the Latin countries) and democracy. Drawing upon his own knowledge of the Mexican case, he preferred a more tough-minded "pragmatism." Even more intensely than Kennedy, he opposed a "second Cuba" in the region; any President who allowed that, in his view, "would be impeached and ought to be."[54] A second Cuba was equated with "another Munich"; a Communist Brazil would be "another China." And whereas Kennedy

[53] This insecurity was only one facet of an exceedingly complex personality, and certainly it was not the only important determinant of his behavior. However, careful reading of the few serious biographies and memoirs about Lyndon Johnson suggests that the harsh, satirical caricatures of the time contained a surprisingly large element of truth. For example, Eric Goldman describes a "downright frightening" Johnson who told White House aides and a cabinet member one day in 1966 that the Russians were behind the criticism of the war, that they were writing speeches for critical Senators, and that they even passed messages of instruction to Senators at hearings (*Tragedy of Johnson*, pp. 499-500 et seq.). Though Goldman had reason to resent Johnson, and in certain respects probably did, in general his treatment of him is sympathetic and balanced; moreover, Goldman's credentials as a historian deserve respect, especially in simple descriptions of events (as distinguished from judgments and interpretations). Goldman also makes it clear that this was only one side of the President's personality.

[54] Goldman, *Tragedy of Johnson*, pp. 76, 381; Geyelin, *Lyndon Johnson*, pp. 69-70, 78-79.

93

had many aides to speak for him on Latin American matters (in the State Department, AID, and the White House staff) Johnson elected to speak with "one voice." That voice belonged to Thomas C. Mann, a foreign service officer, fellow Texan, and former ambassador to Mexico.

Mann was neither the long-time friend of Johnson nor quite the "reactionary" his liberal critics thought him to be. He was Lyndon Johnson's kind of person: "able, industrious, tough-minded, and knowledgeable," as well as "uncommunicative . . . intellectually uninspiring, uncolorful, mechanical, pragmatic. He not only didn't have charisma, he didn't believe in it."[55] Johnson (with Dean Rusk's encouragement) gave him an extraordinary delegation of authority and deliberately publicized the notion that Mann was his "one voice" on hemispheric matters. He took the unprecedented step of appointing Mann to be simultaneously Assistant Secretary for Inter-American Affairs in the Department of State and Special Assistant to the President. He also designated him Coordinator of the Alliance for Progress. Mann was soon dubbed Johnson's "czar" for Latin American affairs; except during major crises, when the President himself took command, the designation was apt.

This background information on Thomas Mann and his role in the Johnson administration[56] is relevant because the

[55] Geyelin, *Lyndon Johnson*, p. 97.

[56] For still more information, see Geyelin, *Lyndon Johnson*, pp. 93-100; and Rowland Evans and Robert Novak, *Lyndon Johnson: The Exercise of Power* (New York: New American Library, 1966), pp. 393-99. The latter source is useful in dispelling the myths that Kennedy had been opposed to Mann (he in fact had tried, unsuccessfully, to recruit Mann as his Assistant Secretary of State for Inter-American Affairs in January 1961) and that Johnson and Mann were old friends (they were not). However, Evans and Novak also affirm that Mann differed from "Kennedy liberals" like Schlesinger, Richard Goodwin, and Ralph Dungan *only* in personal style, and *not* in substance. This goes too far; Mann was more of a "hard-liner" substantively as well.

Mann was appointed Undersecretary of State in February 1965. He was succeeded as Assistant Secretary and Coordinator of the

so-called Mann Doctrine represented a significant change in political development doctrines toward Latin America. Whereas Kennedy had initially taken a fairly extreme position in favor of liberal democracy in the region and then moved to a more moderate stance, Johnson and Mann virtually abandoned constitutional democracy as a standard from the start, and more or less maintained that position throughout their terms.

The changes wrought by the Mann Doctrine were those of substance and of style. The substantive change was that the United States would no longer seek to punish military juntas for overthrowing democratic regimes. Emphasis would be placed instead on four major objectives: economic growth, protection of American investments, nonintervention, and opposition to Communism.[57] (The potential for conflict between the third and fourth of these became actual in the Dominican Republic a year later, in April 1965. In that instance the anti-Communist objective prevailed overwhelmingly over the principle of nonintervention.) The circumstances surrounding the announcement of the Mann Doctrine were equally important. The Doctrine became public through journalistic reports of an off-the-record speech by Mann on March 18, 1964, to all U.S. ambassadors, chargés d'affaires, and chiefs of AID missions in Latin America, who had been called to Washington by the President for a three-day review conference. The fact that Mann had so clearly and emphatically been designated the President's Latin American "voice," and that he spoke off-the-record to an extremely high-level group at an important review conference, heightened the perception among jour-

---

Alliance by Jack Hood Vaughn. Lincoln Gordon replaced Vaughn in January 1966; after a little more than a year Gordon resigned and was succeeded by Covey T. Oliver, who remained until the end of the Johnson administration. Despite these changes in personnel, the policy of the Johnson administration remained closer to the Mann Doctrine than to the diplomacy-for-democracy doctrine of the Kennedy years.

[57] Report by Tad Szulc, *New York Times*, March 19, 1964.

nalists, Latin American leaders, and others that Mann's speech signaled a major change in policy.[58] Moreover, in his entire presentation, Mann made no mention of the Alliance for Progress.[59]

The day after the speech the State Department issued a guarded, ambiguous statement which said on the one hand that "the United States' devotion to the principles of democracy is a historic fact," and, on the other hand, that "United States policy toward unconstitutional governments will, as in the past, be guided by the national interest and the circumstances peculiar to each situation as it arises."[60] The next day it was disclosed that the United States had recently approved a $2.5 million loan by the Inter-American Development Bank to the dictatorship of François Duvalier in Haiti.[61] Less than two weeks later, on April 2, the constitutional regime of President João Goulart of Brazil was overthrown in a coup led by the army; within twelve hours, the United States recognized the provisional military government and made public an unusually warm greeting by President Johnson to the new leaders.[62]

[58] Earlier, in January, Johnson had taken a "hard" line on the crisis in Panama over the question of sovereignty in the Canal Zone, and this crisis simmered through the March announcement of the Mann Doctrine. Moreover, both Latin American and North American policymakers knew Mann's reputation, so that his very appointment also strongly suggested a change. But this speech on March 18 was the first explicit statement of a new doctrine for the region.

[59] Szulc, New York Times, March 19, 1964.

[60] New York Times, March 20, 1964. This was also essentially the position taken by President Nixon in his first major policy statement on Latin America. See his speech to the Inter-American Press Association, October 31, 1969, reprinted in the New York Times, November 1, 1969.

[61] New York Times, March 21, 1964. Policymakers in both northern and southern halves of the hemisphere thought the loan to be technically sound; it was the timing of the disclosure of a loan to the most retrograde dictatorship in the region that deepened feelings and perceptions of the significance of the Mann Doctrine.

[62] For a good discussion of the U.S. role in the Brazilian coup, see Thomas E. Skidmore, Politics in Brazil: 1930-1964 (New York: Oxford

In combination, these changes represented a major shift in U.S. policy toward Latin American political development. Interestingly, the statement by Edwin Martin in October 1963 had received nowhere near the attention that the Mann statement did. Consequently, the gradual shift toward more realistic goals during the Kennedy administration was obscured. Kennedy's policies were seen as uniform, whereas in fact they changed significantly; Johnson's were seen as a complete reversal, when in fact they were merely carrying to an extreme a process already well under way.[63]

The Johnson administration continued its extension and escalation of previous trends in the Dominican Republic and in Vietnam. Bombing of North Vietnam began in February 1965; the commitment of American combat forces to South Vietnam was made a month later; in late April the first contingent of U.S. Marines landed in Santo Domingo—the first overt military intervention in any Latin American country by the United States since 1925. Soon the number of American troops in the Dominican Republic reached 23,850.[64] By August 1965 there were 125,000 American

---

University Press, 1967), pp. 322-30. Cf. Geyelin, *Lyndon Johnson*, p. 122, who suggests that the Johnson administration did use direct but covert means to hasten the coup. Skidmore is correct, however, that there is no public evidence for this view and considerable evidence against it.

[63] For example, Tad Szulc, the able Latin American correspondent for the *New York Times*, reported from Washington the "impression" that "Mr. Mann had started a gradual change of emphasis, leading to a basic modification of the entire United States philosophy of dictatorships" (*New York Times*, March 20, 1964). However, the "gradual" change preceded and was codified in Edwin Martin's little-noted statement; the Mann Doctrine approximated, and to an even greater extent appeared to be, almost a total reversal.

[64] This is the State Department figure for the maximum number of troops on May 17, 1965. *Nomination of Lincoln Gordon to be Assistant Secretary of State for Inter-American Affairs*, Committee on Foreign Relations, U.S. Senate, Hearing, 89th Cong., 2nd Sess., February 7, 1966, p. 6.

troops in South Vietnam and by 1968 the number was over 500,000.

The differences between the Johnson and Kennedy years were mainly those of style, personality, and emphasis, rather than overt doctrines. Many of the permanent bureaucrats in AID and the Department of State who served under both Presidents maintained largely the same doctrines after November 1963 as before. Other continuities were noted earlier. However, in the American political system the President affects the tone and the substance of all foreign policy. The personality of a President and the emphases he chooses to give fixed policies make a big difference. They take over where policy continuity leaves off. For example, if it is true that Kennedy abused the Cold War approach in such countries as Cuba and British Guiana, and was overly optimistic in Latin America and Vietnam, it is also true that Johnson compounded the errors in the Dominican Republic and Vietnam. If it is true that they were both constrained by Congress and public opinion in any desires they may have had to loosen the grip of the Cold War on political development thinking, it is also true that Presidents can alter constraints by skillful leadership. In this respect Kennedy was a somewhat better leader than Johnson.

TITLE IX

Background and Legislation. At the same time that the Johnson administration was intensifying the Cold War approach, sentiment was growing, in and out of the executive branch, for an additional and seemingly very different kind of effort. For many years AID had carried on a number of activities which probably affected the political systems of the recipient countries, but which were not carried out with political development explicitly in mind. Thus, highways and dams may have contributed to political integration; programs in public administration and public safety doubtless strengthened government bureaucracies and law enforcement agencies; programs in health, education, housing, fi-

98

nance, and agriculture may have affected patterns of income distribution and political participation as well as aggregate economic development. However, rather than following a conscious plan explicitly for political development, most of these activities were designed either as part of the attempt to promote economic development, or as part of a vague, "buckshot" effort at general "development."[65] Moreover, since few of these efforts were evaluated systematically, it was difficult to know whether and under what conditions they had positive or negative consequences for political development.

In the early 1960s, pressures had slowly begun building up for a more explicit concern with political development per se. Gradually, more people were becoming aware that economic development did not necessarily lead to all of the good things anticipated in the aid legislation and concepts. Instead of wondering whether these goals were not too ambitious in the first place, however, the main response was to search about for ways in which the aid program might be altered so as to achieve more of the goals, especially democracy.[66]

In the summer of 1966, the House Committee on Foreign Relations accepted a proposal by Congressman Donald Fraser, a Democrat from Minnesota, that a new amendment, Title IX, be added to the Foreign Assistance Act.

[65] See Nelson, *Aid, Influence*, pp. 129-49; Packenham, "Political-Development Doctrines," 209-227.

[66] A brief sketch of these background proposals is given in Nelson, *Aid, Influence*, pp. 142-45. A detailed account of the legislation, its background, amendments to it, and its implementation in AID is provided by Ralph Braibanti, "External Inducement of Political-Administrative Development: An Institutional Strategy," in Ralph Braibanti, ed., *Political and Administrative Development* (Durham, N.C.: Duke University Press, 1969), pp. 4-21. Additional information on the creation and implementation of Title IX is given in Elizabeth Fletcher Crook, "Political Development as a Program Objective of U.S. Foreign Assistance: Title IX of the 1966 Foreign Assistance Act," Ph.D. dissertation, Fletcher School of Law and Diplomacy, Tufts University, 1969, esp. pp. 64-202.

Entitled "Utilization of Democratic Institutions in Development," Title IX was approved by both houses of Congress later that year. It provided that in carrying out development assistance programs, "emphasis shall be placed on assuring maximum participation in the task of economic development on the part of the people of the developing countries, through the encouragement of democratic private and local government institutions." In its report on the aid bill, the committee further directed AID to give new emphasis to the goal of attaining "a larger measure of popular participation in development." It felt that this goal could best be achieved

> . . . through the fostering of cooperatives, labor unions, trade and related associations, community action groups, and other organizations which provide the training ground for leadership and democratic processes; through making possible increased participation of such groups and of individuals in the planning, execution, and evaluation of development undertakings; through broader and more effective utilization of the experience and resources of existing private and voluntary organizations; and, generally, through the building of democratic private and public institutions at all levels—local, state, and national.
>
> . . . AID's reports should evaluate American assistance not only in economic terms, but also in terms of the extent to which our aid encourage democratic political processes.[67]

Thus Title IX was the first explicit legislative injunction to the aid agency to concern itself directly and indirectly with political development in the Third World. The language of the amendment, the report on it by the Committee on Foreign Affairs, the arguments of its principal proponents, subsequent interpretations of it, and indeed its very

[67] Committee of Foreign Affairs, U.S. House of Representatives, "Foreign Assistance Act of 1966," House Report No. 1651, 89th Cong., 2nd Sess., June 23, 1966, pp. 27-28.

title—"Utilization of Democratic Institutions in Development"—all show clearly that the intent and content of Title IX were to make political development, defined in terms of political participation and democratic institutions, a goal of equal rank and salience with economic development. This understanding produced in some quarters the view that Title IX was potentially the most significant and valuable change in the basic concept of foreign aid since at least the Kennedy reforms of 1961.[68] Among others, the same understanding produced indifference, skepticism, or vigorous opposition. And almost everywhere there was uncertainty about the more precise meaning of Title IX and its operational implications for aid programming. Since Title IX was the first and only explicit political development provision in aid legislation, these reactions and interpretations provide important insights into the conscious response of liberal Americans to the problem of political development in the Third World. We shall, therefore, examine them in some detail.

Interpretations. Title IX produced three broad types of interpretations and reactions. One reaction was skepticism, and in some instances hostility. The skeptics doubted the desirability and feasibility of carrying out the congressional

[68] For this view, see among others George C. Lodge, "U.S. Aid to Latin America: Funding Radical Change," *Foreign Affairs*, 47, No. 4 (July 1969), 749; Donald M. Fraser, "New Directions in Foreign Aid," *World Affairs*, 129, No. 4 (March 1967), 245-46 and 250, and the remarks of Congressman Bradford Morse in the *Congressional Record*, February 27, 1967, both quoted in John R. Schott, "Title IX: A New Dimension in U.S. Foreign Aid?" Paper Prepared for Delivery at the Annual Meeting of the International Studies Association, San Francisco, March 27-29, 1969, pp. 7-8; and Princeton Lyman, "Opening Remarks at the Roanoke Conference on Title IX of the Foreign Assistance Act," November 10, 1968 (photocopy of prepared remarks). Mr. Lyman was Chief of the Title IX Division of AID. He reported that the interpretation that "has generally come to be adopted by A.I.D." was that Title IX is "very far-reaching in intent: to reshape A.I.D.'s and the U.S.'s view of the role and objectives of foreign aid" (p. 2).

101

mandate. In this group, the largest number were those officials in AID and the Department of State who maintained the economic and Cold War approaches in a relatively rigid form. A smaller number were not inflexible or doctrinaire but skeptical on different grounds. Among these were AID Administrator William S. Gaud, some economists (Kermit Gordon, Edward Mason, Theodore Schultz, Gustav Ranis) on AID's Advisory Committee on Economic Development, and academic outsiders like Robert O. Tilman (a Yale political scientist and Southeast Asia expert) and Richard N. Adams (a Texas anthropologist and Latin America expert). Their objections were not identical. However, they tended to share the view that implementing Title IX would be difficult and politically dangerous. They also tended to doubt the wisdom of setting up an Office of Political Development in AID, which others had proposed.[69]

The other two groups were favorable to Title IX and to the general idea of an explicit approach to political development defined as democracy and popular participation. The main difference between these two favorable groups was in the degree to which they emphasized a "direct" or "indirect" approach. According to the direct approach, aid should be used to strengthen explicitly political variables: political parties, legislatures, courts, constitutions, electoral laws and practices, bureaucracies. Many of the proposals of Congressmen Fraser and Bradford Morse, a Republican from Mas-

[69] Richard Adams' testimony is in *Survey of the Alliance for Progress*, Subcommittee on American Republics Affairs, Committee on Foreign Relations, U.S. Senate, Hearings, 90th Cong., 2nd Sess., February 27, 28, 29, and March 1, 4, 5 and 6, 1968, pp. 204-225. The testimony by Gaud and Tilman is in *Rural Development in Asia*, Subcommittee on Asian and Pacific Affairs, Committee on Foreign Affairs, U.S. House of Representatives, Hearings, 90th Cong., 1st Sess., Parts 1 and 11, pp. 109ff and 191ff, respectively. For the economists' views, see the minutes of the meeting of the Advisory Committee on Economic Development, Agency for International Development, "M.I.T. Title IX Conference Report and Title IX Policies of AID," October 11, 1968, mimeographed.

sachusetts and another leader in the movement for Title IX, illustrate this approach.[70] Pat Holt, a consultant to the Subcommittee on American Republics Affairs of the Senate Committee on Foreign Relations and a Latin American expert, testified that "the United States needs governments in Latin America which see things more or less like we do. Such governments can only arise from a set of reasonably well-rooted, stable, democratic political institutions." Among the ways the United States could further these ends, Holt thought, was through adding "political content" to the curriculum of American training schools for Latin American military personnel, and "civic education" in adult literacy programs. H. Field Haviland, Jr., of the Brookings Institution seconded Holt's recommendations and urged programs for "civic development" along democratic lines in Latin America, such as by "developing" political parties and by "strengthening" the "civic education" of civilian and military officials.[71] High officials from the State Department and AID in Vietnam described a wide array of activities designed to promote political development in rural areas, such as constitutional changes, more honest elections, strategic hamlet programs, and "nation-building" efforts.[72] An Office of Political Development, either inside or outside of AID, was proposed by Samuel P. Huntington and others; it might be "a new style CIA, more skilled in building governments than in subverting them."[73]

Proponents of the indirect approach, on the other hand,

[70] For these and related proposals, see *Congressional Record*, March 15, 1966, pp. 5,601, 5,605-9; and *ibid.*, July 13, 1966, pp. 14,765-67, 14,773-77.

[71] *Survey of the Alliance for Progress*, pp. 198, 201, 202-4.

[72] *Rural Development in Asia*, pp. 263ff.

[73] Samuel P. Huntington, *Military Intervention, Political Involvement, and the Unlessons of Vietnam* (Chicago: Adlai Stevenson Institute of International Affairs, 1968), p. 28. This monograph originally appeared in fragmented form in Pfeffer, *No More Vietnams?* Of all the proponents of the direct approach, Huntington was one of the least inclined to equate political development exclusively with political democracy.

argued that aid should focus not so much on explicitly political variables as on nonpolitical variables which in turn affected the political system. They stressed the view that virtually all aid activities have a political development dimension, and that AID and other agencies should explicitly consider these dimensions in advance of nearly every decision they made. Political development was defined as more popular participation and democracy. What this group was saying, in other words, was first that policymakers should address and evaluate social and political "aspects" of "development" as well as economic "aspects." Standing alone, this injunction was so vague and benign that it provoked little disagreement. Beyond this, however, there was a corollary: that aid should be especially designed to emphasize popular participation and democracy. The latter view was more controversial. This indirect approach was the principal interpretation adopted by AID (or at least the Title IX Division of AID) in late 1968.[74]

Attempts to Clarify Title IX. In order to clarify the meaning of Title IX, Congress passed several amendments to it in 1967 and 1968.[75] In the latter year AID commissioned the Center for International Studies at MIT to convene a six-week summer conference, the purpose of which was to recommend how broad an interpretation to place on Title IX and how to implement it in the actual operations of the agency.

These efforts at clarification had only limited success. The amendments calling for more evaluation and research were not unpopular but bore no exclusive relationship to Title IX. By 1967 evaluation of the consequences of all aid activities in terms of its most salient objectives was finally becoming a widely recognized need in AID.[76] A provision

[74] Lyman, "Opening Remarks," p. 2.

[75] These are described in Braibanti, "External Inducement," in *Political and Administrative Development*, pp. 19-20.

[76] See David E. Bell, "The Quality of Aid," *Foreign Affairs*, 44, No. 4 (July 1966), 606; Col. George A. Lincoln, "Improving A.I.D. Pro-

for "systematic programs of in-service training" on Title IX objectives was almost meaningless because the "purposes" with which personnel were supposed to be "familiarized" were too vague or, where sharp, controversial and contradictory. The main problem was in the basic concept of Title IX itself. Although it instructed AID to recognize differing needs, desires, and capabilities in different countries, it also instructed that AID encourage democratic institutions and support democratic trends. The tension between these two injunctions was usually resolved by Title IX's supporters in favor of the latter. The difficulty many proponents had in shedding all their optimistic liberal assumptions is well illustrated in the report that came out of the conference held at MIT in the summer of 1968.[77]

The report concluded that the principal theme of Title IX should be "popular participation." Participation had three dimensions: participation in the implementation of economic development; participation in the fruits of economic growth; and participation in political decisionmaking. The last was the "central concept." It covered "more than the political right to vote in elections. It includes, for example, the right of a people to speak to a bureaucracy that is responsive, and the ability to form voluntary organizations to pursue group interests."[78]

This definition was the core of the report, which became the main basis for AID thinking about Title IX in late 1968. According to the report, participation now ranked along with economic development as a principal goal of AID. It

gram Evaluation," Report to the Administrator (Washington, D.C.: Agency for International Development, 1965), *passim*. The Lincoln report helped to increase awareness of the need for more and better evaluation.

[77] *The Role of Popular Participation in Development* (Cambridge: M.I.T., Center for International Studies, 1968). Forty persons, drawn about half and half from universities and government (mainly AID), attended the conference. Professors Max F. Millikan and Lucian W. Pye of M.I.T. were co-chairmen.

[78] *Ibid.*, pp. 1-2.

was recognized that "the goal of participation also requires the development of a wide variety of institutions at all social and political levels from the local community to the national center." Such institutions would supposedly do two things: first, "enable people to articulate their demands effectively"; and, "enable government to respond effectively to those demands." However, while there were a great many suggestions in the report about ways in which aid could increase participation and allow people to articulate demands more effectively, there were very few suggestions about ways in which aid could strengthen the capacity of governmental institutions to respond to these demands. The few proposals advanced to strengthen governmental capacity were even more sensitive and impractical than the many proposals made for increasing participation.

Sensitivity and impracticality were not the only reasons, however, why the report had so little to say about the means by which aid might strengthen political institutions. Equally important was the fact that its authors did not view institutional capacity for coping with demands as a serious problem. The institutions, they felt, would flow automatically from participation and economic development.

> More participation leads, through popular pressure, to improved governmental performance and to more equitable and useful distribution of resources. More economic growth provides both resources to make participation possible and a growing variety of institutions and organizations through which it can be practiced.[79]

Moreover, the distinctions which Title IX supporters attempted to draw between "popular participation" and democracy sometimes were in fact (if not necessarily in intent) little more than verbal sleights of hand. Thus the minutes of a meeting on Title IX of the Advisory Committee on Economic Development of AID recorded the feeling of one

[79] *Ibid.*, pp. 2-3.

member that "the terminology so far developed in regard to Title IX was quite good—for example, the reference to social and civic rather than political development, and participation as a better word than democracy."[80]

The Significance of Title IX. The significance of Title IX does not lie principally in its impact on AID programming, which was quite small.[81] Nor does it necessarily lie in its potential impact. By the end of 1969, Title IX had attracted considerable attention and had generated a flurry of reports, conferences, studies, airgrams to overseas missions, research contracts, interagency committees, an AID Division, and at least one book. But thus far it has had no major impact on policy. Whether Title IX will become "the next basic step" in American foreign aid, on a par with the Marshall Plan, Point Four, and the Kennedy reforms of 1961, seems doubtful; in any event, it remains to be seen.[82]

The significance of Title IX rather is this: when, for the first time, political development per se was made an explicit, high-priority goal in foreign aid legislation,[83] it was defined in terms that reflected the premises of the liberal tradition in America. For it embodied essentially three kinds

[80] Minutes of Advisory Committee on Economic Development, October 11, 1968, p. 7 (cited in n. 70 above).

[81] Everyone agrees on this: see Nelson, *Aid, Influence,* pp. 147-48; Schott, "Title IX," p. 1; *The Role of Popular Participation in Development,* p. 1.

[82] The quoted phrase is from Lyman, "Opening Remarks," p. 12; see also Schott, "Title IX," p. 1.

[83] The economic and Cold War approaches were and are highly significant political development doctrines with infinitely more profound consequences for the Third World. While political development was a salient concern in these two approaches, however, it usually was operationally secondary to and derivative from other objectives (especially economic development and combating Communism). The efforts of President Kennedy to use aid as an instrument with which to promote democracy in Latin America were also more consequential than Title IX and quite explicit. But they were not similarly enshrined in legislation, and they utilized the technique of diplomacy rather than direct and indirect methods in the countries themselves.

of responses to the problem of political development in the Third World. One was the direct approach: strengthen legislatures, "train" Latin American politicians, "create" and "develop" political parties, and the like. With few exceptions, this approach represented an effort to export liberal constitutional and largely American institutions and practices to the Third World. Another response was the indirect approach, as in the report of the MIT study group. It, too, reflected and sought to export the American experience, for it tended to assume that social and political participation, like economic development, lead to "all good things" political in underdeveloped countries much as they did in the United States. It little recognized that economic growth and social and political participation can and sometimes do lead to instability, authoritarianism, radicalism and even, rarely, full-scale revolution. Nor was the indirect approach accompanied by an appreciation of the appropriateness under certain circumstances (circumstances much less rare in poor countries than in the United States) of radical and revolutionary change. Since it did not anticipate these possibilities, it had nothing new to say about how to respond to them. Hence it offered no substitute for the traditional American proclivity to react negatively and sometimes repressively toward certain consequences of the very changes the United States had helped to promote, and would continue to promote, with the indirect approach.

The third and final response was the vague and generally unexceptionable view that the United States should pay more attention to the social and political "aspects" of "development," evaluate aid in these terms, and train people to recognize the importance of these dimensions. There is little to disagree with in this rather vacuous response. However, when it slides, as it did, into the indirect approach, there is more cause for concern.

What Title IX showed, in sum, is that after over two decades of intense world involvement and experience with foreign aid, a significant segment of aid policymakers were still in the grip of a liberal tradition they seldom recognized and little understood. Most proponents of Title IX protested that this was not so and denied that they wished to "export" American institutions and practices. And the denials were sincere. But sincerity is no synonym for accuracy. In general, it seems clear that the power of the liberal tradition on those who disavowed its effect was greater than they knew.

SUMMARY: THREE MAIN DOCTRINES

From 1947 to 1968 there were, broadly speaking, three main types of doctrines about political development in the American aid programs: the economic approach, the Cold War approach, and the explicit democratic approach.

According to the economic approach, aid was to be used to promote long-term economic, social, and political development in the recipient countries. The main emphasis lay on the first of these. Aid would contribute to economic development; and economic development would contribute to a host of good things political—stability, non-Communism, democracy, pro-American attitudes and foreign policies, international understanding, world community, peace. Aid was to take the form mainly of developmental assistance (grants, loans, commodities, and technical assistance) and diplomacy. The salience and explicitness of the various political development goals varied, but the economic approach in one form or other was utilized throughout this period.

The main proposition of the Cold War approach was that aid should be used to enhance political stability, strengthen non-Communist forces, and for other narrowly defined security purposes. According to this doctrine, aid could also be used to win and maintain friends and alliances, military bases, American presence, votes in international organizations, and for other immediate security purposes. Cold War aid might also be used to promote economic development,

109

if this was viewed as compatible with the other objectives and related to American security needs. In all of these cases, the theory was that aid could promote non-Communism, pro-Americanism, and stability, which were viewed as conducive to American security in the context of the Cold War. The main means were defense support (later called supporting assistance) developmental assistance, miscellaneous other kinds of aid (e.g. counter-insurgency programs), and diplomacy. This approach was most salient during the fifties and the middle and late sixties; but it was employed throughout the whole period.

The explicit democratic approach was similar in certain respects to each of the other two main doctrines. It is distinctive in that it specified more explicitly than the others that aid should be used to promote political democracy as well as economic development, non-Communist forces, and the other objectives. The tactics employed for advancing these ends were mainly three: diplomacy (e.g. President Kennedy's attempts to combat military coups in Latin America); direct political development activities (e.g. altering the electoral systems in the Greek and British Guianan cases); and influencing nonpolitical variables which in turn would influence the political system (e.g. the efforts to strengthen cooperatives, trade unions, and other pluralistic organizations). The idea here was that aid properly designed and used might contribute to the emergence and strengthening of constitutionalism and pluralistic democracy. This approach was employed less frequently than the other two, mainly in the Kennedy administration. Support for it grew during the middle and late sixties, especially in the Congress.

3

The Liberal Roots
....   of the Doctrines

ONE can better understand why the doctrines about political development in the American aid program took the
form they did by examining some assumptions implicit in
what Louis Hartz has called the "Liberal Tradition in America."[1] This is not to say that the liberal tradition is the only
explanation for these doctrines. There are other important
causes, but none accounts adequately for the doctrines.
Moreover, the influence of the liberal tradition on these
doctrines has been insufficiently noted and generally under-
estimated. Although some evaluation of the doctrines inevitably enters into this discussion, my principal objective
in this chapter is only to explain them.

Specifically, this chapter will describe in some detail the
content of each of the four main liberal assumptions; examine their genesis in the historical interpretations of the
American exceptionalists; and document (both by sum-
marizing the evidence from Chapters 1 and 2, and by in-
troducing new material) some of the ways in which American political development doctrines since 1947 have reflected
these assumptions. Each component of the liberal tradition
is particularly useful in helping to account for a single major
doctrine; beyond this, the four assumptions "hang together"
in a coherent whole that explains and illuminates the doctrines even more than the simple sum of the parts. This coherence of the assumptions and the doctrines will be the
subject of the first half of Chapter 4.

[1] Louis Hartz, *The Liberal Tradition in America: An Interpretation
of American Political Thought Since the Revolution* (New York:
Harcourt, Brace and World, 1955).

CHANGE AND DEVELOPMENT ARE EASY

The first inarticulate assumption of the liberal tradition, simply put, is that change and development are relatively easy. According to the exceptionalist perspective, this assumption flows in large measure from the fact that social, political, and economic development were relatively easy in the United States, especially for the dominant cultural groups.[2] And this was so in part because there was comparatively little to change.

It was not necessary to change the social order in America because, with the major exceptions of native Americans and black people, Americans were "born equal." Perhaps only in recent years, when the issue of race has become more salient, and other urban, environmental, and international problems have intensified, have Americans begun to appreciate what a genuinely difficult social problem is like. Similarly, except for the Civil War, political change and development in the United States have been relatively easy. Even the American Revolution was a comparatively speedy affair. Most historians now accept the thesis that it was not a "real" revolution such as those in France, Mexico, Russia, China, and Cuba. If there is any analogy in American history to those epochal upheavals, it is more correctly the Civil War than the War of Independence.[3] So, too, the difficulties of estab-

[2] They were not so easy, of course, for *dominated* groups, especially native Americans and black people. However, to a very great extent Americans have been unable or have refused to perceive the burdens American change and development have imposed on these groups. This first liberal premise, like the others, reflects both "objective" conditions and events in America, and the selective interpretations Americans have put on them. See Graham and Gurr, *Violence in America*, pp. xvii, xxix, 7, 788ff; and Hartz, "A Comparative Study of Fragment Cultures," *ibid.*, pp. 107-127.

[3] The Civil War is so treated, for example, in Barrington Moore, Jr., *Social Origins of Dictatorship and Democracy: Lord and Peasant in the Making of the Modern World* (Boston: Beacon Press, 1966), Chap. 3.

lishing a new nation after independence, and the political problems cast up by the Great Depression of the 1930s, while indeed serious in American terms, were easy matters to cope with politically compared to the massive problems confronting the Third World.

Finally, the natural blessings and the achievements of the American economy have been unrivaled in modern world history. Protected from external conflicts, with high agricultural productivity and a low ratio of men to the land, America in its first century of independence experienced relatively easy economic growth. And industrialization, when it came with great force in the latter half of the nineteenth century, was also relatively easy and breathtakingly quick.[4] These happy experiences fostered the assumption, scarcely conscious, that change and development were easy everywhere.

So goes the argument of the exceptionalists, who argue further that this assumption is applied by Americans to foreign countries. The description of foreign aid doctrines in Chapters 1 and 2 provides a considerable amount of evidence suggesting that this assumption was operative from 1947 to 1968.[5] The initial economic aid appropriation to Greece of $300 million swelled to over $1 billion by 1951 and to an estimated $4 billion in total economic and military assistance by 1967. Yet socioeconomic injustices and political instability and repression still plagued Greece at the end of these two decades. The same optimism was evident in ECA aid to East and Southeast Asia in the period from 1948 to 1952. The United States aimed to make South Korea

[4] Degler, "The American Past," p. 198; Louis Hartz, testimony in *The Nature of Revolution*, Committee on Foreign Relations, U.S. Senate, Hearings, 90th Cong., 2nd Sess., February 19, 21, 26, and March 7, 1968 (Washington, D.C.: Government Printing Office, 1968), 120.

[5] The next few paragraphs are mainly a topical review of material presented chronologically in Chapters 1 and 2. Except where indicated otherwise, documentation of specific points and quotations may be found in those chapters. The same applies to the comparable reviews in the next three sections of this chapter.

113

economically self-reliant "within a relatively few years." A major objective of aid to Southeast Asian countries during those years was to insure "the survival of moderate democratic governments" in Burma, Indochina, Thailand, and the Philippines. American officials thought these goals could be achieved through the combination of "relatively small quantities of material aid" and "extensive" but inexpensive technical assistance. Yet after twenty years and an expenditure of far more money than anticipated, only in the Philippines, if there, has the objective been even approximated.

President Truman thought that the Point Four program quite possibly could raise the standard of living of "the rest of the world" by "just" 2%. This optimism continued on a wide scale through at least the first half of the 1950s, as the aid and State Department bureaucracies propounded the doctrine that technical assistance developed economies, promoted democracy and stability, and warded off Communist aggression in more than 50 countries on a budget never exceeding $150 million per year—or, on the average, less than $3 million per country.

The optimism of Millikan and Rostow's famous "banking concept," which was a factor in the establishment of the Development Loan Fund, was based on an ill-advised assessment of the ease with which change and development were occurring in the United States. They wrote, in 1957:

> The United States is now within sight of solutions to the range of issues which have dominated political life since 1865. . . . The farm problem, the status of big business in a democratic society, the status and responsibilities of organized labor, the avoidance of extreme cyclical unemployment, social equity for the Negro, the provision of equal educational opportunity, the equitable distribution of income—none of all these great issues is fully resolved; but a national consensus on them exists within which we are clearly moving forward as a nation. . . . *If we continue*

*to devote our attention in the same proportion to domes-
tic issues as in the past, we run the danger of becoming
a bore to ourselves and the world.*[6]

The Kennedy administration sought to move "more than
half the people of the less developed nations into self-sustained economic growth," and to move "the rest" of them
closer to that goal, with expenditures for economic aid that
never exceeded $4 billion annually. Heavy reliance was
placed on the optimistic concept of a "take-off" stage of
development. The ambitious goals of the Foreign Assistance
Act of 1961 were accepted and echoed by the Secretary
of State, administrators of AID, most of the AID bureaucracy, and the Congress during the Kennedy years. The Alliance for Progress was a particularly good example of a
program that embodied the "Change Is Easy" assumption.
The attempts by President Kennedy to promote constitutional democracy in Latin America also reflected this optimism. And in Vietnam, President Kennedy assumed that
the United States could accomplish with 16,000 men in the
early sixties what France had failed to accomplish with
200,000 men in the early fifties.[7]

President Johnson retained basically the same aid legislation, organization, personnel, and conceptual tools that
he inherited from President Kennedy. Beyond this, he extended to Asian and other Third World countries the techniques and bargaining style that he had used, more or less
effectively, in the Texas hills and on Capitol Hill. These
techniques failed, however, in the Third World, in part because they embodied the assumption that change and development were as easy in the underdeveloped world as they
were in the United States. Title IX, which represented congressional more than presidential initiative, expressed an
awareness that economic development and political democracy did not necessarily go "hand in hand." But instead of

[6] Millikan and Rostow, *A Proposal*, p. 150 (emphasis added).
[7] The latter point is made by Henry Kissinger in Richard M. Pfeffer,
No More Vietnams?, p. 13.

115

insisting on a hard search for necessary priorities, it em-bodied an often almost impossible search for additional steps that would make aid achieve economic development and political democracy simultaneously. In large measure, there-fore, it was excessively optimistic about the possibilities in the Third World for democratic change and development. Some optimism and hope, to be sure, are useful and neces-sary; too much optimism can have negative consequences when frustration inevitably sets in.

The persistence of the assumption that "change and de-velopment are easy" is also seen in the continuing stress in debates about the aid program on means and techniques, which were highly controversial, rather than on ends and goals, which tended to be taken much more for granted. Since the ends were largely "givens" or constants, whenever aid did not produce the desired results the common infer-ence was not that the objectives were out of line but that something was wrong with the techniques. This gave rise to a constant tinkering with aid machinery, personnel, and lower-order concepts. For instance, the Economic Coopera-tion Administration was replaced in 1951 by the Mutual Security Agency, which was replaced in 1953 by the For-eign Operations Administration, which was replaced in 1956 by the International Cooperation Administration, which was replaced in 1961 by the Agency for International De-velopment. From 1948 to 1962, there were ten different ad-ministrators of the American aid agency.

As noted earlier, the main questions in the debate over Point Four in 1949 and 1950 had to do with methods much more than with goals. But the debate on Point Four was only one extreme example of a general tendency. Over the last two decades a variety of "fashions" have been seen as the "crucial" element in development and therefore as the "key" to effective aid programs. Harlan Cleveland has listed no less than twelve such fashions: relief and recovery, in-vestment, technical assistance, planning, education and train-

116

ing, institution building, public administration, social development, community development, population control, internal security, and—alas—political development.[8] No doubt other lists could be made. Until recent years, however, except for critics who were generally regarded as eccentric, reactionary, or hopelessly radical, relatively few persons knowledgeable about and involved in foreign aid matters have seriously challenged the basic assumptions on which the program is based.[9]

[8] Harlan Cleveland, *The Obligations of Power: American Diplomacy in the Search for Peace* (New York: Harper and Row, 1966), pp. 104-113.

[9] Representative Otto Passman, the chairman of the subcommittee dealing with foreign aid of the Appropriations Committee of the House of Representatives, is perhaps the best example of the "eccentric" type of critic; he was also widely regarded as reactionary. Passman is an exception to the foregoing generalization in that he had a significant influence on aid policy. Spokesmen for approximately two dozen private organizations annually testified at great length, and with generally little effect, before congressional committees. Some of them urged the end or drastic curtailment of the aid program; others wanted it to be increased sharply. The former groups tended to be business-oriented and conservative; the latter were heavily religious and humanitarian. The "hopelessly radical" critics would include those who regarded aid as little more than part of the arsenal of American imperialism in the Third World. They, too, had little impact on aid policy.

One of the most interesting challenges to the premises of American aid, which did receive some serious attention, is an article by Edward C. Banfield, "American Foreign Aid Doctrines," in Robert A. Goldwin, ed., *Why Foreign Aid?* (Chicago: Rand McNally, 1963), pp. 10-31. This essay also appeared in slightly different forms in *Public Policy*, C. J. Friedrich and Seymour Harris, eds. (Cambridge: Harvard University Press, 1961), and as a pamphlet published by the American Enterprise Institute, Washington, D.C., in 1963. Banfield's pessimistic conclusions about aid's influence are similar to (though more extreme than) my own. However, he and I draw different policy prescriptions from these rather similar conclusions. He believes that American "survival" requires keeping the Third World underdeveloped (p. 27 in Goldwin). I conclude that the United States should expect less congenial political results from its aid; but that

117

The proclivity to tinker and make marginal adjustments on the basis of constant premises, rather than to question and test the assumptions themselves, is also evident in the types of evaluation carried on in the aid agency. The AID Office of Program Coordination has provided a useful checklist of four different "functions" which the term "evaluation" is used to describe: (1) compliance control, e.g. observance of legislative and administrative requirements; (2) management improvement; (3) assessment of project implementation, e.g. evaluation of the efficiency with which specific assistance activities are being carried out, in terms of the original work plan and targets; and (4) assessment of actual contribution to development.[10]

The first two "evaluation" activities do not yield insights or propositions about economic, social, or political change and development, or, more importantly, about the impact of aid on them. A typical example of compliance control is official visits by individuals or teams "who survey programs and operations for a day or two or more extended periods, and who usually concentrate on finding and boring into soft spots, rather than emphasizing lessons for improvement and transfer to other missions." This approach to evaluation has amusingly but accurately been characterized as the "Aha! Approach": "the visiting team of experts arrives, talks generally and pleasantly about the program until a soft spot is suspected, shouts 'Aha!,' and targets thenceforth on the questionable item." The management improvement mode is concerned strictly with procedures and administration; it includes "efficiency reports" and personnel performance ratings; and it reflects in part the notion (expressed by

---

even so we should continue to promote economic development in the Third World, even more than we do now. For further discussion of these issues, see Chapters 4 and 8.

[10] Office of Program Coordination, AID, "Measures to Ensure the Effective Use of Aid," U.S. Paper Presented to the Conference on Improving the Effectiveness of Aid for Overseas Development, Ditchley Park, Oxfordshire, England, June 3-6, 1966, pp. 15ff.

one State Department official) that evaluation was "having a senior individual visit AID missions and recommend who should be discharged."[11]

The third type of aid evaluation, "assessment of project implementation," was supposed to have been achieved through the process of "country programming." However, a study of AID evaluation in 1965 concluded that "the annual program planning and review process does not, in fact, provide either the time or the climate conducive to an objective appraisal of actual experience with a view toward identifying and transferring lessons learned."[12] Instead, "many of the goals outlined by field missions still serve more as labelled receptacles for the set of projects being carried out under the supervision of the individual technical divisions in the mission, rather than a *de novo* grouping with its own internal logic and strength. The projects may be well or ill-planned individually and as a group, but superficial 'packaging' by itself adds nothing to their effectiveness."[13] Finally, with a few significant exceptions, which came mainly in the middle and late 1960s, there was very little of the fourth type of evaluation, "assessment of actual contribution to development" of American aid. And even when carried on, it was infrequently communicated effectively to decisionmakers; only occasionally and in limited ways did it have a significant impact on the shape of aid policies.[14]

[11] Lincoln, "Improving A.I.D. Program Evaluation," p. 10.

[12] *Ibid.*, p. 13.

[13] Office of Program Coordination, "Measures to Ensure . . ." p. 5. This statement should not necessarily be interpreted to mean that the evaluation process could not have been used more for genuine evaluation efforts. For the paper continues: "On the other hand, where the approach has been taken seriously and supported by adequate analysis, it has led to significant changes in program design, and to better directed and coordinated activities and influence." See also Nelson, *Aid, Influence*, pp. 59-67.

[14] See Lincoln, "Improving A.I.D. Program Evaluation," *passim*, and Bell, "The Quality of Aid," 606. This discussion of evaluation

An important result of this almost complete failure to assess aid's achievements systematically in terms of aid's substantive objectives was that evaluation as a means of correcting erroneous premises was not perceived as useful; and since this kind of evaluation was not perceived as useful, there was little pressure (until about 1966) for more fundamental evaluation. This vicious circle prevented aid officials from learning from experience and thus freeing themselves from the constraints imposed by their inarticulate liberal assumptions.

All of this is not to say either that evidence which contradicted the first liberal premise was totally unperceived, or that it was totally ignored by the policymakers. However, such evidence was interpreted in ways that left the fundamental assumption unshaken. For example, aid officials interviewed in 1962-1963 repeatedly stressed the marginality of American influence on world affairs generally and particularly on internal change in recipient countries.[15] They stated that it is hard to bring about economic development and even harder to effect social and political development. The following remarks were illustrative: "You can't push history too far"; "We can't play God"; "The recipient countries must want to develop for the program to be a success." Officials said they saw the initiative for change resting with the recipient countries; only if they want change can the United States begin to influence them, by saying "Yes" or "No" to their initiative and by setting conditions on the aid. This was the doctrine of "self-help," and no doctrine was more clearly and frequently asserted, publicly and privately, among AID officials. In fact, the doctrine of self-help, in one form or another, has been stressed "time and again" by aid officials since the beginnings of the pro-

draws on my unpublished paper, "Evaluation and Research in AID," where the tendencies described are documented much more extensively, and where a few exceptions are noted.

[15] Packenham, "Political-Development Doctrines," 227-29.

gram in the latter half of the 1940s.[16] Another example of apparently disconfirming evidence is President Kennedy's repeated statements that the United States was "only 6 per cent" of the world's population and therefore its influence could only be marginal.

How can such evidence be squared with the thesis that the first liberal premise was operative? Here the notion of layers of meaning is relevant. Officials, and also wider publics, sometimes learned that change was not so easy as they had thought; but they learned imperfectly and incompletely. If they stripped away one layer of their liberal assumptions, they usually found underneath another form of the same assumption. And the layers were seemingly unending. If the officials were ambivalent about aid's influence, they maintained a tendency to resolve the ambivalence in the direction of the optimistic liberal assumptions rather than by facing up to the inapplicability of the assumptions to much of the Third World.

Moreover, and very importantly, although individuals could learn to change their assumptions to some degree, such changes occurred within the limiting framework of legislative and institutional goals and premises which reflected the optimistic first liberal assumption. Stated differently, the pragmatic learning occurred "on top of" legal and organizational commitments and assumptions that were highly optimistic and not fully amenable to pragmatic revision.

Thus, while some learning surely occurred to correct the excessive optimism of the Truman Doctrine, the same optimism characterized the Point Four program and the transfer of Marshall Plan aid to Asia. Officials learned some lessons from the ECA experience in Asia, but repeated earlier mistakes in their analysis of the road ahead in the Third World (as was illustrated in the case of Harry Bayard Price). President Kennedy thought he was tough-minded and realistic about how much aid could achieve in underdeveloped

[16] Baldwin, *Foreign Aid*, p. 45.

countries, but he substantially overestimated and oversold the Alliance for Progress. President Johnson rejected what he regarded as naïve optimism in the Kennedy aid posture, and then envisioned and began to implement a crash Marshall Plan for Southeast Asia.

Thus the doctrine of self-help, even though it was firm and widespread among aid officials, and seems to rebut the thesis argued here, can be misleading. *Verbal affirmations of the principle of self-help would be more convincing if the principle were not so often violated in practice and if Americans with lengthy, high-level experience with aid programs did not keep repeating year after year that they were* still *learning it.* As noted earlier, President Kennedy could and did make his "only 6 per cent" statements at the same time that he was acting to contradict this maxim in Latin America, Vietnam, and elsewhere. The Johnson administration greatly stressed the doctrine of self-help and made a mockery of it in South Vietnam. Eugene R. Black, the former president of the World Bank and a man with vast experience in foreign aid, could still write in 1969: "Americans *have been learning* at home and overseas that there are few tasks more difficult than that of trying to help others progress. And we *are learning* that efforts to do so can be crippled by misconceptions, a desire for *quick* results, and a tendency to oversimplify."[17] Mr. Black's statement seems quite accurate and wise. But if he could *still* be learning these lessons after so many years from such excellent vantage points, how much less could earlier and less experienced men have learned? And if the lesson of self-help had been truly learned in 1946, or 1956, or 1966, then how could such learning still have been going on in 1969?

According to the authors of the Pearson Report, the "spirit of disenchantment" about foreign aid shared by the United States and other developed countries in the later 1960s was partly due "to the fact that attitudes in donor

[17] "A Message from Eugene R. Black," Pamphlet, Overseas Development Council, Washington, D.C., April 1969 (emphasis added).

countries often have been affected by misconceptions and unrealistic expectations of 'instant development' when we should have known that development was a long-term process."[18] A former AID economist, who was also an economic adviser in Brazil, writes that "AID exerts a lot of verbal pressure for self-help, but not nearly so much pressure in actual policymaking. The few contrary cases cited, such as the Bell-Dantas agreement for Brazil, are atypical and exceptional."[19]

The lessons of self-help and of the limited capacity of American resources to affect the course of events in less developed countries have been learned over and over again, and have been about as quickly ignored, forgotten, or replaced by another layer of the liberal tradition. It is difficult to say whether awareness of the difficulty of change has increased in the two decades of American experience with foreign aid. But even if it has—and this is by no means as certain as we tend to assume—the fact remains that a powerful and dimly perceived assumption keeps pulling Americans back, despite official proclamations and abundant evidence to the contrary, to an unjustified optimism about the processes of change and development and the impact the United States can have on those processes.

ALL GOOD THINGS GO TOGETHER

A second inarticulated assumption of the liberal tradition is the notion that "All Good Things Go Together." Samuel Huntington has well stated the origins and the substance of this assumption:

> In confronting the modernizing countries the United States was handicapped by its happy history. In its de-

[18] Pearson, *Partners in Development*, p. 4.
[19] Letter to the author from Joel Bergsman, December 3, 1968. Dr. Bergsman worked in the Office of Program Coordination in AID in Washington in 1963-1965, and during 1966-1967 he was a member of an advisory group in Brazil from the University of California at Berkeley.

123

velopment the United States was blessed with more than its fair share of economic plenty, social well-being, and political stability. This pleasant conjuncture of blessings led Americans to believe in the unity of goodness: to assume that all good things go together and that the achievement of one desirable social goal aids in the achievement of others. In American policy toward modernizing countries this experience was reflected in the belief that political stability would be the natural and inevitable result of the achievement of, first, economic development and then of social reform. . . . In some instances programs of economic development may promote political stability; in other instances, [however,] they may seriously undermine such stability . . . the relationship between social reform and political stability resembles that between economic development and political stability. In some circumstances reforms may reduce tensions and encourage peaceful rather than violent change. In other circumstances, however, reform may well exacerbate tensions, precipitate violence, and be a catalyst of rather than a substitute for revolution.[20]

Even in the United States, to be sure, certain components of the "pleasant conjuncture of blessings" to which Huntington refers have led to conflicts and tensions, some of the most serious of which Americans are confronting today. It is not necessarily inconsistent, however, to affirm the existence of these problems and also to maintain the exceptionalist perspective. For example, Graham and Gurr, who have criticized Hartz and others (wrongly, I think) for allegedly "celebrating" America's uniqueness, accept and employ the exceptionalist thesis when they suggest that "the seeds of our contemporary discontent were to a large extent deeply embedded in those same ostensibly benevolent forces which contributed to our uniqueness." They then discuss several of the distinctive American characteristics—the Puritan

[20] Huntington, *Political Order*, pp. 5-7.

migration, the frontier, the Lockean consensus, economic abundance, and the doctrines of the Declaration of Independence—which both contributed to our "happy" history and today help account for our deep social and political malaise.[21]

The point is that there is a kind of paradox at work: while our history has been unusually "happy" and "all good things" have gone together to an unusually large degree, at the same time there have been some serious difficulties and tensions. We have managed to forget or ignore many of the latter but some, especially in recent years, have refused to go away. The exceptionalists, by and large, have not denied this. Rather, they have claimed that Americans were lucky in many respects, and they have warned against "celebrating" the American experience and ideology as a model for other countries. Most of them, and certainly Hartz, have cautioned Americans about the capacity of the liberal tradition to obscure and distort the nature of certain kinds of domestic problems as well.[22]

Surely evidence abounds that the "all-good-things" premise was deep and widespread in American foreign aid doctrines from 1947 to 1968. If anything, Huntington's formulation does not go far enough. For the economic approach assumed that economic development leads not only to politi-

[21] Graham and Gurr, *Violence in America*, pp. 793ff.

[22] For Hartz's cautions, see "A Comparative Study of Fragment Cultures," and *The Liberal Tradition*, Chap. 11. For a related argument, which gives even greater emphasis to the potential for conflict among the values embedded in the liberal tradition, see Harry V. Jaffe's discussion in the Symposium on *The Liberal Tradition* in *Comparative Studies in Society and History*, Vol. 5 (1962-1963), 274-78.

Among the exceptionalists cited earlier (in the Introduction, nn. 10-13), Daniel Boorstin seems to me the only one who may fairly be accused of having excessively "celebrated" the American system with respect to its domestic problems. If so, he is hardly guilty of the same sin with respect to foreign countries; indeed, one of the main theses of *The Genius of American Politics* is that American political institutions are not exportable.

cal stability, but also to a host of other good political things. Americans have persisted in this assumption even though the consequences of aid were frequently the opposite of those intended, and even though the goals of aid frequently conflicted among themselves. In reality, aid sometimes led to economic development, and sometimes it did not; economic development (and social reform and political participation) sometimes had the desired consequences, and very often it did not.

To a great extent, aid to Greece, the Marshall Plan, ECA aid to Asia, Point Four, the developmental side of the Mutual Security Program, and the Foreign Assistance Act of 1961 all embodied this assumption that all good things go together. The assumption proved valid on a large scale only in the case of the Marshall Plan; and even there, some Americans felt betrayed when Charles de Gaulle revivified French nationalism in the late fifties and the sixties.[23] The Alliance for Progress added social reform to economic development in the formula for producing all good things; but, as Huntington points out, social reform like economic development did not always have the desired and anticipated consequences.

The Kennedy administration argued that the "fundamental task" of aid was "to make a historical demonstration that in the twentieth century, as in the nineteenth—in the southern half of the globe as well as in the north—economic growth and political democracy can develop hand in hand." Entire books could be written—some have been[24]—about the weaknesses in this analogy between nineteenth-century Europe—which had already experienced its modernizing revolutions and the age of absolutism, and which, in a wholly

[23] It must be noted, however, that few such complaints came from policymakers in the aid agency.

[24] For instance, Rustow, *A World of Nations, passim;* and Huntington, *Political Order,* Chap. 2. Cf. S. M. Lipset, *Political Man: The Social Bases of Politics* (Garden City, N.Y.: Doubleday, 1960), pp. 138-39.

different historical context, could cope with many diverse kinds of social problems and demands sequentially—and the Third World in the twentieth century—where problems of national identity and governmental authority were usually severe and where political systems often faced simultaneously such problems as nationhood, authority, participation, industrialization, and more equitable distribution of resources. The observations of Arthur M. Schlesinger, Jr., noted earlier—that the "Charles River approach" of the Kennedy administration had "a certain blandness" which made the process of development sound "a little too easy and continuous," and that it "represented a very American effort to persuade the developing countries to base their revolutions on Locke rather than Marx"—reveal perhaps more than he knew. And the efforts of the Kennedy administration had a great deal more in common with both earlier and later doctrines than is generally realized.

Similar premises were expressed in the Johnson administration. The list of goals in the Foreign Assistance Act of 1961 continued to grow throughout most of the decade. Even when the whole Statement of Policy was thrown out in 1967, the action was more a result of congressional pique over Vietnam than an explicit rejection of the "all-good-things" assumption. The "larger context" for Lyndon Johnson's approach to foreign policy, according to Eric Goldman, was a "powerful American tradition," which Goldman perceptively sketches thus:

> Over the generations, Democrats and Republicans, liberals and conservatives, had tended to assume a general international trend, a trend so certain in their minds that it took on the cast of a law of history. Human beings everywhere, the law ran, sought peace and democracy, wanted to get ahead to a farm of their own or a house on the right side of the tracks, preferred to do it all gradually and with a decent regard for the amenities. Consequently, the real history of man was a long, slow swing toward a world consisting entirely of middle-class democ-

127

racies. Once in a while trouble came when some country fell under an evil leader or leaders who forced it along a road proscribed by the law of history. Then it was only necessary to remove the pernicious element and let the aspirations flow back along their proper path. . . . Since the natural movement of the world was toward peaceful, democratic, middle-class ways, foreign policy was essentially a problem of encouraging this trend, and when necessary, of removing an unnatural growth by diplomacy or war.[25]

Although Goldman does not use the phrase, the tradition to which he refers is the liberal tradition. And in this passage Goldman has not only identified the "all-good-things" component of that tradition, but also—in his reference to what the liberal tradition implies about "unnatural growths" —put his finger on one of the principal responses of liberal America to events that do not fit this second liberal assumption, as we shall see more fully below.

Title IX also illustrates the "all-good-things" premise, and in a particularly interesting way. Although regarded by its proponents as a radical new departure in foreign aid thinking, it was largely another manifestation of the liberal tradition. The ambitiousness of the goals was never questioned; Title IX merely added participation to the means necessary for their achievement. Some Title IX proponents even argued that the waning of the Cold War presented a new and greater opportunity for "affecting the world environment in order to make it more congenial."[26] In the United States the economy and society had "pushed" government up "after" them, and political participation had seldom posed severe problems for those in authority. The results, to most Americans, seemed not at all bad; and it

[25] Goldman, *Tragedy of Johnson*, p. 385.

[26] Minutes of Meeting of the Advisory Committee on Economic Development, AID "M.I.T. Title IX Conference Report and Title IX Policies of AID," October 11, 1968, pp. 6-7.

seemed reasonable to suppose that by extending these precepts to the Third World similar results would be forthcoming there.

Thus the Development Loan Fund and the economic development impulse of the late fifties, the social reform provisions of the Alliance for Progress, and the participation focus of Title IX were all expressions in part of the "all-good-things" assumption. Significantly, each was considered a "radical" departure from earlier doctrines. And, seen from within the liberal perspective, each was. Seen from without, however, they were only minor variations on the liberal theme.

Some of the basis for criticism of Title IX, of course, was precisely the growing doubt in American society about the adequacy of these assumptions, for the United States as well as for other countries. These doubts were largely spawned by the domestic crises of the mid-sixties and by Vietnam. The fact that the Title IX argument—that participation and economic development are the twin pillars of a policy that leads to all good things—could have been made at such a time in American history is eloquent testimony to the power of the liberal tradition.

RADICALISM AND REVOLUTION ARE BAD

Radicalism and Revolution Defined. A revolution is a rapid, fundamental, and usually violent change in the dominant values and myths, political institutions, social structures, leadership, and governmental policies and activities of a society. Revolutions are to be distinguished from coups, insurrections, rebellions, revolts, and wars of independence. A coup in itself changes only leadership and possibly policies. Insurrections, rebellions, and revolts are not always successful in changing policies, leaders, and political institutions; and even if they are, they do not necessarily change social structure and values. A war of independence is a struggle by one community against rule by another com-

129

munity; it does not necessarily involve large changes in the social structures, values, or even the political institutions and policies of either community. Notable examples of revolutions so defined are the French, Mexican, Russian, Chinese, and Cuban revolutions.[27]

In this century all revolutions have been more or less "left-wing" or "radical" in their ideology, if not always in practice. That is, they have defined such concepts as democracy and liberty largely in terms of social and economic egalitarianism rather than exclusively or predominantly in political terms. Thus it is possible to distinguish twentieth-century revolutions, such as those in Mexico, Russia, China, Cuba, and North Vietnam, from what Barrington Moore, Jr., has called the "bourgeois revolutions" in seventeenth-century England, eighteenth-century France, and the United States in the nineteenth century, as well as from the "capitalist and reactionary revolutions" in late nineteenth-century Germany and Japan.[28]

In the contemporary Third World, as in times past, revolutions have been rare. If one adheres closely to the above definition, revolutions seem to have occurred since 1947 only in China, Cuba, North Vietnam, and perhaps Algeria. (Yugoslavia may also have had a revolution, but it is not a Third World country as defined here.) Bolivia after 1952 had some revolutionary features; however, changes in social structure and national myths were not massive, and there was relatively little violence.[29] Similarly, while Egypt, Indo-

[27] This definition is adapted slightly from the one given by Huntington, *Political Order*, p. 264.

[28] Moore, *Social Origins*, p. xv.

[29] It should be noted that violence in the Cuban Revolution, as in the Bolivian case, was relatively limited. However, the Cuban violence received far more public notice, at least in the United States, than the Bolivian violence. Cuba's revolution was widely perceived as bloody, even though in comparative terms it was not. It is reasonable to suppose that there might have been a good deal more violence in Cuba after 1959 had not the United States opened wide its doors to the

nesia, and some other former European colonies underwent changes that were revolutionary in certain respects, few if any of them fundamentally changed the social order. Whatever the "correct" number of revolutions from 1947 to 1968 may be, it is not very large.[30]

Radicals are those who advocate revolutionary or quasirevolutionary changes. They oppose "the system"; they believe that it should be changed "by any means necessary," including various forms of disorder, intense conflict, and violence. Radicals, as the term is used here, reject exclusively political definitions of freedom, equality, and democracy; for them these concepts are also, or even mainly, defined in social and economic terms. Although many—not all[31]— Communists are radicals (at least up to the time they attain power), only a minority of radicals are Communists in any formal sense. Not many radicals have come to power in underdeveloped countries in the post-independence years. However, almost all underdeveloped countries contain some radicals, and in many of these countries they are an important political force. One of their most significant character-

exiles. Cuba fits the other criteria of revolution used here exceptionally well.

[30] Rigorous descriptive categories for distinguishing revolutionary from nonrevolutionary and prerevolutionary regimes are lacking. Scholars have seemingly devoted more attention to specifying the causes of revolutions, loosely defined, than to the construction of satisfactory typologies. On this point, see Harry Eckstein, ed., *Internal War: Problems and Approaches* (New York: Free Press, 1964), p. 23; Lawrence Stone, "Theories of Revolution," *World Politics*, 18, No. 2 (January 1966), 159-76; and Chalmers Johnson, *Revolutionary Change* (Boston: Little, Brown, 1966), Chap. 1. The list of successful revolutions given above draws on these works and on Huntington, *Political Order*, esp. Chap. 5.

[31] For example, many Latin American Communist parties have chosen for decades to work "within the system" rather than to change it "by any means necessary." This has been especially so with regard to the Moscow-oriented parties as contrasted to those with ties to Peking and Havana. An excellent example is the Brazilian Communist Party under the leadership of Luis Carlos Prestes.

131

istics is that they are almost always strong nationalists. In most countries of the Third World, radicals who are principally agents of foreign powers or international revolutionaries (like Che Guevara) are a definite and rather small minority.

The Third Liberal Premise. The third assumption of the liberal tradition, succinctly stated, is that "radicalism and revolution are bad." More awkward, but more complete and precise, is this formulation: Radical politics, including intense conflict, disorder, violence, and revolution, are unnecessary for economic and political development and therefore are always bad.

To assert that this assumption, stated here as an ideal type, exists and affects the doctrines is not to deny that there has been a considerable amount of intense conflict and violence in the United States. Four points need briefly to be made in this connection. First, the systematic empirical study of violence is still in its infancy, especially as regards historical comparisons among nations. Even though it is becoming increasingly clear that there has been far more violence in the United States than has generally been realized, it remains less clear how violence in America compares with violence in other countries, particularly over long periods of time. Second, as Dahl, Tilly, Gurr, and others have noted, Americans even more than other peoples seem to have had a kind of "historical amnesia" about the violence and intense conflict in their past. Third, domestic violence seems to have been more legitimate in the United States as a means to extend and consolidate the nation and to maintain the "moving equilibrium" of the sociopolitical order than as a means to alter it at a radical pace and in radical directions. Finally, the best available evidence suggests that although the United States ranks high among the world's nations in the number of political assassinations, riots, politically relevant armed group attacks, and demonstrations, it has ranked low compared to Third World countries and about the same as European countries in frequency of "serious conspiratorial and revolutionary movements." As Graham and Gurr put it, "Paradoxically, we have been a turbulent people but a relatively stable republic."[32]

The third liberal premise has in fact affected a great deal of American foreign policy, both historically and in the aid program over the last two decades. It is especially useful in explaining the political development doctrines that favored anti-Communist, stable, pro-American governments in the Third World—in other words, the Cold War approach. Obviously the Cold War approach has causes that extend beyond this particular assumption. A substantial part of the explanation—probably the most important single cause—was the intense preoccupation with security as a problem in international relations. This concern went beyond the antipathy for radicalism and revolution as an aspect of domestic political development in the Third World. Much of this preoccupation was exaggerated and unproductive even from the point of view of U.S. security interests narrowly defined, to say nothing of the broader, developmental view of American national interests. But, justified or not, these perceptions of security needs were pervasive and powerful.

However, although U.S. anti-Communism may have been somewhat obsessive, it was not completely pathological. Whatever revisionists may discover about the origins of the Cold War, it seems dubious in the extreme that fifty or a hundred years from now historians will conclude that this preoccupation was *entirely* manufactured in the United States. Thus the Cold War doctrines also were, in some measure, appropriate responses by the United States to its legitimate security interests.

Finally, intense conflict, disorder, and violence are never costless in terms of humane values and are often harmful for

[32] Graham and Gurr, *Violence in America*, pp. 798-801, 618-20, quotation at p. 799. For Tilly's and Dahl's views, respectively, see *ibid.*, p. 7, and Robert A. Dahl, ed., *Political Oppositions in Western Democracies* (New Haven: Yale University Press, 1966), p. 53.

133

development. By strictly developmental criteria, therefore, the United States has probably been right in some instances to use aid and other instruments, when it was genuinely invited to do so, to help combat these phenomena.

Sometimes, however, radical politics may be appropriate in order to change the institutions, values, policies, and leadership of backward, corrupt, repressive societies. There are conditions under which radical politics may be superior or at least not demonstrably inferior to the politics of reform or evolution. Reasonable people will differ markedly about the conditions under which radical strategies are beneficial, and how often they should be utilized; but few if any reasonable people would affirm that they are never appropriate. (For example, few would argue that the French and Russian revolutions were not justified.)

Under such circumstances, and where our security needs are not significantly threatened, the proper American response would seem to be to accept, and in some cases perhaps even to encourage, radical and revolutionary politics. Yet this has rarely happened. Certainly none of the three main political development doctrines since 1947 has specified support for radicalism or revolution under *any* circumstances. To a surprising degree, the same has been true of American responses to revolutions abroad all the way back to the French Revolution, as we shall see. This inability of Americans to understand the positive role of radicalism under certain conditions, and the almost complete distaste for radical groups abroad, cannot satisfactorily be explained only by reference to American security needs and perceptions, or on the ground that intense conflict is always harmful to development. To explain these things more fully, we need to recall the third component of the liberal tradition.

The Origins of the Premise. The idea that the United States is a revolutionary nation is a persistent myth of our time. "Familiarity with our record," Henry Wriston wrote

134

in *Foreign Affairs* in 1961, "will end much of the difficulty in understanding current revolutions. For 1961 is still a part of the Age of Revolution that was launched in 1776." Later in the same article he added: "Read aright, our Declaration of Independence makes us kin to all the new nations which escaped from the status of wards and attained the posture of independence." A year later, Dean Rusk expressed his "conviction that the ideas which inspired the American Revolution and have guided our national development are the most powerful forces at work in the world today."[33]

But the United States was "born equal"; it needed no profound social revolution to become so. Indeed, "It is the absence of the experience of social revolution which is at the heart of the American dilemma"[34]—that of a liberal nation seeking and needing to understand a world that is largely illiberal. The American Revolution of 1776 is much more correctly described as a war for independence with revolutionary overtones than as a revolution in the grand, social, or fundamental sense. Its main political purpose was to preserve those principles which had guided the governing of America for nearly a hundred and fifty years prior to 1776. "The colonials revolted against British rule in order to keep things as they were, not to initiate a new era." Until the efforts by the British government—especially by George III—to impose taxes on stamps and later on tea, British rule was unobjectionable. The "crimes" of George III listed in the seldom-read body of the Declaration of Independence were those of the ten years before 1776; nothing whatever was said about the previous century and a half of British

[33] These quotations are taken from Degler, "The American Past," p. 192. For similar sentiments, see also Chester Bowles, " 'A Revolution Intended for All Mankind,' " *New York Times Magazine*, December 10, 1961, pp. 12, 107-9; and the material cited in Hartz, *Liberal Tradition*, pp. 305-6, and in Millikan and Rostow, *A Proposal*, pp. 131-32.

[34] Hartz, *Liberal Tradition*, p. 306.

governance. "Americans during their revolutionary decade," Carl Degler and others have pointed out, "argued for the rights of Englishmen; who has ever heard the Algerians plead for the rights of Frenchmen?"[35]

It is true, as some critics of the American exceptionalists have suggested and as the latter have conceded, that some Tories were expelled from America and others emigrated—fled—to Canada and elsewhere; that some estates were confiscated; that primogeniture and quitrents were abolished; that the Anglican Church was disestablished; and that the status atmosphere "generally loosened" during the revolutionary years in America. Thus the liberal doctrines of John Locke did not manifest themselves in absolutely pure form. Doctrines seldom do. The matter is relative. The United States was and has remained extremely liberal and anti-radical on a worldwide scale. If America does not embody the liberal tradition in every particular, it fits that category rather well and certainly infinitely better than it does the "real revolution" category. As Hartz has put it,

> it is ... one thing for a society to be torn between feudalism and liberalism, and another for it to be centrally liberal but feudal at the margins. That is the problem we face here. The Tories tended to be elitist but they were still bourgeois, and even if it could be demonstrated that more acres of land were confiscated in their case than in the case of the French aristocracy, their social status would not be increased by this fact. Quitrents and pri-

[35] Degler, "American Past," pp. 193-94, 196. Almost fifty years after independence, John Adams wrote: "That there existed a general desire of independence of the crown, in any part of America before the Revolution, is as far from the truth as the zenith is from the nadir. For my part, there was not a moment during the Revolution, when I would not have given everything I ever possessed for a restoration to the state of things before the contest began, provided we could have had any sufficient security for its continuance" (quoted in Degler, pp. 193-94).

mogeniture were falling into disuse even where they existed in America in 1776, which is not surprising, since there was neither a true aristocracy nor a true peasantry on the American land. The revolutionary spirit of social democracy, though real, was merely an intensification of a mood in the colonies which every foreign observer . . . had noted since the 17th century. In all of these cases, what we are dealing with is . . . a reflex action, a shaking off by a liberal fragment of Europe of some of the medieval marginalia which clung to it as it migrated across the Atlantic. And this conceptualization, when placed alongside that of the revolutionary archetype, leads us to a conclusion concerning these changes which is not a matter of degree but a matter of kind. The outstanding thing about America's "social revolution," instead of being its break with the past, is its continuity with the past.[36]

[36] Hartz, in *The Nature of Revolution*, p. 113. See also Hartz, *Liberal Tradition*, Chap. 3. Degler writes: "The American Revolution, to be sure, like many other great events, went beyond the intentions of those who started it, but between a revolution that is intended to overthrow the past and one that is intended to perpetuate it lies the vast gulf between a radical and a conservative habit of mind" ("American Past," p. 195). Barrington Moore, Jr., states that the American Revolution was "at bottom . . . a fight between commercial interests in England and America, though certainly more elevated issues played a part as well. The claim that America has had an anticolonial revolution may be good propaganda, but it is bad history and bad sociology. The distinguishing characteristic of twentieth-century anticolonial revolutions is the effort to establish a new form of society with substantial socialist elements. Throwing off the foreign yoke is a means to achieve this end. What radical currents there were in the American Revolution were for the most part unable to break through to the surface. Its main effect was to promote unification of the colonies into a single political unit and the separation of this unit from England" (*Social Origins*, pp. 112-13). See also Huntington, *Political Order*, pp. 134ff. Cf. Dankwart A. Rustow, who stresses "all that recent research has established about the magnitude of Tory emigration to Canada and the extent of property re-allocation among those who stayed behind," and the "troubles" that the United States has had throughout its history (book review in *Journal of Interna-*

I: DOCTRINES

Responses to Revolutionary Regimes in Power. These experiences and beliefs have made it difficult for Americans to perceive, understand, and appreciate the positive role that radicalism and revolution, with the intense conflict and violence that often attend them, may play under certain circumstances in other countries. The typical American response to the great historical revolutions, for example, has been initially favorable and then, when they did not "emulate the American pattern of quickly leading to orderly, democratic societies," one of disappointment and even hostility. This happened in the cases of the French Revolution, the Latin American independence movements of the early nineteenth century (which were not even profound social revolutions but which were followed in most instances by much violence), and the Russian, Mexican, and Cuban revolutions.[37] As Hartz has written, in another apt and telling passage:

> [Americans] welcomed the initial struggle for liberal institutions, especially if it involved the issue of national independence, gathering in public meetings, lighting bonfires, issuing editorials. But when the struggle began to show excessive violence, when it began to involve "hanging and shooting," as one writer noted in the Latin American case, the "mild and merciful" peoples of North America proceeded to withdraw their affection. And, of course, as the current of revolution began to shift from the liberal to the socialist direction, as the Communards appeared in Paris and the Bolsheviks in Moscow, the Americans turned away in practically universal horror.

tional Affairs, 23, No. 1, [1969], 120-21). Yet Hartz contends that today "there are fewer scholars than there would have been 20 years ago who would contend that the American Revolution of the 18th century was itself a social upheaval of the European type" (*The Nature of Revolution*, p. 112). So far as I can learn, Hartz's assessment is correct, and most historians today distinguish the American Revolution from true social revolutions.

[37] Degler, "American Past," p. 194.

138

From the French Revolution onward the American response to revolution abroad is like a love affair which is
constantly turning sour, like an infatuation which is for-
ever ending in disenchantment.[38]

However, when violence has been used by established
governments to put down revolutionary movements abroad,
American reactions have usually been less hostile. "There
was no outcry in America against the suppression of the
Communards in 1871. Here was violence, and plenty of it,
but it was being used for 'order and law,' as one editorial
writer put it."[39] The American press was shocked by the
political executions carried out by Fidel Castro during his
early months in power, but it had paid little attention to the
much larger number of political murders committed during
the Batista period. "Were these executions any different,
many Cubans reasoned, from the executions of German war
criminals after the Nuremberg war trials?"[40]

An uncounted number of Indonesians—estimates range
from a minimum of 300,000 to well over 500,000—were
liquidated as "Communists" by the military government that
overthrew the Sukarno regime in 1965. This purge was far
and away the bloodiest anywhere during the last two decades; even in terms of proportion of population it was many
times more severe than the Cuban violence. But it went relatively unnoticed in the United States compared to the attention bestowed upon such left-wing groups as the Cuban revolutionaries and the Vietcong. One does not have to defend
the latter to wonder why the Indonesian violence was so
little noted or criticized. Part of the answer to this question
lies in the tendency of liberal America to perceive selectively, to filter out disturbing information about relatively

[38] Hartz, in *The Nature of Revolution*, p. 115. Also see *The Liberal
Tradition*, pp. 284-85, 295, 300-306.

[39] Hartz, in *The Nature of Revolution*, p. 117.

[40] Leland L. Johnson, "U.S. Business Interests in Cuba and the Rise
of Castro," *World Politics*, 17, No. 3 (April 1965), 454-55.

right-wing regimes while being strongly affected by negative news about left-wing regimes.[41]

America's responses to revolutionary regimes in power since 1947 have been perhaps more varied than its responses to the great historical revolutions. Yet in the postwar era, as in the earlier periods, the main tendency of U.S. policy seems to have been to react negatively to genuinely revolutionary political systems. As noted above, at most only four regimes that have come to power in the Third World since 1947 are unexceptionable cases of revolutionary political systems: China, Cuba, North Vietnam, and Algeria. American policies toward China, Cuba, and North Vietnam have tended to be hostile, although a thaw occurred in U.S.-China relations after 1971, and comparable changes have been hinted at with regard to the other two countries. U.S. relations with Algeria have been mixed but improving since its revolution. The United States has had relatively good relations with and has supplied significant quantities of economic assistance to Yugoslavia, another Communist country; it is not, however, part of the Third World.

American policies toward the Bolivian regime after 1952 were quite positive. For example, the United States provided more aid per capita to Bolivia than to any other country in Latin America during the decade from 1952 to 1961. But the Bolivian "revolution" had comparatively little violence and

[41] Gurr reports that between 1961 and 1965, there were 4,000 casualties (deaths and injuries) per 100,000 population in Indonesia. Since Indonesia's population during those years was just over 100 million, the total comes to over 4 million casualties. He says that this figure "is probably grossly inflated because it includes an unrealistic estimate of injuries associated with the massacre of several hundred thousand Indonesian Communists." Even if the figure were reduced by a magnitude of four, it would still be 1,000 casualties per 100,000 inhabitants (total one million), or almost 7 times as many as the next most casualty-intensive nation in his table of 22 selected countries. See Ted Robert Gurr, "A Comparative Study of Civil Strife," in Graham and Gurr, *Violence in America*, p. 579.

For further discussion and evidence of this tendency to perceive selectively, see "The Coherence of the Doctrines," Chap. 4, below.

made few fundamental changes in social structure and values. American relations with Egypt under Nasser and Indonesia under Sukarno never were very good; they improved in Indonesia after Sukarno's fall in 1965. Similarly, relations with other "revolutionary" governments in former European colonies have varied considerably by country and over time. But in speaking of these countries, one moves away from the category of truly revolutionary regimes toward other types of political systems.

It is true, of course, that much of the antipathy of the United States toward the regimes in Cuba, China, and North Vietnam stems from causes other than the simple fact that they were revolutionary. They are all Communist regimes. And each was hostile to the United States. However, these causes do not appear sufficient to explain American policies completely. Nor do they satisfactorily account for the typical diagnoses and evaluations of political development in these countries. In the case of Cuba, for instance, the widespread assumption that a Communist regime is evil by definition, plus the perception that Cuba posed a major threat to U.S. security, combined to produce excessively negative assessments of the performance of the Cuban political system, which in turn have reinforced and strengthened anti-Cuban policies.

One does not have to romanticize the regime of Fidel Castro to contend that its achievements in several spheres, including education, health, women's rights, distribution of income and status, national identity and pride, have few if any parallels in Latin America during the last decade. Certainly there have been serious mistakes in the economic realm: the ill-conceived early attempts to industrialize, and the subsequent overly ambitious targets for sugar production are perhaps the two outstanding examples. The presence on the island of an estimated 20,000 political prisoners is also a blight on the regime and a justifiable cause for concern and criticism. Nevertheless, the Cuban polity has shown a remarkable will and capacity to cope with and to generate

141

continuing transformation, and all this without significant domestic strife, counter-revolutionary activity, or, so far as one can tell, any large number of political executions since those of the first few months.[42]

All this has been recognized abroad—in Europe and among Latin American progressives and radicals—to a considerably greater extent than in the United States. With rare exceptions officials in Washington have not examined the balance sheet on political development in Cuba in the same way that they have in other countries. Instead there has been a strong tendency to allow evaluations of Cuba's foreign policy to determine or heavily color evaluations of Cuba's domestic polity. Suggestions that Cuba has on balance one of the more rapidly developing polities in the hemisphere seldom occur and, when they do, tend to be heard with shocked disbelief or scorn, or both. The extent to which future historians will conclude that such suggestions were justified is of course uncertain; but that is not the point. The fact remains that analyses raising this possibility have not received their day in court, while equally or more uncertain analyses about other contemporary but less radical and non-Communist regimes have.[43]

Responses to Radicals. If the record of American foreign policy and doctrines toward revolutionary regimes in power is somewhat mixed, it seems to have been uniformly negative toward those nongovernmental groups who attempt to change the system "by any means necessary," but have not succeeded in doing so—i.e. toward radicals. This uniformity

[42] Lee Lockwood, *Castro's Cuba, Cuba's Fidel* (New York: Random House, Vintage, 1969); Richard R. Fagen, *The Transformation of Political Culture in Cuba* (Stanford: Stanford University Press, 1969). The figure for the number of political prisoners is Fidel's estimate, given in Lockwood at p. 230.

[43] See, for example, Coffin, *Witness for Aid*, p. 256; Nelson, *Aid, Influence*, p. 139; Sorenson, *Kennedy*, p. 343; and, esp. Schlesinger, *A Thousand Days*, pp. 215-32.

is especially significant in light of the fact that since 1947 very few revolutionary regimes have come to power, whereas almost all Third World countries have radical groups or movements. Moreover, most revolutionary regimes in power are Communist governments, whereas only a minority of radical groups are formally tied to Communist organizations. Therefore U.S. attitudes and activities toward the latter are in a sense truer indicators of basic American assumptions regarding radicalism, since they are less contaminated by security needs and perceptions unrelated to conceptions of political development per se.

In terms of actual policies and activities (as distinguished from the doctrines that lie behind them), there may be a country in the Third World where the United States has consistently supported truly radical forces; if so, I have not been able to find it. In most of these countries, the United States has actively opposed such forces in varying degrees, and in many of them active American resistance has been substantial. Richard Barnet has documented these activities in American policy toward Greece, Lebanon, Vietnam, the Dominican Republic, Guatemala, British Guiana, Iran, and the Congo.[44] Similar American efforts have been carried on in Thailand, Laos, and the Philippines. The United States has supported and carried on counter-insurgency programs, whose sweep includes not only apolitical criminals and Communists supported by foreign powers but also indigenous radicals, in a majority of Latin American countries. Even where the American effort is not large and visible, as it is

[44] Barnet, *Intervention and Revolution*. Barnet defines a revolution as "an organized effort of a group to overthrow the established order with a view to bringing about a radical change in the economic or social system" (p. 44). What Barnet defines as a revolution is defined in the present study as the activity of a radical group or movement, since in my definition a revolution occurs only when the effort is successful in attaining power. Barnet's book is probably the most thorough treatment that has yet appeared of American responses to radical politics in underdeveloped countries since 1947.

143

through counter-insurgency programs, the diplomatic posture of the United States seldom has supported truly radical movements and groups.

To note this antipathy for radicalism is, of course, *not* to assert that the United States has only supported right-wing, dictatorial forces. The United States has in fact favored a considerable variety of types of groups and movements, ranging from very conservative to very liberal, from doctrinaire capitalists to doctrinaire socialists, from dictators to democrats. Not infrequently proposals have been made that the United States, governmentally and privately, "go around" conservative central governments to relate to and support private and local government groups which seem to have potential for the creation of pluralistic, democratic governments. Cool responses to right-wing dictators are frequently means of supporting more liberal groups in the society.

So there has been variety. But the range of this variety has seldom if ever extended to truly radical forces. As far as I can tell, nowhere in the Third World has the United States knowingly supported, directly or indirectly, actively or by cool responses to those in power, genuinely radical movements, groups, or individuals. In most of these countries such forces have been opposed in some degree, and in many the United States has acted vigorously—although not always effectively—to cut them down. This seems to be strong evidence indeed to support the proposition that underlying U.S. policy is the assumption that under no circumstances are radicalism and revolution appropriate for economic and political development.

Distaste for radicalism is evident in the political development doctrines as well as in actual policies and activities. The record of these doctrines since 1947 reveals virtually no sympathy for radical causes under any circumstances. Evidence of implicit and explicit hostility to radicalism, however, is abundant. In the case of Greece, for instance, it appears that almost no one in the U.S. government in-

144

quired very deeply into the rebels' case, or tried to verify whether and how much the Soviet Union was in fact aiding and controlling them. In Europe in early 1947, William Clayton reported, any deterioration in the standard of living would result in "revolution," which, he felt, "must not happen." (To cite this piece of evidence is not necessarily, in this and some of the other instances noted here, to assert that the particular doctrine was wrong. The point is that there were situations in which radicalism was either an appropriate or a not necessarily inferior alternative, but the doctrines made no provision whatever for such situations. The value of these doctrines will be assessed in Chapter 4.)

Aid to Korea was aimed at helping to create "peaceful and democratic conditions in the Far East." "Solid advancement" in Asia was, for Harry Bayard Price, equated exclusively with "peaceful consent," and antithetical to "radical revolution." Only "gradual" change brought "genuine fulfillment"; radical change brought only "enslavement." There was little room during the Eisenhower presidency to consider the appropriateness of radical change.

President Kennedy wanted aid to "help reduce the explosiveness of the modernization process." The constant, unvarying emphasis was on reform as a substitute for radicalism and revolution. The Kennedy administration pinned its hopes on the "democratic left" in Latin America, whose exemplars were such men as Víctor Raúl Haya de la Torre, José Figueres, and Rómulo Betancourt.[45] Kennedy told Cheddi Jagan that the principal purpose of American foreign policy to underdeveloped countries was to encourage their "national independence" and create a "world made safe for diversity"; he then cut Jagan down because he seemed to be a radical. President Johnson saw a radical or Communist Dominican Republic as "another Cuba," and a radical or Communist Brazil as "another China." In Brazil, the Dominican Republic, and Vietnam, the Johnson administra-

[45] Schlesinger, *A Thousand Days*, pp. 194-205, 223.

tion sought democratic, constitutional, liberal governments, but it would gladly settle for conservative and/or military governments if necessary to avoid radical or Communist regimes. The Johnson administration, like its predecessors, was uncomfortable with forces that might lead to authoritarianism of either the Left or the Right; but if it had to choose between these two types, it unhesitatingly chose the latter.

In the Title IX legislation and in all the official documentation about it, there is virtually nothing positive about radical forces. Title IX stressed participation but displayed little awareness that increasing participation can produce instability and radicalism. More importantly, it fails to attach a corollary to the stress on participation: that when participation produces radical politics, the United States should in some instances be better prepared to live with the consequences. Lacking this corollary,[46] Title IX simply has nothing to say to inhibit the traditional pattern of negative American responses to the very changes the United States has often helped to create.

The antipathy of the Cold War approach to radicalism is strong and rather obvious. Almost equally strong, but less obvious, is the hostility to radicalism embodied in the economic and explicit democratic approaches. Throughout the post-1947 period, these doctrines have placed the United States against the status quo and in favor of change. But change has had to be "healthy," "constructive," "positive"— as these terms were defined in and by the United States. "The aim of the democracies," Harry Bayard Price wrote, "should not be to buttress the status quo or to prevent overdue changes from taking place, but to help guide genuine revolutionary aspirations into constructive, rather than destructive or retrogressive channels." "Where revolution meant healthy social change," Arthur Schlesinger told the

[46] In the survey of views about Title IX in Chapter 2, the only commentator who advanced this corollary was Professor Richard Adams. See Chap. 2, n. 70.

President of Bolivia, Paz Estenssoro, in 1961, "the Kennedy Administration could be depended on to look on it with sympathy, but not so when revolution meant dictatorship, repression and the entry of alien forces into the hemisphere."[47]

It is important to note, however, that "constructive" and "healthy" are not always defined abroad as they are by American officials, for whom such concepts have been exclusively linked to gradualism, reform, order, consensus, moderate conflict, and nonviolence. Even where Americans have the capacity to direct change through "positive" channels as we define them—which is not everywhere by any means—there are some places where we should not even make the effort. But absence of the radical alternative from the American formula for political development means that we are seldom pleased to allow radical forces to run their course, much less eager to spur them on to victory.

A vivid illustration of much that has been suggested here about the roots of the Cold War doctrines and policies is an article by George C. Lodge, a former Assistant Secretary of Labor for International Affairs, which appeared in *Foreign Affairs* in July 1969 under the title "U.S. Aid to Latin America: Funding Radical Change."[48] Radical change, for Mr. Lodge, is change without violence. As he sees it, there are two—and only two—alternatives for American foreign policy toward Latin America. One is to support the status

[47] Price, *The Marshall Plan*, p. 391; Schlesinger, *A Thousand Days*, p. 182. An AID adviser put it thus: "we are in reality incapable of taking advantage of changes underway, particularly rapid radical change . . . our fear of revolutions [makes] us individually and institutionally unable to become involved with powerful forces which might lead to major change." A fellow adviser commented that if the first man were correct, "then it means that we are capable at best of taking advantage of only very slow evolutionary change" (Minutes of meeting of the Advisory Committee on Economic Development, Agency for International Development, "M.I.T. Title IX Conference Report and Title IX Policies of AID," October 11, 1968, mimeographed, p. 5).

[48] Lodge, "U.S. Aid to Latin America," pp. 735-49.

147

quo in change-resisting societies. (This, he reports, was the traditional American practice, but it is no longer satisfactory.) The other, which he supports, is to reject the status quo. More specifically, he favors American help and encouragement for those nongovernmental groups in Latin America—the "engines of change"—which are the basis for pluralistic democracy and decentralized economic development.

Furthermore, according to Lodge, the United States should be prepared to bypass governments in power in order to reach these groups. He admits, even seems to relish, that such actions would be "controversial," "subversive," "interventionist," and "radical." But he is willing to take the risk, because "It is time to recognize that almost any foreign assistance in Latin America is bound to be interventionary in one way or another." He strongly urges that "we make the most of the pluralism of American society, accentuating its great and varied strength and employing it to connect U.S. groups naturally to Latin American counterparts"; and he applauds Title IX, because it is very much in the spirit of the "radical transformation" of foreign assistance that he proposes.

There are perhaps circumstances under which Mr. Lodge's proposals have merit, just as there may be conditions under which other manifestations of the explicit democratic approach make sense. The article is notable not so much because it provides more evidence of the continuing appeal of the explicit democratic approach, based on the American experience, but rather because of the degree to which it makes explicit Lodge's *total* opposition to *genuine* radicalism under *any* circumstances, and because of the *bases* of this opposition.

What justification, he asks, is there for his "radical" proposal? To answer this question, "we must identify our interests precisely." Anti-Communism is no longer a satisfactory rationale. Rather, "our priorities would seem to be in the following order:"

The chief concern of the Government of the United States must be the survival of the American people. *Survival is threatened by the existence anywhere of chaos and disorganization.* These produce socio-political vacuums which the bully and the predator are tempted to fill aggressively. In this day and age such aggression can bring the threat of total war.

The second concern of the U.S. Government must be the protection of the rights and interests of U.S. citizens in Latin America.

It follows from these primary and secondary objectives that the control of violent conflict is a vital interest of the United States.

Footnote 1 reads: "Some distinction must be made between necessary and avoidable conflict and violence. The Mexican revolution took a million lives; but few today would say that it had not been necessary. The hope must be that communities have become *more sophisticated since then,* more able to make less painful the revolution which nation-building seems to require inevitably."[49]

Now, if "chaos and disorganization" anywhere threaten American "survival," then it is truly a wonder that the U.S. survives, for there has been no lack of disorder in the Third World in the last two decades. If "the control of violent conflict" everywhere is "a vital interest of the United States," then it is difficult to see how Mr. Lodge's assumptions or proposals differ *radically* from the Cold-Warriors who preceded him and whose rationale he claims to reject. But he is at great pains throughout his article to stress and to justify the "radical" nature of his proposals. This is more evidence of the liberal tendency to perceive small alterations as massive changes. "Lawlessness," he says, should not be confused with "revolution"; revolution is what the Founding Fathers talked about in the Declaration of Independence. For him, revolution is permissible to the extent

[49] *Ibid.,* p. 739 and n. 1 (emphasis added).

149

that it is peaceful; the more violent and lawless it becomes, the less justifiable it is. If violence was "necessary" for Mexico, that was fifty years ago; the "hope" must be that "communities have become more sophisticated since then." Here one finds the typical liberal disdain for true revolution and the violence that frequently accompanies it—except, perhaps, in history books, when it is no longer a problem for contemporary policy.[50]

Mr. Lodge's views are perhaps extreme. If so, however, they differ not in kind but only in degree from the modal pattern of American thinking about radicalism and revolution. Sometimes an extreme case serves the same function as an ideal type: it intensifies and sharpens patterns of thought or action which are otherwise blurred and obscured. Much as our policies toward Vietnam were a "blowup"[51] of many flaws in American foreign policy toward other countries, so are Mr. Lodge's views an enlargement of some flawed assumptions in American political development doctrines. They show that the ideal type of the third liberal premise, sketched above, finds at least one complete and exact counterpart in empirical reality. Not all the other evidence offered here fits the ideal type so well, but all approximates it. Lodge's views are only an especially vivid example of the central tendency in American thinking about radicalism and revolution.

[50] The same disdain characterizes some liberals who are also historians. Toward the end of his tortured defense of President Kennedy's Cuban policies, Schlesinger writes: "In spite of a score of disillusionments in Russia, eastern Europe and China—so many eggs broken and so few omelettes—many still cherished the hope that sometime, somewhere, revolution would at last achieve the dream of a truly just and joyous society." Schlesinger appears to be saying that revolutions are never justified under any circumstances. He then adds a long, pretentious quotation from Proust that begins, "The facts of life do not penetrate to the sphere in which our beliefs are cherished" (*A Thousand Days*, p. 223). The quotation applies as beautifully to Schlesinger himself, however, as to anyone else.

[51] See the comments of Stanley Hoffmann, in Pfeffer, *No More Vietnams?*, pp. 5-6.

DISTRIBUTING POWER IS MORE IMPORTANT THAN
ACCUMULATING POWER

In analyzing political systems, especially in underdeveloped countries, at least two questions about power are immediately relevant. One is how power is *distributed*: Is it concentrated in the hands of a relatively few people, or is it dispersed among many? The other question is: *How much* power exists? Is the amount or quantum of power expanding or contracting? How stable is that quantum of power? Both questions are interesting and important, but in developing societies the second is sometimes more important than the first.[52]

Although logically there is no necessary correlation between how power is distributed and the amount of power that exists, empirically the two dimensions are probably related, particularly in the Third World.[53] In many—though not all—underdeveloped countries, power is more readily accumulated if it is concentrated or centralized than if it is widely distributed.[54] (In fact in most European countries, too, centralized power has been necessary at some point in order to facilitate modernization.) Most of the Third World

[52] There is, of course, a third major question: for what ends should power be used? The answers typically given to this question appear throughout this and the preceding two chapters.

[53] This discussion draws heavily on Huntington, *Political Order*, pp. 140-47.

[54] Let me emphasize that I am not arguing that this proposition applies in all times and places. Charles E. Lindblom has been foremost among those who have challenged the traditional notion that things always are done better if nicely coordinated at the top. His critique of that notion is persuasive. However, it is also incorrect to argue the opposite: that things are always done better if they are decentralized. Lindblom at times seems to suggest this. See Charles E. Lindblom, "Policy Analysis," *American Economic Review*, 48 (June 1958), 298-312; "The Science of 'Muddling Through,'" *Public Administration Review*, 19 (Spring 1959), 79-88; *The Intelligence of Democracy: Decision-Making Through Mutual Adjustment* (New York: Free Press, 1965). My own view is that Lindblom's views tend to be less applicable in the Third World than in Western countries.

countries most successful in accumulating power and modernizing have a strong central power system. Almost all Third World countries need more power, and in many this means centralizing power. It is important to note that accumulating power through centralization does not necessarily mean limiting participation. Quite the contrary, expanding participation will often be advantageous and even necessary for the accumulation of power.

However, it is often more difficult to combine increased participation and the accumulation of power within the framework of pluralistic political institutions, which distribute the power, than within the framework of other kinds of political institutions (most typically "mobilization regimes") which concentrate the power. Huntington has suggested a three-stage process of political development in the Third World which relates these three variables (distribution, quantum of power, and participation) to one another:

> Typically, the first challenge of modernization to a dispersed, weakly articulated and organized, feudalistic traditional system is to concentrate the power necessary to produce changes in the traditional society and economy. The second problem is then to expand the power in the system to assimilate the newly mobilized and politically participant groups, thus creating a modern system. This challenge is the predominant one in the modernizing world today. At a later stage the system is confronted with the demands of the participant groups for a greater dispersion of power and for the establishment of reciprocal checks and controls among groups and institutions. Many of the communist states of eastern Europe are grappling with the problem of adaptation to the pressures for the dispersion of power.[55]

The fourth inarticulate assumption of the liberal tradition is that "distributing power is more important than accumu-

[55] Huntington, *Political Order*, p. 146.

lating power." More specifically, Americans pay more attention to how power is distributed than to the amount of power. As far as the distribution question is concerned, Americans tend strongly to prefer that power be distributed rather than concentrated. Often, of course (as in the Cold War approach), Americans have been willing to accept and support groups and regimes that concentrate power. As we have seen, however, this has occurred much more frequently with respect to anti-Communist regimes that tend to limit participation and thus restrict the accumulation of power than with respect to radical or Communist "mobilization" regimes that usually encourage participation and thus increase the quantum of power. Americans tend to favor the accumulation of power only when the power thus accumulated is fairly widely distributed. The main devices or arrangements Americans have favored for accumulating power have been economic development and popular participation within pluralistic political systems. They have not looked with favor upon mobilization regimes, which in the Third World are typically radical or Communist, as devices for maximizing participation and thus for increasing the quantum of power.

Before reviewing the evidence for these generalizations, let us recall the characteristics of U.S. history which the American exceptionalists have cited to explain these tendencies. As everyone knows, the Founding Fathers built into the American Constitution of 1787 a complex set of checks and balances that would widely distribute power and authority. Through the mechanisms of republicanism, federalism, and the separation of powers, they sought to mitigate the evils of faction. They expected "that the social divisions and conflict within American society made necessary a complex set of checks and balances. In reality, however, their Constitution was successful only because their view of American society was erroneous."[56]

[56] The quotation is from *ibid.*, p. 125. Huntington cites Hartz, *Liberal Tradition*, pp. 9-10, 45-46, 85-86, 133-34, 281-82.

The view was erroneous because American society was only superficially divided and in conflict; more profoundly it was unified and consensual around the inarticulate assumptions of the migrant culture of the Lockean, liberal tradition. In America, in Huntington's words:

> . . . the absence of feudal social institutions made the centralization of power unnecessary. Since there was no aristocracy to dislodge, there was no need to call into existence a governmental power capable of dislodging it. . . . Society could develop and change without having to overcome the opposition of social classes with a vested interest in the social and economic status quo. The combination of an egalitarian social inheritance plus the plenitude of land and other resources enabled social and economic development to take place more or less spontaneously. Government often helped to promote economic development, but (apart from the abolition of slavery) it played only a minor role in changing social customs and social structure. In modernizing societies, the centralization of power varies directly with the resistance to social change. In the United States, where the resistance was minimal, so also was the centralization.[57]

Thus American history has not been propitious from the point of view of enabling Americans to understand and appreciate the need in Third World countries for accumulating power and authority. Since Americans have never had to worry greatly about the problem of creating a powerful government, of accumulating a large quantum of power, in order to modernize, they have been peculiarly blind to the problems of "creating effective authority in modernizing countries."

---

[57] Huntington, *Political Order*, p. 126. To assert that power in America has been relatively decentralized is not, of course, to assert that no centralized power and authority existed at all; nor is it to deny that there have been variations over time.

When an American thinks about the problem of government-building, he directs himself not to the creation of authority and the accumulation of power but rather to the limitation of authority and the division of power. Asked to design a government, he comes up with a written constitution, bill of rights, separation of powers, checks and balances, federalism, regular elections, competitive parties—all excellent devices for limiting government. The Lockean American is so fundamentally anti-government that he identifies government with restrictions on government. Confronted with the need to design a political system which will maximize power and authority, he has no ready answer. His general formula is that governments should be based on free and fair elections.

In many modernizing societies this formula is irrelevant . . .[58]

These hypotheses of the "American exceptionalists" are confirmed to a considerable extent by the record of doctrines and policies since 1947, in particular the Latin American diplomacy-for-democracy of the Kennedy administration and Title IX. These actions and doctrines, plus other more diffuse and generalized efforts to "liberalize" right-wing authoritarian regimes (which will be discussed in Chapter 4), all emphasized elections, pluralistic voluntary organizations, more autonomous and powerful legislatures, competitive parties, greater popular participation in decisionmaking, and other devices excellently conceived to distribute power and limit authority.

The main evidence against this view would seem to be the considerable amount of American support for anti-Communist groups and regimes that did not distribute power widely. However, such support was given for Cold War reasons, or to impede radical and revolutionary forces, more than because of an American preference for concentrating and accumulating power per se. Moreover, regimes in which

[58] *Ibid.*, p. 7. See also pp. 125, 126, 135, 143tf.

power is concentrated do not necessarily accumulate power well. Democracy was preferred, but sometimes it was "necessary" to support and encourage more authoritarian forces. Whether supporting democrats or dictators, however, U.S. officials seldom paid a lot of attention to the question of the quantum of power. They were much more preoccupied with the question of the distribution of power, or with anti-Communism.[59]

Clearly President Kennedy's policies toward Latin America in 1962-1963, in which he utilized principally diplomatic techniques to promote liberal democratic rule, were consistent with the fourth liberal assumption. These efforts were designed to discourage military coups and to encourage constitutionalism and elections. Constitutionalism and elections are devices for impeding or prohibiting the arbitrary use of coercion and for ensuring that leaders control followers. In other words, they are mechanisms for distributing power. However "obvious" the universal propriety of these prescriptions may appear, they were not necessarily always the right ones in individual cases, even compared to the prospect of military rule or dominance. In any event, whatever their merit in particular instances, the efforts were made and they reflected the fourth component of the liberal tradition.

The other main expression of the explicit democratic approach to political development was Title IX. Because Title IX was unique as a legislative mandate for political development, it constitutes in a sense the best index we have of how Americans "think about the problem of government-building." The heart of the amendment was the injunction to encourage popular participation and "democratic private and local government institutions," including cooperatives, labor unions, trade associations, and other voluntary organizations. These prescriptions were explicitly defended in terms of the alleged success of such organizations in fostering

[59] For further discussion of the points in this paragraph, see "The Coherence of the Doctrines," Chap. 4, below.

and preserving pluralistic democracy in the United States. Congressman Morse, among others, explicitly cited Tocqueville's view that American associational life was a distinctive feature of democracy in America, in order to give legitimacy to his efforts to promote similar organizations in the Third World. Personal and organizational linkages were urged between politicians and political parties in the United States and in underdeveloped countries.[60] Title IX both followed and generated suggestions that the United States strengthen and improve competitive political parties, local government, courts, constitutions, electoral laws and procedures, and legislatures.

Many of these proposals were little more than attempts to export American institutions and processes to the Third World, without asking very seriously whether they made sense there. An excellent illustration of this ethnocentricity was the suggestion that the United States make available to less developed countries its expertise in creating staff and research support for legislative processes. Further exploration of this proposal was one of the first steps taken by the Title IX Division of AID in late 1966 and 1967 to implement its mandate.[61] The aim of the Legislative Services Project, as it was called, was to establish and finance links between the staffs of selected American state legislatures and those of the national legislatures in underdeveloped countries. By focusing on legislative staff and services rather

[60] *Congressional Record*, March 15, 1966, 5,605-9; *ibid.*, July 13, 1966, 14,773-77.

[61] The program of a planning conference on legislative services sponsored by AID stated: "The project of which this conference is a part marks the beginning of an effort by AID to give effect to the congressional mandate in Title IX" ("Legislative Services Conference," State University of New York, Center for World Affairs and International Studies, Planting Fields, Long Island, December 8-10, 1967, p. 1). For further information about the conference and AID's efforts to explore the Legislative Services Project, see Allan Kornberg and Lloyd D. Musolf, eds., *Legislatures in Developmental Perspective* (Durham, N.C.: Duke University Press, 1970).

157

than on legislators or electoral laws themselves, the hope was to avoid problems of political sensitivity. The opening lines in the original staff proposal were:

> The widespread ineffectiveness of legislatures in the less developed countries hampers both political and administrative development. The political consequences of legislative weakness are self-evident. . . . [Therefore] it is now timely to launch an A.I.D. program dealing with this problem because of the new emphasis on political development under Title IX.[62]

I believe that each of these propositions is probably false. Since relatively little research has been done on legislatures in the less developed countries, the political consequences of legislative ineffectiveness are far from self-evident. It is fairly clear that most national legislatures in such countries are weak and ineffective; the limited evidence available suggests, however, that what power legislatures have is used much more often to resist change than to initiate it. Throughout most of the globe, but especially in the Third World, legislatures tend to represent more conservative interests than executives, especially in presidential political systems. Hence it is not at all clear that strengthening legislatures contributes to political development. In societies that need and want change, and where political development may be defined to include the will and capacity to cope with and to generate continuing transformation, it may not make much sense to increase the power of an institution that is likely to resist change and, in some instances, to take power away from institutions most likely to enhance change.[63]

[62] Comparative Administrative Group, American Society for Public Administration, "Administrative Resources of Legislatures: A Project Proposal with Special Reference to Legislative Reference Services," November 28, 1966, mimeographed, p. 1.

[63] For a discussion of the functions of legislatures in both developed and underdeveloped countries, and a more detailed critique of the legislative services project and its premises, see Robert A. Packenham, "Legislatures and Political Development," in Kornberg and Musolf,

The Legislative Services Project is one example of Title IX's direct approach, which stressed explicitly political variables as targets in a strategy for political development. The other direct approach proposals were also mostly projections on a world screen of the fourth premise of the liberal tradition. It might be objected, however, that some supporters of Title IX urged an indirect approach, focused on nonpolitical variables that could increase popular participation; that participation, like wealth, is a resource for accumulating power; and that therefore in this sense Title IX was not a reflection of the fourth assumption of the liberal tradition.

It is almost certainly true that the greater the number of people who participate in politics, the greater will be the total amount of power in the political system, all other things being equal. However, this statement would have more force if those who defined Title IX in terms of participation had advocated it in the context of mobilization regimes, where power is concentrated (usually for radical ends), as well as in the context of pluralistic regimes, where power is fragmented. Mobilization systems are excellent devices for maximizing participation.[64]

But few if any supporters of Title IX made this kind of argument. The constant emphasis was on participation as a means of increasing popular control over leaders; the idea of expanding participation under conditions in which leaders might retain and even expand their control was little discussed. By implication, if not always explicitly, the desirability of the mobilization path to participation, and thus to the concentrated accumulation of power, was rejected. Thus, a former acting director of the Political Development

Legislatures, pp. 521-82. For evidence of the conservative orientation and effects of legislatures in developing countries, see Huntington, *Political Order*, pp. 388-96.

[64] Fagen, *Political Culture in Cuba*, pp. 7-10; David Apter, *The Politics of Modernization* (Chicago: University of Chicago Press, 1965), Chap. 10.

159

Division in AID writes that to the "more sophisticated" people in the agency, Title IX was the "culmination" of attempts to correct the overemphasis in aid on "actions which tended to strengthen central government institutions at the expense of local, 'grass-roots' democracy."[65] And by "grass-roots democracy," he meant something much closer to pluralistic American democracy than to "mobilization" democracy, where participation is extremely high but where popular control over elite decisionmaking is limited.

More explicitly, the MIT report on Title IX rejected what it called "the pseudo participation of totalitarian mobilist regimes."[66] This characterization implies that "mobilist" regimes are always "totalitarian"; from such a premise it is easy to reject the mobilization path to participation. The premise may, of course, be challenged.[67]

In the indirect approach too, then, Title IX attends so much to the distribution of power that it neglects the importance of accumulating power, and thus again reflects the fourth premise of the liberal tradition.

[65] John R. Schott, "Title IX," p. 2.

[66] *The Role of Popular Participation in Development* (Cambridge: MIT, Center for International Studies, 1968), 21.

[67] For instance, see Fagen, *Political Culture in Cuba*, pp. 159-65.

4

The Coherence and Value
....   of the Doctrines

IF the various manifestations of the explicit democratic
approach constitute the "best" evidence for the continuing
impact of the fourth liberal premise on American political
development doctrines, does not other evidence—notably
the Cold War approach—contradict this hypothesis? That
is, the Cold War approach has often sanctioned American
support for groups and regimes which concentrate power
in order to maintain stability and resist Communism. Thus
the widespread and continuing presence of the Cold War
doctrine seems to be at odds with the idea that Americans
prefer to see power dispersed. Samuel Huntington has put
this objection in the following manner:

> ... it is at times argued that the United States is so much
> a victim of liberal myopia that it is hopelessly incapable
> of understanding the political needs of foreign systems
> and of adapting its own goals and methods to meet those
> needs. Americans, it is said, will inevitably attempt to re-
> produce in the most unsuitable foreign soil all the charac-
> teristics of their own highly distinctive two-party, liberal,
> pluralistic, constitutional democracy. Obviously, Ameri-
> cans, like anyone else, like to see the virtues of their own
> system and to flatter themselves by seeing it reproduced
> elsewhere. On the other hand, however, it is also quite
> clear that Americans have been able to rise above such
> parochialism in the past, and there is no reason why this
> should not be even more of a pattern in the future. In-
> deed, many of those critics who accuse the U.S. of at-
> tempting to export its own institutions at the same time
> also accuse the U.S. of supporting reactionary and re-
> pressive personalistic dictatorships around the world. Such
> critics would be more persuasive if they were less incon-

sistent. In fact, of course, the United States has, wisely or not, supported and attempted to promote the development of the most varied types of political systems around the world . . . [as in] Iran . . . Tunisia . . . Bolivia . . . Korea . . . Thailand . . . Nepal, and . . . a variety of competitive democratic systems in which the dominant groups have been socialist, Catholic and liberal, as well as highly conservative.[1]

The main weakness of the foregoing criticism is that it assumes that the American "liberal myopia" has only one component, namely, the tendency to export pluralistic American democracy. As we have seen, however, the liberal tradition has several components. In the first instance, it specifies that change is easy (premise one) and that all good things go together (premise two). Hence the economic approach, which flows from these premises, is thought by itself to go a long way toward assuring the emergence of stability, democracy, and other good things. When this does not happen, as is often the case, then there are basically two options.

One is the explicit democratic approach, reflecting the fourth assumption of the liberal tradition. In this approach an effort is made to take additional steps beyond the economic doctrine to nurse political systems along the stable democratic path. The other option is the Cold War approach. It reflects especially the third premise of the liberal tradition—the antipathy to radicalism, revolution, violent conflict, and instability generally—and may be employed if both the economic and the explicit democratic approaches fail to produce the desired and anticipated results, and especially if they lead instead to instability and intense conflict involving groups that champion radical or revolution-

[1] Huntington, *Military Intervention*, pp. 25-26. Huntington advances precisely the hypothesis that he rejects here in his *Political Order in Changing Societies*, p. 7. The relevant passage from the latter work was quoted above in Chapter 3, p. 155.

ary goals. Since the first two approaches very often do "fail," the Cold War approach is not infrequently used.

Though ostensibly separate and conflicting, the three approaches are actually integrated and consistent components of a coherent liberal tradition, which grew out of a unique historical experience. America was "born equal"; democracy came "easy"; no profound social revolution was necessary. Hence Americans tend to think that other societies should also fairly easily become wealthier, more equal, and more democratic. If they do not, then the assumption is that something must be wrong with the *societies*, not with the theory. Deviations from the patterns of economic and political development as they occurred in the United States—especially radicalism and revolution—are due to "unnatural growths," which the United States then tries to remove "by diplomacy or war."[2] In this fashion the "right" hand of the liberal tradition (as manifested in the Cold War approach) counters what the "left" hand (the economic and explicit democratic approaches) has helped to create.

The United States has supported and encouraged a considerable variety of political regimes and forces in the Third World.[3] The "liberal myopia" of which Huntington speaks implies not only that the United States will try to duplicate its own democratic institutions abroad; it also means that we will react negatively to extreme instability, radicalism, and revolution, and be willing to countenance and encourage conservative and even reactionary forces and governments—

[2] The phrases quoted are from Goldman, *Tragedy of Johnson*, p. 385. The full quotation is given above in Chapter 2, n. 46.

[3] The United States has necessarily related diplomatically to quite a variety of governments and regimes in power. This results from the obvious diplomatic need for any nation to deal with established regimes to a considerable degree. Still, it is misleading to suggest, as Huntington does, that the United States has "attempted to promote the *most* varied types of political systems around the world." For this ignores the virtually complete antipathy in doctrine and practice to radical groups and forces not in power, and the preponderant, if not unmixed, hostility even to revolutionary governments in power.

even if they concentrate power in conservative dictatorships
—so long as they appear able to compete with and contain
"excessive" instability, radicalism, and revolution. Both of
these responses are, as we have pointed out, perfectly consistent with the liberal tradition, although obviously not
each response is consistent with each component of it. Indeed, there is no *single* assumption in American political
thought which explains all the variety in the American responses. Nor should this be surprising. As a whole, however,
the four assumptions of the liberal tradition account for
much of the variety.

In order to see more clearly the interrelationships among
the components of the liberal tradition, we must also review
the categories of political systems that typically flow from
it, and note the priorities that are typically set among them.
American officials have tended to view the political regimes
of the Third World in terms of three categories: liberal democracies; anti-Communist authoritarian systems; and Communist dictatorships. Clearly this trichotomy greatly over-
simplifies "reality," but it nevertheless is the conceptual
device that has mainly been used.[4] These three categories
have also been employed when analyzing the prospects for
political systems in flux.

[4] In addition to the evidence in Chapters 1, 2, and 3, see the report
of President Kennedy's Task Force on Latin America (chaired by
A. A. Berle, Jr.), discussed in Schlesinger, *A Thousand Days*, pp.
195ff; *Nomination of Lincoln Gordon, passim*; Nelson A. Rockefeller,
The Rockefeller Report on the Americas (Chicago: Quadrangle
Books, 1969), pp. 57-62; Richard M. Nixon, Address to the Inter-
American Press Association, Washington, D.C., October 31, 1969,
printed in *New York Times*, November 1, 1969, p. 14.

Scholars have often employed essentially the same typology. For
example, the dependent variables in Barrington Moore, Jr.'s, celebrated
recent work, *Social Origins of Dictatorship and Democracy*, are
democracy, fascism, and communism. A persuasive plea for more
differentiated typologies is made in Douglas A. Chalmers, "Understanding the Variety of Political Systems: A Necessary Next Step
in Comparative Politics," unpublished paper, Columbia University,
November 1969.

President Kennedy's analysis of the political situation in the Dominican Republic after the assassination of Trujillo in May 1961 is an excellent example of the utilization of these three categories and of the priorities the United States has set among them. It also serves as a paradigm for illuminating the coherence of the three main types of doctrines we have identified in this book, and of the assumptions underlying them.

"There are three possibilities," Kennedy said, "in descending order of preference: a decent democratic regime, a continuation of the Trujillo regime, or a Castro regime. We ought to aim at the first, but we really can't renounce the second until we are sure that we can avoid the third."[5] These three possibilities exhausted the alternatives. It was *either* a "decent democratic regime" *or* a "Trujillo regime." Other categories—notably one to conceptualize non-Communist, indigenous, radical forces—were omitted. To the extent that it was explicitly considered, the indigenous radical category was either rejected on its own merits or blurred into the Communist category. The same alternatives were posed by President Johnson in 1965. At that time too indigenous radicals and progressives were subsumed under the "Castro regime" category. The result was American intervention.[6]

To a considerable extent, the formula Presidents Kennedy and Johnson applied to the Dominican Republic has been writ large—although, except in Vietnam, seldom etched so

[5] Quoted in Schlesinger, *A Thousand Days*, p. 769.

[6] See Slater, *Intervention and Negotiation*, pp. 12-13, 25-26, 39-41, 191-93, 200-202, 215-16. The Dominican case also illustrates very well the *sequence* of political development approaches to which the liberal tradition gives rise: the economic approach, supplemented by the explicit democratic approach, followed (when the first two tactics fail to produce the desired and anticipated objectives) by the Cold War approach. Then the cycle begins again. See especially John Bartlow Martin, *Overtaken by Events: The Dominican Crisis from the Fall of Trujillo to the Civil War* (New York: Doubleday, 1966), for a detailed description of these approaches in action, and Slater, *Intervention and Negotiation*, pp. 48-70, for an overview and theoretical elaboration.

deeply—across American foreign policy toward underdeveloped countries during the last two decades. With few exceptions, the United States has supported liberal, constitutional forces or governments where "possible," and authoritarian, anti-Communist ones where "necessary." Communist regimes have never been permitted if the United States could help it. Radicals (who may be illiberal and authoritarian but progressive in terms of social and economic change) have been a more difficult phenomenon to deal with; they have either been forced into the Communist category eventually or distinguished from Communists but opposed anyway. This last point, about radicals, requires a brief digression.

Like other international actors, Americans seem to perceive and respond to difficult, unfamiliar phenomena—in this case, radicalism—in at least three different ways.[7] One response is simply to omit the category completely, as Presidents Kennedy and Johnson did in the Dominican Republic. Another response is to recognize the existence of such a category but to regard it as specious: e.g. " 'radicals' are really only Communists in disguise." In March 1964, for example, James C. Thomson, Jr., a White House staff expert on Asian affairs, suggested to an Assistant Secretary of State that the conflict in Vietnam was "in some ways . . . a

[7] This and the next paragraph draw upon and modify slightly some hypotheses in Robert Jervis, "Hypotheses on Misperception," *World Politics*, 20, No. 3 (April 1968), 454-79, at pp. 466-67. Jervis suggests three ways in which actors in international relations may perceive and respond to ambiguous, unfamiliar phenomena (his examples are omitted): "First, concepts [which correspond to the phenomena] may be completely missing. . . . Second, the actor can know about a concept but not believe that it reflects an actual phenomenon. . . . Third, the actor may hold a concept, but not believe that another actor fills it at the present moment." He hypothesizes that "misperception is most difficult to correct in the case of a missing concept and least difficult to correct in the case of a recognized but presumably unfilled concept. All other things being equal . . . , the first case requires more cognitive reorganization than does the second, and the second requires more reorganization than does the third."

civil war," and that, by implication, some substantial portion of the Vietcong were indigenous radicals, or at least nationalists before they were Communists. In reply, the Assistant Secretary snapped, "Don't play word games with me!"[8] A third way is to concede that non-Communist radicalism is a genuine category; then the questions are whether a particular group, movement, or individual fits the category and how it is evaluated. Thus some American officials dealing with Vietnam recognized the concept; among them, some thought there were groups who fit the category, while others thought not. Never, however, at least through the end of 1968, did prevailing American doctrine evaluate the radicals positively; it always, on balance, preferred the Diem, Ky, and Thieu regimes to the radical forces opposing them. Similarly, Lincoln Gordon, the American ambassador to Brazil at the time of the overthrow of João Goulart in 1964, recognized the non-Communist radical category and in fact distinguished indigenous radicals in Brazil, such as Goulart and Leonel Brizola, from Communists. But he felt that they planned to transform Brazil unconstitutionally into a "populist" dictatorship along the lines of Argentina under Perón (1945-1955) or Brazil, earlier, under Getúlio Vargas (1937-1945). Hence he welcomed Goulart's overthrow—even though it was equally unconstitutional—and the establishment of the Castello Branco government.[9]

According to the formula outlined above, then, *the United States has been uncomfortable with authoritarian forces and regimes of any kind, but in general it has been more uncomfortable with authoritarianisms of the Left than with authoritarianisms of the Right.*[10] The preference for liberal

[8] James C. Thomson, Jr., in Richard M. Pfeffer, ed., *No More Vietnams?*, p. 48. For another example, in reference to U.S. views of former President Juan Bosch of the Dominican Republic, see Slater, *Intervention and Negotiation*, pp. 12-13.

[9] On Brazil, see *Nomination of Lincoln Gordon*, esp. p. 65; and Skidmore, *Politics in Brazil*, Epilogue.

[10] For a contrary view, asserted without evidence, see Kenneth R. Minogue, *The Liberal Mind* (New York: Random House, 1963,

democratic regimes everywhere, which stems from the fourth liberal postulate, is evidenced in the continuing belief that a world of democratic nations is best for all concerned and in the national interest of the United States. The preference for right-wing over left-wing authoritarianisms stems from the antiradical component of the liberal tradition as well as from security needs and perceptions of those needs arising largely out of the Cold War and from the inherent undesirability under certain conditions of radical politics.

Evidence of American distaste for right-wing authoritarianisms is abundant. It is not limited to those manifestations of the explicit democratic approach which have already been discussed in some detail. It includes also the many U.S. efforts, of varying intensity, to induce relatively conservative authoritarian governments to liberalize their regimes. The United States was not at all happy with the repressive dictatorship it had propped up in Greece in 1949-1950, and it tried (unsuccessfully) to liberalize that dictatorship. Analogous attempts were again made in Greece after the military coup in 1967. In South Vietnam, American policy was, on the one hand, to shore up governments that were manifestly out of touch with and lacking the support of their peoples; on the other hand, there were repeated American efforts to get the South Vietnamese elites to hold competitive elections, make other democratic reforms, and establish more humane mechanisms for economic, social, and political justice. Similar efforts were made in Brazil after 1964, intermittently in the Dominican Republic from 1961 to 1966, and at various times in Taiwan, South Korea, Pakistan, and other countries.

1968): "In general, liberals disapprove of violence. . . . But their disapproval of the violence of others varies according to who carries it out . . . liberals are likely to dismiss [left-wing] violence with gentle regret. The violence of a Mao Tse Tung is more acceptable than that of a Chiang Kai-shek, that of a Castro more than that of a Batista" (pp. 10-11). This thesis is difficult to square with my observations of the United States, although it may better fit the British or Australian cases.

It is true, of course, that such attempts have not always been intense; that with few exceptions they have had limited success; and that the United States has tended to continue (and in some instances increase) its support for the incumbent regimes despite the scarcity or absence of these types of reforms. Such efforts were often either naïve, or hypocritical, or both. The fact remains, however, that some such efforts were made. They have occurred in part because the liberal tradition exerts pressure on any American government not to give strong support to relatively authoritarian regimes unless it also urges such regimes to liberalize themselves.[11]

There is an even larger amount of evidence to support the second part of the proposition, namely, that Americans are more uncomfortable with authoritarianisms of the left than with those of the right. The Cold War approach to political development has been applied with far greater frequency and intensity than has the explicit democratic approach. And when attempts at liberal reforms have not produced the desired constitutionalism and stability but instability and radicalism, the United States has almost without exception reacted negatively. In effect this has usually meant support for relatively right-wing authoritarian forces and governments. One of the important consequences of this pattern of preferences has been a tendency to exaggerate the defects of the radical groups and regimes that we oppose and to minimize the defects of the right-wing groups and regimes we support.[12] We have already noted how much Americans

[11] Wilsonianism, of course, was a powerful earlier manifestation of this same impulse. See N. Gordon Levin, Jr., *Woodrow Wilson and World Politics: America's Response to War and Revolution* (New York: Oxford University Press, 1968). See also Theodore P. Wright, Jr., *American Support of Free Elections Abroad* (Washington, D.C.: Public Affairs Press, 1964).

[12] Stated more formally, we tend to resolve the cognitive dissonance between (a) our goal of democracy, and (b) our support of right-wing forces in order to avoid left-wing forces, by perceiving many

have stressed "what went wrong in Cuba" and how little they have noted what has "gone right" there. Similar kinds of overly pessimistic analyses have been made of Ho Chi Minh's regime in North Vietnam, Cheddi Jagan's government in British Guiana, the Arévalo and Arbenz governments in Guatemala, and the Perón regime in Argentina.[13]

On the other hand, American officials underplayed the repressive and corrupt features of the Greek regime in 1947; they did the same thing after the coup in 1967. Americans scarcely noticed the slaughter of hundreds of thousands of alleged Communists or Communist-sympathizers in Indonesia in 1965. They paid great attention to Castro's show trials and executions but little to the political murders of Batista. At various times in the 1950s the United States had extremely cordial relations with the dictatorships of Trujillo in the Dominican Republic and Pérez Jiménez in Venezuela. South Korea and Taiwan, along with Greece, were probably the three "success stories" most frequently cited by AID officials in the 1960s as evidence of the efficacy of American economic assistance:[14] Korea was governed by a military led dominant-party system, and Taiwan by the personalistic

---

of the negative aspects of left-wing groups and governments while perceiving few of the negative aspects of right-wing groups.

On the notion of cognitive dissonance, see Leon Festinger, *A Theory of Cognitive Dissonance* (Stanford: Stanford University Press, 1957).

[13] On the Guatemalan case, see especially Bryce Wood, "Self-Plagiarism and Foreign Policy," *Latin American Research Review*, 3, No. 3 (Summer 1968), 184-91. On the Perón regime, see Peter H. Smith, "Social Mobilization, Political Participation, and the Rise of Juan Perón," *Political Science Quarterly*, 84, No. 1 (March 1969), 30-49, esp. 31, n. 4.

[14] For example, see Hollis B. Chenery and Alan M. Strout, "Foreign Assistance and Economic Development," *American Economic Review*, 56, No. 4 (September 1966), 679-80; Gustav Ranis, "Why Foreign Aid?," *Ventures: Magazine of the Yale Graduate School*, 8, No. 2 (Fall 1968), 27. Chenery and Ranis were assistant administrators in AID in the 1960s; Strout was on their staff.

dictatorial apparatus of Generalissimo Chiang Kai-shek. The Eisenhower, Kennedy, Johnson, and Nixon administrations have all, in varying degrees, made much of elections in Vietnam; yet seldom if ever have these elections been free expressions of public preferences.

Another example is American policy toward the Brazilian "Revolution" of March 31–April 2, 1964. The United States recognized the new government, and President Johnson sent an unusually cordial greeting to the interim Brazilian President, within twelve hours after he had been sworn in. In May 1964, Lincoln Gordon, the American ambassador, stated to the Superior War College in Rio de Janeiro that the "Revolution," which was essentially a military coup, "can indeed be included along with the Marshall Plan proposal, the Berlin Blockade, the defeat of Communist aggression in Korea, and the resolution of the missile crisis in Cuba as one of the major turning points in world history in the middle of the twentieth century."[15] In February 1966, pressed by the Committee on Foreign Relations of the U.S. Senate to justify the military regime of Castello Branco, Mr. Gordon described it "as a transitional regime with some exceptional arbitrary powers which is moving very rapidly in the direction of full constitutional normality."[16] Contrary to this prediction, however, Brazil moved rather steadily after 1966 in the direction of a full-scale dictatorship, by increasing arbitrary arrests, torturing political prisoners, cancelling popular elections, closing the national congress, and imposing strict censorship on newspapers.[17]

These examples lend support to Hartz's contention that "We [Americans] are not familiar with the deeper social struggles of Asia [and Latin America?] and hence tend to interpret even reactionary regimes as 'democratic.' We fail

[15] Quoted in Skidmore, *Politics in Brazil*, p. 329.

[16] *Nomination of Lincoln Gordon*, p. 65. See also pp. 7-8, 34, 67.

[17] See Alfred Stepan, *The Military in Politics: Changing Patterns in Brazil* (Princeton: Princeton University Press, 1971), pp. 253-66.

171

to appreciate nonpolitical definitions of 'freedom' and hence are baffled by their use."[18] It is true that there are at least some partial exceptions to the foregoing tendencies. The United States has supported Tito in Yugoslavia, Paz Estenssoro in Bolivia, Sekou Touré in Guinea, Sukarno in Indonesia, Nasser in Egypt, and perhaps other "leftist" leaders, in varying degrees. But Tito was supported mainly for strategic reasons (to help "loosen" the Soviet "bloc"); Paz was not so much a radical leader as a moderate arbiter among conflicting factions in a semirevolutionary regime;[19] Touré had ex-

[18] Hartz, *The Liberal Tradition*, p. 306.

[19] The question of the extent to which U.S. aid to Bolivia after 1952 constitutes an exception to the tendencies just discussed deserves further study. The Department of State in 1955 concluded that the Bolivian government was "Marxist rather than Communist and . . . advocated United States support of this regime on the same premise that it advocated support of the preceding military junta—to prevent displacement by more radical elements" (*Critical Materials*, Report of the Senate Economic Subcommittee on Minerals, Materials, and Fuels of the Committee on Interior and Insular Affairs, Doc. No. 83, 84th Cong., 1st Sess. [Washington, D.C.: Government Printing Office, 1956], pp. 116-17, quoted in Richard W. Patch, "Bolivia: U.S. Assistance in a Revolutionary Setting," in Richard Adams, *et al.*, *Social Change in Latin America Today* [New York: Random House, 1960], p. 130). Clearly this Marxist-Communist distinction is important and was not frequently made in the Dulles years. However, Patch throws more light on the situation. He describes President Víctor Paz Estenssoro and Vice President Hernán Siles, whom the United States supported, as "essentially moderates." He also states that "U.S. aid has been of crucial importance in keeping the moderate leaders of the MNR [the National Revolutionary Movement, the governing party] in power." The United States was reported to have made the resignation of Juan Lechín, the radical Minister of Mines, a condition for extension of further U.S. aid in 1955. Patch describes the "original intention" of U.S. aid thus: "to help a group of men who accept the principles of democracy, who reject totalitarianism, whether exercised by a wealthy elite or in the name of the masses, to build a nation dedicated to true democracy and willing to assume a responsible place in the community of nations" (Patch, "Bolivia," pp. 119, 174, 133, 164). The United States also allied itself with the fiscally and monetarily conservative International Monetary Fund in a successful campaign to induce the Bolivian government to stabilize wages and

cellent personal relations with President Kennedy but never received massive American material support; Sukarno got far less American aid than his more conservative successors; and Nasser was tolerated rather than enthusiastically endorsed. By contrast, U.S. support for right-wing authoritarian regimes in the underdeveloped world has been more firm and substantial. The most characteristic patterns are those previously described.

Thus it is not extreme to assert, with Hartz, that the coherent set of assumptions that grow out of the exceptional American experience constitutes a kind of "colossal liberal absolutism . . . [which] hampers creative action abroad by identifying the alien with the unintelligible, and . . . inspires hysteria at home by generating the anxiety that unintelligible things produce."[20] More specifically, the first two liberal premises make the United States excessively optimistic or utopian; the third liberal premise often makes us counterrevolutionary and even reactionary; and the fourth assumption inclines us toward a special kind of pretentiousness and arrogance.

VALUE[21]

The great trouble with the doctrines is not that they are always wrong but that they are not always right—and that Americans seldom realize the latter. The great problem with

---

to postpone or abandon certain welfare programs. These moves exacerbated tensions between the government and the tin miners and thus helped to polarize Bolivian politics. After 1960, the United States helped to build up the army, which overthrew Paz in 1964 (Huntington, *Political Order*, pp. 333-34. See also *ibid.*, pp. 325ff, and James W. Wilkie, *The Bolivian Revolution and U.S. Aid Since 1952: Financial Background and Context of Political Decisions* [Los Angeles: University of California, 1969]).

[20] Hartz, *Liberal Tradition*, p. 285.

[21] What follows is only a brief assessment of the three main political development doctrines. Chapter 6 gives a parallel critique of the theories. Chapter 8 offers a few prescriptions about both doctrines and theories.

the liberal tradition which the doctrines reflect is not its looseness and pragmatism but its coherence and rigidity. Americans need to discover the fallacies in the doctrines and the "colossal liberal absolutism" of the political tradition from which the doctrines flow if they are to act more perceptively, justly, and sensibly in relation to Third World politics. They cannot abandon theorizing, but they can and should expand their theoretical horizons, revise their largely implicit liberal dogma, and open themselves to new data and new values. In policy terms, they should revise sharply their antipathy for radical politics in the Third World and put teeth into their ostensible commitment to a world of diversity.

THE ECONOMIC APPROACH

The economic approach is sometimes valid but more often misleading. Economic development sometimes leads to all good things, but more often it does not. The relationship between economic development and political stability is, in global terms, evidently curvilinear rather than unilinear. Economic development is not a sufficient condition for political democracy; it comes close to being a necessary condition, although a case like India from 1947 to 1968 makes one wonder even about that. Similarly, the relationships between levels and rates of economic development, and anti-Communism and pro-Americanism, also appear to be mixed and nonlinear.

The main weakness of the economic approach is not that it aims at promoting economic development in the Third World; it is rather that it contains expectations about the probable political consequences of economic development that are too optimistic. Levels of economic development in such countries are too low, and the gap between rich and poor countries is too great, for the United States to abandon its commitment to economic development in these regions. Quite the contrary, this commitment should be intensified and expanded rather than weakened or narrowed. At the same

174

time, however, Americans must come to understand that economic growth and development in the Third World very often will not have all the happy consequences they are understood to produce. Often they will produce instability, anti-Americanism, authoritarianism, radicalism, and other behavior that Americans may find distasteful, and which may, in fact, in some instances be regrettable. Americans must learn to understand these consequences of economic development and social change as in some sense "natural." Americans must learn to distinguish more clearly and wisely which consequences are not necessarily bad for the development of the recipient country, and which do not genuinely threaten the vital interests of the United States. Americans must also learn to refrain from seeking to "correct" such occurrences when our efforts might be either undesirable, or unfeasible, or both.

The Desirability of Economic Development. At least two further questions remain. The first relates to the desirability of the economic development objective itself, quite aside from the issue of excessive optimism about its political consequences. One of the many reasons for urging a focus on economic development, and a greater propensity to accept its political consequences, is that the United States and the less developed countries seem more or less agreed on the substance and salience of economic development, whereas they differ much more on the nature of political development and hence on the salience of different political development objectives.

It may be objected, however, that often economic development is also ethnocentrically defined. Anthropologists have long suggested that the quality of life in "underdeveloped" countries is not necessarily worse than it is in "developed" ones. The British economist Barbara Ward once wrote an article on this theme with the disarming title, "We May Be Rich, But They Are Happy."[22] Barrington

[22] *New York Times Magazine*, May 5, 1963, pp. 22-23, 120-21.

175

Moore states flatly that "there is no evidence that the mass of the population anywhere has wanted an industrial society, and plenty of evidence that they [*sic*] did not. At bottom all forms of industrialization so far have been revolutions from above, the work of a ruthless minority."[23]

Of what value is economic development really? The issue is, as the foregoing suggests, not quite so simple as it may appear. Nevertheless, most of the important issues probably have to do not so much with the desire and need of the peoples of these countries for economic development, but rather with the form of and the means to better living standards and other amenities that economic development brings. What little systematic empirical evidence exists suggests that the hopes and fears of peoples in both developed and underdeveloped countries relate first and foremost to their economic well-being. People in subsistence economies want enough to eat; those in slightly wealthier surroundings want decent housing and a regular job; those in affluent societies want the status-bestowing luxuries. Cross-national comparisons of the hopes and fears of people in poor and rich countries indicate that a minimum standard of living seems to be required before other interests and concerns can emerge.[24]

[23] Moore, *Social Origins*, p. 506.

[24] See Hadley Cantril, *The Pattern of Human Concerns* (New Brunswick, N.J.: Rutgers University Press, 1965), *passim*. This book reports the results of a unique survey study of the hopes and fears of almost 20,000 people in thirteen countries at widely varying levels of social and economic development. Although surveys have some serious shortcomings as a tool for tapping hopes and fears, especially in nonindustrial cultures, Cantril's data deserve attention. His study is far and away the most broadly based of its kind.

In this connection, another pertinent study is Daniel Lerner, *The Passing of Traditional Society* (New York: Free Press, 1958), pp. 101-2, 398-99, 430. Lerner analyzed data from a survey of six Middle Eastern countries (Turkey, Lebanon, Egypt, Syria, Jordan, and Iran). One of the questions asked each respondent was whether he was happy or unhappy ("fairly" or "very") with his life. The data support Lerner's conclusion that "those who embody tradition are most unhappy while those seeking to forsake it become increasingly happy in the measure they succeed" (p. 101).

176

Of course it can be misleading to define economic development exclusively in terms of per capita income, ignoring problems of distribution. Of course economic development has—or should have—social, psychological, and cultural as well as strictly economic dimensions. Of course pollution, congestion, and the neurotic personality of our time should be avoided as far as possible. Perhaps most importantly, economic development should be defined in terms of the distinctive characteristics of particular developing countries, rather than simply in the ways it is conventionally defined in the Western industrialized nations.[25] It is true, and obvious, that focusing on economic development is no panacea for all the problems of priorities in American aid and other developmental activities. Nevertheless, it is easier to romanticize Third World poverty in a comfortable urban coffee house or a posh university faculty club than in a *favela* in São Paulo or a rice paddy in Asia. The following affirmation, pronounced many years ago by Francis Hackett, does not meet all the issues posed by the "We Are Rich, But They Are Happy" school; but it responds to, and I think disposes of, a number of them. He said:

> I believe in materialism. I believe in all the proceeds of a healthy materialism—good cooking, dry houses, dry feet, sewers, drain pipes, hot water, baths, electric lights, automobiles, good roads, bright streets, long vacations away from the village pump, new ideas, fast horses, swift conversation, theatres, operas, orchestras, bands—I believe in them all for everybody. The man who dies without knowing these things may be as exquisite as a saint, and as rich as a poet; but it is in spite of, not because of, his deprivation.[26]

[25] A powerful, though controversial, statement of this point is Ivan Illich, "Outwitting the 'Developed' Countries," *New York Review of Books*, November 6, 1969, pp. 20-24. See also his "The Seamy Side of Charity," *America*, 116 (January 21, 1967), 88-91.

[26] Francis Hackett, *Ireland*, quoted in Paul A. Samuelson, *Economics: An Introductory Analysis*, 3rd edn. (New York: McGraw-Hill, 1955), p. 703.

177

The Feasibility of Economic Development and the Question of U.S. Influence. The second question, or rather set of questions, relates to the feasibility of aid as an instrument for promoting Third World economic development. How powerful a tool *is* bilateral aid? What conditions maximize its potential for development, and what conditions obstruct it? Is aid's impact on economic development always positive? How does bilateral aid compare with other forms of aid (e.g. multilateral assistance) and with completely different sets of variables (e.g. international trade patterns and host country characteristics) as causes, or inhibitors, of economic development?

Reliable answers to these questions are in pitifully short supply. For despite the hundreds of books and articles that have been written about aid, the corpus of serious literature dealing with aid's impact on development remains very small.[27] The reasons for the paucity of such studies are not only methodological (e.g. how to isolate the impact of aid on events simultaneously affected by many other variables), political (e.g. in AID, the fear of uncovering mistakes that might be used by critical congressmen to cut appropriations), and economic (evaluation is costly, and therefore the consequences of every aid activity cannot be assessed systematically), but also ideological: the lack of attention to these questions is not wholly unrelated to the first liberal premise.[28]

A further difficulty with existing studies is that different people define influence differently and bring differing value premises to their evaluations of the impact of aid; such differences also are sources of confusion regarding the influence of aid. For example, assessments of impact probably

[27] For instance, the Pearson Report, one of the comprehensive analyses of development aid that has appeared, devotes four and a half pages out of nearly four hundred to the subject of the "contribution" of aid (pp. 48-52). Even this brief discussion is contradictory; see n. 30, below.

[28] See Chapter 3, n. 14.

vary according to where one lives (people in developing countries probably tend to perceive American influence as greater than Americans do) and according to what the assessor thinks of U.S. policies (if he likes them, he probably tends to think our influence is not great enough; if he does not, he probably thinks it is too great). Still further, the magnitude of U.S. influence on Third World economic and political development probably varies quite substantially, both from country to country and within countries over time. The causes of variation are many: they include the amount of American aid relative to host country resources; the state of diplomatic and economic relations between the United States and the recipient; social, economic, and political characteristics of the host country; the type of aid instrument in question.

For all these reasons, assessing the amount of U.S. influence on economic and political development in the Third World is an enormously complicated task.[29] But the magnitude of that influence is not the only complex and problematic issue; the direction of the influence is also unclear in many instances. It is by no means safe to assume that aid necessarily helps economic development, to say nothing of political development. In fact, the variety of answers that are given to just the first of these questions is astounding. And yet until recently most Americans did make this assumption, which was shared and reinforced by most established experts on the aid programs. The spate of official and semiofficial reports that appeared in 1969 and 1970 concurred in general with the conclusion registered in the Pearson Report that aid "helped make possible a good record

[29] Moreover, the degree to which U.S. aid can or cannot influence behavior in recipient countries is not demonstrated merely by indicating the proportions of aid over gross investment, imports, or GNP, or by citing some countries where American financing has apparently contributed to growth. An excellent brief discussion of these and related points is Kenneth N. Waltz, *Foreign Policy and Democratic Politics: The American and British Experiences* (Boston: Little, Brown, 1967), pp. 193-94.

of development in the past two decades."[30] Several empirical studies of narrower scope have also found aid's impact to have been almost exclusively beneficial.[31]

A large and growing number of studies, however, has argued that bilateral and even multilateral aid programs are hindrances to economic development. Studies of this type vary greatly in their methodologies and ideological premises, but they are not to be dismissed as merely polemics. For instance, several single-country case studies find the consequences of aid to have been substantially negative.[32] A Chil-

[30] Pearson, *Partners in Development*, p. 52. It is notable that this conclusion follows upon the statement three pages earlier that "the correlation between the amounts of aid received in the past decades and the growth performance is very weak" (p. 49). This example is illustrative of a wider tendency of the favorable studies to stress the positive evidence and to deemphasize the negative evidence which the authors of such studies are too competent and objective to ignore altogether. For another example of the same tendency, see Robert E. Asher, *Development Assistance in the Seventies: Alternatives for the United States* (Washington, D.C.: The Brookings Institution, 1970), pp. 53, n. 11, 81-84.

The studies and reports done in 1969 and 1970 are reviewed in Willard L. Thorp, "Foreign Aid: A Report on the Reports," *Foreign Affairs*, 48, No. 3 (April 1970), 561-73; Joan M. Nelson, "The Partial Partnership," *International Organization*, 25, No. 1 (Winter 1971), 79-96; and Robert E. Asher, "Development Assistance in DD II," *ibid.*, 97-119.

[31] Irma Adelman and Hollis B. Chenery, "Foreign Aid and Economic Development: The Case of Greece," *Review of Economics and Statistics*, 48 (February 1966), 1-19; Hollis B. Chenery and M. Bruno, "Development Alternatives in An Open Economy: The Case of Israel," *Economic Journal*, 72 (March 1962), 79-103; Hollis B. Chenery and Alan M. Strout, "Foreign Aid and Economic Development," *American Economic Review*, 56, No. 4 (September 1966), 680-733; Charles D. Hyson and Alan M. Strout, "Impact of Foreign Aid on U.S. Exports," *Harvard Business Review*, 46, No. 1 (January-February 1968), 63-71, esp. p. 67; and Neil H. Jacoby, *U.S. Aid to Taiwan: A Study of Foreign Aid, Self-Help, and Development* (New York: Praeger, 1967). Of these, all except Jacoby's book are based largely on aggregate quantitative data, often over relatively short periods of time.

[32] (Senator) Ernest Gruening, *United States Foreign Aid in Action: A Case Study*, Report Submitted to the Subcommittee on Foreign

ean professor of psychiatry, Dr. Vincent Sanchez, concluded after a three-year study of the impacts on youth and family life of eight U.S.-sponsored colleges in Chile that American aid efforts, although they may have helped economic development, also caused a wave of severe personality problems.[33] The Rockefeller Report on Latin America in 1969 and the Peterson Report on foreign aid in general in 1970 both argued that economic aid sometimes had negative consequences.[34] Some conservatives (like Milton Friedman and P. T. Bauer) and most radicals (like Ivan Illich, Andre Gunder Frank, J. P. Morray, and Harry Magdoff) have argued for years that "aid" is an obstacle to development and (in the radical view) an instrument of imperialism.[35] The radical version of this argument has lately been incorporated into an elaborate theory of inter-American and indeed U.S.–Third World relations, the so-called dependency orientation.[36] The view of aid as a hindrance to

---

Aid Expenditures, Committee on Government Operations, U.S. Senate, 89th Cong., 2nd Sess. (Washington, D.C.: Government Printing Office, 1966) (Chile); Huntington, *Political Order*, pp. 325-34 (Bolivia); Eugene Bramer Mihaly, *Foreign Aid and Politics in Nepal: A Case Study* (London: Oxford University Press, 1965); William S. Stokes, "The *Contraproducente* Consequences of Foreign Aid in Bolivia," in Helmut Schoeck and James Wiggins, eds., *The New Argument in Economics: The Public Versus the Private Sector* (New York: Van Nostrand, 1963), pp. 145-84.

[33] A report on the study was given at the Second International Congress for Social Psychiatry in London in August 1969; see the *New York Times*, August 24, 1969, p. 28.

[34] *The Rockefeller Report on the Americas*; *U.S. Foreign Assistance in the 1970s: A New Approach*, Report to the President from the Task Force on International Development, Rudolph A. Peterson, Chairman (Washington, D.C.: Government Printing Office, 1970).

[35] For instance, see Friedman, "Foreign Economic Aid: Means and Objectives," *The Yale Review* (Summer 1958), reprinted in Pincus, *Reshaping the World Economy*, pp. 64-73; Harry Magdoff, *The Age of Imperialism* (New York: Monthly Review Press, 1969), esp. Chap. 4.

[36] An overview of this orientation is Susanne Bodenheimer, "Dependency and Imperialism: The Roots of Latin American Under-

development became sufficiently prominent and widespread in the late 1960s that such "establishment" figures as Dean Acheson and Nelson Rockefeller could support some of its key propositions.[37]

At present, therefore, a fairly impressive case can be made for aid as either a promoter of or an obstacle to economic development. Which case one accepts depends on many variables. Obviously there are variations among countries and over time; the way the questions are posed and the values of the investigator also affect the kinds of answers that are given. In general, however, my own view is that the magnitude of manageable influence wielded by the U.S. government through its aid programs on Third World economic development has probably been marginal in most cases most of the time. U.S. assistance doubtless helps economic development in some instances and hurts it in others. However, I agree with Raymond Mikesell that "As a general proposition, external capital or aid is neither a necessary nor a sufficient condition for development."[38]

Obviously more and better research into the question of aid impact is a high-priority need. In the meantime, given the political, administrative, and economic restrictions the United States has placed on its aid, the increasing debt burden that loans have created for many recipient countries, and the political and/or military consequences U.S. aid may involve, it is quite possible that in certain countries the United States can help development more by decreasing its

---

development," in K. T. Fann and Donald C. Hodges, eds., *Readings in U.S. Imperialism* (Boston: Porter Sargent Publisher, 1971), pp. 155-81. See also Osvaldo Sunkel, "National Development Policy and External Dependence in Latin America," *Journal of Development Studies*, No. 6 (October 1969), 23-48.

[37] *The Rockefeller Report on the Americas*, pp. 80-88; Acheson, *Present at the Creation*, pp. 265-66.

[38] Raymond Mikesell, *The Economics of Foreign Aid* (Chicago: Aldine, 1968), p. 258, quoted in Samuel P. Huntington, "Foreign Aid: For What and For Whom," *Foreign Policy*, No. 1 (Winter 1970-71), 184-85.

aid than by increasing it. As Huntington has observed, "the governments of poor countries may have good reasons to prefer less aid rather than more aid."[39]

It remains very important, however, to distinguish the question of the utility of bilateral economic and technical assistance for Third World development, on the one hand, from questions regarding the desirability and feasibility of rich nations trying *in some fashion* to assist poor nations, on the other. My own view, which I shall not attempt to justify here, is that both morality and political prudence (in the best sense) can be drawn upon to support efforts to transfer resources from the rich to the poor countries, and to increase substantially the rate of the transfer. No one knows at present how this can best be accomplished, or even if it is possible at all. Right now the broader question of how to restructure international economic, political, and social relations so as to increase the economic development potential of the Third World is probably a much more pertinent and pressing focus of analysis and policy innovation than the question of whether to increase or decrease bilateral American aid.

THE COLD WAR APPROACH

The Cold War approach has avoided one of the main weaknesses of the economic approach—the failure to specify priorities—by clearly and unambiguously positing anti-Communism and gradualism as its major objectives. Sometimes this has been justifiable in terms of American security interests and/or developmental needs and wants of people in the Third World. Moreover, the Cold War approach has, in a sense, "succeeded" to a far greater extent than either of the other two approaches. As we have seen, since 1947 only four underdeveloped countries (China, North Korea, Cuba, and North Vietnam) have acquired Communist governments. No country where the United States made a major

---

[39] Huntington, "Foreign Aid," No. 1, 189.

aid effort has "gone Communist."[40] This record may fall in
South Vietnam, Laos, or elsewhere in the future, but it
stands today. Finally, as an implicit theory of political development the Cold War approach has had the virtue of
stressing the capacity of political and bureaucratic organizations, groups, and individuals to govern, to maintain order,
to get things done. In an important if restricted sense, therefore, this feature of the Cold War approach has made it
superior as political development theory to both the economic and explicit democratic approaches, which take capacity to govern more or less for granted.

Yet the shortcomings of the Cold War approach are also
very great. They have to do partly with the feasibility of
the approach, and even more importantly with its desirability. It is an illusion of many Cold Warriors in America
(and many New Leftists as well) to suppose that the lack
of success of Communism in the Third World is exclusively
or mainly a consequence of American efforts. The evidence
does not, I submit, support such a view. In the great majority
of cases at least three forces have been equal or more powerful inhibitors of radical, revolutionary, and Communist
groups. One is the pervasiveness and strength of conservative (in the classic sense of change-resisting) political values,
attitudes, and behavior patterns among almost all social
strata in underdeveloped countries. Resistance to rapid
change in these countries is massive; it confronts Communists just as it confronts liberal reformers. A second force
is the explicitly anti-Communist ideologies of political actors
and wider publics in much of the Third World, again at all
levels of society. Militant anti-Communism is not limited to
State Department officials or "enlightened publics" in Min-
neapolis, Los Angeles, or Dallas; it is equally or more viru-

[40] See Kauffman and Stalson, "U.S. Assistance," 715-25. Their Table
V on p. 721 lists the twenty major recipients of U.S. economic assistance from 1945 to 1965. Aid to China was small in both absolute
and per capita terms (it was not, of course, one of the twenty).

lent among workers and merchants and landowners in Brazil, or in officers' clubs in Buenos Aires and Jakarta. The third force is nationalism. Like traditional conservatism, nationalism is not a phenomenon that obstructs only Americans then melts away conveniently for Communists. They have to contend with it, too—as, for example, Russian leaders dealing with Fidel Castro have learned. What prevents the United States from realizing this simple truth is mainly a national orientation which sometimes seems to verge on paranoia. Thus if the Cold War approach is "feasible" it is also much less necessary than Americans assume it to be.[41]

But however strongly one views the matter of the feasibility of the Cold War approach, even greater objections may be raised regarding its desirability. Evaluations of the desirability of this approach in specific instances depend on how one views the consequences of radicalism and revolution for (a) economic, social, and political development in the country in question, and (b) vital American security interests more narrowly defined. So far as the first of these is concerned, the point to be stressed here is not that radicalism and revolution are always appropriate, but that it is wrong to assume that they are never appropriate. Yet that is precisely the assumption that has been embedded in almost

[41] Robert W. Tucker has taken this point even further. He suggests that American efforts to defeat Communism in the context of nationalism are actually counterproductive: "With few exceptions," he writes, "in the confrontation of communism with nationalism, it is communism that must lose, particularly if we [Americans] will refrain from intervening." Similarly, George F. Kennan, who formulated the "containment" doctrine in 1947, has stated (as quoted by Tucker): ". . . in most of these situations, in the smaller and developing countries, where there seems to be a threat of communism or of forces close to communism taking over, there are usually countervailing forces which, if we keep out, will make themselves felt. If we intervene, we paralyze them" (both quotations are from "The American Outlook," in Robert E. Osgood, *et al., America and the World: From the Truman Doctrine to Vietnam* [Baltimore: Johns Hopkins Press, 1970], p. 69).

185

all of American doctrine and policy toward the Third World during the last two decades. From the point of view of Third World development, exclusive reliance on such an assumption is simply untenable.

Obviously, this is not to say that the only pathway to progress in the Third World is revolution, a centralized one-party system, a socialist economy, etc. The point is that these pathways are by no means always inferior to other ways. Thus the argument advanced here is not refuted by showing that countries X, Y, and Z made great progress with one of the types of political systems sanctioned by American doctrine. To refute it one would have to show that all of the political pathways not sanctioned by the United States made poor progress and/or that each of these constituted genuine threats to the vital security interests of the United States. I doubt very much whether such a refutation is possible.

Moreover, and very importantly, absolute antipathy for radicalism and revolution is untenable because it ignores the historical fact that radical activities and movements, even when they do not fully succeed (i.e. when they do not produce a genuine revolution), may make contributions to evolutionary development which more moderate, gradualist tactics and reformers cannot make themselves. For example, Albert O. Hirschman, a distinguished economic-development theorist who can hardly be characterized as a "knee-jerk radical," concluded almost a decade ago that "decentralized, unrequited violence is frequently found in the role of indispensable midwife to reform." And he drew the relevant policy inference: "To advocate reforms in Latin America without *tolerating, accepting and sometimes even welcoming and promoting* the only kinds of pressures which have proven to be effective in getting reforms through is to risk being accused of hypocrisy and deception: now that the United States has declared itself in favor of a variety of reforms in Latin America, it should perhaps be apprised of the circumstances and hazards usually associated with such an enterprise."[42]

Of course, American policy toward radical forces and regimes must be determined not only by the capacity of such forces and regimes to advance developmental ends, but also by the degree to which they threaten vital U.S. security interests. The foregoing is a truism; the more controversial question is how vital interests are defined.[43] In the past, the main tendency has been to assume that the mere existence of radical forces, especially—but by no means exclusively—if they are "Communist," threatens vital U.S. interests. As late as 1969, the Rockefeller report on the "quality of life in the Americas" treated all radical action as inimical not only to the development of the countries of the region, but also to the security of the United States.[44] This view, also represented by George Lodge and others discussed earlier, is impossible to "disprove" entirely: it is true that the world is increasingly small; that an explosion anywhere can trigger cataclysm everywhere; that, in Mr. Lodge's words, "chaos and disorganization anywhere" can be interpreted as a threat to our most vital interests.

Yet this perspective may be challenged on at least two grounds. First, it provides no basis for distinguishing various degrees of threat. It impels the United States to be an around-the-world policeman, guarding against radicalism, instability, and anti-Americanism. At some point, of course, implementation of this role becomes an impossibility in practical terms; nevertheless, the *definition itself* provides no criteria for determining when we should and should not

[42] Albert O. Hirschman, *Journeys Toward Progress: Studies of Economic Policy-Making in Latin America* (New York: Twentieth Century Fund, 1963), p. 260 (emphasis added). For a similar argument, with illustrative evidence, see Huntington, *Political Order*, pp. 357-62.

[43] See Chapter 1, n. 8, and Chapter 8, pp. 323-27.

[44] *The Rockefeller Report on the Americas*, esp. pp. 59-65.

implement it. The constraints are practical (resources; domestic political pressures against overseas extension; etc.) rather than theoretical (i.e. the degree of the threat).[45] Finer distinctions than these seem essential unless practicality is to be the only de facto criterion limiting counter-revolutionary efforts and if the United States is to avoid a posture approximating paranoia in an admittedly uncertain world.

Second, what of the quality of life, both in the United States and abroad, in a world in which our actions are determined by such broad and undiscriminating definitions of vital interests and threats to them? Even admitting that some hard-to-measure risk to American security inheres in "allowing" radical, unstable political situations to go unchecked, is this risk great enough that the United States has to take on the moral burden of quelling such activities wherever they may break out? President Kennedy used to say that the world is not tidy and orderly, and that "we are going to have to learn to live with it." This would seem to

[45] The policies of the Nixon administration were perhaps not so different from earlier ones as they may appear. In Latin America, the administration said it would not try to export American democratic forms and processes and stressed the modernizing potential of "many" military elites. However, all "subversives"—indigenous radicals as well as agents of foreign powers and apolitical criminals—were lumped into one category and unambiguously opposed. The "Nixon Doctrine" first announced in Guam in the summer of 1969, which states that the U.S. will help Asian governments with materials and money but not with men to deal with insurgencies, set certain vague limits on the willingness of the United States to intervene in the Far East. However, here too all radicals were lumped together and opposed; and the bases for American restraint were practical and political ("no more Vietnams") rather than the result of any changes in notions about desirable modes of political and economic development. In other words, the same formulas for political development were being used; the difference was in the degree to which the administration said it was willing to involve the United States in implementing them.

188

be not only a practical necessity but a moral imperative in some substantial measure if the quality of the "American way of life" is to remain worth preserving. If the price of protecting ourselves from "threats" is opposing instability, radicalism, and anti-Americanism as often as we can afford to, is not that price too high? And what empirical or moral justification is there for assuming that we in the United States know better than they do what is best for Third World countries?

THE EXPLICIT DEMOCRATIC APPROACH

If, roughly speaking, the economic approach is desirable but usually not feasible, and the Cold War approach is feasible but often not desirable, the explicit democratic approach comes close to being neither desirable nor feasible. This is an oversimplification, of course: almost certainly liberal constitutionalism can and should be a high-priority value in some Third World nations, and the United States can perhaps make a positive contribution to the realization of that goal in some of them. Nevertheless, the chances for liberal democracy in most Third World countries in the foreseeable future are not very great; and the chances that the United States can be effective in advancing the cause of democracy through positive action are probably even smaller. The attempt to promote liberal constitutionalism is often both unrealistic from the point of view of feasibility and ethnocentric from the point of view of desirability.

The ethnocentricity inheres partly in the American tendency to define democracy mainly or exclusively in political terms, whereas many people in the Third World define democracy in economic and social terms as well, often giving greater weight to the latter. Also, American democracy is exclusively linked to the norm of gradualism, to the idea of reform and evolution within a "moving equilibrium"; it does not admit the appropriateness under some circumstances of radical or revolutionary patterns of political

189

change. Finally, exporting democracy is ethnocentric insofar as it fails to take into account the possibility that the
political systems of the Third World may be, and quite
possibly should be, changing in ways that are different from
those that have come before, but which may be more appropriate in those settings than any "developed" patterns
they might emulate.

Moreover, the explicit democratic approach is often not
feasible. It is especially difficult to implement via the direct
approach (focusing on explicitly political variables) mainly
because that approach is so politically sensitive. The indirect
approach (focusing on nonpolitical variables) is more feasible in the sense that it is less politically sensitive, but probably more difficult from the point of view of predicting
and controlling the outcomes. The diplomatic approach,
finally, is perhaps the most feasible; however, as President
Kennedy discovered, its potential for promoting democracy
is also limited. In short, the enormous influence, skills, and
knowledge required to make the explicit democratic approach work are in short supply. Employing this approach
without adequate tools may, in many instances, be worse
than not employing it at all.

Some years ago, Daniel Boorstin warned that "if we
[Americans] rely on the 'philosophy of American democracy' as a weapon in the world-wide struggle, we are relying
on a weapon which may prove a dud." Democratic institutions, he observed, "always grow out-of-doors in a particular climate and cannot be carried about in a flower pot."[46]
I believe that his advice is still relevant, largely because it is
based on an explicit awareness of the uniqueness of the
American experience and the peculiar character of its liberal
tradition. By contrast, in 1957—four years after the appear-

[46] Daniel Boorstin, *The Genius of American Politics*, pp. 4, 177.
Where Boorstin says, "a weapon in the world-wide struggle," I should
have preferred "an instrument of foreign policy toward underdeveloped countries."

190

ance of Boorstin's book—Millikan and Rostow concluded their book proposing a new American foreign aid policy with these lines:

> All peoples of the globe together sail,
>   sail the same voyage,
> All bound to the same destination.[47]

But the peoples of the globe are not all bound to the same destination—nor should they be. We in the United States need to be reminded of this.

I am inclined to believe that for the present and the immediate future the United States usually can do better in regard to Third World political development by doing less (especially in counter-revolutionary directions) than by attempting to do more (especially in the way of exporting various aspects of liberal constitutionalism and American pluralism). We must learn to live with a world of diversity; and to do this we must first understand and overcome our own liberal tradition and its absolutism. Until we have made substantial progress along these lines, we are probably well advised to worry more about how to avoid mistakes of commission than about how to correct those of omission.

We cannot, of course, abandon theorizing. Theorizing is inevitable; good theorizing is desirable. Some concepts and doctrines, implicit or explicit, will continue to guide our initiatives and reactions to politics in the Third World. At the same time, we need to learn how to perceive, live with, and even welcome the variety of political systems and solutions in other countries. The theoretical need for abstraction and the need to recognize diversity are in tension, to be sure. To resolve the tensions wisely is to face a dilemma; yet it is a dilemma which all—policymakers and scholars alike—must face. There is no defensible escape.

[47] Millikan and Rostow, *A Proposal*, p. 151. The chapter title is "The American Mission."

We shall return to this theme in the final chapter. Now, let us turn to political development theories among American social scientists; the potential utilities and limitations of these theories for policy; and the extent to which the theories also reflect the inarticulate assumptions of the American liberal tradition.

PART II: Theories

Political Development Theories, 1945-1970

THE preceding chapters have focused on the implicit theories—doctrines—of political development embedded in U.S. aid programs and related policies and activities. In the next three chapters, the focus expands to include the more explicit theories of social scientists.

There are two main reasons why these chapters on theories are relevant and complementary to the materials on doctrines. First, if the thinking of aid officials about Third World political development constitutes one type of "expert" opinion on the subject, the thinking of scholars and social scientists surely constitutes another. The theories are of interest as part of the general body of expert opinion on political development in these countries. They constitute another kind of resource with which Americans can understand political changes in the Third World and assess U.S. policies in relation to such changes. How great a resource were the theories? How useful were they to policymakers? How useful might they have been had they been utilized more thoroughly?

Examining the theories also enables us to determine to what extent theorists, like policymakers, were affected by the largely inarticulated liberal tradition. Surely the argument that American attitudes toward political development have been profoundly affected by the Lockean premises would be strengthened if it could be shown that they also affected the thinking of scholars, whose training and occupational roles were designed to reduce the distortions produced by limited national perspectives. Since Mannheim, certainly, few thoughtful people have doubted that the surroundings of scholars—their social and economic class, their nation, their cultural values, their political ideologies—have effects on their scholarship. But which surroundings? What kinds of effects? To what extent? Chapter 7 in particular explores similarities and differences between the doctrines and the theories, with these questions in mind, and notes some significant implications of the comparisons made.

In order to be able to assess the usefulness of the theories and the degree to which they have reflected the liberal assumptions, it is necessary first to describe the content of the theories—to review and analyze the major ways in which political development was defined and explained (in the causal sense) in the scholarly literature in comparative politics in the United States from 1945 to 1970. This span of years corresponds almost perfectly to the period covered in the treatment of doctrines in the preceding chapters. In order to get a richer sense of these notions of political development, it will be illuminating also to touch briefly on the main kinds of research methods and intellectual styles that the scholars employed.

Overview. Since what follows is abstract and rather detailed, it may be helpful to summarize in advance the basic argument about the main theoretical approaches to political development during this period.[1]

Causal theories of political development between 1945 and 1970 break down into three main types. The first two defined political development as political modernization and political democracy. The main difference between them was in the kinds of causal variables stressed: The first, which was dominant in the literature until the early 1950s at least, stressed legal-formal and various "historical" variables. The second stressed "informal" economic, sociological, and psychological variables. This second type was the most influential during the postwar decades.

The third type, which gained prominence in the mid-1960s, defined political development in terms of will, skill,

[1] See also Table 5 on p. 241; and, for important details about the meaning of the term "theory" in this discussion and about the scope and method of the coverage in this chapter, see the Appendix.

capacity, and choice. Writers in this category treated political development not as dependent on legal-formal factors or vast socioeconomic and psychological forces, but rather as independent variables explaining various social, economic, and other political phenomena. Little attention was devoted to explaining political development, so defined; rather, political development explained other things. Burgess, Friedrich, and Finer are examples of type-one theorists; Lipset, Lerner, Almond, Verba, and Pye are examples of type two; Apter, Eisenstadt, Huntington, Hirschman, and Ilchman are examples of type three.

LEGAL-FORMALISM

At least until 1950, the mainstream of comparative politics scholarship in the United States employed what may be called a legal-formal theory of political development. With qualifications (to be noted), this body of scholarship defined political development as constitutional democracy, and explained it in terms of legal-formal variables and a variety of "historical" factors.

The legal-formal approach had its origins well before the period under review. It had very nearly monopolized American political science from the middle of the nineteenth century—when the discipline may be said to have gotten its start in the United States—to around 1900. It remained the dominant approach, both in political science generally and in comparative politics in particular, through most of the first postwar decade. Indeed, the subsequent impact of behavioral and interdisciplinary research in the field of comparative politics has dimmed memories of the long-standing dominance of the legal-formal approach. The major textbooks in comparative politics until well after 1950, for example, continued to be those authored by Friedrich, by Finer, and by Carter, Ranney, and Herz.[2]

[2] See Claude E. Hawley and Lewis A. Dexter, "Recent Political Science Research in American Universities," *American Political Sci-*

In this literature a consensus on the nature of political development existed. To be sure, the term "political development" was not used often, and the agreement was partly tacit; but this consensus was wide and deep. Political development was identified with the attributes of English and American liberal constitutional democracy. This notion of political progress was simply accepted; it was one of those ideas no one (or almost no one) challenged. Agreement on this proposition was if anything even broader and more solidly based than the consensus on how to explain the main characteristics of political systems and how to do research into such questions.

Having defined and described political development as constitutional democracy, the legal-formal approach explained it in terms of constitutions and "historical" factors. The theory said that democracy was associated with and caused by constitutions and statutes that prescribe such features as separation of powers; federalism; regular, competitive, popular elections; the secret ballot; single-member-district rather than proportional representation; and the like.[3] The "historical" factors included an amorphous and shifting list of contextual variables like ethnicity, religion, race, class, wealth, climate, geography, demography, and political traditions. Among these "historical" explanations,

ence Review, 46, No. 2 (June 1952), 470-85, esp. pp. 484-85; Gabriel A. Almond, The American People and Foreign Policy (New York: Harcourt, Brace, 1950), pp. 154-55; Harry Eckstein, "A Perspective on Comparative Politics, Past and Present," in Harry Eckstein and David E. Apter, eds., Comparative Politics: A Reader (New York: Free Press, 1963), pp. 3-32; Gabriel A. Almond and G. Bingham Powell, Comparative Politics: A Developmental Approach (Boston: Little, Brown, 1966), pp. 1-8.

[3] This theory is not, of course, a tautology. Constitutions are documents or common law rules. Constitutionalism is political behavior that corresponds relatively closely to these documents or rules. In fact, most countries with constitutions do not have constitutionalism. This fact makes the legal-formal theory interesting: it obviously is not true by definition. Whether or not constitutionalism accompanies constitutions is an empirical question which may be confirmed or disconfirmed by evidence.

the economic interpretation was probably stronger than the rest, and the seeds of what came later to be known as social-system and political-culture approaches can be found. But these informal variables were much less emphasized and systematically employed before the early 1950s than after.

Thus, explanations such as these lay at the heart of this literature as theory. To a considerable extent, however, the methodologies and intellectual styles of these writers disguised the theoretical core. Books were generally organized country-by-country rather than topically—this was the "configurative" rather than the comparative style. The methodologies were mainly historical and legalistic. A greater emphasis lay on description than on explanation. Those few quantitative data that were used were rather elementary, descriptive statistics. With few exceptions, experts in comparative politics were not very self-consciously theoretical.[4]

Moreover, the principal geographic focus of these studies was on Europe—the United Kingdom, France, Germany, the U.S.S.R., Italy, and other European countries. In the texts and research reports of the day, mostly ad-hoc contrasts and comparisons were made among these countries or between them and the United States. Since two great wars had been fought over the issues of democracy versus dictatorship of the Right, and since the Cold War seemed to raise the issue of democracy versus dictatorship or totalitarianism of the Left, much scholarship during the early post-1945 period was also designed to illuminate the nature of these two polar types.

THE BREAK WITH FORMALISM

From the early fifties through most of the sixties the most influential writings about political development em-

[4] Bryce's *Modern Democracies* was an early prototype of the modal tendency. Friedrich's *Constitutional Government and Democracy* was an excellent example of a more self-consciously theoretical treatment. Both works are well analyzed in Eckstein, "A Perspective on Comparative Politics," in Eckstein and Apter, *Comparative Politics.*

ployed what I shall call the economic, the social-system, and the political-culture approaches. It is important to underscore the fact that these years comprise much the greater share of the period under review, and that these theories had a more profound and lasting influence on scholarly thinking than any of the others employed during the postwar period.

According to these theories, political development was a dependent variable defined as political modernization and/or political democracy. (The meanings assigned to these terms will be discussed shortly.) In conceptualizing political development as a dependent variable, and in defining it as democracy or movement toward democracy, the "post-formalist" approaches did not differ significantly from the earlier one. They differed very greatly, however, in the types of variables they employed to explain political development thus defined. Not legal-formal variables such as constitutions and statutes and organization charts, but economic variables such as wealth and industrialization, sociological variables such as number of voluntary associations or openness of the class system, and psychological variables such as empathy or egalitarianism were seen as the main determinants of political modernization and democracy. By "the break with formalism" I mean this substantive shift from legal-formal to informal economic, sociological, and psychological explanatory variables that occurred in the fifties and sixties, and that had such a massive influence in American scholarship. Before examining these explanations, however, let us consider the definitions of political development that were used.

DEFINITIONS

The criteria of *political modernization* employed in the 1950s and early 1960s are clearer now than they were then. In those years these definitions were even more ambiguous, imprecise, and confusing than they are today; worse, there

200

was less awareness of the problems, so that the confusion often went unexamined and uncorrected for a long time. Gradually, however, scholars began to address some of these definitional problems. Although it is possible to argue that the more they concerned themselves with definitions, the more they disagreed, this would be a misleading interpretation. Superficially, it appeared that there was little agreement. More profoundly, however, by the mid-1960s scholars had begun to reach a partial consensus about the main components of the phenomenon they were calling political modernization. In retrospect, we can say that the following elements most often went into the broad concept of political modernization: national integration, or nationhood; governmental authority, or statehood; and political participation.[5]

Almost all writers recognized the problem of *nationhood* (national integration, national unity, national identity) as an essential element of political modernization. This meant that for a national political system to be modern, its members had to know that they were part of the nation and have some sort of commitment or loyalty to it. Similarly, almost all writers felt that political modernization involved *statehood*, or governmental capacity, authority, and power to penetrate, regulate, and draw resources from society. The third dimension, political *participation*, has been called by

[5] For a similar list and an excellent discussion, see Samuel P. Huntington, "Political Development and Political Decay," *World Politics*, 17, No. 3 (April 1965), 386-88 and ff. The relatively high degree of consensus emerging among many scholars at this time on the dimensions of political modernization is also reflected in Almond and Powell, *Comparative Politics*, pp. 35ff; Rustow, *A World of Nations*, esp. pp. 35-104, 126-32; Lucian W. Pye, *Aspects of Political Development* (Boston: Little, Brown, 1966), pp. 45-48. In the latter work, before isolating three dimensions of political modernization on which scholars seemed generally agreed, Pye elaborated ten definitions in order to "illuminate a situation of semantic confusion." This widely read list of definitions exaggerated the admittedly substantial confusion since, as Pye noted, the definitions overlapped, and considerable argreement underlay the confusion (*ibid.*, pp. 33-45).

201

one scholar the "one characteristic of political modernization and political development which is most frequently emphasized." The idea was: modernization means mass mobilization; mass mobilization means increased political participation; and increased participation was seen as a key element in political modernization.[6]

But we have said that political development meant not only political modernization but also *political democracy*. In fact, political development in its "highest" or "truest" form was usually equated, implicitly[7] if not explicitly,[8] in

[6] The passage quoted is from Huntington, "Political Development and Political Decay," p. 388. Of course, other concepts than these three were sometimes included as dimensions of political modernization. For example, some writers included "equality" or "welfare" or "distribution"; others, "structural differentiation and specialization." However, these latter concepts were used less consistently than the three I have mentioned; moreover, when they were used, their meanings were even more ambiguous and imprecise than those three.

[7] For example, Gabriel A. Almond, "Introduction," in Almond and James S. Coleman, eds., *The Politics of the Developing Areas* (Princeton: Princeton University Press, 1960), pp. 3-64; Almond and Powell, *Comparative Politics*; Pye, *Aspects of Political Development*, and *Politics, Personality, and Nation Building: Burma's Search for Identity* (New Haven: Yale University Press, 1962); Gabriel A. Almond and Sidney Verba, *The Civic Culture: Political Attitudes and Democracy in Five Nations* (Princeton: Princeton University Press, 1963); and many of the essays in the multivolume Studies in Political Development series sponsored by the Committee on Comparative Politics of the Social Science Research Council and published by Princeton University Press.

[8] For example, Joseph LaPalombara, "Bureaucracy and Political Development: Notes, Queries, Dilemmas," in LaPalombara, ed., *Bureaucracy and Political Development* (Princeton: Princeton University Press, 1963), pp. 35-37; Frederick W. Frey, "Political Development, Power, and Communications in Turkey," in Lucian W. Pye, ed., *Communications and Political Development* (Princeton: Princeton University Press, 1963), p. 301; Harold D. Lasswell, "The Policy Sciences of Development," *World Politics*, 17, No. 2 (January 1965), 290-91; Daniel Lerner, *The Passing of Traditional Society* (Glencoe: Free Press, 1958), p. 64; Fred W. Riggs, "Bureaucrats and Political Development: A Paradoxical View," in LaPalombara, ed., *Bureaucracy and Political Development*, p. 120.

the long run if not in the short run,[9] with liberal, constitutional democracy. The concepts and indices used, in turn, to describe democracy were usually "rough and subjective."[10] Often writers evaded or ignored the problem of definition altogether.[11] Sometimes English or American democracy was explicitly taken as the standard of democracy;[12] when no particular country was cited as the model, usually one of these two countries was still the implicit standard.[13] Thus, in one way or another political development usually turned out to mean democracy;[14] and democracy was almost

[9] For example, Lerner, *Passing of Traditional Society*, p. 64; Lasswell, "The Policy Sciences," 290.

[10] The phrase is used by Everett Hagen with reference to his own classification of political systems ("A Framework for Analyzing Economic and Political Change," in Robert E. Asher, *et al.*, *Development of the Emerging Countries: An Agenda for Research* [Washington, D.C.: The Brookings Institution, 1962], p. 4), but it has wider applicability. It applies, for example, to the following studies: Almond and Verba, *The Civic Culture*; James S. Coleman, "Conclusion," in Almond and Coleman, eds., *The Politics of the Developing Areas*, pp. 532-76; Lipset, *Political Man*, Chap. 2 and *The First New Nation: The United States in Historical and Comparative Perspective* (New York: Basic Books, 1963), Chap. 7.

[11] Thus, some of the contributors to the Princeton series on political development simply refused to define the term, even though they used it frequently. It was not uncommon to see it bandied about without any immediately clear indication of what it stood for. Also, political development has been equated with political change and with political history; for examples and criticism of these usages, see Huntington, "Political Development and Political Decay," pp. 392-93, 390. With relatively few exceptions, however, it was possible to discern at least in a general sense what an author meant by political development, even if he did not give an explicit definition.

[12] For example, see the citations to Frey and LaPalombara in n. 8 above.

[13] For example, the works by Almond and Powell, Almond and Verba, and Lipset, cited in nn. 2, 7, and 10, above.

[14] Exceptions to this general tendency in the literature of the fifties and early sixties existed, of course. Among the exceptions were works by such scholars as David Apter, Zbigniew Brzezinski, Karl W. Deutsch, S. N. Eisenstadt, Rupert Emerson, Guy Pauker, Dankwart

always defined in terms of some characteristic or set of characteristics abstracted from Western, liberal, constitutionalism—e.g. political competitiveness, political pluralism, polyarchy, regular and popular elections, subsystem autonomy, elite responsiveness to popular demands and interest group pressures, and the like. When, on rare occasions, "hard," quantitative, rigorous indices were used instead of the rough and subjective ones, they tended to be formalistic and unrealistic.[15]

Tocqueville's *Democracy in America* (1840), Almond and Verba's *The Civic Culture* (1963), and Lipset's *Political Man* (1960) and *The First New Nation* (1963) illustrate the "rough and subjective" character of definitions of political development as democracy.[16] (We use Tocqueville as an example only to show that the precision of definitions of democracy has not necessarily increased greatly in nearly a century and a half.) Tocqueville believed that democracy was an inevitable and irreversible development throughout the whole Western world. He wanted to understand it in order to ease the transition to democracy in France. He saw

---

A. Rustow, and Howard Wriggins. As will be indicated below, the generalization was less valid in the latter half of the sixties.

[15] See especially Lyle W. Shannon, "Is Level of Development Related to Capacity for Self-Government?" *American Journal of Economics and Sociology*, 17 (July 1958), 367-81; Phillips Cutright, "National Political Development: Measurement and Analysis," *American Sociological Review*, 28 (April 1963), 253-64; and, for a critique of Cutright, Deane E. Neubauer, "Some Conditions of Democracy," *American Political Science Review*, 61, No. 4 (December 1967), 1,002-9. See also the exchange between Cutright and Neubauer, *American Political Science Review*, 62, No. 2 (June 1968), 578-81.

[16] In fairness to Lipset, it should be noted that, to my knowledge, he does not himself employ the term "political development" in his writings. He is normally included, however, in discussions of prominent political development theorists, and his concerns, interests, and values, as manifested in *Political Man* and his other writings, are very similar to those of other social scientists who do use the term, e.g., Almond and Verba in *The Civic Culture*.

in America the finest flowering of the democratic form of government, and from this premise it was logical to study American democracy in order to achieve his larger purpose. There was no problem of defining the characteristics of democracy beforehand; such a definition was already embodied in the American polity. As he says,

> It is not, then, merely to satisfy a legitimate curiosity that I have examined America; my wish has been to find instruction by which we may ourselves profit. . . . I have selected the nation, *from among those who have undergone it, in which its development has been the most peaceful and the most complete,* in order to discern its natural consequences, and, if it be possible, to distinguish the means by which it may be rendered profitable.[17]

Almond and Verba used a similar strategy. They chose five "democratic" countries and analyzed their political cultures, using the similarities and differences to draw inferences about why Britain and the United States have more "stable and democratic" polities than Germany, Italy, and Mexico. They used no rigorous definition or test to show that Britain and the United States are more democratic: theirs was a "rough and subjective"—and in this case valid—judgment.[18]

Lipset, in a well known article later reprinted as part of his book *Political Man*, divided groups of European and Latin American countries into subgroups of more and less democratic countries. He then gathered social and economic data on these countries in order to make a crude test of the hypothesis that economic development and political democracy are positively related. He found that they were. Ostensibly, the criterion Lipset used for democracy in Latin America was "whether a given country has had a history of

[17] Alexis de Tocqueville, *Democracy in America*, Henry Reeve, trans. (New York: Schocken Books, 1961), I, lxxxi-ii (emphasis added).

[18] Almond and Verba, *The Civic Culture*.

more or less free elections for most of the post-World War I period."[19] Yet, by Lipset's own reference, the actual basis for the classifications he made was not this criterion at all, but rather the subjective judgments of a few experts, none of whom wrote after 1950, most of whom wrote in the 1940s, and two of whom (James Bryce and Francisco García Calderón) wrote and thus made their selections of post-World War I democracies before the outbreak of World War I![20] In fact, at least two of the seven Latin American countries that Lipset, with the aid of the experts, finally classified as democratic failed to meet his ostensible standard for inclusion: free elections occurred in Argentina and Brazil substantially less than half the time between the end of World War I and 1960. Moreover, such free elections as occurred in Colombia, another of the seven "democratic" countries, limited participation to a minority of the adult population. A fourth country, Mexico, Lipset called democratic while candidly drawing a more or less accurate sketch of its politics. The other three cases were democratic beyond dispute.

In a subsequent book, using different but similar criteria, Lipset chose four democracies, the United States and three countries from the Old British Commonwealth (Great Britain, Canada, and Australia), and showed how, under varying social conditions and historical circumstances, widely different value patterns can still support a democratic political process.[21] Again, the definition of democracy in the four countries was not rigorous. All of which is not to deny the value of these studies: the strategies adopted were often sensible in terms of the authors' objectives. I mean only to

[19] Lipset, *Political Man*, p. 48.

[20] *Ibid.*, pp. 48, 48n. The views of these experts are summarized in an article, which Lipset cites, by Arthur P. Whitaker, "The Pathology of Democracy in Latin America," *American Political Science Review*, 44, No. 1 (March 1950), esp. pp. 113-14.

[21] Lipset, *The First New Nation*, Chap. 7.

point out that the definitions of the dependent variable are "rough and subjective."

Another group of studies used less open but still "rough and subjective" indices of political development. One of them, by James S. Coleman, may serve as an illustration. Coleman writes, "The political systems covered in this survey are listed . . . according to the degree of competitiveness (competitive, semi-competitive, and authoritarian) and degree of political modernity (modern, mixed, and traditional). These classifications have been made with a profound awareness of the gross character of the judgments they represent, as well as of the fact that most of the systems concerned are in transition. The present classification is regarded as both tentative and disputable."[22] Coleman then investigated the correlations between these categories of political systems and various social and economic variables, in order to test his hypothesis that there is a positive correlation between economic development and political competitiveness.[23]

Still another group used considerably more precise measures, but at the cost of narrowing, formalizing, and reducing the significance of the concepts. Phillips Cutright, for example, wanted to test the hypothesis that political development is "interdependent" with educational systems, economic development, communications systems, urbanization, and labor force distribution. Political development is conceptualized as a relatively high level of "complex and specialized national political institutions." This concept is operationalized in an incredibly complicated manner that is, for all its elaboration, still rather formalistic.[24] As he says,

[22] "Conclusion," in Almond and Coleman, *The Politics of the Developing Areas*, pp. 533-35.

[23] *Ibid.*, p. 538. Another study using essentially the same approach is Hagen, "A Framework for Analyzing Economic and Political Change," pp. 1-8.

[24] Cutright, "National Political Development," p. 256.

207

"Operationally, we bank heavily on the role played by political parties in national political life in measuring political development." As his operational definition indicates, he also relies heavily on parliaments as an indicator. Neither the *number* of parties nor the *number of years* in which parliaments meet are by themselves very good indicators of political development. The reason for these narrow measures is not hard to find: "The index is, of course, heavily dependent upon available data." All of Africa finally had to be omitted, Cutright reports, because of inadequate data.[25] Another scholar with a "hard" but not very meaningful measure of political development is Lyle W. Shannon, who used formal independence from colonialism as an index of "capacity for self-government," and found a correlation with the level of economic development. But his work said nothing about the non-legal-formal characteristics of the polity, nor about political development after independence.[26]

Thus, scholars writing about political development defined it as political modernization and democracy. They did not spend much time elaborating or justifying their definitions, for they believed—most of them—that political modernization and democracy were self-evidently the goals of these political systems. The tacit view seemed to be that it was unnecessary to devote much attention to spelling out the nature and the normative aspects of political development; for everyone "knew" in some intuitive way what political development was. More interesting to them was the question of the conditions of political development thus understood. It was to this question that they devoted most of their attention, and it was here that they were more explicit and precise.

EXPLANATIONS

The well-known article by Lipset referred to above illustrates the kinds of intellectual emphases, focuses, and preoc-

[25] *Ibid.*, pp. 255, 255n.
[26] Shannon, "Is Development Related to Self-Government?"

cupations that were dominant. In this article, as throughout his book *Political Man*, Lipset's main theme is the socio-economic bases or conditions of democracy. It has already been remarked how casually he defined democracy, his dependent variable. The independent variables, however, were elaborated much more carefully, with abundant quantitative information. At the end of the essay Lipset wrote a "methodological appendix" in which he provided a diagram indicating some "possible conditions and consequences" of democracy. The conditions he listed were: an open class system, economic wealth, an "equalitarian" value system, a capitalist economy, literacy, and high participation in voluntary organizations. Lipset's "diagram" or "model" (he uses both terms) of the "syndrome of conditions" most frequently found in democratic regimes represents precisely the array of types of causal variables that were most often relied upon during this period by the majority of influential scholars.[27] Wealth, a capitalist economy, and literacy, are all illustrations of the economic approach. An open class system and participation in voluntary organizations are examples of the social-system approach. And an equalitarian value system is an illustration of the political-culture approach.

Lipset's syndrome is representative of the major types of explanations of political development in at least one other important respect. His set of "possible conditions" of de-

[27] Lipset, *Political Man*, p. 74. We should note Lipset's statement that the diagram "is not intended as a complete model of the general social conditions associated with the emergence of democracy, but as a way of clarifying the methodological point concerning the multivariate character of relationships in a total social system" (p. 75). This statement would not seem to preclude use of the diagram as an illustration of a substantive as well as a methodological argument. In the first place, the examples of conditions and consequences Lipset uses in the model are not just random or fortuitous; they in fact summarize much of his substantive argument. More importantly, Lipset's statement seems directed against the inference that his list of conditions and consequences is complete, rather than against the idea that the specific kinds of conditions and consequences he does list are important and deserve emphasis.

mocracy as a generic phenomenon turns out to be, on close inspection, more nearly approximated in the United States than in any other democracy. In other words, Lipset's extensive comparative research led to the conclusion that the conditions that tend to be associated with democracies (and which in the text he says tend to *cause* democracy) happen to be found most completely and richly in one nation, the United States. It is possible, of course, that Lipset is right on this point; but for him to be right, at a minimum democracy would have to be more fully and richly realized in the United States than in any other nation. If this were not the case, then one would be justified in inferring that Lipset had confused certain social conditions of political life in his own country with the conditions of democracy in most democratic countries.[28]

Lipset's writings, especially *Political Man* and *The First New Nation*, are illustrative of modal tendencies in the theories in other respects too, as we shall see below. Now, however, let us consider the three most prominent types of explanations of political development during the fifties and most or all of the sixties: the economic, the social-system, and the political-culture approaches.

The Economic Approach. The main idea of the economic approach is that there is a positive correlation between level of economic development and the chances for democracy. More precisely: Among the countries of the world, the higher the per capita GNP, the greater the frequency of competitive political systems and polyarchies. Often, in this approach, economic development was seen as the main requisite or cause of political democracy. Actually, there is a great deal of data to support the former (correlational, not causal) proposition. Using slightly different but roughly

[28] In subsequent work, Lipset modified some of these conclusions. Thus, in *The First New Nation*, he found that under certain conditions elitist values could sustain democratic politics as well as egalitarian values could (see n. 21, above).

210

comparable indices of democracy and of economic development, Adelman and Morris, Coleman, Cutright, Dahl, Hagen, Lipset, Russett, and others all have found such a correlation.[29]

However, the correlations between economic development and political democracy are far from perfect, and correlations in and of themselves say nothing about cause. Some countries with a very low level of economic development (e.g. India) are democratic, whereas some well-off countries (e.g. Argentina, the U.S.S.R., France) have had very unstable democracies and even dictatorships. Recent studies seem to suggest that the correlation between level of economic development and prospects for democracy in nation-states is weakest among very poor and relatively rich states and strongest among middle-income nations. For example, Dahl observes that when per capita income is in the vicinity of $200-$250 the chances of competitive politics appear to be so low that variations in per capita GNP do not matter; similarly, where per capita income is in the vicinity of $700-$800 the chances of competitive politics are so high that variations in per capita GNP do not matter.[30] The correlation is strongest (though still not perfect) among countries in the middle range.

It is worthwhile to note some further limitations in this kind of crude correlational analysis. First, the relationships are between *levels* of economic and political development, not *rates*. There is no good reason to suppose that the posi-

[29] Irma Adelman and Cynthia Taft Morris, *Society, Politics, and Economic Development: A Quantitative Approach* (Baltimore: Johns Hopkins Press, 1967); James S. Coleman, "Conclusion," in Almond and Coleman, *The Politics of the Developing Areas*; Cutright, "National Political Development"; Robert A. Dahl, *Modern Political Analysis*, 2nd edn. (Englewood Cliffs, N.J.: Prentice-Hall, 1970), pp. 66-69; Hagen, "A Framework"; Lipset, *Political Man*, Chap. 2; Bruce M. Russett, *Trends in World Politics* (New York: Macmillan, 1965), Chap. 8; Russett, *et al.*, *World Handbook of Political and Social Indicators* (New Haven: Yale University Press, 1964), pp. 293-303.

[30] Dahl, *Political Analysis*, pp. 67-68.

tive relationships that have been identified are necessarily linear; hence at any point in time, increases in the level of economic development are not necessarily associated with increases in the level of democracy. Second, one should not equate political democracy with political stability. Normally, political democracies are by definition stable; but all stable regimes obviously are not democratic. Finally, at high and low extremes economic development is probably positively related to political stability; in the middle range, however, there appears to be no strong relationship. In fact economic development can be a destabilizing force, as numerous authors have shown.[31]

Thus, although there is a firm empirical base for much of the economic theory of political development as just described, the theory is highly imperfect and must be qualified in important respects. How is it, then, that the theory was so influential among scholars in the United States, where it was sometimes used without the appropriate cautions? We can identify at least two major reasons for this influence.

The first is that the theory was congenial to a highly influential strain in the history of American political thought. One immediately thinks of the works of Europeans, especially Karl Marx, as classic cases of the economic approach to politics. But intellectual history in the United States has also been receptive to this idea. There is a long tradition in American social thought regarding the importance of economic factors—notably property—for political liberty and the conduct of political affairs.[32] There is also a tradition, recently rediscovered, of looking at the relations of the

[31] See the recent work of Ivo and Rosalind Feierabend, Francine Frankel, Ted Robert Gurr, Mancur Olson, Jr., and Samuel P. Huntington, some cited in Chap. 1, n. 51.

[32] David Fellman has traced this strain from its origins in seventeenth-century England through the end of the Jacksonian era, which he takes to be about 1850 ("The Economic Interpretation in Early American Political Theory," Ph.D. dissertation, Yale University, 1934).

economy, as the independent variable, to the polity, as the dependent variable.[33]

Coming on the heels of this tradition and himself a part of it, Charles A. Beard presented the economic approach to politics more forcefully than any other prominent American scholar. He also gave it the aura of science.[34] On the research front, this meant that Beard's thesis absorbed much of the interest in the "new science of politics" that was developing as a reaction to the legal-formalism of the time.[35] On the teaching side, Beard has had a pervasive influence on the teaching of American history.[36] For decades American elementary and high school pupils have been socialized to Beard's doctrine, even though the first systematic effort to test Beard's thesis (advanced in his *Economic Interpretation of the Constitution*) was not published until forty years after the book's appearance in 1913.[37] Against this historical

[33] This tradition has been interpreted as a "common theme" in "liberalism, classical economics, Marxism, conservatism and Saint Simonism—[as well as] much of modern sociology" (Reinhard Bendix, *Max Weber: An Intellectual Portrait* [Garden City, N.Y.: Doubleday, Anchor, 1962], pp. 487 88). See also Sheldon S. Wolin, *Politics and Vision* (Boston: Little, Brown, 1960), Chaps. 9, 10.

[34] See Charles A. Beard, *An Economic Interpretation of the Constitution* (New York: Macmillan, 1935), Chap. I, "Historical Interpretation in the United States."

[35] See Morton White, *Social Thought in America: The Revolt Against Formalism* (New York: Viking Press, 1949), pp. 74, 125-27; Lee Benson, *Turner and Beard: American Historical Writing Reconsidered* (New York: Free Press, 1960); and Robert E. Osgood, *Ideals and Self-Interest in America's Foreign Relations: The Great Transformation of the Twentieth Century* (Chicago: University of Chicago Press, 1953, 1955), pp. 371-76.

[36] See Maurice Blinkoff, "The Influence of Charles A. Beard upon American Historiography," *University of Buffalo Studies*, 12 (May 1936), 4-84.

[37] Both Benson and Robert E. Brown, *Charles A. Beard and the Constitution* (Princeton: Princeton University Press, 1956), make this point. Brown's book in 1956 and Forrest McDonald, *We, the People: The Economic Origins of the Constitution* (Chicago: University of Chicago Press, 1958), appear to have been the first systematic tests of Beard's thesis.

213

background, it is not surprising that Americans writing about political development should be very much interested in its economic roots.

A second reason for the strong influence of the economic approach in academic circles, and perhaps indirectly on the policy community as well, was that it had about it the aura of social *science*. This made it appear more rigorous, elegant, and enlightening than it really was. For instance, Lipset made much in his "methodological appendix" of the notions of multicausality (rather than single-factor explanations, like Weber's Protestant ethic), "statistical" (rather than causal) relationships, and other cautions. Yet in the text he repeatedly asserts causality, argues that economic development, education, and other single factors taken by themselves are independent causes of political democracy, and from these premises makes policy inferences which seem to flow naturally enough from his substantive argument but which are unjustified if one takes his methodological remarks seriously.[38]

The stress on science also obscured important weaknesses in the conceptualization and modes of measurement of the dependent variable. Thus, as mentioned earlier, in Lipset's *Political Man* the ostensible criterion of democracy in Latin America was not used in fact, with the result that the number of democracies was exaggerated. Additionally, Lipset used different criteria in Latin America and in Europe, partly in order to increase the number of democratic cases in the former region. The dichotomous classification system he used was a crude instrument which, by forcing countries into one of only two categories, grossly exaggerated both similarities and differences among them. Moreover, some of the classifications were extremely dubious. For example, he classified Argentina, Brazil, Colombia, and Mexico as "democracies and unstable dictatorships," as contrasted with Bolivia, the Dominican Republic, Ecuador, Guatemala, Pan-

---

[38] For instance, see Lipset, *Political Man*, pp. 5on., 57, 417.

ama, Peru, and Venezuela, which are called "stable dictatorships."[39]

The Social-System Approach. According to the social-system approach, the main requisites of political development, defined as constitutional democracy, are to be found in certain attributes of social structure and process. A considerable variety of hypotheses employing this approach have been specified. Here are the more common types.

1. Social Correlates of Democracy. One hypothesis, or set of hypotheses, is this: Political democracy is correlated with and caused by urbanization, education, literacy, exposure to and consumption of mass media, health facilities per capita, good housing, and the like. The view is, in short, that "social development," as indexed by high scores on scales measuring the foregoing kinds of variables, correlates positively with political democracy. These "social correlates of democracy" seem pretty well established empirically.[40] Like the economic correlates of democracy (with which they overlap to some degree), however, these factors are related only very imperfectly and in complex ways to democracy. In other words, the relationship is positive but very general and complicated. It is not "one for one."

2. Equality and Democracy. A second hypothesis is that the more equally resources like land, education, and income are distributed in a society, the greater are the prospects for democracy. Social and economic equality, in other words, is a requisite for democracy. Also, societies where the distribution of socioeconomic resources is greater will tend to be more politically stable. As with the first two hypotheses, this one tends to be generally true, but here again deviant cases are numerous and significant.[41]

---

[39] *Ibid.*, pp. 48-49.

[40] See the items cited in n. 29 above; see also William Buchanan and Hadley Cantril, *How Nations See Each Other* (Urbana: University of Illinois Press, 1953), pp. 30-37.

[41] See, for example, Bruce M. Russett, "Inequality and Instability:

3. Voluntary Associations and Democracy. This approach has a tradition at least as old as Tocqueville and as recent as David Truman. To generalize about so diverse a group is always a mistake in part, but we may gain some understanding if we try to formulate the central theme: A complex infrastructure of groups provides the differential centers of decisionmaking, the shared power base, and the overall social vitality that are required for democracy. The case for this is put not only on moral grounds ("group participation in politics is a good thing because each group ought to have its say"), but also on existential grounds ("group participation is functional because it is necessary for the vitality of the system and because there are serious cognitive limits on men's capacity for central planning").[42] This is the core of the "pluralist" explanation of democracy. A great deal of the literature in the fifties and early sixties was shaped by this theory, which is still influential. Recently, the utility of this approach as a descriptive, analytic, and explanatory tool in non-American cultures has been challenged. Partly for these reasons, and partly because of the paucity of appropriate data, it is hard to assess its standing as empirical theory.[43] At the very minimum, how-

The Relation of Land Tenure to Politics," *World Politics*, 16, No. 3 (April 1964), 442-54; Dahl, *Political Analysis*, pp. 69-74.

[42] On the latter point, see especially Robert A. Dahl and Charles E. Lindblom, *Politics, Economics, and Welfare* (New York: Harper, 1953), pp. 78-88; and two articles by Lindblom, "The Science of Muddling Through," *Public Administration Review*, 19 (Spring 1959), 79-88, and "Policy Analysis," *American Economic Review*, 47 (June 1958), 298-312.

[43] Among the best studies employing this approach are William Kornhauser, *The Politics of Mass Society* (New York: Free Press, 1959); Joseph LaPalombara, *Interest Groups in Italian Politics* (Princeton: Princeton University Press, 1964); Philippe Schmitter, *Interest Conflict and Political Change in Brazil* (Stanford: Stanford University Press, 1971); Robert E. Scott, *Mexican Government in Transition*, rev. edn. (Urbana: University of Illinois Press, 1964); Myron Weiner, *The Politics of Scarcity* (Chicago: University of Chicago Press, 1962). All of these works explicitly employ an interest-group

ever, it seems fair to say that the theory must be adapted for use in non-American settings rather than transferred *in toto*.

4. The Middle Class and Democracy. A fourth manifestation of the social-system approach is the linkage often made between the size of the middle class, or its rate of growth, and democracy. Neither of these two hypotheses is quite the same as Aristotle's proposition that democracy is related to "a class structure bulging toward the middle."[44] But the latter may be considered a third hypothesis of this general type.

Actually, evidence is scarce to support the view that any of these three "causal" variables is independently related to democracy (that is, still related after controls for spurious correlations have been introduced). The first hypothesis, relating the size of the middle class to democracy, is supported by correlational data; but the relationship is probably spurious, since the size of the middle class is highly related to the economic and social correlates of democracy. It is dubious that prospects for democracy increase significantly *as* the size of the middle class grows. For instance, numerous Latin American cases in the last decade—Argentina, Brazil, Mexico, others—have shown that the middle sectors will support authoritarian, status quo forces at least as often as reformist forces and more often by far than radical forces. A major problem with the third hypothesis is that few societies anywhere, and probably none in the Third World, have a "class structure bulging toward the

---

framework of analysis. Additionally, the pluralist theory in its various forms was the basis for a great many other works that did not employ the framework explicitly. The diffuse influence of this theory has been enormous. Reservations about this approach in European and Third World settings have been expressed by LaPalombara, Linz, and Schmitter. For some of the history of this approach in the comparative politics field in the United States, see Gabriel A. Almond, *Political Development: Essays in Heuristic Theory* (Boston: Little, Brown, 1970), pp. 15-17, 51-76.

[44] Lipset, *Political Man*, p. 417, and the quotations from Aristotle in the frontispiece.

middle." In most countries, class structures "bulge" at the bottom. This makes the hypothesis almost untestable, at least by comparing nations. It might be tested more readily with smaller units of analysis than nation-states.

5. Social Cleavages, Integration, and Democracy. National integration, peaceful adjustment of conflicts, and democracy have each been said to be inversely related to the number and kind of social cleavages in a society and directly related to the mechanisms or processes which have potential for bridging the cleavages. According to this view, ethnic, geographic, religious, caste, linguistic, tribal, and other subcultural cleavages impede integration and democracy; networks of "social communication," or "aggregative political structures," facilitate integration and democracy.[45]

Blending some of these notions together, it is possible to construct a rough "model" of the social foundations of political development (defined as democracy) as the social-system theorists view it. The legal-formal approach conceived

[45] See Karl W. Deutsch, "The Growth of Nations," *World Politics*, 5, No. 2 (January 1953), 168-96; *Nationalism and Social Communication* (New York: Wiley, 1953); James S. Coleman, *Nigeria: Background to Nationalism* (Berkeley and Los Angeles: University of California Press, 1960); Rupert Emerson, *From Empire to Nation: The Rise to Self-Assertion of Asian and African Peoples* (Cambridge: Harvard University Press, 1960); Selig Harrison, *India: The Most Dangerous Decades* (Princeton: Princeton University Press, 1960); and Karl Deutsch, *et al., Political Community and the North Atlantic Area* (Princeton: Princeton University Press, 1957); Gabriel A. Almond, "Introduction: A Functional Approach to Comparative Politics," in Almond and Coleman, *The Developing Areas*; Bruce H. Millen, *The Political Role of Labor in Developing Countries* (Washington, D.C.: The Brookings Institution, 1963). For sophisticated recent applications and extensions of this orientation, mainly in the context of Western European political systems, see Dahl, *Political Oppositions*; and S. M. Lipset and Stein Rokkan, eds., *Party Systems and Voter Alignments* (New York: Free Press, 1965). Excellent review essays are Sidney Verba, "Some Dilemmas in Comparative Research," *World Politics*, 20, No. 1 (October 1967), 111-27; Peter H. Merkl, "Political Cleavages and Party Systems," *World Politics*, 21, No. 3 (April 1969), 469-85.

the conditions of democracy primarily in terms of constitutional forms; the economic approach, in terms of economic output. This approach suggests a society in which the processes of social mobilization—urbanization, education, exposure to the mass media, etc.—are proceeding at a rapid rate. A land reform program and a progressive income tax are in the process of implementation. The middle class is growing, and there are relatively large numbers of autonomous and vital groups, organizations, or institutions in the society. People voluntarily join these groups, and they form new groups from time to time. People belong to several groups at one time; in each group the memberships are different; hence there are cross-cutting memberships and multiple loyalties. In addition to these horizontal links, there are vertical links—structured interactions between groups at different levels. Groups at the top of such linkage relationships may be said to perform the aggregation function. They are a point of access for the articulated demands of the lower-level groups in the linkage chain. The class structure is neither polarized nor rigid, which further facilitates access. Through these mechanisms in the developed political system all major groups have reasonable access to political decisions.

The Political-Culture Approach. One of the most widely used definitions of political culture is this one: "The political culture of a society consists of the system of empirical beliefs, expressive symbols, and values which defines the situation in which political action takes place. It provides the subjective orientation to politics."[46] Political culture viewed in this way refers to patterns of attitudes, beliefs, and values that in some measure cause or determine patterns of political behavior. The premise is: attitudes determine behavior rather than vice versa. Political culture is seen as related to the functioning or nonfunctioning of certain kinds of political institutions, and the causal arrow runs

[46] Sidney Verba, "Comparative Political Culture," in Lucian W. Pye and Sidney Verba, eds., *Political Culture*, p. 513.

from "culture," as a psychological variable or set of variables, to political behavior and/or institutions. This is the way the general notion of political culture was almost universally conceived in the 1950s and 1960s.[47] In the political development literature, the main interest has been in finding political cultures which support and maintain modern, democratic, political systems.

Political culture is largely a psychological concept. The psychological mechanisms at work occur on at least two levels: (1) the level of beliefs and attitudes about political roles held by members of the polity, and (2) the level of personality. More research has been done on the attitudinal than on the personality level.

The concept of political culture at the level of beliefs and attitudes was mostly a postwar development, although it obviously had prewar roots. It received its name in a classic formulation in 1956.[48] Other works using it include Leites' and Wylie's studies on France; Banfield's on southern Italy; Lerner's on the Middle (Near) East; Binder's on Iran; Apter's on Africa; Almond's and Verba's on the United States, United Kingdom, Germany, Italy, and Mexico; and Lipset's on the United States as a "new nation."[49] These studies are notable for spotlighting a hitherto neglected dimension of political development. The attitudinal "states of mind" and the personality types named by these authors as requisites or inhibitors of political development go under varied headings: for example, "empathy" (Lerner), "amoral familism" (Banfield), "unwillingness to accept political responsibility" (Leites and Wylie), a mixed "civic culture" (Almond and Verba), "identity" (Pye). While they were

[47] For a different view, which begins from the premise that behavior determines attitudes as well as vice versa, see Fagen, *Political Culture in Cuba*, esp. pp. 4-6.

[48] Gabriel A. Almond, "Comparative Political Systems," *Journal of Politics*, 18 (August 1956), 391-409.

[49] Citations for these works are given in Packenham, "Approaches to the Study of Political Development," 118, n. 45.

differently named partly because they measure slightly different phenomena, they also tapped a common core, namely, the basic psychological predispositions here called the political culture.

Most works at the personality level focused on the American and European political systems rather than the Third World,[50] but there were a few relating personality to Third World political and economic development.[51] Perhaps the most influential of these was Lucian Pye's study of Burmese politicians and administrators.[52] Its thesis was that political development, defined in terms of capacity for nation-building and democracy, is fundamentally a problem of personal identity, trust, and psychic well-being. That is, the politically developed society was seen to be one in which participants' personalities are sufficiently secure and well-integrated that they are psychologically able to accept the privileges and bear the responsibilities of independence and self-government. The hypothesis seemed to be: If a society has enough people with such personalities located in the right places, then national integration and political democracy will obtain. This is an extraordinary thesis if one considers it in light of traditional explanations of nationhood and self-government. Rather than, say, constitutional forms, or class structure, or wealth, according to Pye, identity and psychic health are the priority conditions of political development.

[50] See *ibid.*, n. 46. For a recent analysis of this literature, see Fred I. Greenstein, *Personality and Politics* (Chicago: Markham Publishing Company, 1969).

[51] See especially Lucian W. Pye, *Guerrilla Communism in Malaya: Its Social and Political Meaning* (Princeton: Princeton University Press, 1956) and *Politics, Personality, and Nation Building* (1962); Susanne Hoeber Rudolph, "The New Courage: An Essay on Gandhi's Psychology," *World Politics*, 16, No. 1 (October 1963), 98-117; more recently, Erik H. Erikson, *Gandhi's Truth on the Origins of Militant Nonviolence* (New York: Norton, 1969); and James E. Scott, *Political Ideology in Malaysia: Reality and the Beliefs of an Elite* (New Haven: Yale University Press, 1968).

[52] Pye, *Politics, Personality and Nation Building.*

Two other controversial and influential volumes, both by nonpolitical scientists interested principally in economic development, also employed the personality approach to development: Everett Hagen's *On the Theory of Social Change*, arguing that economic, social, and political development were mainly a function of innovative, entrepreneurial personalities, and David McClelland's *The Achieving Society*, maintaining that the main requisite of development was a particular psychological attribute which he called "need for achievement."[53] Though Pye's work was more focused on political development, these works—especially McClelland's —were more richly documented than Pye's interpretive essay.

METHODS AND INTELLECTUAL STYLES

During the period of dominance of the economic, social-system, and political-culture approaches, scholars became in many respects much more self-consciously theoretical, comparative, and quantitative. More and more they came to perceive themselves, and were so perceived by others, as social *scientists*: people who conceived their role vis-à-vis social phenomena as analogous to that of physical and biological scientists in relation to natural phenomena. While the single-country, configurative monograph was still one of the staples of the field, cross-national studies became a much more important part of comparative politics. Even one-country studies were sometimes better known because of their general theoretical ideas than because of their contribution to knowledge about the particular country.[54] It was now more important for the social scientist to explain than "merely" to describe.

[53] Everett E. Hagen, *On the Theory of Social Change: How Economic Growth Begins* (Homewood, Ill.: Dorsey Press, 1962); David C. McClelland, *The Achieving Society* (Princeton: Van Nostrand, 1961).

[54] Pye's *Politics, Personality, and Nation Building* is an excellent example.

Thus the literature contained a great many works dealing at length and in very precise terms with the conditions for democracy. But there was virtually no scholarship simply describing the incidence of democracy among the world's nations, or indeed among the nations of a single continent or region, over time. Even very crude time-series and distributional data on the incidence of democracy, such as those reported in the Introduction to this book, appeared very rarely in the literature. It seems safe to say that botanists, geologists, or (closer to home) economists would not dream of explaining a phenomenon until they had relatively good descriptions of what they wanted to explain. Economists routinely gather detailed cross-sectional and time-series data on a great variety of matters, including economic development and growth. Among them, the acquisition of "merely" descriptive data as a prelude to explanation is a value so widely agreed upon that it is routinized and institutionalized. The idea scarcely seems to have occurred to political development theorists; if it did, it was a much lower priority for them than "explanatory" studies.

These priorities undoubtedly resulted in part from the complexity of the political systems the scholars were studying and the self-consciousness of the theorists about the relevance of the data itself. They felt a theory was needed in order to approach the data. However, these priorities also probably reflected an uncritical acceptance and distortion of mechanistic scientific principles. In addition, some theorists simply may not have known the countries they were looking at very well. In this situation, theories and explanations were sometimes substitutes for the ability to describe.[55]

Disciplinary lines blurred, especially between political science and sociology, anthropology, and psychology (but

[55] For a provocative discussion of these and related issues and possibilities, see Albert O. Hirschman, "The Search for Paradigms as a Hindrance to Understanding," *World Politics*, 22, No. 3 (April 1970), 329-43. I am also indebted to Henry Bienen for helpful comments on these matters.

much less economics and history). This blending was said by some to be enriching; others saw it as sterilizing since it seemed to take "politics" out of political science. History, ideology, and political institutions like legislatures, courts, and even parties and the bureaucracy were relatively little studied during these years. And the range of places studied widened enormously, so that by the late fifties and early sixties virtually no part of the globe was without its American expert from the discipline of comparative politics.

Among the causes of these transformations were the post-World War II involvement of the United States in international affairs, the independence movements in Asia and Africa, and (later) the increased prominence of Latin America in the world views of both scholars and men of affairs. Another source for the changes was the "behavioral revolution" in American political science. The fifties and sixties saw the consolidation of this "revolution" (and, according to one distinguished scholar, the arrival by 1970 of a second, "post-behavioral" revolution).[56] The seed planted by the so-called Chicago school of political science in the twenties and thirties (Merriam, Gosnell, Lasswell, and others) had grown and blossomed. The break with formalism of the fifties and sixties was to a large extent the manifestation, albeit in somewhat transmuted form, in the study of foreign political systems of the behavioral revolution in the study of American politics.

More concretely, the Committee on Comparative Politics of the Social Science Research Council was the spark which combined with the "tinder" conditions noted above to forge new perspectives and theoretical formulations. The tenure of Professor Gabriel A. Almond as chairman of this committee, from 1954 to 1963, is roughly coincident with the rise of the economic, sociological, and psychological approaches. Few formalized academic groups have so thor-

[56] David Easton, "The New Revolution in Political Science," *American Political Science Review*, 63, No. 4 (December 1969), 1051-61.

oughly set the course of a segment of social science scholarship as did this Committee during that decade. Even so, the Committee by no means completely dominated the field; nor, obviously, did it have coercive powers. Rather, other scholars found the Committee's ideas attractive, employed its concepts in their own research and teaching, and accorded the Committee and its members the most precious rewards of the social system of social science—respect, admiration, and prestige. In short, the break with formalism was the work of no cabal, but an intellectual movement with a base of support that was both deep and wide.

The mood which accompanied the break with formalism was nothing if not optimistic. Partly this optimism was the product of faith that scientific method, interdisciplinary cross-fertilization, a disciplined and rigorous theoretical style, and broader geographic focuses could produce political development theories with a high potential for social engineering. The ends of political development were, as we have seen, little elaborated or defended: the basic elements of the normative dimension seemed more or less self-evident. A more interesting question was: How can these ends be brought closer to realization? Social science theories of political development seemed to provide at least the beginnings of an answer. Lipset wrote in 1960 that his "concern with making explicit the conditions of the democratic order reflects my perhaps overrationalistic belief that a fuller understanding of the various conditions under which democracy has existed may help men to develop it even where it does not now exist." Apter, in a volume published in 1963, stated that "Science cannot determine morality, but it can be placed in its service. The next stage in comparative politics will produce . . . a new era of pragmatic theory and practical reform." And in 1965 Harold Lasswell, in a review of three major books on political development, concluded that they had "brought the time closer when a comprehensive theory of value accumulation and institutional development can provide an inclusive frame of reference for the decision

225

makers and choosers involved in giving or receiving assistance, or in directing self-sustaining and integrated growth." He also emphasized what he called "the gratifying expansion of the policy sciences of development." Thus social science seemed to be constructing the base for a rational approach to humane social engineering.[57]

THE WILL AND CAPACITY APPROACH

The economic, social, and psychological interpretations were innovative, optimistic, and very influential. They represented and stimulated significant advances in knowledge. Yet, as the sixties wore on, a new disquiet emerged among students of political development. A variety of criticisms was directed at the first ten- or fifteen-year wave of post-legal-formal scholarship. It was, the critics said, ahistorical: comparative in space, but not comparative over time. It had gotten tangled up in untestable propositions about system-maintenance and "functional requisites" of society and polity.[58] A preference for liberal democracy often lurked behind a thin veil of scientism. Revolutions were always bad, and reform was always good. Governmental capacity, political choices, leadership, political skill—in short, much

[57] Lipset, *Political Man*, p. 417; David Apter, "Past Influences and Future Development," in Eckstein and Apter, *Comparative Politics*, p. 738; and Lasswell, "The Policy Sciences," 308-9. My own early writings also were overly optimistic; see the citations in the Preface, n. 1.

[58] For helpful discussions of the strengths and weaknesses of "structural-functionalism" or simply "functionalism" in political science, see Eckstein, "A Perspective on Comparative Politics," pp. 26-29; William Flanigan and Edwin Fogelman, "Functionalism in Political Science," in Don Martindale, ed., *Functionalism in the Social Sciences, Annals,* American Academy of Political and Social Science, Monograph 5 (Philadelphia: February 1965), pp. 111-26; Arthur L. Kalleberg, "The Logic of Comparison," *World Politics,* 19, No. 1 (October 1966), 69-82; and A. James Gregor, "Political Science and the Uses of Functional Analysis," *American Political Science Review,* 62, No. 2 (June 1968), 425-39.

226

of the stuff of politics—were often ignored, since political development was seen as dependent on vast social, psychological, and economic forces.

In the middle and late 1960s, writings on political development increasingly came to stress precisely those variables that often (though obviously not always) had been omitted before: the choices, will, skill, and capacity to cope with the demands and needs of society that were cast up by the force of, or the imputed desire for, "modernization." In this perspective, political development was conceptualized not as strictly dependent on socioeconomic forces, but also as an independent, autonomous force in its own right. Writers employing this approach avoided seeing political development as some fixed-end state; rather, they saw it as a continuing process—in Manfred Halpern's words, "a persistent capacity for coping with a permanent revolution."[59] This approach went by various names: "will and capacity" is the generic title given to it here, although others use terms like "problem-solving" capacity, "institutionalization," or "ability to sustain new goals."

Halpern's phrase conveys the central idea of the will and capacity approach: political development as a relational concept involving both mass needs and demands, on the one hand, and the will, skill, and capacity of political leaders and institutions to deal with and generate change, on the other. More specifically, the will and capacity orientation breaks down further into at least three types of studies, here referred to as institutional capacity studies, political economy studies, and political leadership studies.

Institutional Capacity Studies. The principal thesis here was that strong political institutions were requisites for socioeconomic modernization, political stability, and/or political democracy. "Strength" of political institutions was measured by how effectively they could get things done,

[59] Manfred Halpern, "Toward Further Modernization of the Study of New Nations," *World Politics*, 17, No. 1 (October 1964), 179.

adapt to new conditions, innovate for the future, and stay free of outside influences.[60] The political institutions on which these studies tended to focus were three: the military, the civil bureaucracy, and political parties. Let us consider each in turn.

A number of prominent scholars articulated the view that the military plays a stabilizing and/or modernizing role in Third World countries. This view challenged the conventional liberal image of a politicized military as a regressive and reactionary force. It had a number of proponents and variants, and made its biggest impact in the early sixties.[61] In a sense, these writings were a departure from the mainstream of political development studies of those years, for the military-as-modernizer literature did stress the importance of political institutions as autonomous, independent forces at a time when the most prominent theories were conceiving politics and political development as exclusively or principally dependent. Only by the mid-sixties, however, did this eddy in the flow of writing about political development become a powerful competing crosscurrent. By that time, ironically, the military-as-modernizer thesis was less widely accepted.

[60] See especially Huntington, *Political Order*, pp. 12-24. Huntington defines institutional strength in terms of four concepts—complexity, coherence, adaptability, and autonomy—which he explicates at some length. Cf. Nelson W. Polsby, "The Institutionalization of the United States House of Representatives," *American Political Science Review*, 62, No. 1 (March 1968), 144-68. Polsby's concept of institutionalization is less elaborate but more operational than Huntington's.

[61] See Manfred Halpern, *The Politics of Social Change in the Middle East and North Africa* (Princeton: Princeton University Press, 1963); Morris Janowitz, *The Military in the Political Development of New Nations* (Chicago: University of Chicago Press, 1964); John J. Johnson, *The Military and Society in Latin America* (Stanford: Stanford University Press, 1964); Johnson, ed., *The Role of the Military in Underdeveloped Countries* (Princeton: Princeton University Press, 1962), especially the essays by Pye and Shils; Guy Pauker, "Southeast Asia as a Problem Area in the Next Decade," *World Politics*, 11, No. 3 (April 1959), 325-45.

Of secondary but increasing influence during the late 1950s and early 1960s were studies focused on the civil bureaucracy. Under this heading are grouped writers who defined political development in terms of administrative capacity to maintain law and order and to perform governmental output functions rationally, neutrally, and efficiently. Studies employing this approach also appeared in a variety of forms and came from a variety of value orientations, methodological persuasions, and general intellectual styles and traditions. By the mid-1960s this "administrative" or bureaucratic approach to political development was prominent and widespread enough in the literature to be counted in a review of major orientations.[62] However, the bureaucracy was probably even more important, both actually and potentially, as a cause of or an impediment to a host of development goals than the literature suggested. Even today, its full importance is perhaps not adequately appreciated in American social science scholarship.

The most influential manifestation of the will and capacity approach expressed in terms of institutional capacity, however, was the institutionalization theory of Samuel Huntington. Huntington defined political development as "the institutionalization of political organizations and procedures."[63] In oversimplified form, his thesis was that political stability (defined as the absence of coups, insurrections, political riots, and other forms of group violence) depends on the degree to which the growth of political institutions stays equal to or ahead of the processes of social mobilization and political participation. "Institutionalization," he writes, "is the process by which organizations and processes acquire

[62] See Packenham, "Approaches to the Study of Political Development," 113-15. In addition to the items cited there, see the following important works: LaPalombara, *Bureaucracy and Political Development*; Braibanti, et al., *Political and Administrative Development*; S. N. Eisenstadt, *The Political Systems of Empires* (New York: Free Press, 1962).

[63] Huntington, "Political Development and Political Decay," 393.

value and stability. The level of institutionalization of any political system can be defined by the adaptability, complexity, autonomy, and coherence of its organizations and procedures."[64] Moreover, in Huntington's view socioeconomic modernization and democracy are normally possible only in the context of political order; since political order depends on institutionalization, it follows from his theory— and he so argues—that institutionalization is also necessary for modernization and democracy. Huntington applied this theory principally in analyses of political parties, secondarily in analyses of the military, and least of all in analyses of the civil bureaucracy.

Huntington's theory is exceptionally important for several reasons. For one thing, it was unusually influential. Few contributions to the literature were more widely read in the 1960s; among new contributions after 1965, perhaps only Barrington Moore's work compares with Huntington's in impact. Second, Huntington's concept of institutionalization, in his words, "liberates [political] development from [socioeconomic] modernization," so that states like India, which are very underdeveloped socioeconomically, are considered to have been highly developed politically, and states like Argentina, which have high socioeconomic development, are considered poorly developed politically. Another feature of Huntington's theory is that it avoids the implication, so deeply rooted in much of the previous literature, of unilinearity, or movement only toward development (and never toward decay). As Huntington points out, "institutions . . . decay and dissolve as well as grow and mature." Finally, and "most significantly, it focuses attention on the reciprocal interaction between the ongoing social processes of modernization, on the one hand, and the strength, stability, or weakness of political structures, traditional, transitional, or modern, on the other."[65]

[64] Huntington, *Political Order*, p. 12.
[65] Huntington, "Political Development and Political Decay," 393ff. For reviews of Huntington's work which deal with weaknesses as

Political Economy Studies. A second manifestation of the will and capacity approach was the reappearance of a concern with political economy. Of course, classical political economists, like Bentham, John Stuart Mill, and Marx, and contemporary Marxists, like Paul Baran, were still read in the postwar decades—but not much. An indicator of the fate of the formal study of political economy is the fact that the new *International Encyclopedia of the Social Sciences* (1968) contains no article under this heading.[66]

Political economy may be defined as the analysis of the costs and benefits of alternate uses of scarce resources by political leaders, where resources, costs, and benefits are all conceived in both economic and political terms, not just one or the other. This definition distinguishes political economy from either political science or economics. Thus understood, political economy seeks, ultimately, to be able to measure political costs and benefits in economic terms and vice versa. This is a large, difficult, and perhaps impossible task. It is seldom approached directly; operational problems are serious; it demands sophistication in normative theorizing as well as in empirical analysis. Little progress has been made to date in employing this approach in the political development field, although there are some stimulating attempts.[67]

---

well as virtues of the theory, see Dankwart A. Rustow in *Journal of International Affairs*, 23, No. 1 (1969), 119-32; and Robert A. Packenham in *trans action*, 7, No. 1 (November 1969), 56-58.

[66] Warren F. Ilchman and Norman Thomas Uphoff note this surprising fact in their book, *The Political Economy of Change* (Berkeley and Los Angeles: University of California Press, 1969), p. viii.

[67] The most elaborate attempt among non-Marxists is Ilchman and Uphoff. The best Marxist book is Paul Baran, *The Political Economy of Growth* (New York: Monthly Review Press, 1957, 1967). Joyce M. Mitchell and William C. Mitchell, *Political Analysis and Public Policy* (Chicago: Rand McNally, 1969), is a textbook that begins to employ a political economy perspective; and William Mitchell, "The Shape of Political Theory to Come: From Political Sociology to Political Economy," in Lipset, ed., *Politics and the Social Sciences* (New York: Oxford University Press, 1969), pp. 101-36, is a prediction with illustrations. The best applications of political economy in-

Formal rational-choice models are a kind of special case within the political economy approach which deserve mention. These are models which, like functionalist models, aim at the construction of a "general theory of social behavior."[68] They borrow from economics the concept of rational choice (rational behavior, rational decisionmaking) and generalize it to the analysis of noneconomic behavior. According to one of the enthusiasts of this approach, John Harsanyi, the advantages of rational choice theories over functional theories are several.

> Unlike functional theories, theories of rational behavior have a natural tendency to take a hypothetico-deductive form, and to explain a wide variety of empirical facts in terms of a small number of theoretical assumptions. . . . [They] can account for social stability and for social change with equal facility; and, by drawing on . . . modern game theory, they can readily analyze both social conflict and social cooperation, and even those uneasy mixtures of the two that characterize most empirical social situations.[69]

Harsanyi cites some examples of studies that have, in his view, "very successfully" used rigorous, precisely stated rational choice models to analyze political behavior. However, he concedes that "before rational-choice models can achieve reasonably wide use in the social sciences outside economics, we shall have to solve a number of important theoretical problems."[70]

Despite the problems that exist and the very limited progress, on the whole, that has been made with political-

---

sights in research on the Third World probably are found in the works of Albert O. Hirschman and Charles W. Anderson. The items cited are illustrative of the range of studies in the political economy category and guides to further citations; they are not in any sense comprehensive.

[68] John C. Harsanyi, "Rational-Choice Models of Political Behavior vs. Functionalist and Conformist Theories," *World Politics*, 21, No. 4 (July 1969), 513.

[69] *Ibid.*, 515.   [70] *Ibid.*, 517-18.

economy analysis, such studies have some very attractive features. Not the least of these is that they aim at the creation of intellectual tools with which to address the very questions which most preoccupy policymakers: What should be done? How much will be gained or lost in terms of X and Y if I do this? What happens if I do that? Acting so as to improve my situation with respect to X will probably hurt me with respect to Y; if so, is X worth it? What is a better course? And so on. Whatever knowledge the political economy and rational-choice studies could develop would seem to have obvious and immediate policy relevance.[71]

Political Leadership Studies. A third and closely related expression of the will and capacity approach is studies of political leadership. These are studies which stress the importance of the will, skill, and values of leaders. For instance, two unconventional economists, Albert O. Hirschman and Robert L. Heilbroner, have in their writings loose theories incorporating leadership as an important variable. Hirschman tends to proceed from nonrevolutionary assumptions, however, whereas Heilbroner's premises tend to be decidedly pro-revolution.

Hirschman has consistently combatted theories which specify imposing and seemingly unattainable arrays of "necessary" social, economic, and psychological "conditions" of economic growth (or, indeed, of almost anything else). He has argued, for example, that under certain conditions (which unfortunately are not clearly specified), "reformmongers" have been able to make economic and political gains even in the absence of such conditions. His hypotheses about the possible benefits of unbalanced growth, "reformmongering," and side effects are also part of the "will and capacity" approach to political development.[72]

[71] *Ibid.*, 536-38.

[72] Albert O. Hirschman: *The Strategy of Economic Development* (New Haven: Yale University Press, 1958); *Journeys Toward Progress: Studies of Economic Policy-Making in Latin America* (New York: Twentieth Century Fund, 1963); *Development Projects Ob-*

Heilbroner has made some of the most extreme criticisms of prevailing Western models of economic and political development: "... I opt for ... 'total' change. ... if I had to take my chances here and now as an anonymous particle of humanity in China or India or in Cuba or Brazil, I would unhesitatingly choose the Communist side." It is Heilbroner's "main premise that only a Holy War will begin modernization in our time," and that the *"leadership* needed to mount [this] jehad against backwardness ... will be forced to expound a philosophy that approves authoritarian and collectivist measures at home and that utilizes as the target for its national resentment abroad the towering villains of the world, of which the United States is now Number One." He continually emphasizes the critical role of leadership: e.g. "... strong tendencies must exist for extending and deepening the control of leadership, not only over political and economic life but into social and intellectual life as well."[73]

Political Development: Independent and Causal. The most significant shift in political development theory as empirical theory in the latter half of the 1960s was the assertion, or reassertion, of the view that politics shapes as well as reflects socioeconomic reality. According to the break with formalism, politics had been seen as mostly dependent on vast economic, sociological, and psychological forces. One theorist wrote:

---

served (Washington, D.C.: The Brookings Institution, 1967); and "Obstacles to Development: A Classification and a Quasi-Vanishing Act," *Economic Development and Cultural Change*, 13, No. 4 (July 1965), 385-93.

[73] The quotations are from Robert L. Heilbroner, "Counter-revolutionary America," in Irving Howe, ed., *A Dissenter's Guide to Foreign Policy* (New York: Doubleday, Anchor, 1968), pp. 277, 253, 275 (emphasis added). See also Heilbroner, *The Great Ascent: The Struggle for Economic Development in Our Time* (New York: Harper, 1963), esp. Chaps. 7 and 8.

234

A political system as the term is used in this paper is a system of interdependent roles. There are no individuals and personalities in the political system or any other social system. . . . [The] argument that the political system is capable of largely autonomous variation which can result in profound economic, social, and cultural change seems to be based largely on the role of the personal motivation and energy of political leaders. The conceptualization that underlies my work treats these personality characteristics as environmental to any social system.[74]

In the will and capacity approach, by contrast, the notion of politics as an autonomous force returned to political development theorizing.

The will and capacity writers thus treated politics, and political development, "not only as effect but also as cause."[75] Political development was usually not explained in the will and capacity literature; rather, it was seen as an independent variable or set of variables which *explained other things*, or at least aimed to do so. The tendency to examine the consequences more than the causes of political development was less a logical necessity than an empirical attribute of the will and capacity literature, but this tendency was very widespread. For instance, there is a great deal in Huntington's *Political Order in Changing Societies* about the nature and consequences of highly institutionalized political organizations; but there is relatively little in the book about the conditions under which such organizations flourish.

What were these "other things" that were explained by such independent variables as organizational capacity and political leadership? With rare exceptions the dependent variables in the will-skill-capacity-and-choice literature were specified *vaguely*; at best, they were indicated *contextually*.

[74] Robert T. Holt, "Comparative Politics and Comparative Administration," *Occasional Papers*, Comparative Administrative Group, American Society for Public Administration, mimeographed (Bloomington, Indiana: February 1966), p. 25, n. 7.
[75] Rustow, *A World of Nations*, p. 145.

They were vague in that words like "modernization," "economic development," "social development," "justice," "reform," "equality," or just "progress" were used to indicate what it is that regimes with high (or low) will and capacity do (or do not) promote. These dependent variables were no less "rough and subjective" than the dependent variables in the economic, social-system, and political-culture approaches. Most of the "modernization" which these theories purported to explain referred to what might loosely be called social and economic modernization: industrialization, per capita income, transportation, proportion of the population in agriculture, exposure to the media, health, education, land reform, tax reform, etc. When the referent of modernization was not just social and economic but also political, it then encompassed such concepts as national integration and participation. In such instances political participation tended more often than in the earlier literature not to mean just "liberal democratic" participation, but also "mobilized" participation, as in Cuba or China.

In a sense, the will and capacity writers focused on a variable or set of variables that was a prominent dimension of political modernization as defined by the politics-as-dependent school, namely, political capacity, authority, or power. But they did at least three things differently. First, they elaborated and differentiated this element, dealing not just with "capacity" in a general sense, but breaking it down into various more or less discrete elements (will, skill, choice, different kinds of capacity). Second, they viewed capacity not as dependent on socioeconomic and psychological conditions, but as in some sense independent, autonomous, determinative in its own right. Third, on the premise that in politics "the ends are never given," they often almost celebrated the vagueness of the "things" which were explained by capacity, leadership, and choices.

This vagueness of the dependent variables—"modernization," "progress," "socioeconomic reform," etc.—had a variety of sources. On the one hand, the imprecision was probably due in part to sloppy thinking and intellectual laziness. It was also thought that failing to specify the ends of development precisely allowed such goals to be determined contextually by what various actors wanted; what various actors wanted could be seen as an empirical question; hence tough normative questions might be avoided—ends could be determined empirically.[76] On the other hand, defining the ends of "modernization" contextually seemed a fairly sensible way to proceed where good data were lacking, where very different kinds of cultures and societies with conceivably different needs were involved, and where some concepts were not readily amenable to precise, rigorous treatment.

Methods and Intellectual Styles. In a variety of ways, therefore, the will and capacity literature gave evidence that another shift was occurring in the style and methods of political development scholars. This shift was not so massive as that which accompanied the break with formalism, and the impact of the latter movement was deep and enduring in most respects. Nevertheless it is a fact that in the will and capacity studies more humanistic, qualitative, configurative research methods and intellectual styles enjoyed a resurgence. Scholars were still, on the whole, theoretically self-conscious, but they were a little less schematically inclined than before, closer to and more intimately acquainted with their data, and more contextual. Renewed appreciation for the well-handled case study was visible. "Simple description" once again became respectable. There was some reaction against global studies, and some revival of appreciation of diversity and comparative studies of narrower scope, as regions, pairs of countries, or single cases. These trends were occasionally uncertain or obscure, but discernible. As Sidney Verba has pointed out, difficult dilemmas existed still; but

76 On the fallacies involved in this view, see Henry S. Kariel, "Goals for Administrative Reform in Developing States: An Open-Ended Design," in Braibanti, *et al.*, *Political and Administrative Development*, pp. 143-65.

they were being recognized and confronted more squarely and soberly in the late sixties than they had been in the previous ten years or so of optimism and occasional euphoria about the science of comparative politics and the "policy science" of political development.[77]

These changes in mood and style had implications for the handling of normative theory as well as empirical theory. One of the most striking aspects of the new perspectives was that liberal, constitutional democracy became less prominent in the theories—either as attribute, consequence, or cause of political development. It must be emphasized that this was an empirical tendency, not a logical necessity. That is, the will and capacity approaches are not logically wedded to nondemocratic regimes. Rather, it happened that in a subtle way scholars using the will and capacity approaches tended to give a higher priority to social and economic development (or, as Marxists might put it, socioeconomic democracy), and a lower priority to political democracy, than had the break-with-formalism writers. An increasing number of scholars came to believe that such shifts in relative emphases on socioeconomic and political democracy were both normatively and empirically justified. Possibly this trend was part of a partial transcendence of liberal ethnocentricism on the part of the social scientists.

It should not be thought, however, that the normative premises and arguments of the theorists became as sophisti-

[77] For evidence of these trends, see *inter alia*, Hirschman, "The Search for Paradigms as a Hindrance to Understanding," pp. 329-43; Oran R. Young, "Professor Russett: Industrious Tailor to a Naked Emperor," *World Politics*, 21, No. 3 (April 1969), 486-511; Bruce M. Russett, "International Behavior Research: Case Studies and Cumulation," in Michael Haas and Henry S. Kariel, eds., *Approaches to the Study of Political Science* (Scranton, Pa.: Chandler, 1970), pp. 425-43; Verba, "Some Dilemmas in Comparative Research," 111-27; and Douglas A. Chalmers, "Understanding the Variety of Political Systems: A Necessary Next Step in Comparative Politics," unpublished paper, Columbia University, 1969. See also the "Symposium on Scientific Explanation in Political Science," *American Political Science Review*, 63, No. 4 (December 1969), 1233-62, for vigorous discussions of very similar issues, only in more abstract terms.

238

cated as their empirical work (which itself had many weaknesses); nor should one suppose that anywhere near as much time, energy, and prestige were attached to normative theorizing as to empirical work. However, the salience of the moral dimension to the theorists slowly grew. Sensitivity to possible ethnocentrisms heightened. The theorists became aware that recent studies had been ahistorical; that ideology had been neglected; and that the pattern of Third World politics was substantially affected by the international environment. The normative "roots and branches" of earlier theory came in for some analysis and criticism.[78] Rightly or wrongly, there was greater openness to the possible benefits of certain kinds of authoritarian regimes; concomitantly, revolutions were now occasionally seen as preferable, or at least as not necessarily inferior, to evolution and reform.[79] Not least important, normative discourse itself became slightly more respectable again, both explicitly, as in the works of Huntington and Moore, and implicitly, in the sense that unlike correlational theorizing, political-economy theorizing focused on choices, which are inherently normative.[80]

Conclusion

This chapter has purposely related each of three major types of theories of political development to a single historical phase within the whole twenty-five year period. I have argued that the legal-formal approach was dominant in the years from 1945 to the early 1950s (and perhaps later); that the economic, social-system, and political-culture

[78] For example, see Lewis Lipsitz, "If, As Verba Says, The State Functions As A Religion, What Are We To Do Then To Save Our Souls?" *American Political Science Review*, 62, No. 2 (June 1968), 527-35; and the exchange between Lipsitz and Verba, *ibid.*, 576-78.

[79] For instance, Fagen, *The Transformation of Political Culture in Cuba*; Huntington, *Political Order in Changing Societies*, Chap. 5; Moore, *Social Origins of Dictatorship and Democracy*, pp. 505-8.

[80] On the latter point, see Harsanyi, "Rational-Choice Models," 537-38.

approaches were the most prominent in the fifties and probably most of the sixties, and that they were definitely the most powerful intellectual current in the field during the period as a whole; and that the will and capacity approaches became a major influence as the sixties wore on, especially after 1965.

This linkage of type of theory to particular periods of time is, I think, fair and illuminating. It does not, however, imply that during any of these periods only one type of theory existed or was influential. Such an argument would be quite misleading. For example, as noted, bureaucratic and military manifestations of the will and capacity approach were evident from at least the mid-1950s on. The economic, social-system and political-culture approaches were very influential theories throughout the whole decade of the sixties; they continue to be now. Moreover, there were clearly elements of such theories in the work of earlier writers. Nor did the legal-formal approach die in the fifties. It only slumbered. By the latter half of the sixties, scholars were again urging attention to constitutions. So it went. Thus, I do not imply any exclusive quality to the linkages between type-of-theory categories and time-period categories. They tend to be related, but there are exceptions. One can agree with Harry Eckstein's observation that "the predominant style of any one period is still practiced, with less emphasis, in the periods that follow. . . . The development of comparative politics has not proceeded through mutually exclusive phases, but has involved instead a continuous heaping up of strata of analysis, if one may put it that way."[81]

With this caveat in mind, it is possible to summarize schematically the main features of the theories of political development from 1945 to 1970; see Table 5. Having reviewed the substance and style of these theories, we may now inquire how useful they were, actually and potentially, for policy and policymakers.

[81] Eckstein, "A Perspective on Comparative Politics, Past and Present," p. 31.

240

TABLE 5

POLITICAL DEVELOPMENT THEORIES, 1945-1970

Approach	Period	Definition	Explained By	Explains	Style and Method	Normative Emphasis
I. Legal-formal	Pre-1945 to 1950+	Constitutional democracy	Legal-formal and "historical" variables	—	Configurative, atheoretical, qualitative, Europe-centered	Liberal consitutionalism
II. Break with formalism	1950+ to 1965+	Political modernization and democracy	Economic, social-system, and political-culture variables	— "All good things")	Comparative, theoretical, quantitative, worldwide	Pluralistic democracy
III. Will and capacity	1965+	Will, skill, capacity, and choice of political leaders and institutions	—	Economic, social, and political "modernization"; stability; other good things	Contextual, theoretical, quantitative/qualitative, worldwide	Varied greatly, more contextual, more open

6

The Usefulness
of the Theories

THE usefulness of the theories refers to both whether they were actually used by policymakers and whether they should have been. The first question refers to what may be called utilization, or extent of actual use; the second, to their potential usefulness.

UTILIZATION, OR EXTENT OF ACTUAL USE

The utilization of theories may be determined by noting the extent to which policymakers actually use them in making decisions. In this context it is important to make a distinction between use and abuse: a theory is used by a policymaker when it can be said to have an influence on the formulation of his policy; it is abused when it is employed by him only to bolster a position he already supports and would support in any case. In the latter sense social science is indeed "used," but influence on the policymaker is lacking, and the term's meaning is pejorative rather than neutral.

A very important attribute of the notion of actual utilization is that it is more or less amenable to empirical measurement. One discovers whether or not social science is useful in this sense simply by observing policymakers, by interviewing them, etc. It is true, as Lazarsfeld and his colleagues have noted, that in practice the task of discovering the extent of use is surprisingly difficult.[1] Moreover, the notion of "influence" is often anything but unambiguous as an empirical concept.[2] Whatever their importance in other con-

---

[1] See the Introduction by the editors to Paul F. Lazarsfeld, William H. Sewell, and Harold L. Wilensky, eds., *The Uses of Sociology* (New York: Basic Books, 1967), p. xxxi.

[2] See the article by Robert A. Dahl on "Power" in the *Interna-*

texts, however, these problems may properly be minimized here. For by comparison with potential usefulness, which deals with the quality of theories empirically, normatively, and as applied social science, the extent of actual use is more or less an empirical concept.

It is also helpful to make a distinction between direct and indirect utilization. Direct utilization refers to those instances where the policymaker is aware of the influence; he can tell an interviewer, for example, that he has been affected by a certain research report, or theory, or social scientist. Indirect utilization refers to instances of influence in which the actor may not be aware of the effect of the social science upon him. Nor may the social scientists who produced this effect. Most Americans, to give a simple example, have been profoundly influenced by the ideas of Adam Smith and John Locke; but only a few of them are much aware of this, and even fewer are fully aware of the depths and complexities of the impacts of the ideas of these two writers on their thinking. Consequently indirect utilization is harder to detect than direct utilization, although both are amenable in some measure to empirical inquiry.

DIRECT UTILIZATION

The direct effect of political development scholarship—as theory and in other forms—on aid policymakers' thoughts and actions regarding political development appears not to have been very great.[3] In the first place, for most officials most of the time political development per se was not an explicit policy problem. Implicitly, of course, their thoughts and actions contained fairly coherent theories about political development. However, most officials normally assumed that these implicit theories or doctrines were evident. They were

---

tional Encyclopedia of the Social Sciences, ed. David L. Sills (New York: Macmillan and Crowell Collier, 1968).

[3] For more details on the scope of the coverage of political development theories and theorists in this and the preceding chapter, see the Appendix.

not viewed as problems that needed to be analyzed and illuminated by social science.

Social scientists gathered data and did analyses which were used by policymakers in the Department of State, AID, and elsewhere; but political development was almost never a very salient concern in such studies. The *Program Guidance Manual* of AID had an elaborate annex, "Political, Social, and Economic Appraisal," which contained a long list of questions about political development designed to guide officials' analyses and inform their decisions. However, the analyses were frequently not performed; and even when they were, they seldom had much of an impact on policy. In general, neither the minority in AID that was somewhat explicitly concerned about political development (one-third at most), nor the very small minority (6-8 people at most) that was both intensely concerned about political development and wanted to use social science analyses as a way to implement that concern in the Agency, had a very large impact on decisions.[4]

A few studies of the "operational codes" of the aid program with respect to political development were also completed. Although they probably had some small impact on a minority of aid officials, congressmen, and others who were already in favor of innovations regarding political development, they probably had almost no impact on the aid policy community as a whole. In general, the effect of social scientists as critics, through this kind of research or in other ways, was weak.[5]

This brings us to the theories of political development themselves. Conscious utilization of the theories by the

[4] Packenham, "Political-Development Doctrines," 216-25; Nelson, *Aid, Influence*, pp. 147-49.

[5] The "operational code" studies are those of Packenham, *ibid.*, 209-35, and Nelson, *ibid.*, pp. 134-49. An earlier version of the latter is Eugene B. Mihaly and Joan Nelson, "Political Development and U.S. Economic Assistance," paper delivered at the 1966 annual meeting of the American Political Science Association. On the failure of the theorists as critics, see Chapter 7.

policymakers also appears to have been slight. The evidence for this is strong. In AID and the Department of State, the main political development doctrines have overwhelmingly been the economic and Cold War doctrines, which were formulated almost exclusively without reference to academic literature on political development. This generalization is accurate for the whole period under review; it is not substantially altered by the slight increase in attention to social science theory that attended and followed the passage of Title IX in 1966.

Officials normally were not familiar with the names of theorists or with their books and articles. An important group of AID officials interviewed in 1962-1963 knew the name and the work of Professor Hans J. Morgenthau, a major figure in international relations theory but not a political-development theorist. But very few knew the names, works, or even the central concepts of the key figures in the comparative politics field at the time. As the 1960s proceeded, more policymakers became acquainted with these works. By then, however, they were often learning about notions which, in a rapidly changing area of scholarship, had become less central to the field. At least many scholars came to regard much of this work as dated and seriously flawed. Even some of the authors themselves had changed their minds in fairly major respects.[6]

[6] Packenham, "Political-Development Doctrines," 234; "Foreign Aid and the National Interest," 217-18. See also "The Theories as Empirical Theory," below, for further discussion of the changeableness of the theories.

Couloumbis and Moore sent questionnaires to 303 officers in the Foreign Service and received 175 completed replies, for a response rate of 58%. One question asked the respondents to list "any person in the academic community who has influenced you in your capacity as an officer of the Foreign Service." The leading names, and the number of times each was mentioned, were: George Kennan, 23; Hans J. Morgenthau, 19; John Kenneth Galbraith, 14; Henry Kissinger, 13; E. O. Reischauer, 11; Zbigniew Brzezinski, 10; Paul Samuelson, 10; Walt W. Rostow, 7; Gabriel Almond, 6; Herman Kahn, 6;

According to one expert, social science affects foreign policy most powerfully through training and orientation programs for foreign policy personnel.[7] To what extent did political development theories appear in such programs? Some of these theories were included in the orientation and training materials of the State Department, AID, and related agencies. For example, the influential book edited by Almond and Coleman, *The Politics of the Developing Areas* (1960), was required reading at the Foreign Service Institute in the mid-1960s.[8] The Title IX Division of AID circulated a volume of background material, the *Title IX Digest*, on the political development amendment in 1968. It contained scholarly articles, bibliographies, and agency memoranda on the subject of political development. The *Program Guidance Manual*, which was among other things an orientation document, contained some material on political development. The *AID Digest*, a monthly in-house publication, devoted a whole issue to political development in August 1962; so did the *Foreign Service Journal* in March 1970. Other ex-

---

Lucian Pye, 5. No single person was listed by more than 23 of the 175 respondents. Sixty officers, over a third of the sample, listed no one.

Another question provided a list of names of international relations theorists and asked the respondents to list those who had influenced their work. The answers to this question were rather different and more numerous: Hans J. Morgenthau, 61; Karl Deutsch, 37; Gabriel Almond, 35; Thomas Schelling, 35; Stanley Hoffmann, 21; Quincy Wright, 20; Kenneth Boulding, Morton Kaplan, Talcott Parsons, 17 each; Harold Lasswell, 16; Klaus Knorr, 15; Sidney Verba, 9. However, sixty-six respondents listed no one. See Theodore A. Couloumbis and M. David Moore, III, "The Influence of Academicians Upon Foreign Service Officers," *World Affairs*, 134, No. 3 (Winter 1971), 257-260. See also Couloumbis *et al.*, "The 'Influence' of the Academic Community on Foreign Policy Formulators," Paper presented to the Annual Meeting of the International Studies Association, Dallas, Texas, March 14-18, 1972.

[7] W. Phillips Davison, "Foreign Policy," in Lazarsfeld *et al.*, *The Uses of Sociology*, p. 394.

[8] *Ibid.*, p. 395.

amples of the appearance of political development scholarship in government training materials could be cited.

However, the magnitude of this exposure was not very great; and to be exposed to theories is not necessarily to be influenced by them. As mentioned, detailed evidence gathered in 1962-1963 showed little utilization of the political-development theories of social scientists by AID policymakers. The situation was almost certainly very similar in other agencies, with the possible but (for obvious reasons) uncertain exception of the CIA. W. Phillips Davison in an article published in 1967 came to the following conclusion, which is confirmed by the present study:

> The extent to which the behavioral disciplines have been ignored in the conduct of our foreign relations is . . . much more impressive than the degree to which they have been used. Cases of utilization that can be cited tend to be isolated or tenuous; the main stream of foreign policy is affected only sporadically and tangentially by sociological or psychological theory, or by systematic research on individuals or groups. When questioned about their personal experiences, most foreign service officers find it difficult to cite instances where behavioral research or theory have [sic] affected their activities. The Country Desks and Geographic Bureaus of the State Department, where the spadework of foreign policy planning and administration is performed, are influenced at most only marginally by behavioral studies.[9]

Davison added that in AID, efforts to use social science increased after 1961, "but the extent of actual utilization is still very modest. It is the exception, rather than the rule, when cultural and social factors are systematically taken into account in AID activities."[10] The Deputy Director of

[9] *Ibid.*, pp. 395-96.
[10] *Ibid.* See also the schedule of courses at the Foreign Service Institute published in the *Department of State News Letter*, July 1970, p. 38. Administration, consular training, economics, languages,

a regional office in AID wrote me in 1968 as follows: "If the AID Title IX Digest has been helpful to you in putting together your book, I am delighted: I have never been quite sure it was useful to anyone else."[11]

It is not only theories of political development which were ignored or resisted by aid policymakers; most *explicit* abstract, theoretical, deductive constructs or formulations, about other facets of foreign aid policy as well, were similarly ignored and resisted. The point may be illustrated by the fate of AID's *Program Guidance Manual*. This document, intended to orient new employees and provide guidance and ideas for experienced personnel, was comprehensive in scope and encyclopedic in length. When he was the Deputy Administrator of AID, Frank Coffin stated that the *Manual* was "a bible of development eagerly sought by academic institutions, other countries—both developed and developing —and by international organizations."[12] Perhaps so; but it was not "eagerly sought" by people who operated the Agency for International Development. Few people thought it very useful; most used a much more pragmatic decisionmaking style. Among 43 officials interviewed in 1962-1963 who revealed their decisionmaking styles, 6 *volunteered* the information that they had not even read the *Manual*. None of them was prompted on this point; the question was not even raised by the interviewer. It is reasonable to suppose that there were others who did not want to or did think to mention that they had not read it.[13]

Such information about decisionmaking styles in AID is

and area studies all receive much more emphasis than any of the social sciences. There were 3 one-week courses on "political training," including a one-week course in "contemporary political science," compared to 4 courses ranging from 7 to 49 weeks on Vietnam, and 4 courses ranging from 2 to 22 weeks on economic and commercial subjects.

[11] Letter to the author, July 10, 1968.
[12] Speech at Camp David, Maryland, Agency Planning Session, November 3, 1962, AID Information Staff Press Release No. 228.
[13] Packenham, "Foreign Aid and Political Development," p. 250.

consistent with and complementary to the argument made in previous chapters regarding the largely inarticulated but fairly rigid liberal premises underlying U.S. political development doctrines. Aid officials tended to have pragmatic, empirical, inductive decisionmaking styles; but this pragmatism proceeded almost exclusively within parameters set by the implicit premises of the liberal tradition. Within rather wide but seldom-exceeded limits, agency guidelines reflected practice more than they gave rise to action. Guidelines codified pragmatic doctrines, but the assumptions on which the pragmatism existed were seldom made explicit and never codified. Thus, formal guidelines and training devices, not only those few dealing with political development but many others as well, normally had little effect, except marginally on new personnel.

Finally, the impact of political development theories through the scholars themselves—as people—does not seem to have been significantly greater than their impact in other ways. Such theorists as Seymour Martin Lipset, Karl Deutsch, Gabriel Almond, Sidney Verba, Robert Dahl, Daniel Lerner, James S. Coleman, Samuel P. Huntington, Dankwart Rustow, Joseph LaPalombara, Myron Weiner, Albert O. Hirschman, Aristide Zolberg, Leonard Binder, David Apter, Harry Eckstein, Carl Friedrich, Edward Banfield, Barrington Moore, Jr., and Lucian Pye, who were leaders in the academic study of political development, were, with a few exceptions, neither very well-known, nor well-connected in Washington. Nor, indeed, were many of them very much interested in having a direct influence on policy. (Perhaps this disinterest accounts for the relatively low influence even of those who did consulting work or did sit on advisory committees.)[14]

[14] These conclusions are based partly on first-hand observations as an AID employee in Washington, partly on formal interviews, and partly on sheer impressions. For fragmentary documentation, see Packenham, "Foreign Aid and Political Development," *passim*; *idem*, "Political-Development Doctrines in the American Foreign Aid Program," 234.

A different analysis, which is perhaps more widespread in the United States today, holds that theorists interacted with policymakers in certain settings and that the influence of the theorists through these interactions was much more significant than the specific theories they created. The following are examples of ways in which this type of argument is manifested:

1. Intellectual influences are felt in such "establishment" research organizations as the Rand Corporation, the Brookings Institution, and the Council on Foreign Relations.

2. Prestigious academic institutions such as Harvard, MIT, Yale, Columbia, Princeton, Chicago, Michigan, Wisconsin, Berkeley, or Stanford "radiate" influence throughout government, especially through such institutionalized mechanisms as private consultantships, research and policy conferences, and government advisory panels.

3. The great American foundations—especially Ford, Rockefeller, and Carnegie—maintain very close links to academic institutions and like the government are eager to use social science resources in policymaking.

Clearly such interactive influences exist in some measure, and as such they constitute partial exceptions to the "low-influence" generalization made above. In fact, in some other areas of social science and public policy, such influences may be very common. In the area of political development theories and policies, however, these influences are still exceptions. It is very important to note, moreover, that such influence as these relationships do generate is much more a *supportive* and *legitimizing* one than a *positive* and *changing* one, or a critical, negative influence that also changes things. The former kinds of influence are important, to be sure, but they are nonetheless very different from influences that significantly alter the course of events by changing decisionmakers' minds. (In its most extreme and corrupted form, of course, the former kind of influence constitutes abuse rather than use of social science.)

Thus the argument made here is not that policymakers

pay no attention whatever to academicians, but rather that the influence of the social scientists on the policymakers was limited and of a rather special kind. Those who have argued differently often make two mistakes. The first is to ignore the basic distinction between changing and sustaining influence. Some analysts—Noam Chomsky is one of the best known examples[15]—have assumed that social scientists, whose writings and activities reinforced official views that would have obtained in any event, and who were essentially failures (as most theorists were) as critics of basic policy premises, ipso facto had a large positive influence on government. As will be seen in Chapter 7 this argument has considerable merit in terms of opportunities forgone for influence through fundamental reappraisal of premises. But in terms of getting officials to act differently the theorists' influence was generally quite low. (For example, although those social scientists who were powerful in government did not dissent on Vietnam, it is hardly accurate to maintain that it was their arguments which prevailed, and led to the disaster, over the opposition of other, wiser heads. The problem was that there were too few dissenters and wiser heads anywhere, not that the social scientists were the sole or main source of the error.)

The other mistake is to generalize too much: from a few individuals to social scientists generally, and from a few areas of public policy to many areas.[16] Thus Chomsky at

[15] See especially his *American Power and the New Mandarins* (New York: Vintage Books, 1969). It should be noted that one of Chomsky's main complaints seems to be about the failure of criticism, and on this point I think he is quite right. See below, Chapter 7. However, he sometimes confuses matters in the ways indicated, e.g., where he speaks of the "influence" and "access to power" of social scientists (pp. 24-25).

[16] It is almost surely the case, for instance, that theorists of military strategy and deterrence were more influential than the theorists of political development. Thus, Ernest R. May notes that the strategic theorists exercised "important influence," both by "fixing the terms of strategic debate" and by "getting into the muck" of policymaking themselves. However, May also notes that the writings of these think-

times implies that many social scientists had as much influence as a W. W. Rostow or a McGeorge Bundy. In fact, of course, very few had such influence. More significantly, almost none of the prominent political development theorists had anything remotely approaching the influence of a Bundy or a Rostow or a Henry Kissinger. Also, Chomsky assumes that the social scientists he cites who did have influence in government were equally influential in the social science community. The reverse may be much closer to the truth. If so, it is not necessarily true that this relationship results from the involvement with or isolation from government per se. For instance, Rostow's standing as a social theorist had fallen considerably in the social science community well before the implications of Vietnam began to dawn. Finally, authors of descriptive country or regional studies were probably more widely known than the general theorists among country desk officers. In any event, prominent theorists like Lipset, Almond, and Deutsch were on the whole a hundred times more influential—directly—in the social science community than in policy circles; some "action intellectuals" like Bundy, who had great political power, had relatively little prestige or influence in the social science community. Certainly it was less than people outside the academic world tend to infer from the fact of his having been a professor at Harvard.

INDIRECT UTILIZATION

Social science theories may influence policymakers not only in these conscious, direct ways, but also in a more

---

ers "had a significant impact on strategic and diplomatic decisions only in a few isolated instances," and that the influence on foreign policy decisions of Alfred Thayer Mahan alone in the first decades of the twentieth century was greater than the "many Mahans" of the 1950s and 1960s. See Ernest R. May, "Ideas About Military Strategy," in *The Role of Ideas in American Foreign Policy*, ed. Gene M. Lyons (Hanover, New Hampshire: University Press of New England, June 1971), pp. 43, 45.

subtle manner. No one has made the point more eloquently than Lord Keynes:

> The ideas of economists and political philosophers, both when they are right and when they are wrong, are more powerful than is commonly understood. Indeed the world is ruled by little else. Practical men, who believe themselves to be quite exempt from any intellectual influences, are usually the slaves of some defunct economist. Madmen in authority, who hear voices in the air, are distilling their frenzy from some academic scribbler of a few years back. I am sure that the power of vested interests is vastly exaggerated compared with the gradual encroachment of ideas.[17]

Ideas "move around." They have subtle effects. Surely ideas learned in school, university, and private reading and conversation affected the views of aid officials about political development. But which ideas? And how does one know? Precisely because indirect effects are often unknown even to the affected, they are hard to discover and describe. Also, indirect effects are often measurable only after a long period of time. Thus one can be reasonably sure that the ideas of John Locke and Adam Smith have had a powerful, indirect influence on Americans, even among those who never heard their names. But it is harder to confirm or disconfirm Keynes' thesis with respect to recent theories of political development.

My own impression is that these indirect effects have been rather small, and that whatever influence they had was, again, a sustaining, reinforcing, legitimizing influence more than it was a changing one. To a very great extent, the theories were ideas which reflected the liberal tradition and thus helped to maintain it.

[17] Quoted in Samuelson, *Economics: An Introductory Analysis*, 3rd ed. (New York: McGraw-Hill, 1955), p. 12. See also David L. Sills' Introduction to the *International Encyclopedia of the Social Sciences*, pp. xix-xx.

POTENTIAL UTILITIES AND LIMITATIONS OF THE THEORIES

The theories not only *were not* used very much; they also *should not* have been used very much because they had little to offer policymakers and could not have improved policy a great deal even if they had been more widely employed.

The theories had at least three major types of faults. First, they tended to be weak as empirical theory. Key concepts were often imprecisely defined. Hypotheses about empirical relationships between and among variables were often poorly operationalized and fell apart under empirical testing. Theories were often global and undifferentiated. Many key variables were omitted. The research was often ahistorical. Time sequences and rates of change were neglected. Policymakers got little help from them in specifying priorities.

Second, they tended to be weak as normative theory. The normative assumptions and implications of the theories were seldom spelled out in detail and were little defended. Both explicit and implicit normative premises were to a very great extent simply projections of American values. In short, the theory was ethnocentric.

Third, they tended to be weak by the criteria of applied social science. That is, even where the theories could explain what they wanted to explain, they often did so in terms of variables that were not amenable to control by policymakers. Applied social scientists and policymakers need not only to identify explanatory variables; they need also to identify variables which are amenable to purposive control. Since most of the theories of this period explained political development in terms of variables that were not amenable to control, they were often more potentially useful in sensitizing the policymaker to the limits of what he could hope to accomplish through social engineering than in helping him to identify points of access for change.

The discussion that follows deals more fully with the limitations of the theories than with their utilities—mainly because the limitations greatly outweigh the utilities and need to be clarified. At the same time the theories have more potential usefulness than I have been able to indicate. It should also be noted that the main but not exclusive focus of attention will be the economic, social-system, and political-culture theories. The potential utilities of the legal-formal and the will and capacity theories will also be assessed, but they receive less attention because the three break-with-formalism theories were the most influential ones of the period. A final caveat is that this assessment gives greater attention to the potential usefulness of the theories for the United States or another foreign country seeking to promote political development in the Third World, than to their usefulness for indigenous leaders in the Third World. The utilities and limitations of the theories probably differ slightly for the two sets of actors. Foreign powers tend to have less legitimacy, less influence, and less knowledge of the needs of underdeveloped countries than indigenous leaders do; therefore the theories are likely to have a bit greater potential usefulness for the latter than for the former—but not much.

AS EMPIRICAL THEORY

Utilities. Probably the greatest potential utility of the theories for the policymaker is that they can enrich his insights and alter and widen his perspectives. For example, the several manifestations of the social-system and political-culture approaches to political development specify that a variety of social-system characteristics and psychological orientations affect political systems in certain ways. It seems reasonable to conclude that, taken as wholes, these characteristics and orientations *do* affect political systems, and that changes in them are related to changes in political systems. Given the degree of reliance on the economic approach to political development in the aid programs, there does seem to be some utility for policymakers in recognizing the impacts on politics of those other types of conditions. The theories are by no means good enough, as social science, to

255

provide the policymaker with ready-made answers about what to do in specific situations. But social science seldom, if ever, can do that, even where the theory is superior.

One can, of course, regard the foregoing "contribution" as pretty obvious, and thus not much of a contribution at all. There are at least two reasonable responses to this point of view. First, many of the specific and detailed propositions contained within the social-system and political-culture approaches are less "obvious" than the approaches themselves taken as wholes. Second, and more important, even if they were not useful starting points for positive, creative action regarding political development, these broad approaches would still indicate some of the limits within which any political development effort would have to operate. For awareness of the impact of social-system and political-culture variables on political development can (and should) sensitize the policymaker to the limits of what he can do about political development through these (and other) means.

The latter point deserves elaboration. It appears that the *major* potential utility of the social-system and political-culture approaches, insofar as they have scientific merit, is a "negative" contribution. That is, they can sensitize the policymaker to the limits of what he can do (with the instruments at his disposal) consciously and purposefully to shape political systems. The theories suggested that political systems may be affected by economic and mass sociological and psychological phenomena as well as by legal-formal and political-leadership variables. Between countries, these phenomena have impacts on political development which vary according to approach, time, and place. However, *within* any single political system, some of these characteristics— especially political-culture and social-system variables—may be very difficult for policymakers to change. Insofar as this is true, these phenomena are not variables but *constants*, impervious to change by policymakers. Thus the main contribution of this body of knowledge to the policymaker is, in many cases, the "negative" one of telling him how difficult it will usually be to reshape the political system through these particular "levers," were he to make the effort. Since these conditions account for a great deal of the variance among political systems—political development usually is probably at least three parts "situational" and no more than one part "optional," or dependent on leadership[18]—he may do well in many situations to focus his political development efforts on variables which explain less (like leadership) but which are more amenable to control.[19]

The fact that even within any given country sociological and psychological phenomena are not *entirely* constants, and that under some conditions they are amenable to change, means that the potential utility of these approaches is not wholly negative but also positive. There are conditions under which they also constitute a base for positive, creative action, especially if the policymaker is willing to use a healthy portion of his resources. Under such circumstances (which are not well understood at this time) these approaches have some potential utility. However, if political development theories have these kinds of potential utilities for policymakers, they have even greater limitations.

Limitations. One of the major limitations has been the weakness of the theories as social science. This assertion has many facets. Scholars do not fully agree on what political development means, and the definitions utilized are often operationally vague and/or shifting. There is surely no theoretical system about political development analogous, say, to the Keynesian or neo-Keynesian system in economics. There are relatively few "if/then" propositions of the mid-

[18] This is adapted from the observation of Dankwart A. Rustow that "the phenomenon of leadership is three parts setting and one part personality. The leader at times is the script writer but more often the *souffleur* of the historical drama." *A World of Nations*, p. 153.

[19] The amenability-to-control criterion of potentially useful theory is discussed in more detail in "The Theories as Applied Social Science," below.

257

dle range which withstand an empirical test across time and space, especially when controls for other variables are introduced. Those that remain are still probabilistic statements, fine for the social scientist but often of limited utility for the policymaker in dealing with a particular case. Some of this literature is exceedingly loose conceptually. Some "theories" are really ways of looking at the world and "frameworks" for comparison which nevertheless are sometimes treated as theory.[20]

On the other hand, precise, "rigorous" definitions of political development, amenable to operationalization in quantitative terms, often narrowed and reduced the significance of the concept. Cross-sectional studies relying heavily on quantitative sociological, economic, and voting data yielded sometimes interesting but often extremely narrow conclusions, or gross but frequently spurious correlations, or both. Equally distressing was the neglect in most of these studies of the crucial historical dimensions of their problems. As late as 1969, the Director of the Office of External Research in the Department of State, Dr. E. Raymond Platig, could write that not just political development theories but "academic social science [in general] is today acutely method-conscious, fascinated by a range of data-handling techniques, productive of a variety of correlations, long on abstract and esoteric theory, rich in conceptualization, but short on propositions with explanatory power, short on bodies of theory easily applicable to the analysis of concrete situations, and almost devoid of problem-specific conclusions or convincing forecasts or projections."[21]

[20] This has happened, for example, to Gabriel A. Almond's very influential introductory essay in *The Politics of the Developing Areas*. The essay is more a way of looking at political systems comparatively than a theory, although I and others have sometimes treated it as theory.

[21] "Foreign Affairs Analysis: Some Thoughts on Expanding Competence," *International Studies Quarterly*, 13, No. 1 (March 1969), 22-23. See also the exchanges among Platig, Andrew Scott, John Haar, and Raymond Tanter in the same journal, 14, Nos. 1 and 2 (March

One of the unfortunate consequences of the propensity to stress cross-national comparisons and neglect historical variables was the widespread assumption—sometimes presented as a "finding"—of unilinearity, or the idea that there is a uniform, evolutionary sequence of change toward ever "higher" levels of political (and other) development.[22] It is, I believe, a fact that Samuel P. Huntington's article, "Political Development and Political Decay," published in 1965, was the first widely read and influential contribution to the political development literature which, as a central theme of its argument, emphatically and systematically challenged the notion of unilinearity. Amazingly, although we all knew about Gibbon's *Decline and Fall of the Roman Empire* and Toynbee's works, the idea that political systems could "decay" as well as "develop" had simply not been made forcefully before in this literature.[23]

In addition, there was confusion between cause and correlation. Partly due to the impact of other social science disciplines, political scientists in the late 1950s became more reluctant than before to speak of cause. But causal language crept into the discourse as into a vacuum; Rustow's critique

and June 1970). Scott thinks the policy relevance of social science research is "obvious" and therefore does not need to be documented. He sees Tanter's work as "an excellent example" of policy relevant research. Tanter claims to have "demonstrated," through some correlations, the "potential relevance" of a social science approach to policy questions. Platig locates a number of problems with Tanter's correlations and says they are irrelevant and unilluminating for policy. He concludes that social scientists "all have a great deal to be modest about" regarding their potential contributions to policy. In my view, Platig wins the debate hands down.

[22] One of the best examples is Lerner, *Traditional Society*, Chap. 2. This point has been well made by Rustow, *A World of Nations*, pp. 141-42.

[23] Huntington, "Political Development and Political Decay," 386-430. Eisenstadt, in *The Political Systems of Empires* (New York: Free Press, 1962) and in several articles, advanced some similar ideas; his work was not, however, nearly as influential in the United States as Huntington's.

of Lipset—"he time and again slips from the language of correlation into the language of causation"[24]—applies to others as well.[25] The problem was compounded because readers did not necessarily avoid this pitfall even when the writer did.

Two other characteristics of the theoretical literature on political development may be counted either as features or consequences of the relatively tenuous scientific standing of the theories. One is its susceptibility to changes in fashions. The other is its weak capacity to help the policymaker set priorities.

Fads and Faddishness. Theories of political development change rather rapidly, and scholarly writings about political development are subject to fashions and fads.[26] The scientific quality of this literature (its quality as empirical theory) has, I believe, improved over time. Nevertheless, the rapidly changing content of this body of theory is one of its most serious shortcomings for policy and policymakers.

Probably no book in the field of comparative politics over the last ten or fifteen years has had a greater impact than *The Politics of the Developing Areas* (1960), co-authored and edited by Gabriel Almond and James Coleman.[27] Yet only a few years after the book appeared, both Almond and Coleman had considerably changed their own views.

[24] Rustow, *A World of Nations*, p. 144, n. 12, where examples are cited. See also Chapter 5, above.

[25] For instance, see the comment by Tanter and the reply by Platig, esp. p. 230, both cited in n. 21, above.

[26] This is a sociological, not a polemical, statement. These fads and fashions are empirical characteristics of the literature. In very large part they are a consequence of the difficulty of the subject matter and the paucity of dependable theory in the field. I am not asserting that they derive from conscious irresponsibility on the part of the authors.

[27] Cited in n. 20. Robert A. Dahl referred to this book as "far and away the most influential recent work" in the field of comparative politics. *Modern Political Analysis* (Englewood Cliffs, N.J.: Prentice-Hall, 1963), p. 112.

260

Various authors criticized the book, especially its theoretical approach.[28] Almond considerably modified and expanded his theoretical framework in subsequent publications. In 1968, he wrote: "Political development theory, after having drunk deeply from sociological, anthropological, and psychological theory, now must turn to economic theory and methodology, and must learn how to utilize the enormous data bank of history in the development of rigorous theory of political development."[29] All of this was entirely proper and, in a sense, to be expected in a new and uncertain field of scholarship. But what happened to this important book is highly instructive for present purposes. A work which seemed for a few years to be indispensable to the policymaker seeking help from the social sciences was only a few years later seen as a marginal source, more a document for the historian of a scholarly field than a critical part of political development theory.

This point has not gone wholly unnoticed in government. The following statement by Charles Wolf, Jr., an economist from the Rand Corporation, was quoted in a government document in 1964: "The Almond-Coleman book came out in 1960. The work on which it was based was done in the two or three years preceding publication. . . . Now the interesting thing is that the authors of this work have very considerably changed their view of the connections between social and economic phenomena and their political and military consequences in the intervening five or six years. The obvious point is that there's a lag between the findings of scholarship and the influence of those findings on policy. . . . [T]he influence of scholarship . . . on policy . . . frequently is the influence of an outmoded scholarship because the findings of research do and should change."[30]

[28] See the items cited in Chapter 5, n. 58.

[29] Gabriel A. Almond, *Political Development: Essays in Heuristic Theory* (Boston: Little, Brown, 1970), p. 287.

[30] "Political Development: A Bibliography, 1960-1964," External Research Staff Paper No. 159 (August 1964), Department of State,

Just as the most general theoretical approaches are subject to such shifts of mood, so also are empirically based studies. For example, for a number of years the parties of West African states like Ghana, Guinea, Mali, Senegal and the Ivory Coast were seen as powerful, centralized organizations with a great capacity for social mobilization and integration. But in reviewing a new book on these one-party states, a specialist in African politics, Henry Bienen, wrote that "Zolberg's account is a revision of recent West African political history; he makes clear what the parties of Ghana, Guinea, Mali, Senegal, and the Ivory Coast are not, and that even the most effective of the West African national movements were by no means 'organizational juggernauts' as they became ruling parties. . . . on the contrary, both before and after independence, they reflected the pluralism and lack of integration of their societies. *Creating Political Order* is likely to establish a new orthodoxy, since Africanists as well as Africans jump on *bandwagons*, and already many of the arguments that Zolberg so forcefully makes can be heard in the land."[31] I have little doubt that the new orthodoxy will be more informed than the old. But what is notable for our purposes is the propensity for the "orthodoxies" to change so rapidly and the appeal of "bandwagons" among social scientists.

Until the mid-1960s certain variables, perspectives, and

Washington, D.C., p. 2. It is possible that just this kind of lag was reflected in the fact that Title IX, which conceived political development in terms of political participation and democratic institutions, was passed into law in 1966, just as the social science literature was beginning to challenge seriously the equation of political development and liberal constitutionalism.

[31] Henry Bienen, "What Does Political Development Mean in Africa?" *World Politics*, 20, No. 1 (October 1967), 130 (emphasis added), reviewing Aristide Zolberg, *Creating Political Order: The Party-States of West Africa* (Chicago: Rand McNally, 1966). For a review essay that is very explicit and prescient about fads and fashions at a time when relatively few social scientists were, see Herbert Goldhamer, "Fashion and Social Science," *World Politics*, 6, No. 3 (April 1954), 394-404.

data relevant to political development were virtually ignored in the literature, e.g. studies of violence and revolution, historical crises, political rights and freedoms, international influences on domestic political development, and certain political structures, like courts and legislatures. Then in the latter half of the 1960s such areas began to receive more innovative attention.[32] One could simply note these relatively neglected areas, record the innovations, and then conclude that the innovations constituted *the* "answers" to the questions that plagued political development theorizing. But where does the process end? What happens to today's fashion *tomorrow?* The pervasiveness of fads and fashions in political development theorizing cautions us, as it must caution the policymaker, against very firm reliance on formulations or hypotheses current at any given time.

This is not to assert that the theories represented only fashions and subjective preferences. Even granting the numerous and profound shortcomings of the theories as social science and the substantial impact of fashion upon what was written, it remains the case that their quality as empirical theory has increased perceptibly over the years. The economic, social-system, and political-culture approaches represent an increment in quality over the legal-formalism that was dominant before World War II.

Within these approaches, too, scientific progress occurred. As noted in Chapter 5, the theorists have gone beyond stating the conditions of political development vaguely defined to specify with more precision the dimensions of the dependent variable, i.e. nationhood, statehood, participation, and democracy. Finally, the emergence of the will and capacity theories represented not only a shift in vogue, in research styles and personal preferences, but also an increment in the scientific quality of the theory. The prior emphases meant that some of the variance in the performance of po-

[32] For examples and citations, see Packenham, "Political Development Research," in Haas and Kariel, eds., *Approaches to the Study of Political Science* (Scranton, Pa.: Chandler, 1970), p. 182.

litical systems was not explained. There was no explanation, for example, as to why India, so poor, illiterate, and beset by caste, language, ethnic, and other cleavages, was still a stable democracy. Or why Mexico was a stabler polity than richer, more literate, more culturally homogeneous Argentina. Political institutionalization, political leadership, and political choices are factors that help explain such cases, as others.[33]

Weak on Priorities. The other important feature of the theories as empirical theory is their inadequacy in specifying priorities among conflicting political goals (such as participation and authority) and among political and other goals (such as participation and acceptable levels of investment, inflation, and per capita income). Such priorities could not be stated because the theory had very little to say about the costs of achieving one desirable value in terms of other desirable values. Crucial questions were left unanswered: e.g. how much does it "cost" (or benefit) a country to increase, say, political authority, in terms of popular participation? per capita income? "rational" allocation of economic resources? national integration? protection of individual liberties? Instead the literature has usually tended to state or imply long lists of "things to do." It is rich in suggestions—either explicit or implicit—about what might be done to achieve certain political development goals; but, from the point of view of its utility for policy, it has not adequately specified *when* and justified *why* those goals should have priority over other desirable political (and economic and social) goals. This inability to specify and to justify priorities has constituted, and still does, one of the most serious shortcomings of political development theory for policy and policymakers.

Consider, for example, the "broad outlines of policy and strategy" suggested by Professor LaPalombara in order to

[33] For further discussion of the ways in which the will-and-capacity theories represented an improvement over the earlier, politics-as-dependent literature, see Rustow, *A World of Nations*, pp. 142-43.

"build" a "healthy" party system, "strong and responsive legislatures," "vigorous" voluntary associations, "responsive" bureaucracies, and strong restraints on government—in short, if one wanted to achieve "as developmental goals the specific structures that we associate with Western democracy."[34] His first suggestion is "a strong de-emphasis on goals of economic development. . . . *At whatever cost* in delayed material gain may be implied, the elite of the developing newer states might be persuaded to downgrade national plans for economic development and to make [Western] democracy a goal in itself."[35] It is no wonder that LaPalombara provides no examples of political leaders in the Third World who have been or could be persuaded to achieve democracy *no matter what* the economic cost! Second, these elites "should be encouraged to limit the role in economic development of the public sector and to encourage the development of the private sector. . . . This is not to suggest a Spencerian notion regarding the appropriate role of the public sector. Obviously, the politicians and intellectuals of the developing countries who are so hostile to private enterprise would never accept such a state of affairs. But they might accept a greater effort to create genuinely dual economies than is presently the case."[36]

A third suggestion is "to control the demands made upon the political system" by "shifting" these demands "from the economic to the social and political realm." That is, leaders in developing countries should not suppress dissident groups or push for "grandiose schemes of economic development and . . . material well-being"; rather, they should use the "energies" normally devoted to these goals "to generate great national commitment to and demand for democratic development," whatever the economic costs, and despite the fact that "strong psychological motivations" of

[34] Joseph LaPalombara, "Bureacracy and Political Development: Notes, Queries, and Dilemmas," in LaPalombara, ed., *Bureaucracy and Political Development*, p. 56.

[35] *Ibid.*, pp. 56-57 (emphasis added).   [36] *Ibid.*, pp. 57-58.

people in developing countries place higher priorities on economic development than anything else.[37] However, "even if these changes in emphasis could be achieved, they represent *nothing more than temporary measures* alongside the prime need for [and this is suggestion four] a massive program of education," which would increase literacy, "inculcate" a "national sense of secularization," reduce the "great hiatus between elite and masses," teach technical skills, and "socialize people" to "democratic values and democratic roles."[38] It is not specified how demands for economic development might be de-emphasized (suggestion one)—even assuming some success in the substantial task of "shifting" them to the "social and political realms"—at the same time that a "massive" education for democracy program would heighten demands for economic development.

Finally, "In the political realm, the bureaucracy could set an example by spearheading democratization in its own sphere. It could also encourage the healthy growth of legislative and executive power, as well as voluntary associations, by exercising a judicious self-restraint in the use of its own power and capacities. Since it is unreasonable to expect that such a pattern of action would materialize spontaneously, it would be essential for members of the political elite of the newer states to push in this direction."[39] But as Professor La-Palombara himself pointed out earlier in his discussion, "To endow this structure [the bureaucracy] with the major responsibility to set society's goals and to implement them is certain to impede the development of other strong political institutions or other important power centers in the society."[40] It is utopian to suggest that an institution which is defined largely by adherence to hierarchical norms and be-

[37] *Ibid.*, pp. 58-59. For evidence that LaPalombara is right about these "strong psychological motivations," see Hadley Cantril, *The Pattern of Human Concerns* (New Brunswick, N.J.: Rutgers University Press, 1965), *passim.*

[38] *Ibid.*, p. 59 (emphasis added).

[39] *Ibid.*, p. 60.   [40] *Ibid.*, p. 59.

havior patterns might "spearhead democratization in its own sphere," however hard political elites might "push" it in that direction. The tension between bureaucratization and democratization simply cannot be so easily resolved.

The contradictory and utopian character of this set of proposals, and others like it, is apparent. The most useful theories specify sequences of change involving different mixes of components and inputs appropriate for different situations, and they imply or suggest appropriate policy strategies and tactics for those different situations. Such theories are rare in any field; few if any exist in the political development field. Theories that fall short of this difficult standard may still have some policy utility. Even so, if the sequential and contextual kinds of theories just noted are the most useful ones, theories that generate lists of prescriptions without giving serious attention to the problem of priorities are the least useful. In the political development field the theories are heavily concentrated at the latter end of this spectrum, and they are not very useful.

Recently scholars have begun to move again in directions that might make their work more useful in these terms. This trend is particularly evident in the will and capacity theories. Thus far, however, such work is not very advanced. Moreover, in politics the ends are not given. Nor are they easily measured. Even in studies adopting a political economy approach, there is no convenient measure (such as money) or mechanism (such as the market) to measure the costs of economic values in terms of political values as there is for economic values within economics. Therefore the political development theorist, if he is to help illuminate problems of choice for policymakers, must engage in both empirical and normative analysis. That is to say, he may not take his political ends as given but must justify them in normative terms.

Large, difficult, important questions, then, such as what values to maximize in underdeveloped countries, and the relative costs and benefits of democratic and autocratic

267

paths to the realization of these values, are not wholly amenable to scientific resolution. This is so because, first, the questions are so cumbersome and complicated. Social science simply cannot answer them unambiguously, even if the values to be maximized were agreed upon. Second, not all the values to be maximized are agreed upon, nor should they be. Different scholars, like everyone else, have different normative hierarchies. Thus, while normative and empirical discourse can and should inform one another, there is no completely scientific resolution—even in specific contexts— of issues such as the nature and conditions of political development and the appropriate choices to be made in order to move toward it. In dealing with "big" questions of this type, it is impossible not to be a normative theorist, whether or not one chooses to make his values explicit and defend them.[41]

AS NORMATIVE THEORY

What was the normative content of the theories? What were their normative premises and implications? How explicitly spelled out, and how well defended, were they? How appropriate were they with respect to Third World political systems? Answers to these questions help us to assess the quality of the theories in normative terms.

During most of the period under review, political development was commonly defined as liberal constitutionalism along English or American lines. To be sure, some scholars (a minority, certainly) never adopted this point of view.[42] Others held it at first, then changed their views in varying degrees as more evidence came in.[43] But still others had a

[41] For a related argument, see James Q. Wilson, "Violence, Pornography, and Social Science," *The Public Interest*, No. 22 (Winter 1971), 45-61, esp. 57-61.

[42] See the authors cited in Chapter 5, n. 14.

[43] Cf., for example, S. M. Lipset, *Political Man: The Social Bases of Politics* (Garden City, N.Y.: Doubleday, 1960), Chap. 2, with his subsequent *The First New Nation: The United States in Historical and Comparative Perspective* (New York: Basic Books, 1963), pp.

tendency to identify political development with features of the British or American political systems, even in the latter half of the 1960s.[44] In general, this was the main normative thrust of the theories during the whole period.[45]

Much of the intent and spirit of these works is captured in the closing paragraph of Lipset's *Political Man* (1960), a work in which Lipset is, if anything, more cautious than most writers were, or might have been had they written so candidly themselves:

This book's concern with making explicit the conditions of the democratic order reflects my perhaps overrationalistic belief that a fuller understanding of the various conditions under which democracy has existed may help men to develop it where it does not now exist. Although we have concluded that Aristotle's basic hypothesis of the relationship of democracy to a class structure bulging toward the middle . . . is still valid, this does not encourage political optimism, since it implies that political activity should be directed primarily toward assuring economic development. Yet we must not be unduly pessimistic. Democracy has existed in a variety of circumstances, even if

viii, 11; or Gabriel Almond's "Introduction" to *The Politics of the Developing Areas* (1960) with Almond and Powell, *Comparative Politics: A Developmental Approach* (1966). In both instances there is a move toward less complete identification of political development with political democracy.

[44] For instance, W. Arthur Lewis, *Politics in West Africa* (London: Oxford University Press, 1965); Charles C. Moskos, Jr., and Wendell Bell, "Emerging Nations and Ideologies of American Social Scientists," *The American Sociologist*, 2, No. 2 (May 1967), 67-72; Lloyd I. Rudolph and Susanne Hoeber Rudolph, *The Modernity of Tradition: Political Development in India* (Chicago: University of Chicago Press, 1967); Myron Weiner, *Party Building in a New Nation: The Indian National Congress* (Chicago: University of Chicago Press, 1967).

[45] See the perceptive comments of Ali A. Mazrui, "From Social Darwinism to Current Theories of Modernization," *World Politics*, 21, No. 1 (October 1968), esp. 75-78.

it is most commonly sustained by a limited set of conditions. It cannot be achieved by acts of will alone, of course, but men's wills expressed in action can shape institutions and events in directions that reduce or increase the chances for democracy's development and survival. . . . To aid men's actions in furthering democracy in then absolutist Europe was in some measure Tocqueville's purpose in studying the operation of American society in 1830. To clarify the operation of Western democracy in the mid-twentieth century may contribute to the political battle in Asia and Africa.[46]

How appropriate is it thus to equate political development with "Western democracy"? The answer to this normative question depends in large measure on the answers to two further, empirical questions. What has been and what is the incidence of democracy in the Third World? What projections does the historical record suggest about the probable incidence of democracy there in the future? The data presented in the Introduction to this study (Tables 2-4) seem to me adequate to sustain the following two propositions: (1) most Third World countries have not been and are not now democratic; and (2) the historical record suggests strongly that the prospects are not bright for a rapid or substantial increase in the percentage of democracies among Third World countries. These propositions do not add up to "the view that . . . non-democratic political systems are in some sense an *inevitable* outcome," which Moskos and Bell have criticized.[47] (Indeed, few if any theorists have taken this extreme position.) It is fair to say, however, that

[46] Lipset, *Political Man*, p. 417. See also the candid and revealing—and less cautious—statement of his political beliefs which Lipset wrote in 1962 as the Introduction to the Anchor paperback edition of this book.

[47] "Emerging Nations and Ideologies of American Social Scientists," p. 68 (emphasis added). W. Arthur Lewis similarly characterizes and evaluates the views of political scientists in *Politics in West Africa*, p. 89.

democratic regimes are *improbable* for most countries in the Third World. This generalization means little in dealing with a particular country; with respect to a general orientation toward political development in the Third World, it means a great deal. Whether dealing with particular countries or with general policy orientations, social scientists who make prescriptions, and/or do analyses which might contribute to prescriptions, are bound to try to assess probabilities and take them into account.

But serious efforts to estimate these probabilities were rare. Western democracy was assumed to be both feasible and appropriate in the Third World. Such limited debate as did occur seldom went beyond claim and counterclaim to serious, sustained analysis. So much was all of this the case that, as was noted in Chapter 5, systematic data about trends in the incidence of democracy in those countries were almost nonexistent. Since normative and policy judgments almost always depend in part, and often in substantial part, on empirical conditions as well as values, the absence of such data weakened the quality of the normative judgments embodied in the theories.

If in fact the odds are strongly against democratic government in the Third World for the foreseeable future, then the policy utility of theories that try to throw some light on the conditions which support democracy may be low or even negative.[48] Specifically, consider the policy implications of utilizing a concept of political development defined exclusively as liberal democracy. A possible outcome is that such a policy—policy A—would succeed in many or most cases. But a more likely outcome is that it would fail, and have serious costs in most cases. For example, democracy

---

[48] "Frequently one cannot simply apply one's standards of values to the different possible results of a decision, determine which one is 'the best,' and then choose it. For if there is uncertainty about the outcomes, to choose 'the best' might be to adopt a strategy that most people on careful reflection would surely reject" (Dahl, *Political Analysis*, 97). The hypothetical example in this paragraph parallels Dahl's.

is deliberative and often slow to work its will. It often provides ample means for conservative minorities to block rapid economic and social change. However, if mass demands are great, or a counterelite has different ideas, tensions can build to the point where intense conflict and instability, followed by total breakdown of the system, may occur. Then there may be either reaction, revolution, or some other form of illiberal politics. Conceivably, any of these might be good or bad. However, especially if the result is reaction, it is quite possible the result will be neither democracy nor social and economic progress.[49] On the other hand, a more modest policy, policy B, might have a much smaller chance (at least in the short run) of aiding democratic development in most countries of the Third World, but it might help it in a few countries; and it might advance other values, like economic and social welfare, or political integration, or stability, in many countries.[50] As an Indian sociologist has observed:

> It is ironic that the progressives who are the most vocal critics of coup d'etats which bring in military or other dictatorships, and of revivalist, fascist-type movements seem to dismiss entirely the possibility that their efforts might produce the opposite of what they are looking for. Their faith in the inevitable laws of social development working in their favor seems as strong as that of any religious person in his religion. . . . [Moreover] an Indian social scientist who concludes that India's instability arises from her democracy is likely to be dubbed a reactionary or a fascist, or an arrogant intellectual who has contempt

[49] An example of this latter sort is Portugal under Salazar. Brazil since 1964 has had growing and generally high annual rates of economic growth, but in several other respects it too may be a good example.

[50] "On reflection most people would, I suspect, prefer B to A, even though one possible result of A might be, in their view, far and away the 'best' of all solutions" (Dahl, *Political Analysis*, p. 97).

272

for the people. . . . To be aware of the shortcomings of democracy, [however,] is not to be anti-democratic.[51]

The equation of political development with political democracy expresses an implicit concern for the "best" solution rather than for a solution which is "better." This concern betrays a certain ethnocentrism in American political development theories. This ethnocentrism is one of the most important limitations of the theories for policymakers and for policy. Writings on political development which make more modest but perhaps more realistic normative promises often have greater potential utility for policy than writings which define political development as democracy. I refer here specifically to the "will and capacity" and political-economy approaches.

The literature has been criticized for ethnocentrism on another, related ground. Some critics have argued that the preoccupation with Anglo-American democracy has made it more difficult for scholars to perceive political arrangements that are evolving in underdeveloped countries. These arrangements, say the critics, may have no historical precedents, yet they may be more appropriate in those contexts than any they might borrow from the West. Those criticized respond that few indeed are the Third World countries which have more capable and democratic polities than —for all their imperfections—the United States or England. They argue further that if the underdeveloped nations are going to evolve new political forms to rival the Anglo-American models, such new forms are not yet apparent. The critics, in turn, reply that the Western models are shot through with injustices and inequities, and that Americans are much too complacent about their political institutions as well as being culturally and politically imperialistic in trying to export them elsewhere.

[51] M. N. Srinivas, "The Politics of Scarcity," *Times of India*, July 12, 1968. Professor Srinivas was chairman of the Department of Sociology, Delhi School of Economics.

It is impossible to go into all of these issues. The crucial question, for present purposes, is not whether the Anglo-American model is subjected to sufficient self-scrutiny (it probably has not been), or whether it is superior or inferior to others now extant, but whether conscious efforts at political development borrowing from those models may not hinder the emergence of new forms of political organization which could be superior in the context of underdeveloped countries. It seems reasonably clear that many Third World countries would be fortunate indeed if their political systems functioned as well in the service of their peoples as those of America and Great Britain, warts and all, do for theirs. But it is quite another thing to argue that the export of features of Anglo-American democracy to new nations would have equally beneficial consequences in those contexts, and to deny that political changes in the latter countries may produce political models that are superior on either a relative or an absolute scale. Barrington Moore's conclusions, in *Social Origins of Dictatorship and Democracy* (1966), that "both Western liberalism and communism (especially the Russian version) have begun to display many symptoms of historical obsolescence," and that "as successful doctrines they have started to turn into ideologies that justify and conceal numerous forms of repression,"[52] should at least put liberals on guard against tendencies toward ossification in their own systems, and against ethnocentric exportation to other systems.

A third ethnocentric aspect of viewing political development as coterminous with democracy has been the strong tendency to define democracy exclusively in political terms, whereas most of the Third World defines democracy in economic and social terms as well, and often gives greater weight to the latter. For example, American scholarship has tended to view democracy in terms of such procedural characteristics as free, regular, and competitive elections; in-

[52] (Boston: Beacon, 1966), p. 506.

stitutional checks and balances; the procedural (and substantive) safeguards of the law and the courts; the effects on leaders of interest group pressures and of participant, bargaining, pragmatic political cultures. There is considerable variety in these conceptions, but they are all focused on political activities and institutions which enable followers to control leaders in some fashion. In the Third World, however, the scope of the meaning of democracy is often much broader. It extends to a greater stress on economic and social egalitarianism, e.g. economic reforms to redistribute income more equitably, social reforms to provide more education, housing, or health facilities. It is more substantive than procedural, and the substance of democracy is often economic and social rather than political. Thus, Apter's "mobilization regimes,"[53]—e.g. "people's democracies" and "guided democracies,"—are undemocratic in the Anglo-American sense because, procedurally, they involve control by leaders over followers more than control by followers over leaders. But they are democratic in the sense indicated here because they are widely seen as mechanisms for promoting substantive economic and social egalitarianism. American social scientists often resist expanding the boundaries of "democracy" beyond the political system both because of their normative preferences and because it would complicate substantially the already difficult task of dealing operationally with the concept. Insofar as this discrepancy between American and Third World concepts exists, however, it limits the potential utility of the theories.

A fourth ethnocentric aspect has been that democracy has implied gradual, piecemeal change, as contrasted with sudden, radical change, and especially revolution. With rare exceptions, American political development theories have had a strong preference for stability, for change "within the system." For example, books on Latin America are subtitled "Evolution or Revolution?" or "Reform or Revolution?":

[53] David Apter, *The Politics of Modernization* (Chicago: University of Chicago Press, 1965).

"revolution" is clearly considered the less desirable alternative. That this view is slightly less prevalent now is illustrated by Moore's work, published in 1966, which concluded that "the costs of moderation have been at least as atrocious as those of revolution, perhaps a good deal more."[54] Despite this departure from the academic consensus, his book was widely acclaimed and won major prizes from both the American Political Science Association and the American Sociological Association. Nevertheless, gradualist norms were almost unquestioned in the political development literature during the 1950s and 1960s; they still prevail.

The preference in the literature for gradual change is not, of course, always misdirected. Revolutionary change is costly, and in some, perhaps most cases, it is more costly than moderate change. It seems clear, however, that there are conditions under which revolution may be preferable to evolution. Moore's investigation of six major cases of modernization in modern times—England, France, the United States, China, Japan, and India—supports this conclusion. Moreover, the revolutions in Mexico (1910), Russia (1917), and Cuba (1959) were costly but not necessarily more costly than the continuance of the regimes they overthrew might have been. In any event, the potential utility of the theories has been limited in normative terms because their writers have not, with very few exceptions, seriously weighed the relative costs and benefits of revolutionary versus evolutionary change. The literature has tended overwhelmingly to *assume* that evolution is better than revolution under *all* conditions, rather than investigating and evaluating the merits under various conditions of the two paths.

AS APPLIED SOCIAL SCIENCE

The potential utility of the theories also depends on their quality as applied social science. This quality is indexed by the degree to which they explain political development in

[54] Moore, *Social Origins*, p. 505.

terms of variables which are amenable to control or manipulation by policymakers.[55] I shall argue that many of the
theories have conceived and explained political development
largely in terms of variables that are relatively difficult, expensive, or even impossible to control, and that this limited

[55] The theoretical point of departure for this assertion is some
literature in the field of the sociology of science, especially Alvin
W. Gouldner, "Theoretical Requirements of the Applied Social
Sciences," *American Sociological Review*, 22, No. 1 (February
1957), 92-102, reprinted in Warren G. Bennis, Kenneth D. Benne,
and Robert Chin, eds., *The Planning of Change: Readings in the Applied Behavioral Sciences* (New York: Holt, Rinehart and Winston,
1961), pp. 83-95, esp. pp. 88-90. Subsequent citations are to the latter
source. See also Herbert A. Shephard, "Basic Research and the Social
System of Pure Science," *Philosophy of Science*, 23 (January 1956),
48-57; Norman W. Storer, *The Social System of Science* (New York:
Holt, Rinehart and Winston, 1966); and Kathleen Archibald, "The
Utilization of Social Research and Policy Analysis," Ph.D. dissertation, Department of Sociology, Washington University, St. Louis,
January 1968, Chap. 4.

According to Gouldner, the criteria for the selection of possible
explanatory variables in the social system of applied social science
are: (1) the extent to which they are susceptible to control or manipulation; (2) the degree to which such manipulation is consistent with
the policymaker's values; (3) how much it costs to manipulate them
effectively; and (4) often, whether they are related to leadership,
which is a "presumably efficient locus of intervention" or control.
Since the cost of effective manipulation is really only a measure of the
extent of controllability, and leadership is a variable or set of variables
which is relatively easy (or "inexpensive") to control, Gouldner's four
criteria can readily be collapsed into only two: susceptibility to control (1, 3, 4), and compatibility with values (2). I omit discussion of
the latter here because it is not especially interesting or important in
this context, because it was partly covered in the previous section on
normative theory, and because of space limitations.

Although Gouldner says only a little about the scientific quality
of the social science as a theoretical requisite for its potential utility,
this is because he is trying to specify the distinctive theoretical requisites of applied as distinguished from pure social science. But he
agrees ("Theoretical Requirements," p. 83) that scientific quality—
a theory's quality as empirical theory—is also a very important criterion of the potential usefulness of social science, pure or applied.

Gouldner sought to "identify the theoretic and conceptual tools

their potential usefulness for policymakers. This has been especially true of the social-system and political-culture approaches to political development, and in one sense it has also been the case with respect to the will and capacity orientation. However, when political development has been conceived and explained in terms of variables that are easier to control, the potential usefulness of the theory, in terms of the criteria of applied social science, has increased. Such is the case with respect to the legal-formal and economic theories, and also, in a different sense, the will and capacity theories. In these approaches, the other, less manageable variables are not necessarily forgotten or ignored. Rather, the theorists may simply focus on or "discover" other variables that also make a difference and are more subject to purposive control.

The legal-formal approach implies that policymakers should direct their attention to constitutional and statutory provisions about electoral systems, legislatures, executives, bureaucracies, civil liberties, etc. These provisions are, relatively speaking, extremely amenable to control. One has only to influence what is written in constitutions and statutes. The low incidence of this approach among the doctrines of aid policymakers is surely not due to the difficulty of influencing such variables so much as it is due to the policymakers' perceptions concerning the ineffectiveness of such changes, even if they were made. This perception has some foundation: legal-formal variables probably do not explain as much of the variance in political-system characteristics as economic, social, and psychological variables. How-

---

most conducive to the maturation of applied social science. The ultimate objective," he continued, "was to codify these, so that they can constitute a paradigm useful for the systematic inspection of the different applied fields." Almost fifteen years after he wrote this article, I still know of no better effort to do these things. It should be noted that for Gouldner, applied social science was a role orientation. By his criteria, Marx, Durkheim, Freud, and Keynes were all applied social scientists; so also are most contemporary theorists of political development.

ever, legal-formal variables do have some explanatory power. Constitutions and statutes do make a difference in the performance of political systems. For this reason, and because legal-formal variables are relatively amenable to control, theories that use legal-formal variables as explanatory variables have a certain potential utility for policymakers. Gouldner's observations about the utility of this type of knowledge for applied social scientists apply equally to its utility for policymakers. As he points out, the "pure" social scientist "aims at identifying variables with predictive power, and the more powerful and reliable the prediction, the better. The applied social scientist's [and the policymaker's] criteria for assessing the adequacy of an independent variable include predictive potency but go beyond this" to include amenability to control. "Since [their] ultimate objective involves the furtherance of some kind of change, not all independent variables are equally suitable for this purpose, nor is the one with the highest correlation coefficient always the best."[56]

The economic approach implies making capital and technology available to those who can use them. It suggests specific, usually quantitative criteria like capital-output and cost-benefit ratios; foreign exchange position; level and rate of inflation, saving, and investment; national development plans; and the like. The policy implications of the economic approach are relatively unambiguous and seem more amenable to control. They can be implemented by relationships with highly visible and accessible elites in finance and planning ministries. The fact that the economic approach satisfies the criteria of applied social science more fully than the approaches mentioned previously is one of the reasons for its attractiveness to policymakers in the foreign aid program. Incidentally, the fact that psychological and sociological explanations for economic development, like those of McClelland and Hagen, seem to satisfy these criteria less well is probably one reason why such theories are less frequently

[56] "Theoretical Requirements," p. 88.

acted upon by policymakers than the more conventional, purely economic manifestations of the economic approach.[57]

The will and capacity approach focuses on political leaders who make choices. It implies that the way to influence political development is to address principally political leaders and government officials and institutions. It focuses on leadership, which is relatively highly amenable to manipulation or control, rather than on vast social forces, which are not. This approach might be implemented in a variety of specific ways. It might imply offering technical assistance to government officials or other leaders. It might mean devising techniques for identifying leaders and using such techniques to nurture them. For a foreign power like the United States, the main implication may well be that the principal means for influencing political development in the Third World are traditional diplomatic techniques, such as formal and informal diplomacy, setting (or not setting) conditions on aid, and selective support (or nonsupport) of incumbent or (much less frequently) potential officeholders. According to this latter set of tactics, the United States might support and encourage governments with the will and capacity to cope with and to generate continuing transformation toward whichever values seem appropriate in particular contexts. And the United States might put pressure, through normal diplomatic channels and through the use of aid as a bargaining tool, on regimes that do not fit this model.

To be sure, leadership often explains less than vast social forces about political-system behavior. Also, leadership is a

[57] Thus Gouldner suggests that "legal institutions" and "material props" have played a large part in the work of applied social scientists because they are "both instrumentally manageable and technologically controllable" (p. 90). Consider, however, the fascinating work of David C. McClelland and David G. Winter, *Motivating Economic Achievement* (New York: Free Press, 1969). They claim that need-for-achievement causes economic growth and that it can be implanted in businessmen with astounding ease. In India, they argue, only ten days of training sufficed to change men's images of themselves in profound ways.

280

relational phenomenon. Leaders always operate in a socio-cultural milieu; hence leadership is never strictly autonomous but also a function of social-system and political-culture variables.[58] And, like all the other theories, the will and capacity approaches are very imperfect as empirical and normative theory. They too imply policies which are sensitive politically, which may be conservative and/or ethnocentric, which require considerable skill on the part of American officials, and which have limited impacts because U.S. resources are limited. Nevertheless, leaders remain more amenable to purposive control than vast social forces.

The social-system approach, it will be recalled, viewed political development mainly as a function of certain kinds of socioeconomic variables, like urbanization, education, and exposure to mass media; the wide distribution of such values as land or wealth; the number and vitality of voluntary associations; the size of the middle class; social mobility generally; and integrative sociopolitical structures. The policy implications of this approach thus include such ideas as manipulating the degree and quality of urbanization; implementing land and tax reforms; creating and sustaining voluntary organizations; increasing the size of the middle class; increasing social mobility; or creating and sustaining integrative sociopolitical structures. These variables are not often amenable to control; it is usually very difficult and

[58] Thus, insofar as political institutions like bureaucracies, parties, legislatures, and some military organizations are seen as mostly reflections of the political cultures and social systems in which they are enmeshed, they are about as difficult to change as the latter. But, insofar as they are seen as relatively autonomous subsystems of the polity, they are more amenable to control. Warren F. Ilchman ably explicates exactly this distinction for the field of development administration in "Rising Expectations and the Revolution in Development Administration," *Public Administration Review*, 25, No. 4 (December 1965), 314-28. He calls the former orientation the "social systems approach," the latter the "administrative systems approach." See also Alvin W. Gouldner, "Metaphysical Pathos and the Theory of Bureaucracy," *American Political Science Review*, 49, No. 2 (June 1955), 496-507, esp. 505.

costly to affect them. To get these things done, the policy-maker is often well advised to work through the leaders—which is to employ a combination of the social-system and the will and capacity approaches rather than just the former.

According to the political-culture approach, political development is largely caused by certain psychological orientations, either at the level of attitudes or at the level of personality. Therefore, the political implications of this approach relate to changes in mass and elite norms, beliefs and attitudes about politics and the political process. It has implied, for example, that people should learn the norms and skills of bargaining, negotiation, and compromise. Also, because in this approach personality variables are seen as important determinants of political development, it suggests that systematic efforts to shape personality structures in underdeveloped countries are in order.

While some of these ideas are perhaps practical,[59] on the whole, basic norms, beliefs, and attitudes about politics, and basic personality structures, are very difficult to change. Even if these variables explain a great deal about the nature of political systems, such knowledge has limited utility for the policymaker because it would be difficult and expensive to "translate" that knowledge into effective policy. Moreover, while in principle the political-culture approach is applicable either to mass or elites, in fact most political-culture research has been on mass populations. The cost and difficulty of changing the beliefs, norms, and attitudes of masses of people is obviously much greater than the cost of changing those of elites. This is another reason why this research has less utility.

The difficulties of implementing the social-system and political-culture approaches directly, and the necessity of working through leaders, may be illustrated by considering the advice of Professors W. Arthur Lewis and Sidney Verba to African nations that would avoid repression and achieve

[59] See n. 57.

282

pluralistic, competitive political systems. Lewis denies that authoritarianism is necessary in Africa. Pluralism is possible, he says, if leaders follow self-restraint, if the governments are decentralized, and if the elites compromise. Verba, drawing particularly upon the histories of the Netherlands and Sweden, stresses that "subcultures must learn to get along with each other. And the learning is cumulative. Successful experience in resolving one conflict builds the kind of trust across subcultures that makes the resolution of the next conflict easier. Recent experiences in Africa suggest that the opposite lesson is currently being learned. They also suggest that much of Professor Lewis's advice will go unheeded."[60]

But how does one get the Ibos and the Hausas and the Yorubas to "get along"? And to cumulate such experiences? One major option, theoretically, would seem to be massive educational campaigns among all relevant subcultures designed to effect profound changes in perceptions, evaluations, and emotional orientations about other subcultures. Most of the causes of subcultural cleavages, after all, go deep into the histories and consciousnesses of the people. But these main causes are terribly hard to change; even if it were possible, the cost would be prohibitively high and it would require long periods of time. Another option is to encourage trust and cooperation among the leaders. Their behavior explains less of the total variance in the amount and intensity of cleavage. It is, so to speak, only a marginal factor, but marginal factors sometimes are decisive. In any event, policymakers have little choice: they cannot hope to influence the masses to any consequential degree. Even heeding Professor Lewis's advice, prospects for democratic pluralism seem dim in most African countries. It is probably true that "cumulative experiences with democracy" is a variable that helps mightily to explain the persistence of

[60] Verba, "Some Dilemmas in Comparative Research," *World Politics*, 20, No. 1 (October 1967), 127. This is a review of Lewis, *Politics in West Africa*, and Dahl, *Political Oppositions in Western Democracies*.

democracy under conditions of stress, but knowing this does not help the policymaker very much.

In sum, one can *understand* events and still not be able to *control* them. Knowledge is often a useful resource in bringing about change; but it does not necessarily provide the key to change. In fact, knowledge can sometimes be of greater service to the wise policymaker by alerting him to the limits of what he can hope to accomplish through purposive action. Knowledge is not always power.

CONCLUSIONS

The extent of direct use of political development theories by policymakers was very low. In terms of indirect use, which is harder to assess, theories may have been slightly more influential, but the general situation appears to be similar. They may have served to provide meanings and to orient actions in subtle ways; they almost certainly reinforced and sustained ideas already current in the policy community. In normative terms, the theories were very congenial to policymakers; if they influenced the officials at all, it was this attribute more than any other that enabled them to do so. But as empirical theory and applied social science, they had substantially less to offer.

The potential usefulness of the theories increased over time, and varied slightly by approach; on the whole, however, it was and is rather low also. The social-system and political-culture theories were weak on all counts, although there were improvements in them as empirical theory during the period which increased their potential utility somewhat. The legal-formal, economic, and will and capacity theories were superior by the criteria of applied social science, but they still were not very strong as empirical or normative theory, despite, again, some internal variations and improvements over time.

This assessment of the potential usefulness of political development theories runs counter to a number of more

284

optimistic evaluations. In a report published in 1968, for example, the Advisory Committee on Government Programs in the Behavioral Sciences of the National Research Council argued that the "lessons" of "the history of [government] experiences in statistical development, economic evaluation, and psychological testing" are such that "the present task is to extend these lessons to other areas of government and public policy through the greater integration of research into the functioning of federal departments and agencies." More specifically, according to the Committee, "similar developments must be encouraged in other fields of the behavioral sciences, especially in sociology, social psychology, political science, and anthropology, that are relevant to new social science programs at home and to programs of development assistance in the international field."[61] Numerous other optimistic estimates can be cited.[62]

These commentators seem especially conscious of one kind of danger in the relationship between social science and public policy: that of ignoring social science where it might help. Not surprisingly, social scientists themselves are especially prone to stress this type of danger. There is, however, a second danger of the opposite sort: relying too heavily on social science when it cannot help very much. This is the greater danger in the political development field today.

It is true that social science has had considerable utility,

[61] Advisory Committee on Government Programs in the Behavioral Sciences, *The Behavioral Sciences and the Federal Government* (Washington, D.C.: National Academy of Sciences, Publication 1680, 1968), pp. 34, 3-4.
[62] For example, see the Behavioral and Social Sciences Survey (BASS), Political Science Panel, *Political Science* (Englewood Cliffs, N.J.: Prentice-Hall, 1969), p. 36; Davison, "Foreign Policy," in Lazarsfeld, *et al., The Uses of Sociology,* p. 404; Eugene B. Skolnikoff, *Science, Technology, and American Foreign Policy* (Cambridge: M.I.T. Press, 1967), pp. 204-5; Jerome Wiesner, quoted in Michael Reagan, *Science and the Federal Patron* (New York: Oxford University Press, 1969), pp. 154-55. See also Chapter 5, n. 57.

both actual and potential, in such fields as psychological testing, statistics, and economic growth theory as applied in the United States. Even in these fields, however, potential usefulness is not always as great as actual use: witness, for instance, the illusion of precision and validity created by using psychological and intelligence tests in minority sub-cultures. Moreover, success in these fields does not necessarily imply success in others. Optimists have long been drawing on "successes" in statistics, economics, and psychology to show that many other fields of social science can make equal contributions.[63] These other fields, however, are often not so far advanced; thus the analogies drawn between them and the "success" fields are often misleading. Many of the payoffs promised by the earlier optimists have still not materialized. If social scientists make promises they cannot fulfill, they may produce a wave of reaction that could smother the genuine potential that exists within some fields for positive contributions to humane social action.

[63] For example, Harold D. Lasswell, "The Policy Orientation," in Daniel Lerner and Harold D. Lasswell, eds., *The Policy Sciences* (Stanford: Stanford University Press, 1951), pp. 3-15, esp. pp. 5-9; Robert E. Lane, "The Decline of Politics and Ideology in a Knowledgeable Society," *American Sociological Review*, 31, No. 5 (October 1966), 658; Reagan, *Science and the Federal Patron*, p. 165.

7

The Liberal Roots of the Theories

IN many important ways the theories are similar to the doctrines. Like the doctrines, they are consistent with and seem to reflect the four inarticulated premises of the liberal tradition. In other ways the theories differed from the doctrines. But such differences as existed between them were not very great or profound.

The theorists failed to act as searching critics of the fundamental assumptions of government policies. Several plausible explanations have been suggested to account for this weakness. Ultimately, however, this failure is traceable in substantial measure to the agreement produced by the Lockean consensus of the liberal tradition.

THEORIES AND DOCTRINES: SIMILARITIES

The first liberal assumption, it will be recalled, is the optimistic notion that "Change and Development Are Easy." The theories manifested, on the whole, a sanguine view of the patterns of and prospects for political change and development in the Third World. For one thing, many of them fell prey to the fallacy of unilinearity: the idea that political systems always develop and never decay. Thus, at least until the mid-sixties, concepts of political development were usually one-way concepts. Anything political that happened in "developing" countries, from coups to civil wars, was part of the process of political development. There was little or no provision for political decay. Also, liberal constitutionalism was often assumed to be immediately both desirable and feasible in the Third World.

Numerous observers have commented on this optimism. Mazrui speaks of "the self-confidence of ethnocentric achievement" and asserts that the theories were often "inspired" by "an incorrigible scientific optimism," which he attributes to the influence of Charles Darwin.[1] Huntington notes the need for a concept of political development that is "reversible" and suggests that one-way theories "are suffused with what can only be described as 'Webbism': that is, the tendency to ascribe to a political system qualities which are assumed to be its ultimate goals rather than qualities which actually characterize its processes and functions."[2] Another way of accounting for this optimism is to assert that it is a manifestation of the first premise of the liberal tradition.

The second liberal premise is that "All Good Things Go Together." It may fairly be said that until the fundamental reexamination of basic concepts which went on in the middle and later 1960s, a solid majority of the most influential studies in the political development field were based on this assumption. As Huntington observed in 1965:

> . . . the tendency has been to assume that what is true for the broader processes of social modernization is also true for political changes. Modernization, in some degree, is a fact in Asia, Africa, Latin America: urbanization is rapid; literacy is slowly increasing; industrialization is being pushed; per capita gross national product is inching upward; mass media circulation is expanding; political participation is broadening. All these are facts. In contrast, progress toward many of the other goals identified with political development—democracy, stability, structural differentiation, achievement patterns, national integration —often is dubious at best. Yet the tendency is to think that because modernization is taking place, political development also must be taking place.[3]

[1] Mazrui, "From Social Darwinism to Current Theories of Modernization," 82, 83.

[2] Huntington, "Political Development and Political Decay," 391.

[3] *Ibid.*

288

Thus the theories manifested a measure of wishful thinking. For instance, it is asserted that social differentiation is associated with specialization of function, specificity of political roles, and the integration of complex structures and processes. "That is, differentiation is not fragmentation and the isolation of the different parts of the political system but specialization based on an ultimate sense of integration."[4] Or, to take another example, political development has been defined as "the increased differentiation and specialization of political structures and the increased secularization of political culture. The significance of such development is, in general, to increase the effectiveness and efficiency of the performance of the political system: to increase its capabilities."[5] It is probably true that differentiation, specialization, and secularization tend to increase capabilities; but they also tend to increase demands and strains on the capabilities of political systems. The tensions between sociopolitical modernization and governmental modernization are not sufficiently recognized. Also, several theorists have suggested both correlational and causal relationships between democracy and propensity to avoid war. Thus, one writer speaks of the "underlying desire to avoid war, which characterizes democratic regimes," and of "a more democratic and, therefore, more peaceful world."[6] This plausible and highly congenial hypothesis seems to have been neither confirmed nor disconfirmed by data.

Another manifestation of the notion of the unity of goodness is the weak capacity of the theories to specify priorities. As Harsanyi points out:

> . . . in most situations we cannot realize all our social values at the same time . . . a choice among different values is necessary. . . . Such choices are never pleasant

[4] Pye, *Aspects of Political Development*, p. 47.

[5] Almond and Powell, *Comparative Politics*, p. 105.

[6] Lipset, *Political Man*, Anchor paperback edition, 1963, p. xxviii, and the dedication. See also the more qualified version of this thesis by Ithiel de Sola Pool in Pfeffer, ed., *No More Vietnams?*, p. 206.

to make, but no intelligent policy decisions are possible without recognizing that such decisions have to be made. . . . However, the traditional attitude among social scientists . . . has not been favorable to recognizing this. Rather, the implicit assumption has usually been that "all good things come together," all desirable factors have positive correlation with one another. . . . We shall call this implicit assumption the Positive Correlation Fallacy. It has been one of the main obstacles to clear thinking among social scientists, and is probably responsible for a high proportion of the bad policy recommendations we have made. . . .[7]

Very probably the positive correlation fallacy, the weak capacity to stress priorities, and the elements of wishful thinking in the theories all reflect in some degree the second premise of the liberal tradition.

There seems little doubt that the theories were profoundly affected by the third liberal premise, "Radicalism and Revolution Are Bad." So much was this the case, in fact, that, as noted in Chapter 6, almost none of the prominent political development theorists in the United States investigated the merits, under varying circumstances, of reform compared to revolution. Rather, the almost completely unchallenged assumption was that gradualism was always better. Until Barrington Moore's *Social Origins of Dictatorship and Democracy*, which concluded that the "costs of moderation have been at least as atrocious as those of revolution, perhaps a good deal more,"[8] such few radical challenges to the gradualist premises that did appear came not from the most prominent and influential American social scientists, but from social scientists at the margins of the American academic establishment, or from foreigners.[9]

[7] Harsanyi, "Rational-Choice Models," 537-38.

[8] Moore, *Social Origins of Dictatorship and Democracy*, p. 505.

[9] The phrase "margins of the American academic establishment" refers mainly to people teaching in the less prestigious American universities and/or scholars whose works were less widely read than those

Political science was particularly lacking in challengers to this third premise until at least the mid-1960s. Before then, an economist, Robert Heilbroner, a sociologist, Irving Louis Horowitz, and an historian, William Appleman Williams, challenged this aspect of the liberal orthodoxy; what influential writer in the comparative politics field can one name?

It is true that minor differences existed between the doctrines and the theories regarding revolutions and radical movements. Wilensky has suggested that investigations into the relative merits of reform and revolution under various conditions are less likely to be made by a research project "firmly embedded in an operating agency of the military" than by social scientists in universities.[10] Wilensky is right; however, not many academic social scientists made such investigations either in the 1950s and 1960s.

The fourth and final liberal assumption is that "Distributing Power Is More Important Than Accumulating Power." Once again, the degree to which the theories and the doctrines are similar is impressive. The best evidence that the theories reflected the fourth premise is the tendency in them to define political development as constitutional democracy, especially the American version. The theories stressed bargaining, accommodation, competition, checks-and-balances, and other characteristics of a system of dispersed power as attributes of the ideal patterns of political development. To a greater extent even than the doctrines, the theories tended to neglect the importance of authority. They paid even less attention to the need for a certain quantum of power and capacity to get things done in Third World political sys-

---

reviewed above. I do not mean to imply that these social scientists were marginal in this sense solely or even mainly because of their radical views. The roots of this marginality are manifold and too complicated for treatment here. This subject merits further study. A good brief discussion is C. Vann Woodward, "Our Own Herrenvolk," *New York Review of Books*, April 12, 1971, pp. 12-13.

[10] Harold L. Wilensky, *Organizational Intelligence: Knowledge and Policy in Government and Industry* (New York: Basic Books, 1967), p. 108, n. 12.

tems. This tendency was dominant through the early 1960s and very strong, perhaps still dominant, even later.

The stress on distribution of power and the neglect of the accumulation of power may also be seen in the proclivity to conceptualize political development mainly as a dependent phenomenon rather than as an independent, autonomous variable or complex of variables. This tendency was not inevitable or required by logic. The theorist can treat democracy as independent, intervening, or dependent. However, in practice, the theorists tended overwhelmingly to treat democracy as dependent. Thus understood, vaguely defined as democracy, and little defended in normative terms, political development was assumed to have happy consequences in terms of a wide array of other aspects of overall "modernization" like economic development, social change, and political integration and legitimacy. Political development was self-justifying; hence it was unnecessary to inquire into and appraise critically its consequences. This neglect of consequences had in fact a hidden premise: authority takes care of itself. The problem of accumulating power was not regarded as important.

The previous chapters contain ample documentation of these assertions about the theories and the fourth liberal premise. Vivid illustrations of these points are also provided by two recent books on political development in India (and, as the authors themselves note, on political development theory in general).[11]

The thesis of each volume is that in India economic development, overall socioeconomic modernization, and political integration and legitimacy—and indeed all other goals of

[11] The books are Rudolph and Rudolph, *Modernity of Tradition: Political Development in India* (Chicago: University of Chicago Press, 1967); Myron Weiner, *Party Building in a New Nation: The Indian National Congress* (Chicago: University of Chicago Press, 1967). These works have been the subject of a superb review essay by another expert on India, Francine R. Frankel, "Democracy and Political Development: Perspectives from the Indian Experience," *World Politics*, 21, No. 3 (April 1969), 448-68.

"modernization"—are compatible with and in fact maximized by the politics of accommodation, bargaining, and dispersion of power. One of the books even purports to see, in the system of caste pluralism in India, the conditions for "Madisonian democracy."[12] From this thesis flows the more general theoretical theme to the effect that political development (Madisonian and/or other types of democracy) and socioeconomic modernization (industrialization, more productive agriculture, social mobilization, education, etc.) are compatible with one another and are enhanced by the fusion of traditional structures and processes such as caste with modern structures and processes such as those of the Congress Party.

The authors of these books find a great deal of fragmentation of power in the Indian political system in general and the Congress Party in particular. The main agents of this fragmentation are caste associations and subnational units of the Congress Party. The authors also evaluate these tendencies. In both books the criteria for these evaluations are attributes of the structures and processes for making "inputs" into the political system. By these criteria, which are implicitly or explicitly those of the American political system, political development in India is proceeding rather well. However, the authors pay almost no attention to the question of outputs or, even more importantly, out*comes* or consequences. Thus, neither book gives "independent consideration to the consequences of these patterns of action [the input activities] for the Indian political system [and economic and social systems] as a whole. Rather, the outcomes appear to be extrapolated from the political systems that provided the original model for the input categories, i.e. the modern Western democracies."[13] This neglect of consequences is associated with a neglect of the importance of accumulating power. Stressing inputs, and judging a political system solely in terms of how well it performs input

[12] See Frankel, "Democracy and Political Development," 461.
[13] *Ibid.*, pp. 460-61.

functions, is another way of manifesting the belief that distributing power matters more than accumulating power. Again, authority is supposed to take care of itself.

A final striking parallel between the theories and the doctrines is illustrated by these books. It was asserted earlier that the liberal tradition has "layers of meaning": it is so powerful that stripping away one layer of ethnocentrism only reveals yet another underneath. This aspect of the liberal tradition was apparent in the doctrines; it appears also in the theories. As Frankel observes:

> While the authors [of these books on India] conscientiously strive to avoid Western biases—by arguing that varying historical sequences and combinations of events can bring about modern democratic structures and norms —they inexplicably assume that, once established, these processes will generate the same kind of adaptive responses to social pressures on the political system of India—a country in the early stages of modernization—as they did in the West. Moreover, it is the American political model that exerts the major influence on these extrapolations.[14]

It is suggested that the Lockean consensus in America is one of the forces that accounts for the assumptions Frankel says are "inexplicable."

Other parallels between the theories and the doctrines could be enumerated. For instance, neither of them gave sufficient attention to the great diversity of political systems in the Third World. The diversity that actually existed was forced into typologies which were simply too crude for their data. When data were scarce or difficult to obtain or unfamiliar, the theorists no less than the policymakers sometimes projected onto the Third World characteristics of political development in Europe or the United States that simply were not present.

Hopefully, however, enough has been said to make the

[14] *Ibid.*, p. 461.

case for the great similarities between doctrines and theories. Let us now turn briefly to some differences.

THEORIES AND DOCTRINES: DIFFERENCES

On the whole the doctrines paid more extensive attention to the will, skill, and capacity of government leaders and institutions than did the theories. Attention to these variables was a prominent feature of the Cold War doctrines in the whole decade of the fifties; in the theories, by contrast, such attention only became prominent later, in the sixties. But it was not only the Cold War which impelled policymakers to perceive and implicitly theorize about aspects of political development which were largely ignored by the social scientists. It was also the very nature of the officials' policymaking role. They had to deal with leaders. They knew from day-to-day experience that leaders made choices which had important consequences. On the whole, they knew this better than the theorists did. Just as it is wrong to assume that social scientists as a group are always better theorists than practitioners, it is also wrong to assume that the interests of pure theory cannot be advanced by contact with applied perspectives and concerns. As Gouldner has observed:

> It is likely . . . that even the most inveterate of pure theorists will profit from examining the hiatuses between the needs of applied fields and the accomplishments of the basic ones. For it may be that these gaps signalize, not only a handicap of the applied social scientist, but also an unnecessary defect in pure theory itself.[15]

But in certain other respects the theories were superior to the doctrines. The doctrines and the theories were similar as empirical theory in that both gave great emphasis to what has been called the economic approach, i.e. the view that politics is more than anything else a function of changes in

---

[15] Gouldner, "Theoretical Requirements," in Bennis, Benne, and Chin, *The Planning of Change*, pp. 94-95.

economic variables, and that a host of dependent variables like political participation, democracy, and stability depend on economic development. However, the theories were rather more attentive than the doctrines to social-system and political-culture variables as additional determinants of the characteristics of political systems. This was especially true in the late 1950s and early 1960s. Since these latter variables were sometimes powerful causal agents as well, the social scientists were able to explain a bit more of the variance in political-system performance than those policymakers who relied exclusively on economic variables.

As normative theory, too, the theories were probably slightly superior to the doctrines. The policymakers, it is true, were marginally more likely to understand that political democracy very often would be unfeasible in the Third World. However, some of the theorists—only a minority, but more than among the officials—realized in the middle and late 1960s that the prevailing assumptions on the appropriateness of radicalism and revolution in the Third World needed to be challenged.

Overall, there was not a great deal to recommend one over the other. The theories were superior in certain ways, but inferior in others, to the doctrines. Much more widespread, profound, and important than the differences between them were the similarities.

THE FAILURE OF THE THEORIES AS CRITICISM:
POSSIBLE EXPLANATIONS

There can be little doubt that as probing critics of the assumptions underlying American foreign policy regarding political development in the Third World, the theorists were failures throughout almost all of the postwar years. Not only were studies lacking which directly challenged those policy assumptions; more importantly, in the vast scholarly literature on political development almost all of the social scientists operated from similar premises *and reached similar con-*

296

clusions for a full two decades. Therefore a very important kind of *indirect* criticism was lacking as well. Until Barrington Moore's book,[16] radical challenges to such assumptions tended to come not from the most prominent American social scientists but largely from social scientists at the margins of the American academic establishment, and of course some foreigners and a few scholars in other fields.[17] Answers to the question of why this was so may have relevance not just for the subject matter of the present book, but also for the broader topic of the relationship between intellectuals and power in the United States.

COERCION AND COOPTATION

One type of explanation focuses on the policymakers and their relationships to academicians. This is the argument that, in one form or another, officialdom influences academe in such a way as to stifle criticism. The range of governmental and political mechanisms and processes that are allegedly used or exploited for this end is broad: it includes foreign affairs research review committees, informal cooptation of independent intellectuals into the government establishment, moral suasion, financial sanctions, McCarthyite witchhunts, and traditional American anti-intellectualism.

Some of these explanations probably have some validity. Yet they are not fully satisfying, and some of them are dubious. Governmental research review committees are a very recent phenomenon in the foreign affairs field; the poverty of criticism antedated them by some time. (In fact, social scientists have been much more critical since these committees came into existence—in the wake of the ill-designed and ill-fated Project Camelot.)[18] The hypothesis

---

[16] *Social Origins of Dictatorship and Democracy.*

[17] See n. 9, above.

[18] See Irving Louis Horowitz, ed., *The Rise and Fall of Project Camelot: Studies in the Relationship Between Social Science and Practical Politics* (Cambridge: M.I.T. Press, 1967).

of restriction by partial incorporation, or cooptation, is at odds with the fact that relatively few of the most prominent theorists were actually involved with or even known in the government. Most of them were simply not interested enough, or the objects of sufficient interest, to be coopted. As shall be seen shortly, moreover, social science in the United States enjoyed a great deal of autonomy, even though it did not use this autonomy very much as a vantage point for basic criticism in the political development field.

The argument about financial sanctions—a favorite explanation of the New Left—may bear greater weight. Nonetheless, it remains to be demonstrated that social scientists in America—in the political development field and most others as well—had adopted a more critical stance before the U.S. government became a major source of funds for social science research. Indeed, the opposite case can be made persuasively: social scientists and intellectuals initiated basic challenges to government policies at precisely the high-water mark of government expenditures for social science research, in the middle and late 1960s.[19] Actually, the vast majority of research that led to the major political development theories was privately financed.[20]

[19] National Academy of Sciences, Advisory Committee on Government Programs in the Behavioral Sciences, *The Behavioral Sciences and the Federal Government*, pp. 38-42, 91-96; Behavioral and Social Sciences Survey Committee, *The Behavioral and Social Sciences: Outlook and Needs* (Washington, D.C.: National Academy of Sciences, 1969), p. 226.

[20] Some of this research was financed by the great private foundations—Ford, Rockefeller, Carnegie, etc.—and some people would include them as part of a governmental or power-elite apparatus that coopts researchers and stifles criticism. It is true that, with some rather significant exceptions, the federal government and the foundations have tended to work toward common goals. However, this working together occurred not so much because the foundations were instruments of the government as because their people and the government people tended more or less naturally to agree on what needed to be done. They shared basic values; they were both products of the liberal tradition.

Finally, it is true that anti-intellectualism has been a force in American life; it was one of the social impulses that McCarthyism capitalized upon,[21] and that politicians like Spiro Agnew and George Wallace seem to have exploited. But it seems doubtful that this type of inhibition can totally explain the feebleness of the critical role. Indeed, anti-intellectualism can just as easily be a force in favor of irrational critical perspectives—most notably ill-formed and emotional criticism from either the Right or the Left—as it can be an inhibitor of intelligent criticism.

"BEHAVIORISM"

A second type of explanation focuses on the scholars themselves and on the professional norms of the social sciences. The substantive norms of political science and other disciplines concerned with political development were profoundly affected in the postwar period by what Easton has called the "behavioral credo." This credo emphasized regularities, verification, techniques, quantification, separation of facts and values, systematization, pure science rather than applied science, and the integration of the social sciences.[22] Political scientists and other social scientists drew analogies between social science and the natural sciences, or at least certain conceptions of the natural sciences. In one of its most powerful variants, political behaviorism stressed the necessity of many studies on narrow topics which, when "cumulated," would provide the basis for the construction of more general theory, up to and including global theories of societies. Most of all, perhaps, the behavioral revolution was an attempt to counter an earlier tendency among political scientists to prescribe freely without knowing the facts and without understanding the possible hidden rationality of the "evils" they sought to reform.

[21] See Richard Hofstadter, *Anti-Intellectualism in American Life* (New York: Alfred A. Knopf, 1963), pp. 3, 4, 12-13.
[22] David Easton, *A Framework for Political Analysis* (Englewood Cliffs, N.J.: Prentice-Hall, 1965), p. 7.

Key goals in all of this were greater objectivity, precision, and better empirical theory. To a large extent, questions of political morality were considered improper subjects for the social scientist. As a normative theorist and prescriber, the political scientist saw himself as no abler than the man in the street. He restricted himself to the study of human behavior in an effort to acquire information and to generate and test theories about empirical relationships. By providing more facts and better empirical theory, he could help reduce caprice and whimsy and error in decisionmaking. It seemed better to concentrate on those aspects of politics which were inherently objective and with respect to which the social scientist's training gave him some expertise, rather than to deal in matters that were subjective and where his voice was not necessarily more expert than that of the neighborhood grocer.

According to this second broad type of explanation, then, the view of the nature of politics and of political and social science just described was widespread and prohibited the theorists from playing a more vital role as critics. The theorists were simply too occupied with their "strictly social-scientific" kinds of activities to be critics. Indeed, in its extreme form the behavioral credo disparaged explicit value-judgments and assumed naïvely that it was possible to be completely value free in the study of politics.

This explanation is partly valid but has some serious weaknesses; in the end it is more useful to see both the lack of criticism and these features of behaviorism as consequences of an antecedent third factor—the liberal tradition—than to treat the former as a consequence of the latter.

It is true that it is impossible to be completely objective in the social sciences. Values affect the topics chosen, the methods of study employed, the data perceived, the inferences made, and so on.

It is also the case that exclusive attention to the study of actual behavior, and the neglect of potential or ideal behavior, is often conservative in its consequences rather than

300

strictly neutral.[23] The behavioral movement was associated in many instances with discovering the hidden rationality of existing institutions and processes rather than discovering their weaknesses and shortcomings. Also, the premises of the theories favored equilibrium, consensus, and order more than persistent disequilibrium and disorder. Conflict models were lacking. In all these respects the theories were not completely neutral but highly value-laden.

On the other hand, despite its inhibitions about explicit value statements, behaviorism did not, strictly speaking, prohibit such statements from being made. Thus, Easton included in his "behaviorial credo" an injunction against mixing "ethical evaluation" and "empirical explanation"; but he added that "a student of political behavior is not prohibited from asserting propositions of either kind separately or in combination as long as he does not mistake one for the other."[24] The behavior of political scientists conformed to the credo on this latter point. The majority of the theorists

[23] See Robert S. Lynd, *Knowledge for What? The Place of Social Science in American Culture* (Princeton: Princeton University Press, 1939, 1967, 1970), esp. Chap. 5. This discussion is still pertinent despite the fact that the lectures on which it is based were delivered in 1938.

On the other hand, as Robert E. Lane has suggested, under some circumstances knowledge can represent a kind of "pressure without pressure groups," so that social science which generates such knowledge is an agent of change rather than a conservative force. See his "The Decline of Politics and Ideology in a Knowledgeable Society," *American Sociological Review*, 31, No. 5 (October 1966), 661-62. Lynd and Lane are both right some of the time, but neither is right all of the time. It depends on the circumstances. One contextual variable that matters is type of knowledge. The type of knowledge most likely to create such pressures in the United States probably has less often been scholarly than professional or journalistic knowledge. For instance, a work like Michael Harrington's *The Other America* is an excellent example of such disequilibrium-producing knowledge. However, while most scholars would probably call it a good, important, general book, few would regard it as an important scholarly book. It seems fair to say that in the United States most scholarly books in the social sciences have tended to be conservative.

[24] Easton, *A Framework for Political Analysis*, p. 7.

had specific prescriptions and pieces of practical advice to offer policymakers. The prescriptions were of the type indicated above—supportive of American policies, or mildly critical at most—but they existed.

Also, it is hard to square this second explanation for the paucity of criticism with the fact that so-called traditionalists (who were pre- and/or anti-behaviorist) were not significantly more inclined to be serious critics than the behaviorists were.

Thus, to say that the "behavioral credo," and the cult of objectivity which it sometimes expressed, are what prevented a larger measure of critical appraisal of the roots of American foreign policy in general and political development doctrines in particular is to utter at best a half-truth. These social-scientific norms of the theorists did not in fact prohibit prescription, for prescriptions there were. What was missing were perspectives that enabled genuinely critical views of premises and prescriptions to emerge. Theorists may have been, because of the behavioral revolution, ambivalent about expressing their values; and it is true that detailed, explicit treatments of values and political philosophies in the classic sense were scarce. But values were abundantly expressed and there were many suggestions about how the government could do its job better. Nor was it a lack of autonomy, of which the theorists had a considerable amount, that inhibited criticism.

From all this it should be clear that the weakness of the critical function stemmed not so much from the total absence of prescriptions as it did from the *content of the prescriptions*. It derived not so much from a lack of autonomy for scholars as from their *disinclination to use the autonomy they had* as a haven from which to question seriously and if necessary to challenge and reject basic assumptions. We still need to account for that content and for that disinclination. And to do this, we need to look to the premises that underlay the theories, the theorists, and the behavioral credo. We need to look again, that is to say, at the liberal tradition.

302

THE LIBERAL CONSENSUS

The main reason why the theories and the theorists did not exercise more "critical rationality"[25] over the doctrines is that both doctrines and theories proceeded on the basis of the same basic premises: namely, those of the liberal tradition. This explanation seems more compelling than either of those previously discussed. It is not only more persuasive than the others but probably also antecedent to parts of them.

In a society where social scientists see their relationship to their government as one of co-workers, the government does not need to coerce or buy off the social scientists in order to inhibit criticism. When scholars and officials share basic values, no theories of conspiratorial power elites and military-industrial-multiversity complexes are necessary to account for the low incidence of ideological conflict and tension between the two groups, whatever merit such theories may have in other contexts. The liberal tradition has already precluded such conflicts. Amos Perlmutter has gone to the heart of the matter. He refers to members of three groups who were interested in the Middle East in the fifties and sixties; but his remarks apply more broadly:

> I am not arguing that there existed a cabal among the CIA, the social scientists, and the State Department. In fact, not only was the convergence of their views unpremeditated but the conflicts and disagreements between Dulles and his State Department advisers were notorious. In many cases, moreover, one group was hardly aware of its fundamental agreement with the others. What held them together was a common political Weltanschauung . . . the ideological convergence made bedfellows of these three typological groups.
>
> What all shared was a belief that America's national interests were benign and enlightened. Except for the CIA . . . all were dedicated to the international status quo, to

[25] This term was suggested to me by Richard Fagen.

area stability and tranquility and to mildly progressive regimes . . . the regimes were to be styled the American way. . . . This enlightened and disinterested support of progressive anti-Communists was believed . . . to be workable, if only because its intentions were good. In the end, these policies achieved the opposite of what was intended.[26]

It is notable how many of the phrases Perlmutter uses echo major themes in this book: "ideological convergence," "unpremeditated," "hardly aware of its fundamental agreement," "common political Weltanschauung," "dedicated to . . . stability and tranquility and to mildly progressive regimes," "styled the American way," "disinterested support of progressive anti-Communists."

Once one perceives that the liberal tradition is an important part of any satisfactory explanation of the feebleness of the theorists' critical judgments, then a number of related matters fall into place. First of all, it is easier to understand why the behavioral approach has had such a warm reception in the United States, and why there has been such optimism and naïveté about the possibilities for both objectively constructed, "value-free" theories of society, and an empirically based "policy science." For it is especially easy to miss the relationship of social science to national ideology and values in a consensual political system.[27]

[26] Amos Perlmutter, "Big Power Games, Small Power Wars," *transaction*, 7, No. 9/10 (July/August, 1970), 74-75.

[27] On "value-freedom," see Alvin W. Gouldner, "Anti-Minataur: The Myth of a Value-Free Sociology," in Maurice Stein and Arthur Vidich, eds., *Sociology on Trial* (Englewood Cliffs, N.J.: Prentice-Hall, 1963), pp. 35-52. For an excellent critique of the "policy sciences" approach, see Duncan MacRae, Jr., "Social Science and the Sources of Policy: 1951-1970," *P.S.*, Publication of the American Political Science Association, 3, No. 3 (Summer 1970), 294-309. For an Englishman's critique of both "Value-freedom" and the "policy sciences," see T. S. Simey, *Social Science and Social Purposes* (London: Constable, 1968), esp. Chaps. 3-5.

All of these are good critiques, but none of them relates the weak-

Second, in a society where ends tend to be widely agreed upon, appeals by the government to the public interest can be successful.[28] Such control over social science as exists is achieved more by these moral appeals to the public than through coercion. In the face of such appeals, the social scientist faces a dilemma. He perceives it, however, not so much as a moral dilemma as a pragmatic one. Under these conditions, the questions the social scientist asks himself are not: Am I contaminated by contact with power? Does power compromise independent, critical judgment? But rather: Can I afford to spend time solving policy problems when I have scholarly work to finish? What effect will a stint in government have on my standing in my discipline? When the scholar by and large agrees with the values of his government and society, it is hard for him to refuse a call to serve. He has to invent justifications for saying no. This may be one of the functions of the new professionalization of the disciplines.

Under these circumstances, moreover, the scholar who refuses to respond to the appeal to public interest, who prefers instead to maintain a critical distance, can be accused of carping from the sidelines, of refusing to face up to the "real, tough, practical problems." Such a critical scholar is liable, in other words, to stereotyping. He may be called unconstructive, impractical, ivory-towered, elitist, and—at the extreme—unpatriotic. Under these conditions politicians,

nesses to the liberal American ideology. A work which does relate the liberal tradition to American political science generally is Bernard Crick, *The American Science of Politics: Its Origins and Conditions* (Berkeley and Los Angeles: University of California Press, 1959, 1967). Crick deals mainly with authors who wrote prior to the years covered in this study, and he has almost nothing to say about the literature on political development. Nevertheless, his thesis that the American science of politics has roots in the liberal tradition is consistent with and complementary to the argument of this book.

[28] This point is also made by Michael Paul Rogin, *The Intellectuals and McCarthy: The Radical Specter* (Cambridge: M.I.T. Press, 1967), p. 38.

bureaucrats, and even some other academicians may have little or no conception of the usefulness for policy and policymakers of genuinely detached, probing criticism, or of scholars trying to exert influence from the outside rather than from within.

The liberal consensus also helps to account for other related phenomena, too numerous to examine in detail here: e.g. the shocked reactions of American scholars to the revelations in 1967 of covert government infiltration of all manner of "private" U.S. organizations—educational, scholarly, labor, business, charities (Latin Americans and Europeans, by contrast, were less shocked and angered than the Americans, for they had long suspected such activity); the low level of interest in explicitly normative theorizing; and the poor quality of that theorizing.[29]

The Theorist's Proper Role

The first and foremost obligation of the theorist, and of the intellectual more generally, is neither to be critical nor supportive of the status quo; it is, rather, to be devoted to the search for truth. It is this quality which principally defines (or should define) the theorist's role in society. In the search for truth, the theorist may start from premises and come to conclusions that are either critical or supportive of society. Either position is acceptable for an individual so long as he is engaged honestly and rigorously in the pursuit of truth and so long as no aspect of reality and no societal assumption germane to that pursuit are immune from scrutiny.[30]

[29] On the latter two points, see Duncan MacRae, Jr., "Scientific Communication, Ethical Argument, and Public Policy," *American Political Science Review*, 65, No. 1 (March 1971), 38-50.

[30] See Richard Hofstadter, "A Note on Intellect and Power," *The American Scholar*, 30, No. 4 (Autumn 1961), 588-98, reproduced in Volume III of *The Use of Social Research in Federal Domestic Programs*, A Staff Study for the Research and Technical Programs Sub-

It is useful, however, to make distinctions between individual theorists and theorists as a group, and between the intentions of individual theorists and the substantive conclusions and consequences of the work of many individuals. Surely individuals pursuing truth may reach conclusions which are either critical or supportive of prevailing assumptions. In fact, if more than a few theorists seek truth in a reasonably unfettered way, they presumably will produce not just criticism, and not just support, but some of each. This happens not because scholars necessarily define themselves as critics or supporters, but simply in the natural course of events. At least, this would seem to be the case in any society where both correct and errant features and assumptions are present, where the search for truth is reasonably free, and where more than a very few scholars are at work. But this is precisely where the record in America, with respect to the theories of political development, is poor.

What has been the record in the United States? According to Lipset and Hofstadter, a great many intellectuals in America in the 1950s and the early 1960s adopted the critical role and rejected the supportive stance out of hand. Lipset states, "*The* common definition of intellectuals, especially by their own spokesmen, is that they are critics of society and necessarily detached from it." Hofstadter was very concerned with what he called "a powerful fetishism of alienation that is widely prevalent in contemporary thought."[31] Yet the most striking feature of the social sci-

committee of the Committee on Government Operations, U.S. House of Representatives, 90th Cong., 1st Sess. (Washington, D.C.: Government Printing Office, 1967), pp. 536-43 (subsequent references to this article will cite the page numbers of the reproduction); Hofstadter, *Anti-Intellectualism*, Chap. 15; and Lipset, *Political Man*, Chap. 10.

[31] Lipset, *Political Man*, Anchor edition, p. 333 (emphasis added); Hofstadter, "A Note on Intellect and Power," p. 540. Lipset defines intellectuals as "all those who create, distribute, and apply culture, that is, the symbolic world of man, including art, science, and religion" (p. 333). The political development theorists clearly fall well

307

ence literature on political development was not that it expressed a "fetishism of alienation." Far from it! Whatever the situation was with respect to intellectuals generally,[32] political development theorists hardly viewed themselves as necessarily alienated or critics of their society. Indeed, it is difficult to name a single prominent theorist who wrote before 1965 and more than a few who wrote after that date who felt that he had "a primary responsibility to repudiate

---

within the limits of this very broad definition, which is basically a vocational or occupational one. Hofstadter's definition of intellectual is more ambiguous. In principle he rejects the occupational type of definition that Lipset uses. Intellectuals, he says, are those who live *for* ideas, not *off* them. In fact, however, very often Hofstadter also defines intellectuals in occupational terms. For instance, he distinguishes intellectuals from experts and then uses the two terms synonymously. See *Anti-Intellectualism*, pp. 26-44, esp. pp. 34-35, 428-29. Because of these inconsistencies in usage, all that can be said is that sometimes the theorists qualify as intellectuals in terms of Hofstadter's definition, and sometimes they do not.

[32] At this more general level too it is hard to know, even from Hofstadter's own writings, just where this "fetishism of alienation" was manifested among intellectuals, just what demons he was concerned to exorcize. He relies heavily on a symposium sponsored by the *Partisan Review* in 1952 for evidence and illustration of his argument. Yet by his own account only three of the twenty-five contributors to the symposium were seriously at odds with the supportive orientation. These three—Irving Howe, Norman Mailer, and C. Wright Mills— and a young historian, Loren Baritz, who in 1960 had published a book (*The Servants of Power*) critical of the abuse of social science by American industry, are all the evidence he presents for his assertion that a "fetishism of alienation" was "widely prevalent." He refers to an article by Howe as "not an entirely personal document, but a kind of manifesto of the intellectuals of the left." Yet again there is no evidence that the article in question represented a group larger than the four people he mentions. Given the ratio of "clerics" (people with a supportive orientation) to "heretics" (people with a critical orientation) at the *Partisan Review* symposium, the complacency of American intellectuals in general during the whole decade of the fifties and early sixties, and the advantages (and disadvantages) of hindsight, it is hard today to know what Hofstadter was so upset about. See Hofstadter, *Anti-Intellectualism*, pp. 393-432, esp. pp. 394-98.

. . . his society."[33] If anything, the prevailing sense of responsibility ran the other way.

Almost none of the theorists either began from very critical assumptions or, more importantly, reached very critical conclusions. What is disturbing is not that so few defined themselves as alienated, but that so few reached more searching conclusions simply as a natural consequence of their research. Surely there was no shortage of dubious premises and hypotheses, both empirical and normative, with which to find fault. Nor was there a scarcity of scholars.

One, therefore, must conclude that they were not unfettered in their quest for truth. But the constraint came not so much in the form of government coercion, financial pressures, or the norms of "behaviorism"; much more important was the subtle constraint of the liberal tradition. In his presidential address to the American Political Science Association in 1969, David Easton observed that "political scientists have still to escape the crippling effects for scholarship of unwitting commitment to national goals and perspectives."[34] Whether or not this judgment is valid for American political scientists generally (probably it is), it surely applies with considerable force to the political development theorists.

The scholars who analyzed the role of intellectuals and social scientists in America during the fifties and early sixties may have worried too much about what was then a relatively small problem (excessive alienation) and too little about the more serious problem of the inability of the theorists and intellectuals to explore critically their own ethnocentric premises and to allow their empirical research to lead them to more challenging conclusions. The exaggerated concern among some of these scholars with alienation, their eagerness to justify the supportive role of the intellec-

[33] *Ibid.*, p. 420.

[34] David Easton, "The New Revolution in Political Science," *American Political Science Review*, 63, No. 4 (December 1969), 1061.

tual in society, and their tacit minimization of the utilities of criticism, may themselves have been manifestations of the liberal tradition.

At any rate, it is sadly ironic that the failure of the theorists and others as a group to question basic assumptions for so long may well have helped to bring about the state of affairs which the critics of alienation feared the most, namely, the numerous recent manifestations of a rejection of reason and authority. Not in the late 1950s and early 1960s, when these critics wrote, but in the late 1960s and early 1970s, a mood that approximates a "fetishism of alienation" has become somewhat widespread in American political and intellectual life. Some of these anti-intellectual tendencies have been exaggerated, yet it is misleading to view them out of historical context. Some of the irrational romanticism and corrosion of authority of the last few years may be in part responses and overreactions to a period in which social scientists and other intellectuals were too complacent, too technocratic, and too unquestioning in their views about political development and in their relations with political power.

PART III: Conclusion

| 8 | Conclusions and |
| .... | Prescriptions |

Something is eating me. I have the conviction, and it grows rather than lessens, that we are living in a profoundly decadent society. Worse, I suspect that some of the very things that are taken as symbols of transformation are themselves further signs of decline. . . . Our radicalism, in short, is permeated by many of the failures that characterize our society as a whole. . . . if we do not try to purify radical politics through frank analysis and honest criticism, then the politics of the country will remain precisely the same, regardless of who takes power. The disease is at the roots. Until we are willing to see how it affects everything and everybody, we are doomed to a repetition of the very errors we are trying to reform.[1]

THIS book has criticized the extension and application of the liberal American ideology to Third World contexts. These criticisms are such that in some circles the book will be seen as a revisionist work. This is not inappropriate, and I am willing to accept the responsibilities, as well as any pleasures and opportunities, that may attend that designation.

However, just as the views expressed in this book diverge in important ways from the dominant doctrines and theories about political development in the United States during the last twenty-five years, so do they differ also in some important respects from a number of revisionist interpretations of American foreign policy that have become fairly prominent recently, particularly certain radical interpreta-

[1] Robert Brustein, *Revolution as Theatre: Notes on the New Radical Style* (New York: Liveright, 1971), pp. 4, 6, 7.

313

tions.[2] In this chapter, therefore, in the course of sum-marizing certain themes, drawing conclusions, and offering prescriptions, the discussion will touch more than once on ways in which the present analysis not only parallels but also diverges from some of these other critical orientations. For this book fits neatly into neither the liberal nor the radical categories of perspectives on contemporary U.S. ideology and foreign policy, although it is consistent with elements from each of them.

AN OVERVIEW

Political development has not been the only goal of U.S. foreign policy in the Third World, and to suggest that it has would be foolish. It would be equally foolish, however, to deny that economic and political development have ever been significant goals of American policy during the period from 1947 to 1968. Especially when "notions of political development" refers, as it does in this book, not only to highly explicit and precisely stated goals (the explicit democratic approach) but also to partly implicit and imprecise yet still salient goals (the economic and Cold War approaches), it is clear that political development has been a very important concern of American policy and policy-

[2] See the works of such authors as Noam Chomsky, Gabriel Kolko, David Horowitz, Walter LaFeber, Harry Magdoff, and William Appleman Williams. An excellent survey, analysis, and critique of the ideas of these authors is Robert W. Tucker, *The Radical Left and American Foreign Policy* (Baltimore: Johns Hopkins Press, 1971). It should be noted that the scope of their analyses is in many respects broader than that of the present analysis. They tend to deal with the causes and consequences of overall U.S. involvement in global political and economic relationships, whereas the present focus is on the substance and ideological roots of U.S. political development doctrines, policies, and theories. Nevertheless, there is enough overlap so that it is important to distinguish my position from theirs (as well as from more conventional liberal analyses).

See also n. 29, below.

314

makers during this period. It is, in short, just as unrealistic, ill-informed, and dogmatic to affirm that developmental ideas played no significant part in American policies and actions toward poor countries[3] as it would be to affirm that they occupied the only (or always the major) significant place in official thinking.

The aid doctrines and social science theories have provided a window on the nature of American political values and ideology regarding political development. In this sense they have served to illuminate the liberal tradition, just as, in another sense, the liberal tradition casts light on the reasons why the doctrines and theories took the shape they did. The goals and theories embodied in the doctrines need not have been universal, unique, or overwhelming for them to be able to provide this window. It is necessary only that they were genuine and salient for a substantial number of actors with regard to a substantial number of countries during a substantial part of the time. There can be no doubt whatever that the political development goals and ideas were sufficiently pervasive and salient to go well beyond that minimal threshold.

The liberal tradition is one important explanation for political development doctrines and theories. Clearly, however, the Lockean ideology is not the only determinant.

[3] For example, Harry Magdoff affirms that "*the* underlying purpose" of all U.S. foreign economic policy "is nothing less than keeping as much as possible of the world open for trade and investment by the giant multinational corporations" (*The Age of Imperialism: The Economics of U.S. Foreign Policy* [New York: Monthly Review Press, 1969], p. 14, emphasis added). Magdoff further alleges that "throughout *all* its variations" aid has had only two "dominant and interrelated ends": to keep poor countries dependent, and to promote capitalism for the benefit of the international corporations (p. 139, emphasis added). As for the argument that the United States has "sincerely encouraged social and economic development abroad," Magdoff says that this amounts to "obscuring economic and commercial interests by covering them up with idealistic and religious motivations" (p. 173).

Many other forces and factors—at the regional, national, and international levels—also come into play. The aim here is not to suggest that all policies can be explained in terms of the liberal tradition, but simply to establish that both the doctrines and the theories have been significantly influenced by it.

The liberal consensus had been exposed to obdurate foreign realities once before in the twentieth century, after World War I. But Woodrow Wilson's efforts to involve the United States internationally failed; the United States was isolationist in its foreign policy for two decades;[4] and therefore the liberal premises for the most part sank beneath the surface of the American consciousness. There they remained, as before, relatively firm and unchallenged.

After World War II, however, especially beginning with the Truman Doctrine, the U.S. government once again became deeply involved in world affairs. This time it was there to stay. It became a major power, the biggest in the world. This internationalism gave rise to a situation in which the liberal premises became more visible. American globalism meant contact (and usually clashes) between the liberal American ideology and illiberal societies and ideologies throughout most of the rest of the world. The latter were conservative or reactionary more often than they were radical, but they were still illiberal. Vietnam became a quintessential case, a "blow-up," of this type of contact, and as such it helped bring the liberal premises into sharp focus. In this fashion American internationalism after 1945 forced the implicit premises and implications of the liberal tradition into fuller view than they had ever been before. This is one of the major reasons why it is possible for us to discover (or rediscover) them now. In the words of N. Gordon Levin, who has made a thorough study of the earlier Wilsonian encounter between American liberalism and a largely illiberal world, "Ultimately, in the post-World War II period,

[4] Cf. the radical position, summarized in Tucker, *The Radical Left*, p. 34, and Tucker's rebuttal, with which I agree, pp. 83-88.

316

Wilsonian values would have their complete triumph in the bipartisan Cold War consensus."[5]

The consensus that emerged had to do with developmental values as well as the Cold War. As Joseph Jones, the foremost chronicler of the Fifteen Weeks that produced both the Truman Doctrine and the Marshall Plan, saw it, U.S. officials believed in 1947 that the United States would "fail to preserve peace and maintain security unless it continually enlists the active cooperation of free men, drawing upon their latent desire for sacrifice and for effort beyond the ordinary, in specific projects for building a better life for all, and [unless it] shares the effort and sacrifice of the building."[6] Jones goes on at some length in the same vein, becoming almost rhapsodic at times:

> . . . The United States, declaring that freedom and democracy within democratic nations and the independence of nations from outside control depend on the maintenance of healthy and self-supporting national economies, challenged the Marxist creed by advancing the proposal that nations work together in unity, using their economic and financial resources in concert for a common economic recovery that would safeguard their common democracy, independence, and free institutions; and by pledging the great economic, financial, administrative, and technical resources of the world's leading capitalist democracy to assistance in the common effort. Inspired self-help, mutual aid, and United States aid!

This rhetoric, even though it is overblown, is itself of interest; and there is no doubt about the accuracy of Jones's conclusion that the officials involved, from President Truman and Secretary Marshall on down, regarded the new policy as "infinitely more than a policy of containment of Soviet-Communist expansion." They saw it also as "a con-

[5] Levin, *Woodrow Wilson and World Politics*, p. 260.
[6] Jones, *The Fifteen Weeks*, p. 265.

317

structive policy of building throughout the free world the conditions not only of peace but of a good life."[7]

In terms of political development goals, a "good life" meant democracy, stability, anti-Communism, pro-Americanism, and peaceful foreign policies. The main instruments of U.S. foreign policy for achieving those goals were economic and technical assistance programs. The main conceptual tools for bringing these goals into being were the economic, Cold War, and explicit democratic approaches.

Underlying these three doctrines were, among other things, the four liberal premises: "Change and Development Are Easy," "All Good Things Go Together," "Radicalism and Revolution Are Bad," and "Distributing Power Is More Important Than Accumulating Power." The first two premises are especially helpful in explaining the economic approach; the third premise is especially helpful in accounting for the Cold War approach; and the fourth premise is especially helpful in explaining the explicit democratic approach. At the same time, the four liberal premises and the three doctrines are coherent: they relate to one another systematically and harmoniously once one understands their origins in the exceptional American experience, and once one sees the priorities under various conditions of the different values embodied in the premises and of the different goals embodied in the doctrines.

In other words, the liberal tradition, as a coherent whole emanating from a specific, unique, and unrepeatable historical experience—the Puritan migration to an abundant, nonfeudal, new world—illuminates and accounts for the doctrines even more than any single one of its four component parts, or the simple sum of the parts, could explain them. In similar though less powerful ways the liberal tradition helps shed light on the nature of the social science theories of political development.

Although, as noted earlier, these developmental aspects

[7] *Ibid.*, pp. 265-66.

of the liberal consensus had surfaced and been discernible before in American history,[8] the Fifteen Weeks and the subsequent global involvements of the United States enabled them to become more clearly visible than they had ever been before. The specific doctrines and theoretical perspectives forged during those weeks constituted the main lines of continuity in American foreign policy and in American views of the world for most of the next twenty-five years. Insofar as these policies and perspectives had a developmental dimension, they provided a window on the deeper liberal consensus. In a broader context they revealed once again the relation of doctrine, policy, and theory to national values and ideology.

IDEAS AS EXPLANATIONS

Explaining the origins and persistence of the doctrines and theories by reference to these liberal premises is to focus on ideas rather than economic factors (the need for external markets, for raw materials, etc.) as explanations. It is true that economic needs and demands were occasionally important determinants of American doctrines and policies of political development. Scattered throughout the first two chapters, in fact, is some evidence to support this view. However, economic factors fall far short of explaining all that needs to be explained. Moreover, the liberal premises, although not such powerful causal variables as perceptions of security needs and interests were, are relatively neglected as explanations. Often they are more powerful than the eco-

---

[8] They are, for instance, clearly evident in the thought and action of President Woodrow Wilson. His well-known stress on "self-determination" and "a world made safe for democracy" reflect the fourth premise. Less well-known, perhaps, is Wilson's opposition to revolution: "Revolutions always put things back, and sensible reforms are postponed" (quoted by William Appleman Williams, "Wilson," *New York Review of Books*, December 2, 1971, p. 4). It would be interesting and worthwhile to explore systematically the degree to which Wilson's thought reflected the four liberal premises.

319

nomic factors. This brings up another distinction between the present book and some other revisionist works.

It is certainly true that ideas are conditioned by historical, economic, and sociocultural forces. In this book, for instance, considerable care and attention have been devoted to showing how in the United States economic abundance, social fluidity, and political decentralization, among other factors, have powerfully affected the nature of the dominant ideology about political development. At the same time, however, especially under the press of historical crises, ideas can also acquire autonomy. In this sense it is no contradiction to affirm simultaneously that ideas are conditioned and that ideas have a life of their own. It is noteworthy that this view of ideas as both conditioned *and* autonomous, although rejected by some economic determinists and idealists alike, is prominent in the writings of sophisticated Marxists as well as non-Marxists. The four assumptions of the liberal tradition seem to me to be examples of just such conditioned yet autonomous ideas.

A recent case in point is Vietnam. It seems extremely difficult if not impossible, despite the many efforts in this direction of late,[9] to explain satisfactorily American policy toward Vietnam by reference to either the actual or the perceived economic interests of the United States. On the other hand, American policy becomes much more intelligible—not to say intelligent—once one has grasped the meaning of the liberal premises and seen how they are extended to our relations with Third World countries. The liberal premises are surely not a complete explanation of U.S. policies toward Vietnam. They are not even the most important determinants of those policies.[10] Yet no thorough accounting of the

[9] For instance, Gabriel Kolko, *The Roots of American Foreign Policy: An Analysis of Power and Purpose* (Boston: Beacon Press, 1969), pp. 88-132, esp. p. 90. For other examples, see Tucker, *The Radical Left*, pp. 16-17, 46-54.

[10] In my judgment, perceptions of security needs were much more important than developmental ideas in determining overall U.S. policies toward Vietnam.

320

reasons for the Vietnam morass can leave these assumptions out; and if one moves from overall U.S. policies to the narrower but still major topic of U.S. thinking and perceptions specifically about political development in Vietnam, then the liberal tradition becomes a prominent part of the explanation, perhaps the most important part.

Analogies make the point even clearer. It would be foolish to affirm that Soviet foreign policy is adequately accounted for simply by reference to the ideas of Karl Marx, Friedrich Engels, or V. I. Lenin. A great many other factors come into account—and even then one does not have a complete understanding. (One never does in the social sciences.) However, it would be equally foolish to ignore their ideas completely. This is especially true if one is to understand Soviet political development policies toward poor countries. Then the explanatory power of the Marxist-Leninist ideological background becomes very obvious and very great. Russian elites nearly always view political development through the theoretical, conceptual, and prescriptive framework of Marxism-Leninism. In a parallel sense the liberal tradition, while less explicit, less self-consciously applied, less tightly constructed, and (perhaps) less detailed and specific than Marxism-Leninism, is an indispensable explanation for U.S. doctrines, policies, and theories regarding political development.

Another parallel is the case of Bismarck, Nietzsche, and Adolf Hitler. It would be quite wrong to ascribe the regime and policies of Hitler exclusively to notions of Bismarckian discipline, racial superiority, and Nietzschean supermen that were prominent in the nineteenth century. But these ideas are not irrelevant, either, to an understanding of the theory and practice of Nazism. The point that needs to be emphasized is that an ideology also lies behind American thinking and actions in many if not all instances. It is not quite the same type of ideology, and of course the substantive content differs enormously. But it is of the same genus if not the same species.

We Americans are used to conceding the importance of

321

Marxist theory in Russian thinking and behavior and of certain nineteenth-century German ideas on twentieth-century German politics. We are less used to recognizing the impact of the liberal tradition on our own foreign policy.

The perspective presented here on the relationship between ideas, perceptions, and actions is evidently shared by at least some people who are perhaps generally more sympathetic than I am to the thesis that private (capitalist) economic needs and interests are the main or exclusive cause of American foreign policy. For instance, Eqbal Ahmad, a Pakistani social scientist whom most Americans would probably classify as a political radical, recently made essentially the same point.[11] He was commenting on a letter by Richard M. Nixon published in the *New York Times* in October 1965. The letter had warned that "victory for the Vietcong . . . would mean ultimately the destruction of freedom of speech for all men for all time not only in Asia but the United States as well. . . . We must never forget that if the war in Vietnam is lost . . . the right of free speech will be extinguished throughout the world."[12] Mr. Ahmad observes, "Whatever opinion one may hold of the military-industrial complex or of economic imperialism in American foreign policy, it would be difficult indeed to deny that such a statement by the most durable and successful of contemporary American politicians reveals more about the political pathology of this society than do the economic interests of its ruling class."[13]

[11] These lines were written before Mr. Ahmad became widely known because of his indictment along with the Berrigan brothers and others for conspiracy to kidnap National Security Adviser Henry Kissinger.

[12] *New York Times*, October 29, 1965, p. 42. I have verified the quotation, which is cited by Mr. Ahmad. The letter was written, it may be noted, before its author became President of the United States.

[13] Eqbal Ahmad, "How We Look to the Third World," *The Nation* (March 3, 1969), 265.

322

U.S. NATIONAL INTERESTS AND THE THIRD WORLD

Once it is understood that political development is just one goal among many; that the major benefit of analyzing those goals is to gain insight into the values and ideology of American political culture; and that the liberal tradition is seen not as a single cause for all U.S. policies toward the Third World but as a prominent cause with respect to political development doctrines and activities and as perhaps the single most important ideological and perceptual lens through which Americans perceive, evaluate, and understand political development in poor countries—once these points are clear, it would seem apparent that questions about whether U.S. foreign policy is guided by "the national interest" or by "humanitarianism," or whether it is "benevolent" or "malevolent," are not so important. Nevertheless, because these topics keep coming up in discussions about aid, and because analyses that draw on these concepts often confuse more than they clarify, it may be useful to say a word more about them here. At the same time this discussion provides an opportunity to say something about U.S. interests in the less developed parts of the world.

The Concept of National Interest. Most of the "debate" about whether U.S. aid, and U.S. foreign policy generally, are based on "humanitarianism" or on "national interest" is sterile and unproductive because of the loose ways in which the terms are employed and the uncertain standards that are offered to evaluate the truth or falsity of the allegations. In the first place, it is almost certainly true, and may therefore be taken as a kind of working assumption, that the U.S. government, and all other governments, do in fact base their foreign policies on the notion that these policies advance their national interests.[14] This information does not help us

[14] Thus, analyses that have tried to explain the shortcomings in U.S. foreign policy by reference to its alleged neglect of the criterion of

analytically, however, for the concept of national interest is anything but a sure guide to policy. In fact, except within very broad limits, the national interest is no guide to policy at all. Within these limits—which are not trivial but are not very discriminating either—national interest means whatever different people want it to mean. As a symbol for justifying actions and for rallying or mobilizing support, the notion of national interest has considerable power; its role in this respect is perhaps indispensable. As an analytic concept from which one can deduce or predict behavior, however, the concept has very little utility.[15] And this is where both conventional and radical analyses have not infrequently gone wrong. Such conventional analysts as Morgenthau and Banfield have contended that American foreign policy was based too much on a concept of global humanitarianism, a negation of the concept of national interest. They argue that this failure to stick to the national interest criterion produced unwise aid policies and undesirable consequences.[16] I believe this hypothesis is false. Of course, officials may have humanitarian goals, but their *sine qua non* goal and justification for aid is that it be an instrument of foreign policy and justifiable in terms of the national interest. If other goals and justifications can be added, all

national interest are not helpful because their "explanation" proceeds from a faulty empirical premise. Evidence to support this view is presented in Packenham, "Foreign Aid and the National Interest," 214-21. See also Kautsky, "The National Interest: The Entomologist and the Beetle," 222-31, and the essay by James N. Rosenau on "National Interest" in the *International Encyclopedia of the Social Sciences*.

[15] For further discussion, see Kautsky and Rosenau. See also Robert A. Dahl, *Polyarchy*, pp. 163-65.

[16] See especially Hans J. Morgenthau, "A Political Theory of Foreign Aid," *American Political Science Review*, 56, No. 2 (June 1962), 301-9, and Edward C. Banfield, "American Foreign Aid Doctrines," in Goldwin, ed., *Why Foreign Aid?*, pp. 10-31. For additional citations and discussion, see Packenham, "Foreign Aid and the National Interest."

the better; if they cannot, the decision is made to go ahead anyway.[17]

The radical analysts are correct that decisionmakers have acted in such a way as to maximize or optimize the national interest *as they saw it*. But this view is dead wrong in supposing that the substance of the national interest is something engraved in rock, some "essence" which is necessarily at odds with the well-being or the interests of other actors (notably Third World peoples). The content of "national interest" is not an objective thing identifiable empirically or deductively but a representation of the normative and policy preferences of individuals or groups. The editors of the American journal *The Public Interest* come close to the heart of the matter when they state that "the public interest is not some kind of pre-existing, platonic ideal; rather, it emerges [if it emerges at all] out of differences of opinion, reasonably propounded."[18]

Differences in the United States about the merits of the war in Vietnam, and about the appropriate purposes of U.S. aid programs, illustrate the thesis propounded here that the content of the national interest is anything but self-evident. Passionate defenders of the war and passionate critics of it all thought they were representing and advancing the national interests of the United States by their arguments, just as each thought that the policies favored by the other side would lead to the opposite of the national interest, namely, national decay and decline. Another example is found in the aid field. Many aid officials, especially those from the State Department and the Pentagon, thought that the way to use aid to advance the national interest was to reward friends and punish enemies in terms of fairly narrow Cold War criteria. Many other officials, especially those in AID, preferred to use aid for what they considered to be longer-term developmental ends, including political development. In both these examples the policies advocated by the various

---

[17] Packenham, *ibid.*, 218.
[18] From the editors' prospectus for *The Public Interest*.

groups are very different, but they all have the same justification—the national interest.[19]

These examples show why it is so wrong to suggest, as
some revisionists do, that anyone who says that political development was a prominent U.S. goal is ipso facto affirming
that the United States was uniquely benevolent in its foreign policy.[20] Obviously the second part of this statement
does not follow, since those officials who supported developmental ends relied on the concept of national interest to
justify their position just as much as did those who supported security goals more narrowly defined.

To the extent that serious students of U.S. foreign policy
have alleged that American motives were purely, mainly,
or uniquely "benevolent," their allegations need correcting.
However, it seems doubtful whether anyone today could
seriously argue that the policies of the United States (or
of any other nation) were designed simply to spread benevolence around the world. In any event, the radical perspective is by no means the only intellectual base from which
to reject the hypotheses of unique American humanitarianism and benevolence.

The concept of "benevolence" has in fact rather serious
limitations as a tool for describing or analyzing the motives
and goals of U.S. officials. For instance, some of those who
deny that the aims and motives of U.S. decisionmakers were
benevolent also affirm, or at the very least strongly imply,
that they were in fact malevolent—that instead of wanting
to do good, they wanted to do harm, to punish. But this
proposition is not tenable either. All governments and almost all political actors—whether capitalist or socialist,
democracies or dictatorships, reactionary or progressive—
seek to "do good," and all justify their actions by this standard. The benevolence-malevolence dichotomy is simply

[19] For additional information and documentation on these and other
examples, see Kautsky and Packenham.

[20] For example, Magdoff, *The Age of Imperialism*, esp. pp. 139, 173-
75. See also n. 3, above.

not very useful in analyzing the motives and goals of international actors.

Especially insofar as *intentions* (as distinguished from *consequences*) are concerned, it would appear much more likely that benevolence and malevolence are rather evenly spread around among North Americans and others, capitalists and socialists, etc. In general, if one seeks to account for good and evil in politics, the subtle works of a social philosopher and theologian like Reinhold Niebuhr would seem to be much more useful than the rather heavy-handed, moralistic analyses cum polemics of the Old Right or the New Left. Both the latter types of writings see a world of sharp ethical dichotomies that does not exist and that probably never will exist, whereas Niebuhr saw the moral ambiguity that lies near the heart of all genuine political decisionmaking and action. Of course, simple, though nonexistent worlds make potent political weapons, and these have their place in political life. That is beyond question. But they come at an analytic price, and it does little good to pretend otherwise.[21]

U.S. Interests in Third World Development. Although the concept of national interest is ambiguous as a guide to policies, estimates of national interest still need to be made. It seems to me the United States has at least three main and rather distinct types of interests in Third World development. First, we have a moral interest. It is very much in the interest of the United States to maintain and revitalize its moral consciousness. A nation that is in moral decay can decline just as surely as—though more subtly than—a nation with deficient military defenses. It seems dubious that the

---

[21] There are some fanatics, for instance, who think that capitalism is a source only of good and that socialism is a source only of evil. There are other fanatics who think only the reverse. Both are, of course, quite wrong. Their simplistic formulas may meet various political needs or psychic and quasi-religious drives. They doubtless help to satisfy urges for intellectual order, simplicity, and assurance. But they do little to advance serious scholarship or analysis.

United States can maintain its moral sensitivity, and live up to its ideals, if it ignores the poverty of poor nations. We are, along with a few other nations, an island of affluence in a sea of poverty. Even if this situation posed no security threat, it would pose a moral threat—indeed, it already does.

There are no easy answers to the question of how to translate moral concern into effective action, but the first step is to recognize the legitimacy, precisely in terms of the national interest, of the moral concern.[22] The alternative is increasing isolation in an affluent but ethically impoverished America. It is conceivable that American "survival" requires that the Third World remain poor,[23] but this does not seem probable. There are other possibilities and probabilities. We can and should act on them. It is in our national interest, in my judgment, to do so.

A second aspect of the interests of the United States in

[22] As has already been implied, morality is often separated from national interest in discussions of the rationales for foreign aid. Specifically, see Samuel P. Huntington, "Foreign Aid: For What and For Whom," *Foreign Policy*, No. 1 (Winter 1970-71), 174-76. Certainly it is wrong to equate individual morality with virtue in politics. However, it is also wrong to ignore the moral dimension of both political virtue and the national interest. It is well understood that the stress given here on the ethical dimension of U.S. national interest is unconventional and unfashionable. This emphasis seems necessary precisely because the distinction between morality and the national interest, while obviously necessary, is *too* sharp in the literature.

[23] In the opinion of Edward Banfield, writing in 1963, the "tragic facts" are these: that "vast areas of the world will probably not achieve a very significant and widespread improvement in levels of living for at least several generations; that they will probably not learn to govern themselves even tolerably well; that such development as occurs is as likely to be inspired by hate as by good will or moral respect; that it [i.e., development] may therefore prove to be a disaster for the United States and for all mankind; and that the measures which promise the most present advantage to the West in its struggle for survival are in general the ones that are least likely to lead to self-sustained economic growth in the underdeveloped countries . . ." ("American Foreign Aid Doctrines," in Goldwin, ed., *Why Foreign Aid?*, pp. 27-28).

328

Third World development is military security. It happens that the poor countries of the world are also the nonwhite countries. These countries are largely black, brown, red, and yellow in ethnic composition. They are also southern, rural, and *relatively* sympathetic to socialism. In short, there are a number of respects besides wealth in which the poor countries differ from the rich. And it is possible—though not probable—that these differences could one day result in a kind of race and class war, the consequences of which could be disastrous. Just one nuclear weapon delivered by just one hostile poor country could do considerable damage in the urbanized, technology-dependent United States. It is worth remembering that the poor countries would have a lot less to lose than the rich ones from starting a war or from launching nuclear missiles.[24] Moreover, such initiatives would not have to be those of a rational actor; their effectiveness would be no less for all that.

[24] Huntington writes: "In a sense, the United States is a tenant occupying the largest, most elegant, most luxuriously furnished penthouse suite in a global cooperative apartment house. The hundred or so other tenants occupy premises of varying sizes and degrees of attractiveness. As one tenant among many, the United States does not have any direct concern with how other tenants decorate their apartments. That is basically their responsibility, although the United States may wish to help out in the case of special friends and neighbors. The United States does, however, have a basic interest in the soundness of the building as a whole. It is precisely that soundness which is in question. The condition of the building is beginning to deteriorate rapidly, and drastic action is needed to correct crumbling foundations, defective wiring, corroded plumbing, leaking roofs, not to mention overcrowding in some apartments and muggings in some stairwells. Unless these basic repairs and maintenance are undertaken, the building is liable to collapse or to go up in smoke. As the wealthiest tenant in the building, the United States has more to lose than anyone else from the deterioration of the living conditions in the building. The United States has a clear interest in insuring that the structure as a whole is sound and that minimum conditions for decent human existence prevail in the building" (Samuel P. Huntington, "Foreign Aid: For What and For Whom [II]," *Foreign Policy*, No. 2 [Spring 1971], 130-31).

But what has all this to do with development? Does increasing development reduce the likelihood of race and class war against the United States—or does it increase threats to U.S. security? To my knowledge, no systematic studies exist to answer this question. Studies of intranation violence and instability, however, invite the speculation that sometimes development will be a substitute for war-making behavior and anti-Americanism, and sometimes it will be a catalyst. When it is a substitute, the United States has every reason to support development. When it is a catalyst, the United States should weigh the costs of such outcomes against the positive consequences of development. Clearly, the fact that development is no guarantee against international conflict is, by itself, no reason to forego the objective. Finally, although development probably increases the capacity of poor countries to wage war, it does not necessarily increase their will to do so. In fact, other variables—such as the skill of political leaders, their ideologies, strategic and diplomatic pressures on them, domestic political forces —may be more immediate determinants of propensity for war-like behavior than level and rate of economic development. At the same time, however, in the long run the more the United States is supportive of Third World development, the more political leaders are likely to be favorably disposed toward the United States in terms of these variables.[25]

Third, the United States has an economic stake in the economic development of poor countries. The richer they become, the more these countries can buy our products, the more investment opportunities will be available to American

[25] On the notion of development as a substitute or a catalyst, see Huntington, *Political Order*, pp. 362-69 and ff. For a thoughtful essay on prospects for conflict and cooperation between rich and poor countries, see Ali A. Mazrui, "The Political Economy of World Order: Modernization and Reform in Africa," in Jagdish N. Bhagwati, ed., *Economics and World Order* (New York: Macmillan, 1972), pp. 287-319.

entrepreneurs, and so on. This argument, so close to the hearts of the radical analysts, has a measure of truth, although it is not nearly so prominent as they would have it. There are also some conflicts between our economic interests and theirs, just as there are conflicts of economic interest among the rich nations. Yet on balance a good case can still be made on strictly economic grounds for Third World development.[26]

Degree of Overlap of Interests. Now, to what extent are the interests of the United States consistent with the interests of the Third World, especially the latter's interests in development? As one might expect given the earlier comments on the concept of national interest, the answers to this question vary greatly depending on who is giving the answer. Some observers—the U.S. Chamber of Commerce, and occasionally the Department of State, to say nothing of various liberal intellectuals—have answered that basically the interests of the United States and the poor countries are congruent (a manifestation in the international sphere of the "All Good Things Go Together" premise). Thus, Millikan and Blackmer write that "as long as our policies are designed to help these societies develop in directions which meet the real interests of their own people, our political and moral interests coincide."[27]

At the opposite extreme, some other analysts say that the interests of the United States and the Third World are almost completely incongruent. This is a position taken by both conservatives and radicals. Thus, the conservative American political scientist Edward Banfield argues that the "struggle for survival" of the West, and "the welfare of

[26] See Huntington, "Foreign Aid: For What and For Whom," No. 1, 174-81, for a persuasive statement of one view of U.S. interests in economic development in the Third World.

[27] Max F. Millikan and Donald L. M. Blackmer, eds., *The Emerging Nations: Their Growth and United States Policy* (Boston: Little, Brown, 1961), p. 145.

mankind," require that poor countries remain poor.[28] At the other end of the political spectrum, radicals such as Frantz Fanon, Andre Gunder Frank, and Harry Magdoff contend that the survival of poor countries, as well as their autonomy and their economic and social well-being, require nothing less than socialist revolutions, often violent ones, all over the Third World.[29] In all of these analyses, the interests of the United States (and, usually, other wealthy, capitalist nations) are viewed as totally at odds (or nearly so) with those of Third World countries.

There is a third position somewhere between the two extremes which recognizes an overlap of interests. (It is this position I have chosen to adopt.) This overlap is not complete, by any means, but it is substantial, and it could be even greater (as well as much less). Since interests are largely in the eyes of the beholders, the degree of overlap depends on the views and actions of leaders and peoples in both the rich and the poor countries. The radical analysts have made a valuable contribution to understanding the relationship between rich and poor countries by emphasizing the conflicts and incompatibilities that may exist between the interests of the two sets of countries. But they obscure the truth if, in understandably rejecting the idea of total harmony of interests, they go to the opposite extreme of affirm-

[28] Edward C. Banfield, "American Foreign Aid Doctrines," in Robert A. Goldwin, ed., *Why Foreign Aid?*, pp. 27, 31.

[29] See, among other works, Frantz Fanon, *The Wretched of the Earth* (New York: Grove Press, 1963); Andre Gunder Frank, *Capitalism and Underdevelopment in Latin America: Historical Studies of Chile and Brazil* (New York: Monthly Review Press, 1967); Harry Magdoff, *The Age of Imperialism*. This view is also often expressed in the so-called dependency theories. For a summary of the dependency literature which is based on the premise of incompatibility of interests see Susanne Bodenheimer, "Dependency and Imperialism: The Roots of Latin American Underdevelopment," in K. T. Fann and Donald C. Hodges, eds., *Readings in U.S. Imperialism* (Boston: Porter Sargent Publisher, 1971), pp. 155-81.

ing that the situation is inescapably one of total disharmony.[30]

GOALS

What can the United States do to increase the amount of overlap between the interests of rich and poor countries? This question is much too large to be answered here. However, it is necessary to explore here the slightly more manageable topic of goals, tactics, and strategies of American aid and aid-related diplomacy (rather than all U.S. policy instruments) toward political development (rather than all types of development). This topic is significant in its own right; its greater importance, however, probably lies in the fact that other types of goals (economic development, social justice, and personal freedom) depend in substantial measure on the types of political systems that the poor countries have.

Insofar as the United States has influence on political development in the Third World, two questions are pertinent: For what ends should this influence be used? By what tactics and strategies should these ends be pursued?

The Notion of Oscillation. In one sense it is almost axiomatic that the statement of a general set of political development goals for the Third World is an extremely difficult task. This is so for all sorts of reasons, especially the enormous number and variety of political systems in the Third World and of U.S. relations with these countries. In another sense, however, this task is, if not easy, at least much less complex and difficult than one might expect.

The conventional view is that the way to deal with the problem of general prescriptions for a complex, variegated world is to make contextual, conditional statements about

[30] For the author's views on the national interests of poor countries, see pp. 336-40, below, and Chapter 4, esp. pp. 173-91 above.

optimal states, and then to make differentiated sets of prescriptions based on these statements. As I have written elsewhere:

> . . . no single prescription will serve for all times or
> places. There is no panacea for the political ills of devel-
> oping countries, and the search for a single solution is
> futile. This is as true regarding the party solution as for
> other single solutions such as the military, the charismatic
> leader, traditional institutions, wider electoral participa-
> tion, or whatever. The theorist's problem remains to find
> a model that leaves room for *varying* patterns of political
> development and a typology of developing political sys-
> tems that suggests *different categories* of specific policies
> and programs appropriated to the various system types.[31]

However, theories of this sort are very difficult to achieve.
What to do in their absence? A very useful suggestion has
been made by Albert O. Hirschman: the notion of alternation or oscillation as an alternative to the idea of optimality.
This notion was first elaborated by Hirschman in his discussion of "exit" versus "voice" as ways of expressing dissatisfaction with organizations. (Exit occurs when a member quits the organization or a customer switches to a
competing product; voice occurs when a member or customer agitates and exerts influence from within.) As Hirschman puts it, his approach

> does not come out with a firm prescription for some
> optimal mix of exit or voice, nor does it wish to accredit
> the notion that each institution requires its own mix that
> could be gradually approached by trial and error. At any
> one point of time, it is possible to say that there is a defi-
> ciency of one or the other of our two mechanisms; but it
> is very unlikely that one could specify a most efficient
> mix of the two that would be stable over time. The rea-

[31] Packenham, "Political-Development Doctrines," 203 (emphasis
in original).

son is simple: each recovery mechanism is itself subject to the forces of decay which have been invoked here all along. . . .

. . . conditions are seldom favorable for the emergence of any stable and optimally effective mixes of exit and voice. Tendencies toward exclusive reliance on one mode and toward a decline in its effectiveness are likely to develop and only when the dominant mode plainly reveals its inadequacy will [should?] the other mode eventually be injected once again.[32]

The idea becomes clearer and much more general in its applicability in *A Bias for Hope*, where Hirschman argues that

the relentless search for permanently optimal policies and institutions which characterizes much of social science is often misdirected. In many situations, it may be possible to define optimality only with respect to the width and frequency of periodically needed reversals of policies and changes in institutions. . . .

This conclusion upsets deeply rooted modes of thought. Everywhere, not only in relation to the international economic policy of the developing countries, social scientists are looking for optimal policies and states, and that generally means that they are looking for optimal combinations of desirable, but mutually antagonistic ingredients of such states. Thus we look for the correct combination not only of contact and insulation, but of central control and decentralized initiative, of moral and material incentives, of technical progress and social justice, and so on.

It is here suggested that we devote at least a portion of our time and efforts to understanding the possible usefulness of alternation and oscillation, as opposed to optimal

---

[32] Albert O. Hirschman, *Exit, Voice, and Loyalty: Responses to Decline in Firms, Organizations, and States* (Cambridge: Harvard University Press, 1970), pp. 124-25.

combination. In the first place, it is possible . . . that certain patterns of alternation would yield results superior to the best that could be obtained by stable combination. Secondly, the focus on alternation would permit one to acquire a feeling for the right amplitudes of the many swings that do occur anyway in the real world.[33]

In the present context Hirschman's notion of alternation or oscillation means that while it is very difficult to specify, *in terms of an optimal equilibrium*, what political development ought to look like generally in the Third World, what it should be under conditions A, B, and C, or what U.S. postures ought generally to be toward such countries, it is nevertheless a good deal easier to say something about what has been wrong with definitions and theories *in the past*, and in general *in which directions* theorists and operators ought to be moving *next*.

Using the concept of oscillation, then, here is a sketch of some types of political development goals toward which the United States should begin to move in a majority of Third World countries. These remarks are intended to indicate the sorts of directions in which the United States should tend to move, for a while anyway, and a cast of mind about these problems, rather than any blueprint or inflexible set of objectives.

Political Development Goals: New Directions.[34] In the Third World it has usually been unwise to equate political development exclusively or even principally with political democracy, especially political democracy modeled after the United States. In many—probably most—of these countries the odds are against democracy as a viable form of government. In these nations, where economic and social develop-

[33] Hirschman, *A Bias for Hope: Essays on Development and Latin America* (New Haven: Yale University Press, 1971), pp. 25, 26.

[34] Portions of the next five paragraphs are adapted from my essay, "Legislatures and Political Development," in Kornberg and Musolf, eds., *Legislatures in Developmental Perspective*, pp. 576-79.

ment is such a critical and pressing task, political systems which are less ambitious and less desirable (from the American point of view) are not only more feasible but probably preferable for achieving these economic and social goals—and in the long run, perhaps, even the political goals of freedom and equality.

In these countries, greater national integration and identity, more governmental capacity and authority, and increased participation in national affairs (which sometimes may be "mobilized" participation as well as democratic participation in the Western sense) tend to be more realistic and appropriate goals of political development than many characteristics of American political democracy upon which social scientists have focused their attention. Just as other nations have developed politically without being democratic—European states during the age of absolutism, Mexico after 1910, Turkey after 1920, Russia between 1917 and the mid-1920s, and Cuba from 1959 to at least the middle or late 1960s—so also political development for most Third World countries will not necessarily be democratic, if indeed it occurs at all. Lipset was moving in the correct direction when he suggested in 1963 that "Instead of speaking generally about democracy, it may be advisable to focus on the conditions which protect personal liberty, that is, on due process and the rule of law."[35]

In societies like these that need and want change, moreover, political development should be seen not only as an end in itself but also, and *even more significantly*, as a means to achieve those values—economic, social, or political—which progressive leaders and the mass of the people regard

[35] S. M. Lipset, *The First New Nation: The United States in Historical and Comparative Perspective* (New York: Basic Books, 1963), p. 11. It is even problematic whether due process, the rule of law, privacy, and protection of the individual are realistically achieveable goals in the Third World, or should be. See Adda Bozeman, *The Future of Law in a Multicultural World* (Princeton: Princeton University Press, 1971).

as most important. No one can say with certainty which values are the highest priorities, or answer the even more difficult question of what the costs and benefits of realizing one value are in terms of other values. It is reasonable to judge, however, that they would include economic development, personal freedom from capricious or pervasive governmental control (though not necessarily Western democracy), equitable distribution of economic and social values, and the other political values previously mentioned. It seems extremely unlikely that Western democracy would rank higher than these values. In this sense, political development may usefully be defined in many instances as *the will and capacity to cope with and to generate continuing transformation toward whichever values seem appropriate in the particular context.* Among these, we suggest that three types of values, especially—economic development, personal freedom, and socioeconomic justice—would usually rank higher than other values. It should be emphasized again, however, that the specific values to be pursued in particular instances would have to vary significantly from situation to situation.[36]

Which types of political systems are most likely to be willing and able to achieve the appropriate values? The answers to this question will also vary greatly over time and space. Most of the evidence, however, seems to support the view that in the majority of cases liberal democratic political systems are not as likely to realize acceptable combinations of these values as relatively authoritarian regimes.[37]

[36] Obviously, appropriate values will vary considerably from place to place and over time. The three broad types of values suggested here are those that seem likely to rank highest most of the time among the masses and progressive leaders of poor countries. For some evidence supporting such a ranking, see Hadley Cantril, *The Pattern of Human Concerns.* See also Chapter 4, above, pp. 173-91. Of course, these three values are only suggestive; even more important is the point about diversity and contextual variation.

[37] As noted earlier, the "will and capacity" orientation is not logically wedded to authoritarian regimes. Rather the linkage is one of

This is not to say that authoritarian regimes are more likely to maximize personal liberty, either in the sense of formal due process and the rule of law, or in the looser sense of any constraint on arbitrary state action. However, in poor countries relatively authoritarian regimes are usually less likely than democratic ones to fail in advancing the ends of economic development and socioeconomic justice. When the maximization of the latter two values conflicts too sharply with the protection of personal freedom in these senses, the price may be too high. In such instances it might well be necessary to accept lower rates of progress in economic development and socioeconomic justice. But if personal freedom justifies such a cutback, the wider ranges of values associated with Western liberal political democracy— such as regular and honest elections, elected legislatures, separation of powers, competitive political parties, autonomous interest groups, a free press—usually do not. Usually these democratic features are not sufficiently feasible or desirable in Third World countries to justify the relatively high cost they imply in terms of economic and social development. This is why relatively authoritarian regimes are often a better, if not the best, alternative for poor nations. For the "best" alternative may be utopian and quite inappropriate if it means political democracy "at any price" while ignoring the negative consequences of this democracy for other desirable goals—such as economic and social democracy—which may compete with it.

In this connection, moreover, it is important to point out that even authoritarian regimes often maintain, through a variety of devices, a substantial (and to my mind healthy) measure of noncentralized socioeconomic, cultural, and organizational vitality and diversity. Some of them also protect and even nurture certain forms of privacy and/or personal

---

a tendency in poor countries toward an empirical association. Democratic regimes that truly have the desirable will and capacity are all the better.

freedom—if not through formal due process, then through other mechanisms. Cuba, Mexico, Peru (since 1968), and Yugoslavia are just a few examples of political systems with quite varied ideological orientations all of which have emphasized capacity over popular participation in decision-making while at the same time encouraging some (though not necessarily enough) regional or local autonomy and protection of personal liberties. Therefore the conception of political development adopted here, while it surely could be abused, does not necessarily opt callously for order over liberty.

The label of authoritarianism tends to conjure up harsh images of totalitarian control, which are often misleading. For one thing, the inefficiencies of life in poor countries affect the police as well as the telephone service or the railroad schedules. And while it is true that economic development and other aspects of modernization increase the efficiencies of the system and thus the possibilities for state control, these same forces also generate pressures for more pluralism, participation, and decentralization. In short, it is unwise to view either the single party or the dominant military organizations as total monoliths. This can lead to a confusion of form with substance. As Hartz has observed, "we [Americans] tend to assume that formal incarnations of the experience of liberty that we know are the only possible ones when, in fact, there is quite a lot of liberty that we have never tasted."[38]

The Dilemma of Probabilistic Social Science and Good Policy Prescription. The foregoing goals, though not applicable to *all* poor countries, are, in the vast majority of cases, more relevant and appropriate than those goals that derive from the example of the United States. These prescriptions are based not only on normative preferences but also on a social scientist's estimate of probabilities. Democracy, stabil-

[38] Hartz, in *The Nature of Revolution*, p. 146.

CONCLUSIONS AND PRESCRIPTIONS

ity, and other goals may all be feasible, but the probabilities indicate otherwise. And good policy must take probabilities into account.

Still, there is a danger in reliance on probabilities. One might respond in the following manner to the suggestions about political development goals just made: Even if one were to accept economic development, socioeconomic justice, and personal freedom as generally the most salient values to be pursued; grant the premise that democracy is usually improbable in the Third World; and concede that relatively authoritarian regimes will generally be necessary to achieve acceptable combinations of the values mentioned —still it is unhappily the case that policy based on probabilities is inherently conservative. That is, one who relies on probabilities may be "scientifically" correct, but there is a tendency to overlook an improbable policy that may just work. Especially in the social sciences where laboratory controls are impossible, and where the scholar is inevitably also a political actor at some level, reliance on probability-based theory as a guide to policy prescription is inherently a conservative posture and has pessimistic overtones.[39] At

---

[39] For example, Albert O. Hirschman has referred to the "vital, though dismal, contribution" of research about economic development which specifies arrays of "pre-requisites" to economic development. See *Journeys Toward Progress: Studies of Economic Policy-Making in Latin America* (New York: Twentieth Century Fund, 1963), pp. 6-7; and, for the quotation cited, his "Foreword" to Judith D. Tendler, *Electric Power in Brazil* (Cambridge: Harvard University Press, 1969), p. vii. Such theorizing is vital because it reveals the seriousness and profundity of the development problem; dismal because solutions seem so difficult ("nothing short of revolution" will suffice, and revolutions are difficult to bring about); and conservative because inferences about what to do tend to be based upon historical experience and the probabilities that seem to emerge from that experience. In the same sense, the social-system and political-culture approaches to political development are also vital, dismal, and conservative. See also Alvin W. Gouldner, "Metaphysical Pathos and the Theory of Bureaucracy," *American Political Science Review*, 49, No. 2 (June 1955), 496-507.

341

least this seems to be the case in a nondialectical, "equilibrium" social science, or one in which "thresholds" of change are not clearly specified. These features tend to characterize American political development theory and American social science generally.[40]

These are important objections; they are both true and relevant. But it is also true and relevant that the social scientist *always* deals in probabilities on one level or another. It is inherent in the social scientist's task. Even those social scientists who theorize about, and base their policy prescriptions upon possibilities within the context of limiting probabilities (Hirschman is the preeminent example), are ultimately, as social scientists, either responsible for specifying the conditions (in terms of probabilities!) under which it is possible to "beat the odds," as it were,[41] or they are

[40] Cf. dialectical, conflict theorists like Marx or Dahrendorf. Hirschman seems to suggest that much of the same pessimism and conservatism adheres even to conflict theorists in the periods between massive transitions. Referring to "the current of social thought leading from Montesquieu via Marx to such contemporaries as Wittfogel and McLuhan," he observes that "everything is movement and even upheaval when a transition occurs . . . but the room for maneuver and change is minimal during the very long stretches of historical time that lie between such transitions" ("Foreword," in Tendler, *Electric Power*, p. ix). The difference between the theories of which Hirschman speaks and American political development theory is that in the latter there tend not to be even any grand transitions!

With reference to American social science generally, Ralf Dahrendorf has suggested that "American values are characterized by the desire to preserve progress rather than any particular state of affairs. But this attitude is nonetheless conservative for its progressiveness . . . this is an attitude ill-prepared for radical change. . . . Like every conservatism, that of American values is vulnerable to the exigencies of history, and betrays traces of anxiety and insecurity" ("European Sociology and the American Self-Image," *Archives Européenes de Sociologie*, No. 2 [1961], 364).

[41] For example, Hirschman wrote, in *Development Projects Observed* (Washington, D.C.: The Brookings Institution, 1967): ". . . this book should be regarded as an attempt to reclaim at least part of [the] vast domain of intuitive discretion for the usual processes of

342

postulating a continuing probability (under conditions which must also be specified) that new possibilities will emerge.[42] In either case the social scientist is driven back to the requirement imposed by the norms of the social scientific enterprise to state some kind of probability. This is true because these

---

the *raison raisonnante*" (p. 8); ". . . I was seeking to provide project planners and operators with a large set of glasses with which to discern *probable* lines of project behavior" (p. 186, emphasis added); "Much remains to be done in understanding the conditions for failure and success of projects—and, in general, of new economic activities—within this wider setting. I hope to have provided *for this purpose*, as a result of close observation of actual project behavior, some useful principles of classification and analysis" (p. 188, emphasis added).

[42] This latter postulate is even more consistently emphasized than the former in Hirschman's work: ". . . if one wishes to dispense with the concept of a unique and universally required pre-condition, change is once again unintelligible and inconceivable *unless* some of the very ingredients of the old order can be shown to be ambivalent and to possess some progress- and growth-promoting potential. Hence the close attention I pay to possible blessings in disguise and the collector's interest I take in constellations which permit strength to be drawn from alleged weaknesses do not spring from infatuation with paradox; rather they are dictated by the essence of the process of change as I am able to understand it" (*Journeys Toward Progress*, pp. 6-7, emphasis in original). "Some of the most characteristic and significant events in the career of projects are ambiguous. . . . and the decision whether to give them a positive or a negative sign in the course of project appraisal requires considerable knowledge of the country, no doubt, but also—and this is what I have been trying to convey— an awareness of the ways in which projects create entirely new openings for change" (*Development Projects Observed*, pp. 187-88), Hirschman says that Tendler's study of electric power in Brazil "demonstrates that the Brazilian solution was unique and cannot easily be applied or reproduced elsewhere. But . . . she makes us suspect that similarly change-promoting configurations of technology must from time to time become available in other sectors and in other countries" (*Electric Power in Brazil*, p. x). The predominance of this second postulate becomes very explicit in Hirschman's recent collection of essays, *A Bias for Hope*, which contains an introductory essay with the subtitle, "Political Economics and Possibilism."

343

types of judgments are based not just on norms but also on estimates of empirical conditions, trends, and relationships which are probabilistic.

Thus the social scientist as policy scientist faces a dilemma: to the extent that he utilizes his social science expertise, he is liable to the charge of defending the status quo; to the extent that he "dreams dreams that never were,"[43] he is liable to the charge of irresponsibility as a social scientist until he specifies the conditions under which these dreams *probably* could become a reality. In other words, if the social scientist relies on probabilities, he can be criticized for the conservative posture of "betting only a sure thing," of "refusing to take risks"; if he relies on possibilities, he can be faulted for being unrealistic, fuzzy-minded, softheaded.

For example, the social scientist who would have told Senator Eugene McCarthy in November 1967, that he probably could force the incumbent President, Lyndon Johnson, not to run for reelection the following year would, in most social scientists' judgment, have made an irresponsible prediction. Clearly the probabilities, in terms of historical precedents, ran the other way. If there were any dialectic or "threshold" theories abroad in the land which would have enabled a social scientist to make such a prediction based on probabilities, I am not aware of them. Nevertheless, it was possible, and that in fact is what happened. It happened not because the social scientists were wrong in their appraisal, and not even because they were wrong in stating it to the Senator (if indeed any did and he listened). Rather, it happened because (among other reasons) Senator McCarthy saw the possibility and chose to act upon it. That the possibility became a reality despite its improbability does not imply that the social scientist was wrong in his assessment any more than Senator McCarthy was in his.

[43] "Never" here is not necessarily meant literally. I use this admittedly rich metaphor to refer to anything from improbable possibilities for which there are some precedents to the type of wholly unprecedented possibilities postulated by Hirschman.

344

The analogy to politics in the Third World is easy to make. If democratic governments are improbable in most underdeveloped countries, and if they are less likely to achieve the most salient objectives of their peoples than more autocratic regimes, the social scientist has to recognize these probabilities. At the same time, it remains possible that democratic government has a chance. The social scientist must, however, specify the conditions under which it is likely that a country can "beat the odds" against democracy before he can predict its occurrence, unless he wants to face the charge of dreaming dreams. The more social scientists can describe the circumstances under which improbable but possible outcomes are more and less likely to occur, the more useful their theory will be to policymakers.[44] However, as noted earlier, such theories are hard to come by. And they are also based on probabilities; hence the dilemma still exists. It is in fact unavoidable given that (a) social scientists always have to deal with probabilities at one level or another, yet (b) social reality is never as predictable as social scientists have to assume it is in order to make their probabilistic statements!

One good way to cope with the dilemma would seem to be to apply to it Hirschman's notion of oscillation. This concept can be applied to the "metatheoretical" issue of possibilities versus probabilities as well as to substantive theoretical questions like exit versus voice or centralization versus decentralization.[45] Both doctrines and theories have stressed

[44] For example, the more social scientists can describe the conditions under which democracy (or any other desired goal) will be more (and less) likely to occur in particular cases, despite its improbability in the Third World generally, the more useful their work will be for policymakers who wish to promote it. This requires more differentiated theory about the conditions of democracy, or whatever value is sought, under particular circumstances, than is usually available at this time. It follows that social scientists who seek to make their work more useful should try to develop more differentiated theory.

[45] Interestingly, Hirschman, who for present purposes "invented" the concept of oscillation and who has applied it to various sub-

345

the possibilities that democracy and stability could be realized on a wide scale and simultaneously. In fact, the possibility that these happy outcomes might occur was stressed so much in American policy and theory that the probability (or rather, the improbability) of their occurrence was given relatively little attention. In fact, however, the probabilities that these goals would be achieved were really rather low. It now seems time to redress the balance, to stress probabilities for a time—even though there are obvious risks in this strategy, just as there were risks under the policy of emphasizing possibilities. Any policy has risks.

Policymakers know this. It is their job to decide which risks to take. The social scientist can, at best, hope to illuminate the policymaker's problems; he cannot make choices for him.

---

stantive problems, has not applied it to the metatheoretical issue of possibilities versus probabilities. This is perhaps explained in part by his "passion for the possible," his "bias for hope." Although Hirschman concedes the necessity of probabilistic theorizing, and although he inevitably engages in some of it himself, the overwhelming emphasis in his own work is on possibilities and the art of "possibilism."

Hirschman's possibilism is a useful reminder of the uniqueness of each historical event, of the openness of the future, of our inability fully to predict human behavior. However, his failure to apply his own notion of oscillation to the issue of probabilities versus possibilities seems to me to be on balance unfortunate. Hirschman's very strong emphasis on possibilism comes close to violating his own stricture against the specification of states of optimal equilibrium: since he talks almost exclusively about possibilities, and writes about probabilistic statements mainly to criticize them, the implication is that possibilistic statements are optimal whereas probabilistic ones are not. Moreover, as Hirschman himself has pointed out, his approach is "open to the criticism that it is unduly tolerant of existing flaws and failings." Sometimes his "possibilities," "openings," and "opportunities" turn out badly. His "blessings in disguise" may turn out to be "curses" instead. By not applying the notion of oscillation to the dilemma of probabilities versus possibilities, Hirschman may be throwing away one of the most useful instruments available to him for coping with the dilemma and for answering his critics. This is ironic because—if we momentarily ignore Hegel, Engels, and Marx, among others—it is his own instrument.

346

Intuition, vision, courage, good luck—all these and more are characteristics of or factors affecting statesmen which the social scientist cannot replace. It may be that the best he can do is state probabilities, indicate possibilities, state conditions under which improbable possibilities are more and less likely, use the notion of oscillation where possible, and then hope that able statesmen will make the right choices. If some find this conclusion a gloomy one, it may indicate that they over-estimated the potential utility of social science for public policy in the first place.

Means[46]

Tactics. In the past the main tactical mechanisms for implementing political development goals have been the diplomatic, indirect, and direct approaches.[47] In general the first technique is much more desirable and feasible than either the second or the third, although the indirect approach is slightly better than the direct one. The further down this

[46] The sections on tactics and strategies deal only with the question of ways to implement the political development goals through aid and aid-related diplomacy, rather than the much broader question of ways to transfer resources more effectively to poor countries. The latter question would involve a discussion of general diplomacy, military aid, private investment, trade, international organizations, various kinds of transnational organizations like foundations, unions, and corporations, covert activities, national security policies, alliance politics, etc. Obviously it cannot be taken up here.

Tactics are treated before strategies partly because strategic issues already have been discussed in Chapter 4 and earlier in this chapter, but also because tactical considerations affect the choice of goals and strategies as well as the reverse (goals and strategies determining tactics).

[47] These techniques were described in Chapters 2, 3, and 4. The diplomatic approach, it will be recalled, refers to diplomatic relations at the level of the central government; the indirect approach refers to efforts focused on nonpolitical variables, like the economy, or schools, or trade associations, or unions, which might affect political development; the direct approach refers to efforts focused on explicitly political variables like legislatures, constitutions, or political parties.

347

list of techniques one goes, the more problems of political sensitivity one encounters; the more acute and damaging the scarcity of relevant knowledge and skills becomes; and the more ethnocentric the goals associated with the tactics are likely to be.

The diplomatic approach employs the standard instruments of government-to-government diplomacy: varying degrees of support or nonsupport for the central government, and different kinds of diplomatic pressure, such as using aid as a bargaining tool.[48] As long as this tactic is applied to optimize the proper goals (which, by the criteria of the goals just elaborated in this chapter, has often not been the case), it is our best instrument. Its practical advantages are several. It does not require an inordinate amount of skill or knowledge on the part of the American officials, because it uses the standard, commonly accepted and practiced technique of addressing the central government through diplomacy. Thus it is far easier to implement than the indirect or direct approaches, both of which assume that very skilled officials are available—more skilled than they either are now or could reasonably be expected to become. Moreover, because it is a legitimate instrument in international relations, diplomacy is less sensitive politically. The indirect and direct tactics are much more likely (and properly so) to generate charges of intervention in the internal affairs of the poor country.

Finally, the diplomatic approach is less likely to be wedded to ethnocentric goals than the other techniques. It is true, of course, that one can use diplomacy to support various kinds of developmental ends, including parochial ones. President Kennedy's Latin American diplomacy-for-democracy made this clear. But at least through this approach there is a possibility of taking a broader view and transcending our narrow national biases. What is needed is only to convince

[48] See Huntington, "Foreign Aid: For What and For Whom," No. 1, 170-71, for a good brief discussion of these instruments.

U.S. leaders who wield diplomatic instruments that greater receptivity, say, to left-wing regimes is appropriate, or that, as Kennedy learned, American capacity to foster democracy in Latin America is limited. These lessons may be hard to learn, but they are at least conceivable. Diplomacy is a tactic for relating to all kinds of regimes—those we like and those we do not like, those similar to us and those different from us. In and of itself it is a relatively neutral instrument that can be used for different types of ends.

By contrast, use of the indirect and direct techniques makes it more difficult for Americans to avoid their national parochialisms. These tactics are, so to speak, nation-building and state-building techniques. They relate to parts of the political system, not to the whole system (or the most significant single representation thereof, namely, the central government) as is the case through the diplomatic tactic. How else would Americans know how to go about the business of state-building and nation-building, of putting together the pieces of a political system, except with nuts and bolts cast out of the American mold? Virtually the only kinds of goals for which Americans would be able to use such tactics are, on a world scale, rather ethnocentric ones.

The diplomatic approach provides no guarantee that ethnocentric ends will not be pursued, but at least there is a possibility for this to occur. The indirect and direct approaches, by contrast, do provide a guarantee: that U.S. political development policies will have a large measure of parochialism. With these approaches American officials would have to learn an extraordinarily large number of lessons in order to escape their parochialism. Using diplomacy, officials would still have to learn, but their task would be less herculean. And the lesson would have to be learned mainly by the few leaders who shape broad policy (especially the President) rather than by a large number of lesser officials who work at the more specific level of day-to-day decisions and activities.

Strategies: A Summary. With the foregoing tactical considerations in mind, and drawing on the goals stated earlier and the evaluations in Chapter 4 of previous doctrines, activities, and policies, one can restate in summary fashion an appropriate array of strategic objectives for U.S. policies regarding Third World political development. The same caveats apply here as when stating goals: there are risks in all policies; and these suggestions are not timeless but rather an indication, using the concept of oscillation as a guide, of directions in which to move.

The United States should "get out of the way" of certain kinds of Third World political changes and developments. It should encourage and support governments with the will and capacity to cope with and generate continuing transformation toward economic development, social equity, and certain kinds of political freedoms, among other values. It should abstain from embracing governments that are weak in terms of these criteria. The specific goals to be pursued, however, will and should vary considerably in different contexts. We should learn to live more comfortably with a world of diversity and to allow political systems to evolve in their own ways. When in doubt we should restrain ourselves more and seek to impose our own preferences less. In particular we Americans should avoid the tendency, so often manifested in the past, to allow the "right" hand of the Cold War approach to negate what the "left" hand of the economic and explicit democratic approaches may have helped to generate. Perhaps most important, we need to gain a new appreciation of the appropriateness under certain circumstances of radical and revolutionary modes of political change. Finally, we should take sides much less often when indigenous forces clash within Third World countries.[49]

In large part, such a reorientation would probably imply not so much taking new steps in the future but rather *not*

[49] For some fairly similar proposals, see Robert L. Heilbroner, "Making a Rational Foreign Policy Now," *Harper's Magazine*, September 1968, pp. 64-71.

taking certain steps which we have taken in the past. The influence of the United States on the rest of the world has limits and is hard to manage; yet we sometimes produce negative effects without even realizing it. Our actions may have unanticipated consequences that can be very harmful as well as helpful. Some of these influences are almost impossible to change. The type of reorientation here suggested, however, might help to make that influence somewhat less unfortunate than it has sometimes been in the past. For example, at a minimum the United States might avoid interventions such as those in Guatemala in 1954, Cuba and British Guiana in 1961, or the Dominican Republic in 1965 —to say nothing of Vietnam since at least 1962—when our vital interests were not threatened to the degree we assumed. In such cases the United States might serve the people of these countries and our own interests as well by avoiding automatic, conditioned responses. In some such cases, or with respect to political regimes like those of Allende in Chile or the generals in Peru, we might better do nothing or support them if, as seems to be the case, they promise to provide the will and capacity for continuing transformation toward desirable combinations of ends.

Reorienting American foreign policy in these directions would not be easy. Fear of Communism and distaste for instability are deeply rooted in the American experience, and constrain political leadership in efforts at reorientation. Different leaders, however, would have varying success in such efforts: it made a difference whether John Kennedy or Lyndon Johnson or Richard Nixon was President in the degree to which these constraints limited policymakers' options. The same will be true of Nixon's successors. While reorientation would require efforts at a variety of levels, it could make little headway unless the President supported it. In the making of American foreign policy, even more than in shaping political systems, the variable most amenable to purposive change is leadership.

The diplomatic approach might also be used to put pressure on unconstitutional governments to return to democracy. However, this posture should normally be limited to those cases in which the country has a reasonable chance of making constitutional democracy work toward acceptable economic, social, and political values. Unfortunately there are many fewer countries in this situation than there are countries whose political lot is some sort of authoritarian system.

In those relatively few countries where liberal democracy has a good chance, the indirect and direct approaches may occasionally be appropriate. However, as Robert Dahl has pointed out, if the democratic forces in such countries "have the popular base necessary for a polyarchy, they do not need much outside support, and if they do not have a popular base then no amount of outside support short of outright invasion and occupation (and not necessarily even that) will enable them to build a polyarchy." Further, Dahl seems justified in his conclusion that "whatever the long-run effects may be on the conditions for polyarchy in various countries, as a strategy for transforming nonpolyarchies into polyarchies the American foreign aid program must be adjudged a total failure. So far as I am aware it has not a single such success to its credit."[50]

The strategies sketched in this book, especially those related to "getting out of the way," may seem to some people overly modest for a great, powerful nation. They may seem to smack of isolationism. Four points may be made in this connection.

First, in a strict sense, the analysis and prescriptions about the doctrines per se have nothing to do with isolationism/internationalism, since they are about U.S. views of and responses to Third World political systems whatever the level of U.S. involvement internationally. Second, insofar as

[50] Dahl, *Polyarchy*, pp. 212, 213.

the issue does arise, the plea in Chapter 4 for restructuring global relationships in order to increase the transfer of resources from rich to poor countries is scarcely an isolationist prescription. Third, reorienting U.S. policy in the direction of greater tolerance for leftist regimes and instability in the Third World is a big task. This suggestion would probably not be seen as either prosaic or overly modest or isolationist in Washington or Moscow or Peking, or, indeed, in Middle America.

Fourth, and more generally, we Americans badly need to get away from the presumption that we must always be "doing something." To be sure, it is better to do the appropriate thing (if it is known and feasible) than nothing at all. But to do the wrong thing is worse than nothing. What is known now provides little guidance—beyond the types of goals, strategies, and tactics indicated above—about desirable and feasible steps for the United States to take. In my judgment, the direct and indirect tactics should almost never be used. The diplomatic approach, properly oriented, might well be used. However, it is better to renounce even diplomatic means than to use them for the wrong ends. If these prescriptions amount to a policy of isolationism, so be it.

Theories. We have suggested some directions in which Americans ought to be moving in their thinking about political development in poor countries. It is possible to go too far in these directions. Some components of the contemporary New Left, both academicians and activists, have made just this mistake: in rejecting the dogmatic features of American liberalism, they have embraced a more rigid, simplistic, vulgar Marxism which surely impedes understanding and which very likely impedes wise political action as well. Among the prominent manifestations of these overreactions and overoscillations have been some of the dependency theories advanced to understand especially U.S.-Latin Amer-

353

ican relations.[51] Surely it is the case, as noted in Chapter 6, that political development theories paid too little attention to external variables in the international environment as determinants of political development or decay in Third World countries. This neglect was serious and long-standing, and has yet to be corrected. Moreover, it is appropriate, as the dependency perspective suggests, not simply to graft variables from the international context onto extant theories of national development, like branches onto a bush, but also to formulate theories from the initial premise that the international context can have manifold, powerful, and complex impacts on Third World politics.

Granting all this, the fact remains that the basic political unit in world politics is still the nation-state. Especially among the larger countries of the Third World, internal factors are still far more significant causal variables than international ones. Some versions of the dependency theory seek to avoid this conclusion by the partially semantic device of turning all decisionmaking nationals in poor countries who have positive relations with rich countries into nonnationals or fifth-columnists for foreign powers and international capitalism.[52] This formulation pays too little attention to nationalism in Third World countries. In its most extreme form it becomes a classic instance of saving the hypothesis by redefining all empirical cases that do not fit it in ways that always sustain the hypothesis. Indeed, one of the gravest weaknesses of much dependency theory is that it is unrejectable. It fails to specify the types of evidence that would disconfirm the hypotheses. Ironically, this same criticism has also been made of the systems and functional theories against which dependency theory was, in part, a reaction.

The extreme versions of dependency theory are only one

[51] For a survey of the literature and citations to prominent works, see Bodenheimer, "Dependency and Imperialism," in Fann and Hodges, *Readings in U.S. Imperialism.*

[52] For instance, Bodenheimer, "Dependency and Imperialism," pp. 162-65.

354

example of the tendency to oscillate too far, to go from one ideological perspective to an opposite extreme that is if anything more dogmatic, simplistic, and often self-righteous than the initial position. Thus, whereas the largely implicit liberal dogma could assume that "all reform is good, and all revolution is bad," the highly explicit radical dogma affirms in some instances the even more erroneous proposition that "all reform is bad, and all attempts at revolution are good." A similar tendency toward overoscillation is evident in academic analyses of the possibility of objective truth in social science. Until the middle 1960s, many social scientists held a somewhat naive view about the possibility of value-free social research. Then a counter trend began. For instance, after rightly noting that social science is, as Mannheim suggested, "handicapped by the narrow focus and distortions implicit in ideological thought," and that these ideological influences are related to the social settings and goals of the groups in which the social science is created, LaPalombara went further than Mannheim himself ever would have by asserting that "it is difficult to imagine how the social scientist in the United States would now go about rebutting the reiterated Russian claim that Western social science is not much more than thinly veiled bourgeois ideology."[53] After making some important criticisms of the idea of objectivity in the social sciences, some analysts proceeded to affirm a posture of radical subjectivism which seems to deny the possibility of fair or objective analysis of any kind—except, of course, with respect to their own types of declarations, which somehow escape the universal law they have just articulated.[54]

Interestingly, Karl Mannheim, one of the originators and probably the most important student of the sociology of

[53] Joseph LaPalombara, "Decline of Ideology: A Dissent and an Interpretation," *American Political Science Review*, 60, No. 1 (March 1966), 5, 14-15.

[54] This seems to be the position of Alvin W. Gouldner, *The Coming Crisis of Western Sociology* (New York: Basic Books, 1970).

knowledge, cautioned against these forms of extreme subjectivism and relativism. For him the very task of the sociology of knowledge was that of "solving the problem of the social conditioning of knowledge by boldly recognizing these relations [between ideas and their social foundations] and drawing them into the horizon of science itself and using them as checks on the conclusions of our research. . . . The sociology of knowledge aims at reducing the conclusions derived to their most tenable truths and thereby to come closer to methodological mastery over the problems involved." He also said: "Only in this way can we hope to overcome the vague, ill-considered, and sterile form of relativism with regard to scientific knowledge which is increasingly prevalent today."[55] These lines might well have been written yesterday. Mannheim's greatest contribution, perhaps, was to clarify the relations between social structure and knowledge. He thus made it easier to reduce the distorting effect of these sociologically conditioned biases, which probably can never be eliminated completely. But any extreme relativism always leads to the "familiar vicious circle in which the very propositions asserting such relativism are *ipso facto* invalid."[56] Ideology, in Mannheim's sense (which is also the sense of this book), handicaps the social scientist; but it does not completely shackle him.

The oscillations from one extreme to another may reflect, among other things, a desire for comprehensiveness, for intellectual simplicity and coherence, for a total picture, for something to believe in. These desires, if indeed they do exist, are understandable. But they probably cannot be met. The world is simply too complex and variegated to be satisfactorily ordered in terms of any of the extant total pictures.

[55] Karl Mannheim, *Ideology and Utopia*, Louis Wirth and Edward Shils, trans. (New York: Harcourt, Brace, n.d.), pp. 237, 87-96, esp. pp. 89n., 95-96, 171, 264. The quotations are both at p. 237. See also Robert K. Merton, *Social Theory and Social Structure*, rev. ed. (New York: Free Press, 1957), pp. 502-8.

[56] Merton, *Social Theory*, p. 503.

The present ideologies and paradigms—liberalism and Marxism are in broad terms the most prominent ones—are deeply flawed; but no very adequate replacements have yet been formulated. The "ideologies" and "paradigms" of the New Left in the United States are not truly "coherent and comprehensive theory"; much more often they represent "a mood, a feeling of rage and revulsion, which is . . . impatient with theory, or even thought and argument."[57]

It is possible that we are at one of those junctures in political and intellectual history that cries out for the brilliant theoretical innovator with a talent for creative synthesis. In certain respects the time seems ripe for going beyond the rigid established ideologies and paradigms and elaborating more fruitful and compelling new ones. But if a latter-day Hobbes or Locke or Rousseau or Marx lurks in the historical wings, he is not yet discernible. Failing the advent of such a comprehensive theoretical innovator, we shall have to make do with messy approximations of partial truths.[58] One can criticize the liberal models, as in the present study. Critiques of the radical paradigms have also appeared.[59] Partial syntheses might be in order, drawing on the best of each orientation, and putting together coherent wholes

[57] John H. Schaar and Sheldon S. Wolin, "Where We Are Now," *New York Review of Books*, May 7, 1970, p. 3.

[58] I am grateful to David Abernethy for helpful discussions of this point.

[59] For instance, see Tucker, *The Radical Left and American Foreign Policy*, and Robert A. Dahl, *After the Revolution: Authority in a Good Society* (New Haven: Yale University Press, 1970). Tucker deals with revisionist interpretations of U.S. foreign policy, and Dahl with radical critics of American democracy and American democratic theory. Both authors are generally fair in their descriptions of the theories they criticize, and both are somewhat sympathetic to the theories, despite their criticisms. See also Robert James Maddox, *The New Left and the Origins of the Cold War* (Princeton: Princeton University Press, 1973); and David Ray, "The Dependency Model of Latin American Underdevelopment: Three Basic Fallacies," *Journal of Interamerican Studies and World Affairs*, 15, No. 1 (February 1973), 4-20.

357

as best one can from the broken pieces of the liberal, Marxist, and other ideologies, models, and paradigms. But this is slow and difficult work. And it is inherently unsatisfying, since a total vision probably does not come from adding up and collating the discarded elements from shattered images. It does come from the creative effort of a brilliant mind that has grappled with both the old ideas and new data and re-ordered both in fundamentally different ways.

Ultimately, discovering satisfactory new paradigms and ideologies will probably require original research, a penetrating vision, a powerful creative thrust, rigor, logic, and a capacity for integration and synthesis. These are demanding requirements, and call for a transcendence of narrow academic professionalism; for a revitalization of certain humanistic skills and inclinations, such as competence in the area of ethical and normative discourse; and for an awareness that mechanistic physical science is not an adequate model for the social sciences.

Conclusion

In the years ahead there will be times when the major distorting influences on American thinking will seem to be coming from the extreme Left, with its crude formulas, its anti-intellectualism, its Manichaean ethics, and its own proclivity for the worst forms of inhumanity to man. It would be tragic, however, to allow an understandable distaste for these excesses to dull awareness of the rigidities that stem from the liberal tradition itself. With respect strictly to Third World political development, the most severe intellectual "hang up" of American officialdom and public opinion, if not also of its academic community, is not an excessively dogmatic Marxism but an excessively dogmatic liberal tradition. These ideas remain today, and will doubtless remain for some time to come, the most profound ideological contributors to American misconceptions about political development in poor countries.

358

It is worth emphasizing that the foregoing conclusions do not necessarily imply an abandonment of liberal constitutionalism as an appropriate standard of political development in the United States. Quite the contrary. The United States falls far short of the democratic ideal, but it approximates that ideal more closely than most national polities do, and existing conditions make that ideal a highly appropriate one to work toward. In most of the Third World, however, the conditions necessary for political democracy or even for reasonable approximations of it usually do not obtain. This is the main reason why it is possible to argue simultaneously for liberal constitutionalism at home and against the export of liberal constitutionalism and other features of the liberal tradition to most of the Third World.

All of this means neither that democracy is impossible in all of the Third World, nor that one should never strive for democracy when the apparent conditions for it are partially absent, nor that it is always unwise to strive to create such conditions. Rather, it is suggested that historical legacies and socioeconomic conditions in most Third World societies are not propitious from the point of view of establishing and maintaining stable democratic political systems. Nor are such systems necessarily the more desirable ones in such settings. At the same time these legacies and conditions offer opportunities for innovations in political arrangements which can enrich not only their own cultures but the more industrialized ones as well.

Can we Americans transcend the liberal tradition? Equally importantly, can we do so without abandoning all that is worth saving in it—which is to say a great deal? It is impossible to tell. Whatever the answers turn out to be, however, it seems safe to speculate that America's future success abroad will depend greatly on how well it performs with respect to parallel if not identical challenges at home. The most critical dimension of the domestic parallel is of course the question of race relations and all the other social ills and injustices associated with this complex issue.

359

It is no accident that many Afro-Americans, Chicanos, Puerto Ricans, native Americans, and other nonwhite minorities have employed the Third World symbol and have stressed their links to the world's popular majority in poor countries. Although there are significant differences between the two situations, there are also many parallels. Both political elites and the majority of the citizenry in the United States have a lot to learn from these minorities—about themselves, about the minorities, and about the peoples and governments of the Third World. What is at stake in the confrontation between the liberal tradition and illiberal forces at home and abroad is in Hartz's words, "nothing less than a new level of consciousness, a transcending of irrational Lockianism, in which an understanding of self and an understanding of others go hand in hand."[60]

[60] Hartz, *The Liberal Tradition*, p. 308.

Appendix
Selected Bibliography
Index

Appendix: A Note on Definitions, Scope, and Method

DOCTRINES (CHAPTERS 1-4)

THE MOST important methodological and definitional points about the doctrines were discussed in the Preface and the Introduction. I shall add here only a few remarks about scope and a word on terminology.

Foreign aid refers mainly to the economic and technical assistance programs administered by the Agency for International Development (AID) and its predecessor agencies, and to the diplomacy associated with those programs. The specific instruments of aid so defined are grants, loans, commodities, and technical assistance. Sometimes other types of aid, like military assistance, special programs (e.g., counter-insurgency), and various covert activities are referred to; but they are not the main concern here. Nor have I studied systematically the doctrines and activities of certain other elements of U.S. aid, such as the Food-for-Peace Program, the Export-Import Bank, the Peace Corps, and the Treasury Department. U.S. contributions to multilateral aid agencies, like the World Bank, and private American efforts, are also generally outside the scope of this book.[1] However, having set these limits, I may note that there is little reason to suspect that detailed study of these programs would alter significantly the main conclusions presented here.

Although it is officials in the aid agency who administer the programs, they are not the only ones who make aid policy. For aid is an instrument of U.S. foreign policy, and

---

[1] The delineation of aid presented here is a conventional one. See, for example, Nelson, *Aid, Influence,* esp. pp. 1-2, 7-10; and John D. Montgomery, *Foreign Aid in International Politics* (Englewood Cliffs, N.J.: Prentice-Hall, 1967), esp. Chap. 2.

is so perceived by aid officials.[2] Other officials—especially the President, the Secretary of State, the Secretary of Defense, Congressmen, and their staffs and organizations—who shape foreign policy also shape and reflect the doctrines in which we are interested. Hence their views and actions are also essential data for this book. Since aid was a principal instrument of American policy vis-à-vis the Third World, the focus on aid provides a good index of the broader policy. At the same time, this book goes beyond the aid doctrines per se to political development doctrines more generally in U.S. foreign policy.

I have selected the period from 1947 to 1968 for several reasons: 1947 was the year in which large-scale American aid programs began and the development of underdeveloped areas through economic assistance began to be a national policy of the United States. That year also marked the beginning of the policy of containment and of the Cold-War period. By the end of 1968, the size of aid programs was sharply reduced, the commitment of the United States to Third World economic development was waning, and the premises of the Cold War—and even some elements of the liberal tradition itself—were under review. Moreover, it was an election year in which the President and the party both changed. All these factors made 1968 a good cutoff point. At the same time, although the challenges to the liberal tradition at home and abroad were stronger in the late 1960s and early 1970s than they had been in years, it seems clear that the liberal assumptions will continue to have a powerful impact on American foreign policy in the future, even if the size and scope of U.S. aid continue to decline. The most important reason for stopping in 1968, in other words, was that I saw little benefit, in terms of the conclusions I had reached, in carrying the study further.

[2] For data substantiating this point, see Packenham, "Foreign Aid and the National Interest," 214-21.

THEORIES (CHAPTERS 5-7)

Defining "Theory." In the theory chapters as in the earlier ones, the term "theory" is used in a looser sense than that of formal definitions, axioms, and integrated, deductive hypotheses relatively well verified through systematic empirical study. There is no political development theory in the latter sense. On the other hand, we do not use the term in a completely amorphous or open-ended way. It refers both to statements about causal relationships among classes of variables (which Homans has called "orienting statements" or "approaches") and to statements about more specific causal relationships between single variables (which Homans calls "propositions"). For example, Marx's statement that the organization of the means of production determines the other features of a society, including characteristics of the polity, is an "approach." Boyle's law that the volume of a gas in an enclosed space is inversely proportional to the pressure on it, and the statement that level of education is directly and positively related to level of voting, or to membership in voluntary associations, or to interest in national political events are propositions.[3] Chapters 5 through 7 deal with both approaches and propositions, but they are necessarily more thorough and systematic about the former than the latter.

Scope of Coverage. The main focus is on social scientists for whom studies of the nature, conditions, and consequences of highly valued types of political systems were a central concern. Social scientists whose writings contained theories of political development but who were mainly concerned with other problems are of less interest here. More attention

---

[3] George C. Homans, *The Nature of Social Science* (New York: Harcourt, Brace and World, Inc., 1967), pp. 7-18. Of course, Boyle's law differs from the propositions about education and political participation in that it is both logically related to a deductive system and is very well confirmed so far by empirical data. None of the propositions discussed in this chapter is nearly as good as Boyle's law in terms of these two criteria, although some are less bad than others.

is given to political scientists and sociologists who directed their energies primarily to political development. Thus political scientists and sociologists like Carl J. Friedrich, Gabriel A. Almond, Seymour Martin Lipset, and Samuel P. Huntington are considered clear and unambiguous examples of political development theorists; whereas economists like John Kenneth Galbraith, Max Millikan, and Walt W. Rostow are excluded or seen as more marginal (as theorists) because their works are largely concerned with other matters, and such theories of political development as exist in their work usually appear as byproducts of these other concerns. The line between these two types is not always sharp, but it exists and serves to set serviceable boundaries on the scope of coverage.

Method. Any review of theories is necessarily abstract and thus inevitably involves some oversimplification. However, although scholars have disagreed on what political development means, their writings are not so divergent as they may at first appear. A distillation of these writings can help to reveal the main currents that have existed.

In analyzing this literature, I sought conceptual clarity and tried to maintain a minimal level of theoretical rigor by employing consistently a simple paradigm of independent, intervening, and dependent variables. I endeavored to identify, as objectively as possible, which were which in the literature and to keep them separate in my exposition. On the whole, this analytic strategy posed no great difficulties, since most of the literature was written this way in the first place. Moreover, most theorists did keep causes, intervening conditions, and effects from overlapping.

But here the initial caveat about abstraction and inevitable oversimplification is relevant. Applying this paradigm to the literature was sometimes easier said than done. Some of the theory was written in functional or descriptive rather than causal language. Such theories I either excluded or reformulated in causal terms. The authors whose work I analyzed did not always consistently implement the paradigm which they ostensibly employed. In these instances, I tried to clean up or sharpen their argument. A small share of the items in the literature did contain out and out tautologies. These I eliminated or tried to revise in nontautological form. Nevertheless, it should be made clear that for such reasons as these other scholars surveying this same body of literature might have identified and defined variables and specified dependent-independent relationships slightly differently.[4]

[4] Some other analyses of the political-development literature which make the same basic distinction as the one used here between politics-as-dependent and politics-as-independent theories, are Alfred Diamant, "Political Development: Approaches to Theory and Strategy," in John D. Montgomery and William J. Siffin, eds., *Approaches to Development: Politics, Administration, and Change* (New York: McGraw-Hill, 1966), pp. 15-48; Glenn D. Paige, "The Rediscovery of Politics," in *ibid.*, pp. 49-58; J. P. Nettl, "Strategies in The Study of Political Development," in Colin Leys, ed., *Politics and Change in Developing Countries: Studies in the Theory and Practice of Development* (Cambridge, England: Cambridge University Press, 1969), pp. 13-34, esp. pp. 31-34; Rustow, *A World of Nations*, esp. pp. 136-45; Giovanni Sartori, "From the Sociology of Politics to Political Sociology," in S. M. Lipset, ed., *Politics and the Social Sciences* (New York: Oxford University Press, 1969), pp. 65-100; Packenham, "Political-Development Doctrines," 195-205; "Political Development Research," in Haas and Kariel, eds., *Approaches to the Study of Political Science*, pp. 169-93.

Selected
Bibliography
....

THIS BIBLIOGRAPHY contains all items cited more than once in the same chapter as well as a few other especially important sources.

Act for International Development. Hearings. Committee on Foreign Relations. U.S. Senate, 81st Cong., 2nd Sess., March 30 and April 3, 1950. Washington, D.C.: Government Printing Office, 1950.

"Act for International Development" (Title IV, Foreign Economic Operations Act of 1950), June 5, 1950, in *American Foreign Policy, 1950-1955.* Washington, D.C.: Government Printing Office, 1956. II, 3,047-54.

Almond, Gabriel A. *Political Development: Essays in Heuristic Theory.* Boston: Little, Brown, 1970.

————, and James S. Coleman, eds. *The Politics of the Developing Areas.* Princeton: Princeton University Press, 1960.

————, and G. Bingham Powell. *Comparative Politics: A Developmental Approach.* Boston: Little, Brown, 1966.

————, and Sidney Verba. *The Civic Culture: Political Attitudes and Democracy in Five Nations.* Princeton: Princeton University Press, 1963.

Anderson, Charles W. *Politics and Economic Change in Latin America.* Princeton, N.J.: Van Nostrand, 1967.

Apter, David. *The Politics of Modernization.* Chicago: University of Chicago Press, 1965.

Banfield, Edward C. "American Foreign Aid Doctrines," in Robert A. Goldwin, ed., *Why Foreign Aid?* Chicago: Rand McNally, 1963.

Barnet, Richard J. *Intervention and Revolution: The United States in the Third World.* New York: World, 1968.

Bodenheimer, Susanne. "Dependency and Imperialism: The Roots of Latin American Underdevelopment," in K. T. Fann and Donald C. Hodges, eds. *Readings in U.S. Imperialism.* Boston: Porter Sargent Publisher, 1971.

Boorstin, Daniel J. *The Genius of American Politics.* Chicago: University of Chicago Press, 1953.

Braibanti, Ralph, ed. *Political and Administrative Development.* Durham, N.C.: Duke University Press, 1969.

Brown, William Adams, Jr., and Redvers Opie. *American Foreign Assistance.* Washington, D.C.: The Brookings Institution, 1953.

Coffin, Frank M. *Witness for Aid.* Boston: Houghton Mifflin, 1964.

Committee on Foreign Affairs, U.S. House of Representatives. "Foreign Assistance Act of 1966." House Report No. 1651. 89th Cong., 2nd Sess., June 23, 1966.

Cutright, Phillips. "National Political Development: Measurement and Analysis," *American Sociological Review,* 28, No. 2 (April 1963), 253-64.

Dahl, Robert A. *Modern Political Analysis.* Englewood Cliffs, N.J.: Prentice-Hall, 1963. 2nd edn., 1970.

———, ed. *Political Oppositions in Western Democracies.* New Haven: Yale University Press, 1966.

———. *Polyarchy: Participation and Opposition.* New Haven: Yale University Press, 1971.

Degler, Carl N. "The American Past: An Unsuspected Obstacle in Foreign Affairs," *The American Scholar,* 32, No. 2 (Spring 1963), 192-209.

Despres, Leo A. *Cultural Pluralism and Nationalist Politics in British Guiana.* Chicago: Rand McNally, 1967.

Easton, David. *A Framework for Political Analysis.* Englewood Cliffs, N.J.: Prentice-Hall, 1965.

Eckstein, Harry. "A Perspective on Comparative Politics, Past and Present," in Harry Eckstein and David Apter, eds. *Comparative Politics: A Reader*. New York: Free Press, 1963, pp. 3-32.

Fagen, Richard R. *The Transformation of Political Culture in Cuba*. Stanford: Stanford University Press, 1969.

Frankel, Francine R. "Democracy and Political Development: Perspectives from the Indian Experience," *World Politics*. 21, No. 4 (April 1969), pp. 448-68.

Frey, Frederick W. "Political Development, Power, and Communications in Turkey," in Lucian W. Pye, ed. *Communications and Political Development*. Princeton: Princeton University Press, 1963, pp. 298-326.

Geyelin, Philip. *Lyndon B. Johnson and the World*. New York: Praeger, 1966.

Goldman, Eric F. *The Tragedy of Lyndon Johnson*. New York: Knopf, 1969.

Goldwin, Robert A., ed. *Why Foreign Aid?* Chicago: Rand McNally, 1963.

Gouldner, Alvin W. "Theoretical Requirements of the Applied Social Sciences," in Warren G. Bennis, Kenneth D. Benne, and Robert Chin, eds. *The Planning of Change: Readings in the Applied Behavioral Sciences*. New York: Holt, Rinehart, and Winston, 1961, pp. 83-95.

Graham, Hugh Davis, and Ted Robert Gurr, eds. *Violence in America: Historical and Comparative Perspectives*. A Report Submitted to the National Commission on the Causes and Prevention of Violence. New York: Bantam, 1969.

Gurr, Ted Robert. *Why Men Rebel*. Princeton: Princeton University Press, 1970.

Hagen, Everett E. "A Framework for Analyzing Economic and Political Change," in Robert E. Asher, *et al.*, *Development of the Emerging Countries: An Agenda for Research*. Washington, D.C.: The Brookings Institution, 1962, pp. 1-8.

Harsanyi, John C. "Rational-Choice Models of Political Behavior vs. Functionalist and Conformist Theories," *World Politics*. 21, No. 4 (July 1969), 513-38.

Hartz, Louis. "A Comparative Study of Fragment Cultures," in Hugh Davis Graham and Ted Robert Gurr, eds. *Violence in America: Historical and Comparative Perspectives.* A Report Submitted to the National Commission on the Causes and Prevention of Violence. New York: Bantam, 1969, pp. 107-127.

―――. *The Liberal Tradition in America: An Interpretation of American Political Thought Since the Revolution.* New York: Harcourt, Brace and World, 1955.

Hirschman, Albert O. *A Bias for Hope: Essays on Development and Latin America.* New Haven: Yale University Press, 1971.

―――. *Development Projects Observed.* Washington, D.C.: The Brookings Institution, 1967.

―――. *Journeys Toward Progress: Studies of Economic Policy Making in Latin America.* New York: Twentieth Century Fund, 1963.

―――. "The Search for Paradigms as a Hindrance to Understanding," *World Politics.* 22, No. 3 (April 1970), 329-43.

Hofstadter, Richard. *Anti-Intellectualism in American Life.* New York: Knopf, 1963.

―――. "A Note on Intellect and Power," *The American Scholar.* 30, No. 4 (Autumn 1961), 588-98. Reproduced in Vol. III of *The Use of Social Research in Federal Domestic Programs.* A Staff Study for the Research and Technical Programs Subcommittee of the Committee on Government Operations, U.S. House of Representatives, 90th Cong., 1st Sess. Washington, D.C.: Government Printing Office, 1967, pp. 536-43.

Huntington, Samuel P. "Foreign Aid: For What and For Whom," *Foreign Policy.* No. 1 (Winter 1970-71), 161-89.

―――. "Foreign Aid: For What and For Whom (II)," *Foreign Policy.* No. 2 (Spring 1971), 114-34.

―――. *Military Intervention, Political Involvement, and the Unlessons of Vietnam.* Chicago: Adlai Stevenson Institute of International Affairs, 1968.

372

————. "Political Development and Political Decay," *World Politics.* 17, No. 3 (April 1965), 386-430.

————. *Political Order in Changing Societies.* New Haven: Yale University Press, 1968.

Ilchman, Warren F., and Norman Thomas Uphoff. *The Political Economy of Change.* Berkeley and Los Angeles: University of California Press, 1969.

Jones, Joseph Marion. *The Fifteen Weeks: February 21–June 5, 1947.* New York: Harcourt, Brace and World, 1955.

Kauffman, Kenneth M., and Helena Stalson. "U.S. Assistance to Less Developed Countries, 1956-65," *Foreign Affairs.* 45, No. 4 (July 1967), 715-25.

Kautsky, John. "The National Interest: The Entomologist and the Beetle," *Midwest Journal of Political Science.* 10, No. 2 (May 1966), 222-31.

Kennan, George F. *Memoirs: 1925-1950.* Boston: Little, Brown, 1967.

Kornberg, Allan, and Lloyd D. Musolf, eds. *Legislatures in Developmental Perspective.* Durham, N.C.: Duke University Press, 1970.

LaPalombara, Joseph, "Bureaucracy and Political Development: Notes, Queries, and Dilemmas," in Joseph LaPalombara, ed. *Bureaucracy and Political Development.* Princeton: Princeton University Press, 1963, pp. 34-61.

Lasswell, Harold D. "The Policy Sciences of Development," *World Politics.* 17, No. 2 (January 1965), 286-309.

Lazarsfeld, Paul F., William H. Sewell, and Harold L. Wilensky, eds. *The Uses of Sociology.* New York: Basic Books, 1967.

Legislative Reference Service, Library of Congress. *U.S. Foreign Aid: Its Purposes, Scope, Administration, and Related Information.* House Document No. 116, 86th Cong., 1st Sess. Washington, D.C.: Government Printing Office, 1959.

Lerner, Daniel. *The Passing of Traditional Society.* New York: Free Press, 1958.

373

Lewis, W. Arthur. *Politics in West Africa.* London: Oxford University Press, 1965.

Lincoln, Col. George A. "Improving A.I.D. Program Evaluation," Report to the Administrator. Washington, D.C.: Agency for International Development, 1965.

Lipset, Seymour Martin. *The First New Nation: The United States in Historical and Comparative Perspective.* New York: Basic Books, 1963.

————. *Political Man: The Social Bases of Politics.* Garden City, N.Y.: Doubleday, 1960. Doubleday Anchor paperback edn., with a new introduction by the author, 1963.

Lodge, George C. "U.S. Aid to Latin America: Funding Radical Change," *Foreign Affairs.* 47, No. 4 (July 1969), 735-49.

Lyman, Princeton. "Opening Remarks at the Roanoke Conference on Title IX of the Foreign Assistance Act." November 10, 1968.

Mazrui, Ali A. "From Social Darwinism to Current Theories of Modernization," *World Politics.* 21, No. 1 (October 1968), 69-83.

McNeill, William Hardy. *Greece: American Aid in Action, 1947-1956.* New York: Twentieth Century Fund, 1957.

Merton, Robert K. *Social Theory and Social Structure.* rev. and enlarged edn. New York: Free Press, 1957.

Millikan, Max F., and W. W. Rostow. *A Proposal: Key to an Effective Foreign Policy.* New York: Harper, 1957.

Minutes of the Meeting of the Advisory Committee on Economic Development, Agency for International Development. "M.I.T. Title IX Conference Report and Title IX Policies of AID." October 11, 1968.

Montgomery, John D., and William J. Siffin, eds. *Approaches to Development: Politics, Administration, and Change.* New York: McGraw-Hill, 1966.

Moore, Barrington, Jr. *Social Origins of Dictatorship and Democracy: Lord and Peasant in the Making of the Modern World.* Boston: Beacon Press, 1966.

Moskos, Charles C., Jr., and Wendell Bell, "Emerging Nations and Ideologies of American Social Scientists," *The American Sociologist*. 2, No. 2 (May 1967), 67-72.

The Nature of Revolution. Hearings. Committee on Foreign Relations. U.S. Senate. 90th Cong., 2nd Sess. February 19, 21, 26, and March 7, 1968. Washington, D.C.: Government Printing Office, 1968.

Nelson, Joan M. *Aid, Influence, and Foreign Policy*. New York: Macmillan, 1968.

Nomination of Lincoln Gordon to be Assistant Secretary of State for Inter-American Affairs. Hearings. Committee on Foreign Relations. U.S. Senate. 89th Cong., 2nd Sess., February 7, 1966.

Office of Program Coordination. Agency for International Development. "Measures to Ensure the Effective Use of Aid." U.S. Paper Presented to the Conference on Improving the Effectiveness of Aid for Overseas Development. Ditchley Park, Oxfordshire, England. June 3-6, 1966.

Olson, Mancur, Jr. "Rapid Economic Growth as a Destabilizing Force." *Journal of Economic History*, 23, No. 4 (December 1963), 529-52.

Packenham, Robert A. "Approaches to the Study of Political Development," *World Politics*. 17, No. 1 (October 1964), 108-120.

———. "Foreign Aid and the National Interest," *Midwest Journal of Political Science*. 10, No. 2 (May 1966), 214-21.

———. "Legislatures and Political Development," in Allan Kornberg and Lloyd D. Musolf, eds. *Legislatures in Developmental Perspective*. Durham, N.C.: Duke University Press, 1970, pp. 521-82.

———. "Political-Development Doctrines in the American Foreign Aid Program," *World Politics*. 18, No. 2 (January 1966), 194-235.

Partners in Development. Report of the Commission on International Development, Lester B. Pearson, Chairman. New York: Praeger, 1969.

Pfeffer, Richard M., ed. *No More Vietnams? The War and*

the Future of American Foreign Policy. New York: Harper and Row, 1968.

Potter, David. *People of Plenty: Economic Abundance and the American Character.* Chicago: University of Chicago Press, 1954.

Price, Harry Bayard. *The Marshall Plan and Its Meaning.* Ithaca: Cornell University Press, 1955.

Public Papers of the Presidents of the United States, Harry S. Truman, 1947. Washington, D.C.: Government Printing Office, 1963.

Public Papers of the Presidents of the United States, Harry S. Truman, 1948. Washington, D.C.: Government Printing Office, 1964.

Public Papers of the Presidents of the United States, Harry S. Truman, 1949. Washington, D.C.: Government Printing Office, 1964.

Pye, Lucian W. *Aspects of Political Development.* Boston: Little, Brown, 1966.

———. *Politics, Personality and Nation Building.* New Haven: Yale University Press, 1962.

Reagan, Michael. *Science and the Federal Patron.* New York: Oxford University Press, 1969.

Rockefeller, Nelson A. *The Rockefeller Report on the Americas.* The Official Report of a United States Presidential Mission for the Western Hemisphere. Chicago: Quadrangle Books, 1969.

The Role of Popular Participation in Development. Cambridge: MIT, Center for International Studies, 1968.

Rosenau, James N. "National Interest," in David L. Sills, ed. *International Encyclopedia of the Social Sciences.* New York: Macmillan and Crowell Collier, 1968.

Rural Development in Asia. Hearings. Subcommittee on Asian and Pacific Affairs, Committee on Foreign Affairs, U.S. House of Representatives. 90th Cong., 1st Sess. Parts I and II. Washington, D.C.: Government Printing Office, 1967.

Rustow, Dankwart A. *A World of Nations: Problems of*

Political Modernization. Washington, D.C.: The Brookings Institution, 1967.

Schlesinger, Arthur M., Jr. *A Thousand Days: John F. Kennedy in the White House.* Boston: Houghton Mifflin, 1965.

Schott, John R. "Title IX: A New Dimension in U.S. Foreign Aid?" Paper Delivered at the Annual Meeting of the International Studies Association, San Francisco, March 27-29, 1969.

Skidmore, Thomas E. *Politics in Brazil, 1930-1964: An Experiment in Democracy.* New York: Oxford University Press, 1967.

Slater, Jerome. *Intervention and Negotiation: The United States and the Dominican Revolution.* New York: Harper and Row, 1970.

Sorensen, Theodore C. *Kennedy.* New York: Bantam, 1966.

Survey of the Alliance for Progress. Hearings. Subcommittee on American Republics Affairs, Committee on Foreign Relations, U.S. Senate. 90th Cong., 2nd Sess., February 27, 28, 29 and March 1, 4, 5, and 6, 1968. Washington, D.C.: Government Printing Office, 1968.

Symposium on *The Liberal Tradition in America.* Marvin Meyers, Leonard Krieger, Harry V. Jaffe, and Louis Hartz. *Comparative Studies in Society and History.* Vol. v (1962-1963), pp. 261-84, 365-77.

Tendler, Judith D. *Electric Power in Brazil.* Cambridge: Harvard University Press, 1969.

Tucker, Robert W. *The Radical Left and American Foreign Policy.* Baltimore: Johns Hopkins Press, 1971.

U.S. Foreign Assistance in the 1970s: A New Approach. Report to the President from the Task Force on International Development, Rudolph A. Peterson, Chairman. Washington, D.C.: Government Printing Office, March 4, 1970.

Verba, Sidney. "Some Dilemmas in Comparative Research," *World Politics.* 20, No. 1 (October 1967), 111-27.

Ward, Barbara, J. D. Runnalls, and Lenore D'Anjou, eds.

The Widening Gap: Development in the 1970's. New York: Columbia University Press, 1971.

Westerfield, H. Bradford. *The Instruments of America's Foreign Policy.* New York: Thomas Crowell, 1963.

Wolf, Charles, Jr. *Foreign Aid: Theory and Practice in Southern Asia.* Princeton: Princeton University Press, 1960.

Index*

Prepared by Mary van Tamelen, Jeanne Kennedy, and Robert Packenham

* In this index 40f means separate references on pp. 40 and 41; 40ff means separate references on pp. 40, 41, and 42; 40-42 means a continuous discussion. *Passim*, meaning "here and there," is used for a cluster of references in close but not consecutive sequence (for example, 40, 41, 43, 44, 47, would be written as 40-47 *passim*).